RECKONING WITH THE DEAD

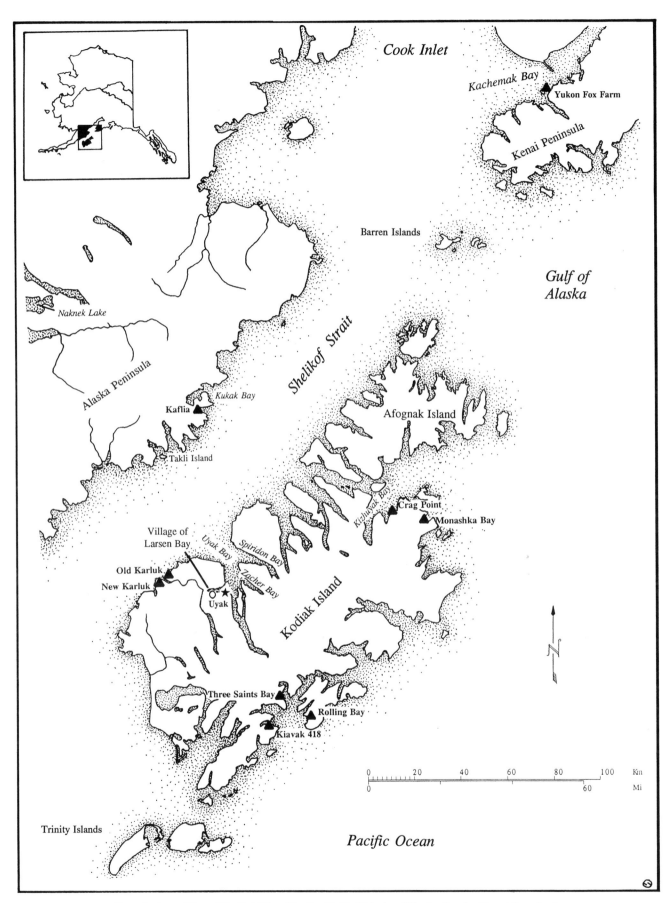

Frontispiece. Map of Kodiak Island in the Gulf of Alaska. (Illustration by Stuart Speaker)

RECKONING WITH THE DEAD

The Larsen Bay Repatriation and the Smithsonian Institution

EDITED BY TAMARA L. BRAY AND THOMAS W. KILLION

SMITHSONIAN INSTITUTION PRESS

Washington and London

Library of Congress Cataloging-in-Publication Data

Reckoning with the dead : the Larsen Bay repatriation and the Smithsonian
    Institution / edited by Tamara L. Bray and Thomas W. Killion.
       p. cm.
      Includes bibliographical references and index.
      ISBN 1-56098-365-5 (paper : alk. paper)
      1. Koniagmiut Eskimos—Antiquities—Collection and
preservation.   2. Freedom of religion—United States.   3. Koniagmiut
Eskimos—Civil rights.   4. Koniagmiut Eskimos—Funeral customs and
rites.   5. Human remains (Archaeology)—Alaska—Larsen Bay (Kodiak
Island)   6. Archaeology—Moral and ethical aspects.
7. Repatriation—Alaska—Larsen Bay (Kodiak Island)   8. Smithsonian
Institution—History.   I. Bray, Tamara L.   II. Killion, Thomas W.
E99.E7R39   1994
979.8′4—dc20   94-2652

British Library Cataloguing-in-Publication Data is available

Manufactured in the United States of America
01 00 99 98 97 96 95 94 5 4 3 2 1

⊗ The paper used in this publication meets the minimum requirements of
the American National Standard for Permanence of Paper for Printed
Library Materials Z39.48-1984.

For permission to reproduce illustrations appearing in this book, please
correspond directly with the owners of the works, as listed in the individual
captions. The Smithsonian Institution Press does not retain reproduction
rights for these illustrations individually, or maintain a file of addresses for
photo sources.

PUBLISHER'S NOTE: This book was copy edited by Nancy Benco for the
Repatriation Office at the National Museum of Natural History, which is
responsible for its content and accuracy.

CONTENTS

FOREWORD

One can rarely pinpoint watershed events in the history of social science, but that is the probable significance of the Larsen Bay repatriation case at the Smithsonian Institution. This case so challenged established attitudes and practices in how anthropologists approach the study of human remains and mortuary artifacts that it constitutes a sea change in the history of American anthropology. For anthropologists, the case brought the realization that a century-old tradition of Native American burial studies had been challenged and changed forever. For museum curators, the sacrosanct principle of protecting valuable scientific collections was replaced by a new set of untested and vaguely defined guidelines. For Native Americans, the case was a turning point in a long, painful history of invasive studies conducted by an often insensitive scientific establishment. Larsen Bay changed this and more.

The process by which these changes occurred strained the Smithsonian's national reputation and its relationships with its native constituency. It placed anthropologists and curators in the awkward position of defending the scientific value of collections while acknowledging the unethical collecting practices of one of the Smithsonian's founding fathers, Aleš Hrdlička, who excavated the Larsen Bay site in the 1930s. Curators attempting to justify academic research discovered most Native Americans had little interest in the history of ancient disease and cared less about its potential contributions to Indian health

than about restoring spiritual harmony and respect for Indian beliefs. For the first time anthropologists confronted serious challenges to the retention of a large and important skeletal collection. It was also the first time curators experienced active alienation from the public and politicians. Numerous other repatriation cases had been settled by the Smithsonian and other institutions prior to Larsen Bay. But the high-profile controversy that developed around this case, which pitted the Smithsonian scientific establishment against a small outraged village that wanted to rebury its ancestors, thrust the practice of collecting and studying native human remains into the public domain in a highly dramatic way, with major political consequences. For these reasons, and because of the unique history, national prominence, and notoriety of the collection, the Larsen Bay repatriation marks a major event in the history of museum anthropology.

Despite its many negative aspects, the Larsen Bay case may nonetheless be considered a turning point and a positive force in the normalization of Native American-museum anthropology relations and has already precipitated new and productive relationships. Scientists and museums have learned lessons about local issues and native concerns. Channels of communication that had long been closed, in some cases for decades, have been cleared, opening the way for interaction and collaboration. It must also be noted, however, that the Larsen Bay case was settled by an administrative decision made by Smithsonian Secretary

Robert McC. Adams when the case was at its most critical stage and not through the review procedure established to resolve disputes. Consequently, the case does not stand as the legal precedent that may eventually be needed to settle ambiguities concerning such terms as "cultural affiliation" and "preponderance of evidence" contained in the language of recent repatriation legislation. Nevertheless, the case offers guidelines and insight into the types of issues that may be expected to arise in future repatriation actions. For these and other reasons, this volume is an important documentary record and case study.

One of the principle issues in the Larsen Bay case concerns the role of anthropology and anthropologists—especially archaeologists and physical anthropologists—in American society at a time of increased awareness of Native American heritage and political power. After generations of public disinterest in the more esoteric aspects of anthropological scholarship, the repatriation issue has attracted public attention and has forced scholars to participate in a broad-ranging reevaluation of the ethics of and justification for studying human skeletal remains and mortuary practices. No longer is the pursuit of knowledge for its own sake sufficient to justify practices considered intrusive or disrespectful to native cultural and religious beliefs.

This volume presents a history of the Larsen Bay case from Aleš Hrdlička's excavations at the Uyak Bay site (known to Hrdlička as "Our Point") in the 1930s to the return and reburial of the skeletal and mortuary collections on October 6, 1991. The site was important in having once been a large village whose middens and houses were scattered over several acres. It had been used by Kachemak and Koniag cultures as a cemetery and a village for more than 3,000 years until its abandonment about A.D. 1500. Hrdlička believed that the large number of skeletons he discovered at the site would allow him to reconstruct the biological history of America's native peoples and those of their northeastern Asia homeland. In the course of excavating a large portion of the site he collected 756 skeletal lots, 144 associated mortuary items, and thousands of other artifacts from three stratigraphic levels.

Hrdlička's work at Uyak Bay, in which he used a small railway to remove dirt from the site, remains one of the largest excavations ever conducted in Alaska. His skeletal collection not only dwarfed those from other Alaskan sites but also for decades remained the largest in the Smithsonian from any site in the Americas, representing 5 percent of the Institution's physical anthropology holdings. It can be said that Hrdlička's work at Larsen Bay produced an important body of archaeological information about a site that was being rapidly eroded by the sea.

In time, Hrdlička and others published extensively on the skeletal remains and other archaeological finds from the site. While these reports were important in defining Kodiak's early Kachemak and Koniag cultures, recent decades have seen Hrdlička's work cited more often for its shortcomings than its accomplishments due to his abominable documentation and excavation techniques (even for his day). In addition, his diaries, published nearly verbatim, detail his gruff and belligerent manner of dealing with native peoples who appeared at the dig site to protest the disturbance of their ancestors. Hrdlička was a walking public-relations disaster and his own worst enemy. He would have been the last to imagine that a day would come when he would see his specimens repatriated by the testimony of his own words and the painful memories of his then young informants.

As is clear in the following pages, a review of the Larsen Bay case is instructive in what to *avoid* in repatriation proceedings. In hindsight, the Smithsonian made many errors in its response to the Larsen Bay community's request for repatriation. Today, its initial obstinacy seems to have been unjustified. It must be pointed out, however, that when the proceedings began in 1987 there was, from anybody's point of view, no known legal or institutional policy for such a massive and unprecedented repatriation action. For these reasons alone it was probably inevitable that the Larsen Bay request would lead to confrontation. The Smithsonian had already established a policy for repatriating human remains of named, known individuals and ethnological materials of a religious nature that had been improperly (and/or unethically) collected. But the request for reburial of 5 percent of the Smithsonian's "scientifically excavated" physical anthropological collection, containing the longest record of human populations in Alaska and one used extensively in modern research, was so far from established norms that curators could not consider such action without opening themselves to serious fiduciary repercussions, to say nothing of its broader impact at the national level. Aspects of the controversy might have been avoided had both sides listened more carefully to the other, but the differences between Larsen Bay and the Smithsonian were already so deep, and being driven further apart by political action, that satisfactory resolution was probably impossible without direct legislative intervention.

At the time, in 1987, when the initial Larsen Bay request was made, my views as a Smithsonian curator reflected these concerns. While it was the physical anthropologists in the department who were most directly affected by the request, both myself and the other curators were aware of the issue and its significance. All curators were. We had been schooled on Hrdlička's misdeeds and the effect of his Prussian arrogance on an earlier generation of curators. To curators, his insensitivity in dealing with the Larsen Bay community seemed more remote than the scientific importance of the collection. Since there was no clear legal or moral basis for repatriation without evidence of direct historical linkage to living descendants, there was no principle on which to decide the case in favor of Larsen Bay. We also had to determine whether the motive was religious or political in nature.

I had a chance to discover this personally during the spring of 1988 while attending a symposium in Kodiak, Alaska, where a large group of arctic specialists had gathered to discuss the traditional cultures of Kodiak Island in connection with the opening of the Inua exhibition in Anchorage. Richard H. Jordan, a friend and former student who had recently begun excavations at Karluk, near Larsen Bay, asked me to take a few minutes from the meetings to meet with Frank Carlson outside in the school parking lot. Frank was the leading figure in Larsen Bay's repatriation request. Knowing that I would be present, Dick had asked Frank to come in from Larsen Bay to present his case.

The meeting was brief. We both explained our positions. It quickly became obvious to Frank that the Smithsonian could not move swiftly in his favor, if at all, and that there would many practical obstacles even if we were to reach an agreement on repatriating the Koniag materials, the later component of the collection. That there were serious obstacles to accommodation on both sides was evident to both. My most vivid recollection of that meeting today is an awareness of the deep personal commitment Frank Carlson felt about the necessity to rectify what he perceived as a serious injustice to his people. There could be no compromises in the rightful treatment of the dead.

I returned and reported on the outcome of the meeting to the anthropology department, but it seemed that by that point the die had already been cast. Discussion and compromises seemed futile, and the process recounted in these pages began to unfold. Later, Jordan tried to arrange a second meeting between Larsen Bay officials and Dennis Stanford, then head of the Archaeology Division at the Smithsonian, but when Stanford arrived on Kodiak in the summer of 1990 the Larsen Bay Council refused to see him. By this time the Larsen Bay community seemed to have decided to proceed toward a political rather than a negotiated settlement.

As Pullar notes in his chapter, the forces driving the Smithsonian and Larsen Bay apart grew out of a clash between deeply held beliefs rooted in scholarly activity and museum policy on one hand and native attitudes and religious beliefs on the other. The case provides a perspective on how science has often been conducted on native subjects in the past and demon-

strates the process of "re-education" underway at the Smithsonian and among the wider scientific establishment. Together with a few other landmark cases, like the protection of Native American religious sites and the repatriation of sacred relics like the Zuni war gods, the Larsen Bay case unfolded during a time of major social change involving the rights of ethnic and cultural groups. It is remarkable that it has taken this long and required the stimulus and sanction of legislative action to move a community whose very purpose has been to preserve and protect native cultures and histories toward rapprochement with those native groups. As is clearly shown here, the issue did not arise out of malice or conscious scientific exploitation. It resulted from a clash of western and native world views that pitted scientists and native peoples as antagonists who had philosophically different approaches to the question of repatriation. Given the isolation of research and museum anthropology from the social milieu of the native community in North America, this clash was probably unavoidable and inevitable. The fact that those actually conducting the research on skeletal remains—the physical anthropologists—often did not participate in the initial collection of remains and frequently had little contact with native communities further distanced curators from native interests, physically and philosophically.

The Larsen Bay story is not unique in demonstrating how native community interests have suffered indignities at the hands of anthropologists. There are many others like it. The case of Minik, the Greenlander whose father and a group of relatives died while being studied at the American Museum of Natural History in New York and who was led to believe that his relatives were "buried" on the museum grounds but later accidentally discovered his father's bones on display, is a singularly gruesome episode in museum-based native studies. This case has done much to damage relations between anthropologists and native peoples and further alienated the public. A common thread existed in both these stories in the person of Aleš Hrdlička, who also played an important role in the anthropometric study of Minik's relatives under Franz Boas's supervision. Here, as in the Larsen Bay case, the human element has been as much a part of the proceedings as arguments about morality, scholarly issues, or legalities have been. Unfortunately, while Boas, Hrdlička, and others can be faulted for insensitivity in their dealings with native peoples in their day, it is more tragic that modern scholars and museum officials have continued to take refuge in the edifice of the ivory tower and failed to recognize the need to develop new perspectives and museum practices.

Larsen Bay brings the repatriation process in step with other consciousness-raising events taking place in other areas of anthropological concern. The incorporation of native voices within the profession of anthropology, as consultants in exhibit production, as promoters and instigators of educational programs, and as colleagues in field studies, has helped remove racist overtones that have been recurrent themes in anthropological science through much of its first century. Today, fieldworkers routinely consult with native communities for permission to conduct research, and guidelines to this effect have been established as policy for federal grant support. Political empowerment at regional and local levels has been evolving to protect native interests, while at the same time fruitful collaboration between anthropologists and native groups is becoming more widespread.

The Larsen Bay case offers a rather negative view of how (some) anthropologists collected data in the past. More recent decades seem to offer many examples of how anthropology and museums abused a special relationship with native society, and in so doing came perilously close to losing respectability. But in the aftermath of Larsen Bay, the enactment of the Indian Religious Freedom Act, and movements to remake museum displays and rewrite history, seeds of a new relationship between anthropologists and Native Americans are being sown. We may hope that this rendering of a difficult chapter in that catharsis will contribute to this process of renewal.

WILLIAM W. FITZHUGH
Director, Arctic Studies Center
Smithsonian Institution

NOTE FROM THE DIRECTOR

The symposium presented at the American Anthropological Association's annual meeting in San Francisco in 1992 proved to be an important meeting for all of us who were involved in the Larsen Bay repatriation. The value of this meeting lay not so much in revisiting the pain of the process, for it was often painful for all sides, but in seeing where we made mistakes and how we could better work together in the future.

I came to my position as director of the National Museum of Natural History (NMNH) in January 1989, 18 months after the museum had received the request from the Larsen Bay Tribal Council for the return of human remains and associated grave goods from the Uyak site. This request had come in the form of a Tribal Council resolution (see the Appendix). When P.L. 101-185, the National Museum of the American Indian Act, was signed into law in November 1989, I was asked to act for the Secretary of the Smithsonian Institution to oversee repatriation and thus became part of the process. Although I am not an anthropologist, I had worked in museums and universities for 30 years and was deeply interested in this issue.

At least two opposing and interacting forces were at work in the Larsen Bay case. The first was a resurgence in the expression of Native American ethnic and cultural identity. This was manifested in a demand to have their views heard, especially on the disposition of human remains, grave goods, and special artifacts that they claimed were improperly held in museums. This reemerging cultural movement was strongly supported by most of the museum's anthropologists, many of whom had actively worked to support other Native American issues, such as land rights, over many years.

The opposing force was based on the deep-seated scientific view that the study of human remains and associated material is a public good, worthy of dedication, and capable of leading to an understanding of humanity that is valuable to all humankind. Within this perspective, museum collections were considered a vital resource that needed to be carefully curated and reassessed as new ideas appeared.

By the time the Larsen Bay case emerged, the NMNH had already changed its views about human remains dating to the historic period. In 1984 it had repatriated a number of Modoc Indian remains, and in 1988 it had returned Blackfeet Indian remains and sacred objects, such as the Zuni war gods. Human remains that were thousands of years old, however, were considered more problematical.

The passage of the National Museum of the American Indian Act in 1989 was a watershed. As the NMNH began the process of complying with the new law, its staff had to change their attitudes even more than before, methods for the repatriation process had to be developed, and discussions with Native Americans became vital. Since then, we have met and discussed repatriation issues with many Native American groups. Some have come to the museum to talk with us, and others we have traveled to see—the Cherokee in North Carolina; the Five Civilized Tribes in Sulphur, Oklahoma; the Warm Springs Confederated Tribes of Oregon; and the Inupiat Communities of the North Slope Borough, Alaska, among others. Some of us also participated in the important reburial ceremony in Larsen Bay. All this has been helpful to us, and I have personally been taught a great deal by the interaction.

In the past few years we have also begun several outreach programs for Native Americans. We are working with native groups as partners in setting up museum displays and we have developed a program to bring Native Americans to Washington to work on our collections under the guidance of Dr. JoAllyn Archambault, a Standing Rock Sioux and an anthropologist on our staff.

Although the Smithsonian was excluded from P.L. 101-601, the Native American Graves Protection and Repatriation Act, due to the fact that the National Museum of the American Indian was still in the process of developing its repatriation policy, NMNH has formally accepted the 1990 Act as its policy. As a result, the NMNH falls under the auspices of P.L. 101-185 and also uses P.L. 101-601 as formal repatriation policy.

We at NMNH look forward to working with Native Americans on repatriation issues in the future. We encourage more use of the national collections of Native American materials to better understand a varied and wonderful cultural past. And we offer help to those who wish to use the National Anthropological Archives with its strong focus on Native American history.

FRANK H. TALBOT
Director, National Museum of Natural History
Smithsonian Institution

NOTE FROM THE SMITHSONIAN REPATRIATION REVIEW COMMITTEE

The National Museum of the American Indian Act (P.L. 101-185, Sec. 12) called for the establishment of a special committee of five individuals to monitor and to review the inventory, the identification, and the return of Native American human remains and funerary objects in the possession of the Smithsonian Institution. Following the provisions of this act, the secretary of the Smithsonian, Robert McC. Adams, appointed five individuals to serve on this committee, four of whom were selected from nominations submitted by the Native American community. The committee was constituted in March 1991 but did not convene for its first meeting until September of that year.

The Smithsonian Institution Repatriation Review Committee members are Russell Thornton (Cherokee), professor, University of California at Berkeley; Andrea Hunter (Osage), assistant professor, University of Northern Arizona; Roger Anyon, dirctor of the Zuni Heritage and Historic Preservation Office; Lynne Goldstein, professor, University of Wisconsin, Milwaukee; and Christy Turner, professor, Arizona State University.

In addition to its oversight responsibilities, the National Museum of the American Indian Act stipulates that the committee may facilitate the resolution of any disputes that may arise between Native American groups and the museum over the return of human remains or objects. The Smithsonian Repatriation Review Committee wishes to note that although it had been formally constituted prior to the secretary's final decision on the Larsen Bay return, it was not called upon to facilitate the resolution of this case and regrets that it was unable to play the role envisioned for this body in this particular instance.

RUSSELL THORNTON
Chairman, Smithsonian Repatriation Review Committee
Smithsonian Institution

CHRONOLOGY OF EVENTS

May 87 Larsen Bay Tribal Council passes resolution calling for return of all Uyak site materials in possession of National Museum of Natural History (NMNH).

July 87 Tribal Council sends resolution to Adrienne Kaeppler, NMNH Anthropology Department Chairwoman.

Sept 87 Kaeppler responds to Larsen Bay request for repatriation of Uyak site remains; states there is no indication that the modern peoples were related to the remains in the collection; also suggests that Hrdlička had permission of local residents to excavate at site.

Oct 87 Tribal Council takes offense at Kaeppler's suggestion that they are not descendants of the remains in the NMNH collections; also deny that permission was ever granted Hrdlička to excavate their burial grounds.

Feb 88 Letter from Kaeppler to Larsen Bay restating that the human remains from the Uyak site represent an ancient population and, therefore, are not considered directly related to the modern inhabitants; stresses scientific value of collection.

Feb 88 Senator Stevens of Alaska writes Smithsonian on behalf of the Larsen Bay village.

Apr 88 William Fitzhugh, NMNH curator, meets with various people from Kodiak Island during visit to Alaska; reports that meeting was friendly but that the question of repatriating the Uyak materials remained unresolved.

Apr 88 Tribal Council writes Kaeppler again stating its wish that the Uyak site remains be returned for reburial.

Oct 88 Donald Ortner appointed Chairman of the Department of Anthropology at the NMNH.

Sept 89 Letter from Henry Sockbeson, lawyer for the Native American Rights Fund (NARF), to Smithsonian Secretary Robert McC. Adams informing the Smithsonian that he is now representing the village of Larsen Bay in their quest for the return of the Uyak site materials.

Oct 89 Donald Ortner appointed Acting Director of the Repatriation Program at the NMNH.

Nov 89 P.L. 101-185, National Museum of American Indian (NMAI) Act, signed into law.

Nov 89 Secretary Adams responds to Sockbeson. Notes that the Smithsonian anthropologists continue to believe that there is no direct link between the NMNH materials and the modern Larsen Bay population; stresses that this question will be investigated further, but that limited funds are available to conduct the work; suggests different possible options for disposition of the remains; asks for their patience.

Jan 90　Letter from Sockbeson to Secretary Adams indicating that the only requirement standing in the way of repatriation is the establishment of a cultural link between the modern residents and the archaeological remains; asks the Smithsonian to provide him with whatever information they have bearing on this question.

Jan 90　Consultants for NARF, Gordon Pullar and Philomena Knecht, prepare a report entitled "Continuous Occupation of Larsen Bay by the Qikertarmiut." Sockbeson forwards copy of report to the Smithsonian, believing that cultural affiliation has been established based on a "preponderance of the evidence."

Apr 90　Letter from Secretary Adams to Sockbeson. Notes that the archaeological history of the Uyak site collection is complex; materials in question range in age from the historic period to 800 B.C.; notes that the evidence presented by the NARF consultants is equivocal and the question of continuity still remains. Offers to repatriate the post-contact burials; again suggests alternative possibilities for disposition of the remains be considered.

May 90　Secretary Adams appoints Smithsonian's Repatriation Review Committee (5 people).

June 90　NARF rejects Secretary's offer to return only post-contact remains; also indicates there is no room for negotiation on disposition of remains as their clients wish to rebury everything. Sockbeson requests that the Repatriation Review Committee be invoked to arbitrate the case.

Aug 90　Department of Anthropology retains services of two experts, Don Dumond and Richard Scott, to evaluate the available biological and archaeological evidence relevant to the question of cultural continuity at the Uyak site and prepare a report.

Sept 90　Letter from Secretary Adams to Sockbeson. Concurs with suggestion to convene Repatriation Review Committee.

Oct 90　Reports of outside experts Dumond and Scott submitted to Department of Anthropology.

Oct 90　P.L. 101-601, Native American Graves Protection and Repatriation Act (NAGPRA), passed by Congress.

Nov 90　Copies of Dumond's and Scott's reports forwarded to NARF.

Nov 90　NARF sends Dumond's and Scott's reports out for review to anthropologists Philomena Knecht and Bill Laughlin.

Jan 91　Laughlin and Knecht provide written comments on Dumond's and Scott's reports. They disagree with their findings and/or say that the data presented strengthen NARF's contention that there is continuity between the prehistoric and modern populations.

Feb 91　Letter from Sockbeson to Secretary Adams. Addresses findings of Dumond's and Scott's reports; provides copies of Knecht's and Laughlin's comments; suggests that all the evidence supports a determination of cultural affiliation and reiterates request for return.

Feb–
Mar 91　Both Dumond and Scott have opportunity to respond to Knecht's and Laughlin's comments; neither Dumond nor Scott support NARF consultants' reading of the data as indicative of cultural affiliation.

Mar 91　Memo from Ortner to Secretary Adams outlining options for proceeding with the Larsen Bay repatriation request: (1) return the remains, (2) keep the remains for lack of evidence of continuity, or (3) convene the Repatriation Review Committee to consider case; presses for the third option.

Apr 91　Letter from Secretary Adams to Sockbeson. States that the Smithsonian has concluded that the materials should be repatriated to the Larsen Bay people on the basis of the evidence.

Aug–
Sept 91　Deaccession of Uyak site skeletal remains conducted with help of contractors.

Sept 91　Return of skeletal remains to Larsen Bay, Kodiak Island, Alaska.

Oct 91　Skeletal remains reburied in ceremony at Larsen Bay.

Jan 92　Return of 144 associated funerary objects (95 catalog entries) to Larsen Bay.

Part 1

The Larsen Bay Repatriation Request

1

LOOKING TOWARD LARSEN BAY

Evolving Attitudes at the Smithsonian Institution

To some, Kodiak Island may seem a lonely place lost to time in a far away corner of the globe. On the map it hugs the coast of southwestern Alaska, about as far away from the temperate centers of late twentieth-century commerce and politics as one could imagine. On closer examination, however, this remote section of the North Pacific reveals living communities of long tradition, concerned with the presentation and disposition of their unique cultural heritage beyond the confines of Kodiak Island. Scratch a little deeper and one begins to see the outline of a richly textured past, for Kodiak has been continuously inhabited by maritime hunting peoples for at least the last 7,000 years (Clark 1984:136).

Throughout this long period, the inhabitants of Kodiak have remained a dynamic force within the teeming cultural cross-currents of northernmost North America. During the last 250 years of "historic time" the area has experienced episodes of western attention and exploitation through exploration, commercial development, missionary work, scientific study, and government administrative efforts. With the exception of a few ethnographic mentions (Davis 1984), however, the native history of Kodiak has been largely ignored. This is particularly true of the American period following the purchase of Alaska from Russia in the mid-nineteenth century. Research expeditions, natural disasters, and military relocation programs carried out in the region during World War II are all events that have remained well beyond the con-

sciousness of the American mainstream. One native community on Kodiak Island has recently reinserted itself into the history of the North Pacific, however, and attracted international attention through its protracted efforts to have ancient remains removed from a local archaeological site repatriated.

The modern community of Larsen Bay is tucked into a secluded inlet on the northern side of Kodiak Island that forms one edge of the Straits of Shelikof (fig. 1.1). This coastal zone enjoys a surprisingly mild climate in comparison to the freezing conditions of greater interior Alaska. Fog, rain, and wind (along with an occasional spectacularly clear day) dominate the days and lives of the Larsen Bay villagers who rely on commercial fishing, crabbing, and canning for their livelihoods. The scene today is much the same as it was over 50 years ago when Aleš Hrdlička of the Smithsonian Institution first arrived to probe the eroding shoreline.

Hrdlička, who was by then well on his way to becoming the undisputed patriarch of physical anthropology in the United States, was hot on the trail of the "first Americans" whom he believed had arrived on the continent relatively recently. He had searched far and wide for their remains across the Alaskan "gateway" to the New World, from the Aleut burial caves on Kagamil Island in the far Aleutians, to Athapaskan cemeteries along the Yukon River in central Alaska. Hrdlička sought proof for his arguments of antiquity, migration, and settlement in the physical characteris-

Figure 1.1. View of modern-day Larsen Bay. (Photograph by Miroslav Prokopec)

tics of the human cranium. Unlike most physical anthropologists and archaeologists of today, however, Hrdlička's interests did not extend much beyond his precious crania. He was generally unconcerned with either the archaeological history of the places he excavated or the concerns of the native peoples who lived there. The breadth and depth of his work on the description of human crania remain unparalleled within the discipline of physical anthropology but his mode of operation in the field, tacitly accepted by most at the time, has come to haunt us.

His insensitivity to the human context of his work must be seen as a symptom of the prevailing attitudes of his era. It was a time when American society paid scant attention to the rights of native peoples, and anthropologists, as members of that society, more frequently exploited indigenous cultures than thought about contributing to their survival. As the chapters assembled in this volume reveal, anthropology still bears the burden of that time. It is a legacy that continues to plague the establishment of an anthropology concerned as much with the rights of contemporary Native Americans as with the explication of their past.

Significance of the Larsen Bay Case

The return of ancestral skeletal remains and funerary objects by the Smithsonian Institution to the people of Larsen Bay represents an important and highly visible event in the history of American anthropology. Since the conscious shedding of the colonial mantle, anthropologists have frequently assumed the role of advocate for the disenfranchised with whom they traditionally work. The dedicated efforts of archaeologists to substantiate native land claims in the Arctic, for instance, and the direct political engagement of anthropologists working on behalf of indigenous peoples in Amazonia, are but two examples.

The perpetrators of violations against native peoples are today more typically construed as external entities such as governments or large corporations. Such entities are almost always seen as separate from the academy, and especially far removed from anthropology. The Larsen Bay repatriation case, however, reversed what we like to think of as the customary relationship of advocacy between anthropology and native peoples. The self-image many of us hold as liberal, activist, and altruistic social scientists is not what

Thomas W. Killion and Tamara L. Bray

was reflected back in the mirror of Larsen Bay. The "institutional enemy" in this case was the anthropological profession itself, and the native peoples involved proved to be fully capable of assembling their own team of professional experts and advocates to challenge the institution. The Larsen Bay repatriation alters in a fundamental way our understanding of the role of museums and their relationship to the Native American community. The lesson is all the more poignant as it involves the Smithsonian Institution, the archetype of the American museum and the repository of some of the nation's most treasured artifacts.

The question of native rights with regard to the disposition of aboriginal burials and sacred objects have been issues of growing concern in the United States over the past twenty years. Following trends in state legislation (see Price 1991), federal repatriation laws were enacted in 1989 (Public Law 101-185, National Museum of the American Indian Act) and 1990 (Public Law 101-601, Native American Graves Protection and Repatriation Act) that required anthropologists to begin to work collaboratively with Native American groups to determine the disposition of culturally affiliated human remains, funerary objects, and items of cultural patrimony. This unprecedented legal mandate has, not unexpectedly, been difficult for the various parties involved as they take their first tentative steps toward developing new kinds of working relationships.

The Request from Larsen Bay and the Smithsonian Response

The Larsen Bay case was initiated in 1987 when the residents of this small village on Kodiak Island presented the Smithsonian with a formal request (see the Appendix) for the return of burial remains removed by Aleš Hrdlička in the 1930s from a local archaeological site known as Uyak. (The chronology of events that followed the request is presented in the front of this volume.) At the time, the Smithsonian's policy regarding the return of skeletal remains extended only to direct lineal descendants of known individuals. The people of Larsen Bay sought the repatriation of all human remains removed from the site, most of which were from one to several thousand years old. The museum had no established guidelines for evaluating requests for the return of ancient remains. The time depth of the Uyak material clearly challenged available methods for establishing cultural or biological affinity. The request fell outside any familiar categories of action recognized by the museum's scientific staff and demanded a broader per-

spective that would encompass an anthropological understanding of the contemporary concerns and sensitivities of the people living at Larsen Bay.

Given the problems posed by the antiquity of the remains, together with the natural tendency of bureaucracies towards inertia, it should come as no surprise to learn that the people of Larsen Bay ultimately waited four years for resolution of their request. It is fair to say that the "speed" with which this case was resolved had to do, in large part, with the passage of relevant legislation and the political pressures brought to bear by the Native American Rights Fund. It should be noted, however, that aggressive legal action has not been the only, or even the most common, approach to the resolution of repatriation requests at the Smithsonian. The return of the Zuni War Gods in 1984 provides an important counterpoint to the Larsen Bay case. Negotiations for the return of the War Gods were also conducted prior to enactment of federal repatriation legislation. Although resolution of this request ultimately took seven years, discussions between the Zuni and the Smithsonian were carried out in a spirit of mutual respect and cooperation, without the intervention of lawyers, and resulted in relationships of lasting importance (Merrill, Ladd, and Ferguson 1993).

Because it came at a time of heightened awareness of and concern about reburial issues, the Larsen Bay request plunged the Smithsonian into an intense period of self-examination during which time some of the most fundamental premises of museum practice and scholarly research were critically evaluated. Hard questions about the museum's obligation to the public trust, minority rights vis-à-vis the dominant culture, and the public value of scientific research forced many of those in the institution to reassess many basic assumptions. The Larsen Bay petition was the catalyst for an evolution of attitudes within the museum that is still ongoing. Though the collections are gone, the changes set in motion by this request remain with the Smithsonian as the legacy of Larsen Bay.

The Larsen Bay Return at the Museum

The human remains from the Uyak site represented a significant proportion, nearly 5 percent, of the Smithsonian's skeletal collection from North America. Beyond the actual loss of an important biological collection, the Larsen Bay case has had a direct and profound impact on how the National Museum of Natural History (NMNH) functions as an international research institution. The repatriation laws mandated the development of a whole new set of guiding principles, the adoption of which forever altered the way in which scientific research may be conducted. The Larsen Bay repatriation is a direct material consequence of the disjuncture that Gordon Pullar describes in this volume as a "clash of world views." Seen in the context of ongoing debate over America's "contested past" (Hill 1992) and the role of living and vocal, rather than "vanished" and silenced, native peoples in the stewardship of that past (McGuire 1992), Larsen Bay stands as a strong indicator of the need for an adjustment of attitudes and behaviors on the part of America's "gatekeepers" to the past.

The Larsen Bay request involved the return of 756 sets of skeletal remains, comprising an estimated 1,000 individuals, and 95 lots of associated funerary objects. Because the Repatriation Office was not yet operational when the decision to repatriate the collection was made, the responsibility for the inventory and actual return of materials fell to the Department of Anthropology at the NMNH. Due to the protracted and, at times, hostile nature of the negotiations leading up to the repatriation decision, both the museum's administrators and the Larsen Bay representatives were eager to expedite the actual transfer of the collections.

To meet the institutional and legal requirements of the repatriation, the scale of which was unprecedented in the history of the museum, a team of five professionals was hired on a contract basis for a period of two and a half months. Under the supervision of Anthropology Department staff, the contractors conducted the physical inventory and partial documentation of the human remains from the Uyak site. The documentation protocols developed during this deaccessioning project formed the basis of the inventory and recording system now in use in the NMNH Repatriation Office. Even with the adoption of abbreviated recording procedures and an assembly-line approach, the contract team was still hard-pressed to meet the agreed upon deadline. The skeletal remains were, nonetheless, readied for shipment by the appointed day. The remains were transferred from the Smithsonian to Kodiak Island early in September 1991 and reburied near the original site of their disinterment on October 6, 1991. The Russian Orthodox service held at the grave site for the reinterred remains was attended by members of the Larsen Bay community, Smithsonian officials, the Native American Rights Fund attorney, state government representatives, and the media.

The identification and return of associated funerary objects from the Uyak site was handled separately due to the lack of available personnel to examine the collection. Difficulties arose in identifying the exact objects that had come from funerary contexts. According to the archaeological evidence, items found in burial contexts were similar to those used in everyday life. This lack of formal differentiation in the mortuary assemblage, in combination with the minimal amount of provenience data recorded in the original field notes, made the precise identification of associated funerary objects problematic. By using Hrdlička's handwritten journals, site photographs, and catalog records, together with the artifacts themselves, however, it eventually proved possible to isolate most of the grave goods. Again, the inventory and documentation of the cultural objects for deaccession purposes was a learning experience, and recording methodologies and protocols were formulated as part of the process. The associated funerary objects from the Uyak site collection were returned to Larsen Bay in January 1992.

Larsen Bay's Aftermath: Challenging Issues for Repatriation at the NMNH

The editors of this volume, together with other staff, were hired specifically to implement the NMNH's repatriation program. At the time of our arrival late in the summer of 1991 the Larsen Bay repatriation was just nearing completion. Although the confrontational atmosphere surrounding the case had largely subsided, it was obvious that a strong sense of urgency and anxiety over the Larsen Bay return still remained in the Department of Anthropology where the collections had been stored, studied, and cared for over a period of 50 years.

As we became immersed in the politics of repatriation during our first months at the Smithsonian, we gradually became aware of the impact that the Larsen Bay case had on the department and more generally on the institution as a whole. It was apparent to us that the policies and attitudes concerning repatriation were extremely new, sometimes contradictory, and still evolving in the crucible of the Larsen Bay repatriation and other less problematic cases. Many of the issues that arose out of the Larsen Bay case remained critical points of concern as we began to develop the repatriation program mandated by law.

One of the key issues had revolved around the question of cultural affiliation and continuity. For the anthropologists involved, the decision of whether or not to repatriate the Uyak site burials hinged on the demonstration of cultural continuity between the ancient remains and the modern Larsen Bay population. For the native residents of Larsen Bay, it was sufficient to know that the burials had been removed from their traditional village area. The remains were considered ancestral to the modern population by vir-

Thomas W. Killion and Tamara L. Bray

tue of their provenience alone, since the inhabitants of the village considered themselves to have been resident there since time immemorial.

This issue was far less clear-cut from an archaeological point of view. It was this lack of agreement over the cultural linkage between the archaeological remains from the site and the modern population that became the primary point of contention in the case. Both the Smithsonian and the Native American Rights Fund engaged outside experts to assess the evidence for cultural affiliation. Given the fuzzy nature of the concept and the time depth involved, it should come as no surprise to learn that the sum of the evidence brought to bear on the case did not lend conclusive support to a determination of cultural continuity at the site one way or the other.

Because the question of cultural linkage remained in dispute, the Larsen Bay case would have been a clear candidate for review by the newly established, but not yet convened, Repatriation Review Committee. This panel, comprised of four individuals nominated by the Native American community and one selected by the Secretary of the Smithsonian in accordance with the provisions of the National Museum of the American Indian Act, was established precisely for the purpose of facilitating the resolution of such disputes. The Secretary of the Smithsonian, however, ultimately made the decision himself, ruling in favor of the Larsen Bay community's claim, without the benefit of the Review Committee's input. Thus, the actual process, as envisioned in the law, was not fully tested and no independent assessment of the evidence for cultural continuity at Larsen Bay was obtained. The variety of data, some new and some reworked, presented in the chapters in this volume, tend to lend overall support to the Secretary's determination that the sum of the evidence argued in favor of repatriation to the Larsen Bay community.

This volume uses the example of Larsen Bay as a case study to illustrate the complexity and consequences of repatriation. It provides a forum for the various perspectives that coalesced around and constituted the Larsen Bay case, juxtaposing the divergent positions of Native Alaskans, members of the legal profession, anthropologists, and museum personnel. The volume strives to mirror the reality of a situation in which a diverse array of interest groups was thrust into a new set of relations defined by the repatriation issue. In permitting these groups to voice their opinion, the volume offers no final solutions. It does, however, provide a starting point for dialogue about a complex and evolving issue that will continue to affect native peoples and anthropologists for many years to come.

The volume is divided into four parts. The first deals with the history of the Larsen Bay repatriation request. This is followed by a review of the evidence brought to bear on the question of cultural continuity. The next section focuses on the various legal, political, and procedural issues that evolved out of the case, while the final one offers the reflections of three outside observers on the significance of the Larsen Bay return. Several of the chapters included here were first presented as papers in a symposium at the American Anthropological Association's annual meeting in San Francisco in December 1992. Additional papers were solicited from Donald Ortner, Chairperson of the Department of Anthropology during the period in which the Larsen Bay case unfolded, and Stephen Loring and Miroslav Prokopec, two scholars intimately familiar with the life and work of Aleš Hrdlička, a key figure in the story of the Larsen Bay repatriation.

In Part 1, The Larsen Bay Repatriation Request, Donald Ortner, a physical anthropologist at the Smithsonian, offers his views on the history and significance of this particular repatriation. He focuses on the uniqueness of the challenge to the institution and the inability of the system to cope, initially, with the political immediacy of the repatriation issue. He cautions that the consequences of the legislative mandate are still unfolding and will continue to pose a challenge as museum administrators and scientists attempt to carry out the law. Gordon Pullar, former president of the Kodiak Area Native Association, an anthropologist, and one of the initiators of the petition presented to the Smithsonian, chronicles the history of the case from the point of view of a Native Alaskan and resident of Kodiak Island. Pullar elucidates the pain and resentment harbored by people at Larsen Bay over Hrdlička's actions and the frustration the community experienced in their attempt to recover the remains he removed in the 1930s. Stephen Loring and Miroslav Prokopec consider Aleš Hrdlička, the man and his times. Clearly an eccentric and zealous personality, the aloof authority he projected as a scientist from the Smithsonian coupled with his odd European mannerisms have made him an easy target for ridicule and contempt in our more "enlightened" times. The authors remind us that what is often lacking from the current critique is a historical perspective that situates Hrdlička within the western intellectual and social climate of his day.

Part 2, The Uyak Site and Evidence for Cultural Continuity, focuses on our understanding of the cultural history of the region and on the different types of evidence brought to bear on the question of cultural continuity. Don Dumond, an expert on the prehistory of southern Alaska, draws on his extensive experience in the region to provide an assessment of cultural continuity at Larsen Bay based on the archaeological evidence. He examines Hrdlička's original formulation of separate and distinct Koniag and Pre-Koniag cultural traditions and Don Clark's later proposal of absorption of most, if not all, of the earlier Koniag culture into the widespread Kachemak tradition. According to Dumond, the Uyak site may well have been abandoned sometime in the fifteenth century. This view must eventually be tempered with a knowledge of coeval and later occupations on Kodiak Island. Stuart Speaker, who was involved with the examination and deaccession of the funerary objects from the Uyak burials, sorts through Hrdlička's field records and notes on Uyak to salvage information of contemporary value on site structure and site formation processes.

Moving to the osteological data, two separate chapters, one by Jim Simon and Amy Steffian, both of whom have recently conducted archaeological investigations on Kodiak Island, and the other by Javier Urcid, a physical anthropologist with the Repatriation Office at the Museum of Natural History involved with the Larsen Bay deaccession, examine the skeletal remains from Larsen Bay in light of Hrdlička's cannibalism hypothesis. The authors arrive at similar conclusions utilizing different sets of data. They suggest that Hrdlička's hypothesis ignores more compelling evidence for the protracted, possibly transgenerational, mortuary treatment of the dead. Richard Scott, a physical anthropologist at the University of Alaska, considers the question of biological continuity at Larsen Bay through a comparison of dental traits found among modern and prehistoric populations. Chris Donta of Bryn Mawr College compares ethnohistoric information on Koniag ceremonial objects with archaeological data in order to evaluate the evidence for continuity in ceremonial life. Donald Clark, a senior scholar in the field of Pacific Eskimo archaeology, concludes the section with a critique of the papers presented and some of his own thoughts on the prehistory of the region and the arguments for and against cultural continuity.

Part 3, The Lessons of Larsen Bay, examines legal issues, practical considerations, and the repatriation program at the NMNH in the wake of the Larsen Bay case. Tamara Bray and Lauryn Grant, both of the Smithsonian, offer an analysis of the problems entailed in the legislative attempt to transform the anthropologically grounded notion of cultural affiliation into an operative legal standard. Henry Sockbeson, the Native American Rights Fund attorney who represented the Larsen Bay community, provides his assessment of recent repatriation legislation and its ramifications for the future of anthropology. Carol Butler, a museum specialist in the Department of Anthropology, pragmatically reviews the operational considerations for museums involved in repatriation, from time schedules and shipping containers to native sensitivities surrounding the treatment of the dead. Melinda Zeder, an archaeologist in the Department of Anthropology and former Deputy Chairperson, offers an overview of the administrative and technical plan for the repatriation program and outlines efforts now underway to further involve Native Americans in the repatriation program at the museum.

Part 4, Reflections on Larsen Bay, situates the event in its broader sociopolitical context. Three scholars with long histories of involvement in the repatriation issue offer their views on the significance of this case and consider its implications for the future of archaeology and museums in this country. Lynne Goldstein, an archaeologist at the University of Wisconsin at Milwaukee and a member of the Smithsonian's Repatriation Review Committee, comments directly on the papers presented in the volume, drawing out the main themes and discussing them in light of the larger repatriation issue. Randall McGuire, professor of anthropology at the State University of New York at Binghamton and an important voice within the critical thinking movement in archaeology, looks at the Larsen Bay repatriation in terms of its implications for the practice of archaeology in the United States. For him, Larsen Bay is both a poignant example of the contradictions between the stated intent and practical methods of American archaeology, and an illustration of the way in which interpretation of the past is informed by present interests. In the final paper of this volume, Rick Hill, a member of the Tuscarora Nation, activist scholar, and museum professional, looks at the Larsen Bay repatriation as both a wake up call for the western repositories of American Indian objects and as a sign of a kind of coming of age within the museum world. Calling upon museums to acknowledge their responsibilities to Native American communities, he urges the establishment of new partnerships to help rejuvenate the rapidly disappearing traditions of Native American cultures.

This volume makes a contribution to the anthropological understanding of repatriation, offers guidelines for future repatriations, and augments our understanding of culture history in southern Alaska. Anthropologists interested in issues as diverse as intellectual property rights, scientific ethics, and culture change should find the volume of value to their own work. We anticipate that it will be useful as a case study for a variety of undergraduate and graduate courses as a new generation of anthropologists and archaeologists are prepared to confront the reality of repatriation. Museum personnel and policy makers concerned with the issues of repatriation, native rights, and tribal sovereignty may also find this study of interest.

The torturous and at times frustrating path leading to the decision to repatriate the Larsen Bay collection took the Smithsonian into terra incognita where landmarks were few and crossings often painful. In the end, the Larsen Bay return, as one of the earliest and largest to date, has become a landmark in itself. It marks the beginning of a new chapter in the history of Native American rights vis-à-vis museums in general, and the Smithsonian Institution, in particular. The Larsen Bay return, "with all its warts," provides an important case study from which other institutions, organizations, and communities concerned with the issues and implementation of the repatriation mandate will ultimately benefit.

Acknowledgments

We would like to thank William Fitzhugh, Daniel Goodwin, and Donald Ortner for their initial support of this project and the encouragement they offered along the way. A measure of thanks is also due Martha Ward, 1992 Program Chair of the American Anthropological Association meeting, who obligingly accommodated many last minute changes to the symposium in which the papers and participants were originally assembled. Don Clark, William Fitzhugh, Margaret Lantis, Randall McGuire, and Dan Rogers read the papers included in this volume at various stages of their development and offered useful comments for their improvement. Nancy Benco provided professional expertise throughout the revision process and a sensitive handling of the issues involved. The authors also thank Leon Simpson and Ernest Ostro, who assisted in the typesetting of the tables, and Stuart Speaker, who drafted the map that appears at the front of this volume.

References Cited

Clark, Donald W.
1984   Prehistory of the Pacific Eskimo Region. In *Handbook of North American Indians,* vol. 5, Arctic. David Damas, ed., pp 136–48. Washington, D.C.: Smithsonian Institution Press.

Davis, Nancy Yaw
1984   Contemporary Pacific Eskimo. In *Handbook of North American Indians,* vol. 5, Arctic. David Damas, ed., pp 198–204. Washington, D.C.: Smithsonian Institution Press.

Hill, Jonathan
1992   Overview: Contested Pasts and the Practice of Anthropology. *American Anthropologist* 94(4):809–15.

McGuire, Randall
1992   Archaeology and the First Americans. *American Anthropologist* 94(4):816–36.

Merrill, William, Edmund Ladd, and T. J. Ferguson
1993   The Return of the Ahayu:da: Lessons for Repatriation from Zuni Pueblo and the Smithsonian Institution. *Current Anthropology* 34 (5): 523–67.

Price, H. Marcus
1991   *Disputing the Dead: U.S. Law on Aboriginal Remains and Grave Goods.* Columbia: University of Missouri Press.

2

SCIENTIFIC POLICY AND PUBLIC INTEREST

Perspectives on the Larsen Bay Repatriation Case

The full account of the Larsen Bay repatriation case begins with the fieldwork and excavations conducted at the Uyak site by Dr. Aleš Hrdlička in the early 1930s. Because of his highly focused and energetic quest for human skeletal samples for the research collections of the National Museum, Hrdlička was often perceived as insensitive to the interests and concerns of people living in the area. There was deeply felt resentment by some people in the Larsen Bay community over Hrdlička's methods and mannerisms that was harbored for well over half a century by the Alaska Native people of Larsen Bay. This undoubtedly was a major factor in the return and reburial of a significant mortuary assemblage from an important archaeological site on Kodiak Island.

In July 1987, the Larsen Bay Tribal Council formally requested the return of all materials excavated from the cemetery at the Uyak site (see the Appendix). This request posed a major challenge to collections management philosophy and policies of the Department of Anthropology in the National Museum of Natural History (NMNH). There was little precedent and few established administrative procedures to serve as guidelines in responding effectively to the request. Revision of institutional policy and formulation of national law related to repatriation was just beginning to be discussed. Given the unprecedented nature of this repatriation request, it is not surprising that the museum was deliberate in formulating its response. This situation may have given the appearance

of purposeful delay and neglect that further exacerbated the communications gap between the Larsen Bay people and the scientific community.

My involvement with the Larsen Bay case began in October 1988 when I assumed administrative responsibilities as chairperson of the Department of Anthropology. My predecessor, Dr. Adrienne Kaeppler, had resigned her responsibilities as head of the department in May 1988. During the period between my appointment and Dr. Kaeppler's resignation, administrative responsibility for the department fell to a series of acting chairmen.

Since I had been out of the country during the first half of 1988, I had limited involvement in the initial exchanges with the Larsen Bay Tribal Council, though I was certainly aware of the request and had discussed it with colleagues. Despite my position as a civil servant, I, too, share the deep suspicion that many people have toward government bureaucracy and am equally frustrated by bureaucratic foot-dragging and gamesmanship that is sometimes a substitute for much needed action.

It is one of the uncomfortable ironies of my life that my role in the Larsen Bay repatriation case was viewed by some as simply another example of the unresponsiveness of a government administrator. I feel that I did my best to move fairly, thoughtfully, and as quickly as possible to resolve the issues inherent in a case for which there were no established institutional policies or precedents. While I have little interest in justifying my actions in relation to this case, I do think it is useful to review the administrative and scientific contexts in which the decisions surrounding the Larsen Bay case were formulated. It is my hope that the museum and scientific communities will look to the lessons of this experience as we work toward creating improved relations with Native Americans. It is my belief that a clearer understanding of the issues and circumstances involved in this case may be helpful in developing a more effective partnership, an objective that is clearly in the best interests of all concerned.

Museum staff, regardless of the specific role they have, are charged with the responsibility to care for the museum collections for which they have custody. Many of us have active research programs based on the collections and are thus unusually qualified to understand and appreciate their value. Materials in our care enlighten our past, enrich our present, and help us understand our future. Because we value these materials, we take our curatorial responsibilities seriously and are deeply troubled by actions that jeopardize their integrity and future accessibility. I will never forget the tremendous sense of loss I felt as I turned over the remains of a woman from the Uyak site for packing and return for reburial. Before I had studied the remains, which represented a possible case of juvenile rheumatoid arthritis, I had spent many hours carefully conserving them so that they could be handled without damage. After I published a report on them (Ortner and Utermohle 1981), many biomedical colleagues had come to study the remains. I obtained as much additional information as I could before the remains were packed, but many questions still remain about the nature of the disease that caused the multiple joint problems.

Clearly, scientists have always operated in a social milieu that requires accountability and responsibility to the society as a whole, and this is as it should be. Currently, we see the tension that can arise between science and society being played out in the debate over the use of foetal tissue in biomedical research. Few scientists question the fact that useful biomedical knowledge has been gained through this research. Nevertheless, very strong opinions exist about the ethics of engaging in it or performing this surgical procedure.

In addition to research conducted by our own staff (e.g., Ortner and Putschar 1981), an average of about 300 scientists a year visit the Smithsonian to conduct research on the incomparable biomedical collection of human skeletal remains, about half of which come from North American archaeological sites. Many of these visiting scientists are medically trained and specialize in biomedical research. Their research has contributed to a greater understanding of the anatomy associated with several biomedical problems, in-cluding chronic back pain, rheumatoid arthritis, various types of infectious diseases, and surgical repair of congenital defects. Hundreds of papers have been published on the results of this research.

Has this research benefitted the Native American community? Clearly in some areas, such as forensic anthropology, the answer is yes, it has. In other areas of research, the answer to this question is more difficult to assess since one rarely knows what chain of evidence has led to a given beneficial biomedical outcome. To close off any avenue of investigation in science, however, involves risks and a potential loss of knowledge that need to be considered carefully. Those of us engaged in such research clearly need to do a more effective job of conveying this information to the broader society of which we are a part.

During the past five years, I have met with dozens of Native American tribal leaders. Nearly all of them value the research done by archaeologists and physical anthropologists. Most recognize that this research has given back to Native American groups something of their history that would have been lost otherwise. During these meetings, tribal leaders have often expressed two specific concerns. One is the failure of anthropologists to seek more active participation of the Native American communities that are the focus of their research and to communicate the results of that research more effectively to them. The other concern is whether human remains need to be kept permanently in museums.

The first issue is one that is central to the Larsen Bay case. The Larsen Bay community accused Hrdlička of removing human remains without their permission and without any attempt to inform the community about the nature of his research. In addition, they often cite evidence indicating that Hrdlička attempted to excavate the bodies of known community members. What tends to be omitted, however, is the fact that on at least one occasion Hrdlička stopped the excavations when this association was made known to him (Hrdlička 1929:139).

I do not wish to engage in a lengthy defense of Hrdlička's field methods or treatment of local people. As a trained physician, he did provide limited medical care for people in the communities where he worked, and he also attempted to explain the nature of his research (Hrdlička 1929:139). Nevertheless, compared with the criteria by which such fieldwork is judged today, Hrdlička engaged in field procedures that would not be accepted today. I would not be surprised to learn that other scientists of his day engaged in similar procedures.

Hrdlička, however, was a pioneer in the development of the discipline of physical anthropology in the New World. Although we find some of his research methods and opinions untenable today, it is also true that he displayed remarkable insight in other contexts. Whether he was right or wrong on specific issues, there can be little doubt that he laid a solid foundation for future research in many areas of human biology.

The second concern arises out of a common misunderstanding about the fundamental nature of scientific research. It is unusual for any research project to resolve, once and for all time, all of the scientific issues and questions that may be important. Far more often, scientific research is an iterative process in which the old research provides a foundation for the new. Scientists often complete a research project only to discover that there are more questions that need to be investigated and more data that need to be collected. It is also the case that the methods of science are continually improving, and the limits of what can be examined are constantly expanding. Physical anthropologists, for example, have begun to recover DNA from archeological human bone tissue only in the past few years (Ortner et al. 1992). This research did not become feasible until 1986 when the PCR technique for replicating DNA, the molecule that contains each person's genetic code, was developed.

Administrative Context of the Larsen Bay Request

At the time the Larsen Bay Tribal Council made its request, the Department of Anthropology had a policy regarding the return of human remains. This policy had been developed in the 1970s as a response to a request by the descendants of four Modoc Indian men. The four Modoc men—Captain Jack, Schonchin John, Black Jim, and Boston Charlie—had been hanged by the U.S. Army in 1873 for the murders of Brigadier General Edward R. A. Canby and Eleaser Thomas, a Methodist minister who served on the Peace Commission that was trying to negotiate a settlement with the Modoc Tribe. The heads of the executed men were removed for anatomical study, a common practice at that time. The skulls were taken to the Army Medical Museum in Washington, D.C., and were accessioned in 1874. In 1904 the remains were transferred to the Smithsonian Institution for permanent curation and storage. The first request for their repatriation, which dates to the early 1970s, was turned down by the institution.[1] Continuing review of the request, stimulated by the ongoing interest and concern of the descendants, eventually resulted in the development of a departmental policy on the return of human remains. The policy stated that human remains in the department's collections would be returned if they were known (named) individuals and were claimed by identifiable descendants. The policy also included a provision for the return to known descendants of remains that had been obtained in a manner that was illegal or patently unethical.

This policy was articulated in the first letter of response to the request from the Larsen Bay Tribal Council.[2] (See the Appendix.) There were a few burials from the Uyak site that were known to be from the historic period and that might be affected by this policy, and further review was needed to determine if this was the case. While the previously established policy on the return of named individuals in the collection was in effect when I became chairman a few months later, changes were on the horizon. The creation of a new policy on repatriation, one that was likely to broaden the existing approach, was being discussed in connection with the development of a new museum for and about Native Americans within the Smithsonian Institution. The new policy was expected to cover human remains and associated funerary artifacts that could be culturally linked to extant Native American groups, going well beyond descendants of named individuals.

During a meeting in Santa Fe, New Mexico, in August 1989, representatives of the Smithsonian Institution and the Native American community agreed on the outline of this new repatriation policy. This agreement was subsequently embodied in Public Law 101-185, which was passed by the U.S. Congress in November 1989 and signed into law by President Bush on November 28, 1989.

Shortly after the Santa Fe meeting, the head of the Smithsonian, Robert McC. Adams, made several public statements about the agreement. A New York Times article[3] quoted Adams as stating that most of the human remains in the department's collection would not be affected by the agreement. During a press conference at the Smithsonian, Secretary Adams[4] speculated that about 5 to 10 percent of the National Museum of Natural History (NMNH) collection might be subject to repatriation, although this might increase as new scientific methods improved the available information. Congressman Ben Nighthorse Campbell,[5] now a U.S. Senator from Colorado who had been one of the key congressmen in the negotiations and passage of the law, estimated that one-fourth of the Smithsonian's collections might be subject to reburial.

What had the new agreement and new law done to resolve the conflict between scientists, who felt that permanent collections of human remains were an important legacy for future biomedical and anthropological research, and Native Americans, who felt that the continuing storage and study of human remains was offensive and that human remains of tribal ancestors should be returned for reburial? The law leaves most of the procedural aspects unspecified. It does provide, in Section 11 (a)(2), that the inventory

Donald J. Ortner

and identification process use "the best available scientific and historical documentation" to identify the association of human remains and associated objects with tribal groups living today. This seems to imply that scientific and scholarly methods would be used both to obtain and evaluate evidence relevant to resolving a question of tribal affiliation.

Having administrative responsibility for implementing the repatriation provisions contained in the new law, my interpretation was that the requirement of demonstrable cultural linkage necessitated rigorous and substantial evidence. At the operational level, where an actual recommendation must be made by museum staff regarding a specific request, the many ambiguities of such a mandate quickly became clear. What constitutes the best available scientific and historical documentation? Are we talking about field reports or the analysis of cultural and biological data? What happens if experts disagree or the published sources are inconclusive? How do we go about evaluating the opinions of the experts? Some experts are likely to be more authoritative than others. How do we go about weighing the importance of different types of data?

The law specifies that a decision on tribal affiliation is to be made on the basis of a "preponderance of the evidence." I have learned that, in a legal context, this phrase has a specific meaning in which anything more than 50 percent is decisive. But in the scientific realm, it immediately begs the question—50 percent of what? If I, as an administrator, have six scientists who say that no affiliation can be demonstrated on the basis of the evidence and a group requesting repatriation has five experts who say that it can, do I reject the claim?

In a letter to Mr. Sockbeson, a lawyer with the Native American Rights Fund and legal representative for the Larsen Bay Tribal Council, in which Secretary Adams agrees to return all the Uyak site human remains (see the Appendix), he notes the complexity of issues involved in this particular request and alludes to factors beyond the scientific evidence that weighed in his decision. One of these considerations was the amount of time the decision-making process had already taken and the ill will this had created in the Native American community.

Many scientists base their conclusions on probability statements in which a hypothesis is rejected if the potential error in accepting it is greater than 5 percent. If we applied this statistical methodology to making decisions about the mandate of the new law, we would immediately be placed in potential conflict with the "preponderance of evidence" clause in the law. This uncomfortable mixture of legal and scientific criteria is almost certain to be an ongoing source of misunderstanding.

Discussion and Conclusions

A number of unfortunate conditions and circumstances contributed to an almost classic example of a serious breakdown in communication between two groups of people who share a substantial mutual interest in the cultural and biological history of Kodiak Island. The response by the Department of Anthropology to the request from the Larsen Bay Tribal Council came during a transitional period in the department's administrative leadership. This was further complicated by the fact that federal legislation addressing repatriation issues was only in the process of being drafted at the time, becoming law (P.L. 101-185) more than two years after the initial request. Both departmental and institutional policies were also being re-formulated during this period.

It is clear that few people fully anticipated the impact that P.L. 101-185 would have on the museum's biomedical collections. I had been operating on the assumption that the total number of human remains that would probably be returned for reburial would be limited by the criteria that had been agreed upon in negotiations and specified in law. The Larsen Bay claim encompassed almost 5 percent of all the Native American human skeletal remains in the departmental collections; thus, it comprised a substantial proportion of the total human remains that we had expected to be repatriated. Furthermore, the size and complexity of the request was unprecedented, and we had minimal experience regarding the procedures for both assembling the relevant information and for reaching a reasonable decision.

The effort the departmental staff was required to undertake in responding responsibly to the Larsen Bay claim required time and substantial staff resources, neither of which existed until about the time the decision was made to return the entire collection. Curators and administrators were caught in the conflict between the real but undefined rights of the Native American communities, on the one hand, and the concerns of the international scientific community on the other.

Thus, what may have had the appearance of administrative delay and stonewalling was in reality the result of genuine concern about curatorial responsibility to future biomedical and anthropological research on one of the most intensely studied skeletal samples in the NMNH collections. It is also easy to see how the delays could be interpreted as just another example of unresponsive and insensitive governmental bureaucracy by the people of Larsen Bay.

One of the many ironies in this case is that anthropologists at the Smithsonian have a long and well-established record of activist interest in and concern for the rights and welfare of Native American people.

In one of the most well-known cases of the nineteenth century, Frank Hamilton Cushing provided strong support to the Zuni Pueblo against an attempt by a politically powerful outsider to take over its land. In another example, James Mooney courageously, and at great personal cost, succeeded in preventing repression of the Native American Church by religious and governmental officials in the 1890s. During this century, the legendary research conducted among the Blackfeet by John C. Ewers, who is retired but still active, resulted in a book that is used to teach tribal history today. These are only a few examples in a rich tradition of friendship and mutual assistance that continues today.

This heritage should have formed a basis of trust between the anthropology department at the NMNH and the Larsen Bay Tribal Council. Unfortunately, the ill will created by Hrdlička during his first years of fieldwork was exacerbated by a perception of administrative unresponsiveness. It is one of the fundamental axioms of management that perception is reality. How the scientific community is perceived is one of the critical problems facing anthropology today. The Larsen Bay case illustrates just how important it is to ensure that public perception of scientific research does not develop in an environment of hostility where the scientists are seen as arrogant and insensitive.

I imagine that the outcome of the Larsen Bay case might have been different if Hrdlička had established another kind of relationship with the local people and this had been carefully nurtured by his successors in subsequent decades. It is worth noting that Zuni Pueblo, which has had a long and cordial relationship with several anthropologists in the Smithsonian and in other institutions, has a different policy that states it will not request the return of human remains currently being cared for in museums.

This relationship of mutual trust and cooperation is in marked contrast with the one that developed with the Larsen Bay community. The Zuni experience provides a model for the direction these relationships should develop in the future.

Notes

1. Letter from S. D. Ripley, Secretary, Smithsonian Institution, to Senator Mark Hatfield, August 9, 1973.
2. Letter from Adrienne Kaeppler, Chair, Department of Anthropology, NMNH, to Mr. Frank M. Carlson, Larsen Bay Tribal Council, February 16, 1988.
3. Major Accord Likely on Indian Remains, by F. Barringer. *New York Times*, August 20, 1989.
4. Press Conference, Smithsonian Institution, September 12, 1989.
5. Interview with Jane Pauley on the Today Show, National Broadcasting Company, September 13, 1989.

References Cited

Hrdlička, Aleš
1929   The Ancient and Modern Inhabitants of the Yukon. *Smithsonian Explorations* 1929:137–46.

Ortner, D. J., and Putschar, W. G. J.
1981   *Identification of Pathological Conditions in Human Skeletal Remains.* Washington, D.C.: Smithsonian Institution Press.

Ortner D. J., N. Tuross, and A. I. Stix
1992   New Approaches to the Study of Disease in Archeological New World Populations. *Human Biology* 64:337–60.

Ortner, D. J., and C. J. Utermohle
1981   Polyarticular Inflammatory Arthritis in a Pre-Columbian Skeleton from Kodiak Island, Alaska. *American Journal of Physical Anthropology* 56:23–31.

3

THE QIKERTARMIUT AND THE SCIENTIST

Fifty Years of Clashing World Views

They were put in the ground to rest in peace. It doesn't seem right that someone would come along and dig them up to study. (Valen Reft, former president, Larsen Bay Tribal Council)[1]

Scientists learn a great deal by studying living and past populations, the latter being completely dependent on the preservation of well documented human remains in museum collections. (Adrienne L. Kaeppler, Chair, Department of Anthropology, National Museum of Natural History)[2]

On October 5, 1991, in the Alutiiq village of Larsen Bay,[3] Kodiak Island, Alaska, the skeletal remains of about 1,000 indigenous people were buried in a common grave a few hundred feet from where they had been dug up by a Smithsonian Institution scientist more than 50 years before.[4] Packed in cardboard boxes, they had arrived by boat from Seattle after having spent a half century at the Smithsonian in Washington, D.C. The burial took place more than two years after the people of Larsen Bay felt the Smithsonian had agreed to return them.[5]

The solemn burial ceremony was officiated over by three priests of the Russian Orthodox Church (fig. 3.1),[6] which for the past 200 years has served as the primary religion for the indigenous people of Kodiak Island. A small group of women elders from the village, dressed in their "Sunday best," sang in Alutiiq, Russian, and English. A few brief presentations followed. Frank Carlson, a resident of the village and

president of the village tribal council when the official effort to repatriate the skeletons began, spoke first. He was followed by Frank Talbot, director of the Smithsonian Institution's National Museum of Natural History (NMNH); Henry Sockbeson, an attorney for the Native American Rights Fund, who led the legal component of the repatriation case against the Smithsonian; and the author, who had been president of the island-wide Kodiak Area Native Association (KANA) when the repatriation effort began.

The event was attended by as many "outsiders" as members of the small village community. Network television cameras rolled and numerous newspaper and radio reporters sought out village elders for interviews (figs. 3.2 and 3.3). Among the visiting dignitaries were Kodiak Island's representatives to the state legislature: Senator Fred Zharoff, the only Alutiiq in the legislature; and Representative Cliff Davidson, who had taken a special interest in the repatriation issue and had twice unsuccessfully introduced legislation that would have protected unmarked Alaska Native burials on state lands and provided for repatriation of Alaska Native human remains currently held in Alaska (fig. 3.4).

The boxes that contained the remains were passed from the back of pickup trucks to the open grave by a human chain made up of village residents, including children, as well some of the guests, such as Sockbeson and Talbot. Talbot's participation was particularly symbolic since it was his distant predecessor at

Figure 3.1. Three priests from the Russian Orthodox Church officiate at the burial ceremony. (All photographs in this chapter by Gordon L. Pullar)

Figure 3.2. *Tundra Times* reporter Holly Reimer interviews Marina Waselie, an elder from Larsen Bay.

Figure 3.3. Larry Waselie, an elder from Larsen Bay, is interviewed by a local radio reporter.

Figure 3.4. Larsen Bay village matriarch Dora Aga poses with Alaska State Senator Fred Zharoff (left) and Alaska State Representative Cliff Davidson in Aga's home on the day of the burial.

Figure 3.5. Charles Christiansen, an elder and the mayor of Larsen Bay, throws a handful of dirt into the grave.

the NMNH, Aleš Hrdlička, who had excavated the skeletons and taken them to the Smithsonian.

At the conclusion of the ceremony, both villagers and guests threw handfuls of dirt into the grave (fig. 3.5) and then traveled the short distance to the village's Senior/Youth Center for a traditional feast of salmon, halibut, king crab, and venison, as well as "non-traditional" turkeys, hams, pies, and cakes. Unlike the sadness and grief that would be present at a funeral for a current loved one, there was an atmosphere of relief at the accomplishment of an obligation or the completion of serious "unfinished business." One Larsen Bay resident, Alex Panamaroff, articulated this feeling in an interview, October 17, 1992: "It didn't really hit me until the actual burial. There was a burden lifted off our shoulders."

From a personal viewpoint, I reflected on the process that I had been involved in for nearly eight years. I realized it had not been simply a dispute between the interests of modern western science and the right of Native Americans to bury their dead. Nor had it been a struggle between good and evil. It had not been a disagreement over what constituted a matter of respect or disrespect, nor an issue that had a right or wrong answer. The dispute over the repatriation of the human remains to Larsen Bay, as it likely is in other cases, was dominated by a fundamental difference in world views. Indigenous people and western scientists have very different ways of seeing time, family, and the universe.

Events Leading to the Reburial

Not long after I became president of Kodiak Area Native Association (KANA)[7] in 1983, its board and staff began a conscious effort to focus on the revitalization of the culture of the region. We proposed to accomplish this by implementing a series of programs that would emphasize cultural preservation and provide the people, especially the youth, with the opportunity to learn of the various aspects of Alutiiq culture, both past and present.

Among the first projects we undertook was involvement in an archaeological excavation in the village of Karluk at the south end of the island. This project, conducted in partnership with Bryn Mawr College and under the direction of the late Richard H. Jordan, involved the participation of Alutiiq youth from many villages in Kodiak through KANA's Summer Youth Employment Program (Pullar and Jordan 1986). Their participation helped them to learn how their ancestors had lived before the arrival of the Russians 200 years earlier. We believed that by learning about this complex and difficult way of life the youth would develop a stronger sense of Alutiiq identity and feel better about who they were. With this heightened self-esteem they would be less likely to join the epidemic of self-destructive behavior that had been sweeping across Alaska's villages over the past several years. The possibility of encountering human remains in the archaeological excavation was dealt with at the outset. Jordan,[8] who went on to become head of the Anthropology Department at the University of Alaska at Fairbanks before his untimely death in 1991, agreed that any skeletal remains found would be reburied the following season, allowing a year for scientific study. In reality, only bone fragments were removed and they were subsequently reburied (Pullar 1990:273).

In the process of recruiting Alaska Native youth for the archaeological project, I first learned of the lingering resentment in the village of Larsen Bay where 50 years earlier Hrdlička had excavated hundreds of skeletal remains from a single burial area. Because this was the only exposure that village residents had to an "archaeologist," the idea of young people from the village participating in an archaeological project did not have much appeal. Village elders remembered Hrdlička as a man who seemed to respect neither the living nor the dead of the Kodiak Island Alutiit (Pullar 1989:10). According to Dora Aga, Larsen Bay elder, "He [Hrdlička] had no regard for the people here. And we had no laws, of course. None that we knew about. We just stood by."[9]

As I listened to the stories of Hrdlička's activities, my naive response was to ask if a request had ever been made to the Smithsonian to return the skeletons and artifacts. I learned that, while people in the village had expressed anger and resentment among themselves for over 50 years, they had never made such a request. (This is not surprising if one is aware of the indirect styles of communication within the island's culture.) I then suggested that the village tribal council simply request the return of the skeletons so they could be reburied. I assumed that because the excavations had taken place in another era when attitudes were far different, Smithsonian officials, in order to avoid embarrassment by the insensitive acts committed a half century before, would simply send the remains back. After private discussions and considerable deliberation, the tribal council, in 1987, sent a letter to the Smithsonian requesting the return of the skeletons. I could not imagine at that time the chain of events that this request would generate.

The initial Smithsonian response seemed to indicate that the request was not being taken seriously. In a September 25, 1987, letter from Adrienne L. Kaeppler, Chair, Department of Anthropology, to the council's repatriation request, she wrote that "the issue of deaccession is a complex one, which the Smithsonian must consider in light of the Institution's responsibility to hold its collections in trust for the benefit of all people, not just discrete interest groups." The issue of the return of the human remains to Larsen Bay became a cause for the entire island Alaska Native community. A second letter, dated October 27, 1987, was sent by Carlson as president of the tribal council to the Smithsonian: "We the Native People of Larsen Bay again respectfully request the return of all human skeletons taken from our region along with the artifacts."

Because there had always been, and continues to be, considerable moving about of and intermarriage among people on the island, people were well aware that these remains represented the ancestors of all indigenous people on the island. It was left to the Larsen Bay Tribal Council, however, to lead the strug-

gle for their return since federal law only recognizes "Indian tribes," and under federal law, the Native Village of Larsen Bay is recognized as an "Indian tribe." It was also appropriate for Larsen Bay to lead this effort since it was the contemporary village that had experienced the trauma of Hrdlička's transgressions.

The repatriation issue was closely related to efforts to promote a strong identity and self-esteem among youth through cultural revitalization on Kodiak Island. At the same time, the Smithsonian, as an agency of the federal government, was claiming "ownership" of the skeletal remains that Hrdlička had removed. It became clear that, if Alaska Native youth were allowed to believe that it was somehow acceptable for the government of the United States to "own" the bodies of their ancestors, then they would have a very difficult time developing the self-esteem that would permit them to feel equal to all others in this country. Battle lines were drawn. From the Alaska Native viewpoint, more was at stake than the right to bury dead ancestors.

Contrasting World Views

The world view of a people is their way of looking at reality. (Michael Kearney, anthropologist)[10]

Entire worldviews can appear at times to be butting against each other: for a curator or researcher, to rebury something is to destroy it. (Douglas J. Preston, former manager of the department of publications, American Museum of Natural History)[11]

At the outset, to the Alaska Native peoples of Kodiak Island, including myself, the Larsen Bay repatriation effort seemed like a righteous effort. The controversy was usually framed within the context of the interests of science against the right of indigenous people to bury their dead. How could anyone object to a people wanting to bury their dead? In a simple dispute between the rights of scientists and the rights of indigenous people to respect their ancestors, it seemed obvious that the indigenous position held the "high ground." But it was far more complex than that. Different concepts of time, death, and sense of identity were at the core of this emotional issue that would eventually test who could make the most effective use of the American political system. Many of the fundamental differences between indigenous world views and the world views of western industrialized society would be clearly demonstrated before the Larsen Bay case was resolved.

Time

Conflicting concepts of time permeated the dispute between the people of Larsen Bay and the scientists of the Smithsonian Institution. Western scientists see time as linear. It is a sequence of events containing generations of people. In the western world people are usually concerned with only a very few generations into their past, rarely further back than their grandparents. To them, it is inconceivable that anyone could claim to be concerned about the treatment of burials of people who died centuries ago.

To indigenous people, time is circular. Those ancestors who may have died hundreds of years ago are still a part of the circle. They are still members of the group of people living today. They may have passed to another world but they remain full members of the group. The indigenous concept of time is often difficult to understand and if understood, difficult to articulate. As an Alaska Native educated almost totally in the western system, I have experienced this difficulty myself. After contemplating the concept for some time, I had an enlightening moment at a planning meeting for the Smithsonian's new National Museum for the American Indian in May 1991. A middle-aged Native American woman, after listening quietly to the discussions for perhaps two hours, expressed her concept of time in a way that felt totally understandable. While her eloquent statement undoubtedly suffers some minor discrepancies due to the limitations of my memory, what I recall her saying is: "You people keep talking about preserving the past. Can't you see that there is no past. Can't you see that the past is today and the past is tomorrow? It's all the same! Can't you see that?" From that moment on, I had a much clearer idea of what the people of Larsen Bay were feeling when they thought of their ancestors and the need to rebury their remains.

During the repatriation efforts, and again during efforts to get a law passed by the Alaska State Legislature to protect unmarked Alaska Native burials, scientists repeatedly brought up the topic of time. While they might understand Alaska Natives peoples wanting to protect recent burials, the idea of protecting burials of people who had lived so long ago that no one knew their names seemed illogical. For example, William Workman, an archaeologist at the University of Alaska, Anchorage, stated, during legislative proceedings to protect Alaska Native unmarked burials: "As a practical matter, this zone of precedence for deference to the wishes of living natives will cover the entire last 200 years plus extent of the historic period . . ."[12]

Individualism versus Tribalism

To tribal people, the tribe is seen in terms of "family." Death within the tribe is like death within a family. "We're all just one family. Each tribe is a family. We all know and love each other," remarked Larsen Bay resi-

dent Alex Panamaroff in a personal interview.[13] And Larsen Bay elder Fred Katelnikoff noted: "There was a lot of closeness. Not just with one village, but with all the villages [on Kodiak Island].[14] These viewpoints, together with the differing concepts of time, reveal how tribal people of today have feelings for their long deceased ancestors, while the individualistic members of western society seldom do. It is not surprising then that family terminology is often used by the people of Larsen Bay when speaking of the remains taken by Hrdlička. For example, Marina Waselie, a village elder, said, "We don't even know who they are. It could be our aunts, uncles, or cousins."[15] Or Roy Jones, tribal council president, explained, "It's got to do with people's uncles and aunts. It's our people and our heritage."[16]

A Matter of Respect

To many people, the issue of repatriation of human remains was a simple matter of respect. But there seemed to be a vast difference between what the archaeologists and physical anthropologists and the Alaska Natives saw as "respect." To the scientists, respect was related to the way they handled the remains during examination. "Please reassure the Koniag people represented by the Kodiak Area Native Association," Ortner wrote to me in a 1989 letter, "that the collection is carefully maintained and is only examined for medical and scientific research. It is not subject to any mishandling."[17] (See the Appendix.) One might imagine a scene of a Smithsonian scientist gently and carefully removing an Alaska Native skull from one of the storage drawers and carrying it with a sense of reverence to an examination table, where it would be carefully studied under bright lights. To most indigenous people, including the people of Larsen Bay, the mere storage of ancestors' remains in drawers located thousands of miles from their burial place was the height of disrespect.

In conversations with Smithsonian staff, all of us involved in the Larsen Bay repatriation request were assured that no skeletal material from Kodiak Island was on display. While I am quite certain that this was believed to be true by the staff people making the statements, I learned that it was not true. I visited the NMNH and closely examined each display of human skeletal material for identifiable markings. In a display titled, "Back defects among Eskimos have increased through inbreeding," I found some spinal columns with the "Kodiak Island" identifying markings. I did not consider the display respectful at all and it helped strengthen my resolve to support the repatriation effort.

The differences over the issue of respect and maintenance of values overlaps with the differences over the concept of time and the dead. As members of western society, archaeologists and physical anthropologists grieve over the death of family and friends, participate in funerals, and maintain well-groomed cemeteries where they can continue to visit the graves of and pay respects to those they have lost. The differences become apparent, however, when the dead are from many generations in the past and are not known by name. To the scientists, as perhaps to most people in western society, there is little, if any, attachment to these people. There is tremendous attention paid to the dead of current loved ones, however. Hrdlička, himself, clearly demonstrated this difference. While he seemed to have no emotion towards any of the people represented by the skeletal remains he excavated, it is apparent that he did grieve over the death of a personal loved one—his wife:

> She was dressed by me in her loveliest red. She was laid on a bed of sweet smelling green covered in flowers. About her face I dropped rose after rose until they covered her ears, face, eyes, and lips—and I loved her more than ever . . . I kissed those sweet lips that seemed to live longest for me until the touch of fire was near . . . and then she went to the grave to the strains of Chopin . . . I gave her to the fire—I gave her to God, mind and body—and then I went slow, shivering into the lone wilderness. (Hrdlička, December 28, 1918, on the death of his wife, as quoted in Spencer 1979:64)

Some of the terminology used by scientists in referring to burials has been offensive to Native American peoples. The insistence on referring to skeletal remains as "resources" has particularly aggravated some (Deloria 1989:2).

Early in 1989, I testified before the U.S. Senate Select Committee on Indian Affairs in Washington in a hearing chaired by Senator Daniel Inouye. My testimony was on behalf of both KANA and the statewide Alaska Federation of Natives; it addressed the crisis of social problems facing Alaska Natives. As usual, I did not miss an opportunity to keep the issue of the Larsen Bay case before the members of the committee and included it, once again, in my testimony. Senator Inouye acknowledged this mention, which indicated that he was continuing to support repatriation efforts (U.S. Government Printing Office 1989:17).

Following the hearing, I visited the Smithsonian's NMNH with Rick Knecht, KANA's cultural heritage program director and archaeologist. The Smithsonian is a huge bureaucracy with literally thousands of staff members. It was common to meet museum personnel who were in disagreement with the Smithsonian's policy on repatriation. As we chatted with one

of these staff people, she asked, "Would you like to see where the skeletal remains are kept?" This was not something I had thought about before, but I agreed to go. The Smithsonian had in storage some 18,500 Native American skeletal remains ranging from bone fragments to complete skeletons, of which about 4,000 were from Alaska and nearly 800 were from Larsen Bay. I was not prepared for what I saw. I had not developed a mental picture of this many skeletons: hallways of wooden drawers, floor to ceiling, with labels identifying the origin of the contents. When we reached the Kodiak Island section, I was overwhelmed. Row after row of drawers were marked "Kodiak Island, Alaska." I hadn't realized just how much space it took to store the remains of 800 people. I left there in stunned silence, not knowing whether to cry or scream out in rage. But at that moment I was convinced, in my own mind, that they would be brought home where they belonged.

The Scientific Argument

Through research based on the Smithsonian collections, scientists have contributed an enormous and diverse array of information about human behavior, the epidemiological history of many diseases, and biological similarity and diversity. (Kaeppler in a letter to Frank M. Carlson, February 16, 1988)

The words of Dr. Kaeppler were, of course, true. The skeletons of human beings can be tremendous sources of information. But there was no need to prove this point as no one was disputing it.

The very basis of western culture is logic. It was therefore not surprising that the Smithsonian would present logical reasons why the skeletal remains should not be returned.

There were three "logical" arguments that were most often stated in making a case against the repatriation of the Larsen Bay remains. The first was the claim that only very old skeletal remains had been taken. The second was the position that Hrdlička had received permission to take remains from Larsen Bay, or, if not, at least no objections had been voiced by the Alaska Native residents. The third was that the skeletal remains taken from Larsen Bay did not represent the ancestors of the village's contemporary residents.

The Smithsonian maintained a position for some time that Hrdlička excavated only very "old" sites. This was reaffirmed in a 1988 letter from Kaeppler to Carlson: "Judged by both the documentation and the artifactual materials, our conclusion that the sites excavated by Dr. Hrdlička are not recent is well supported."[18] (See the Appendix.) And again, in a 1990 letter from Secretary Adams to Sockbeson, the lawyer who represented the tribal council: ". . . the Institution is certainly prepared to transfer all materials reliably associated with the historic period, i.e., since 1750 A.D., which is not to suggest that we would not go further as various questions are answered. One burial in this period is associated with a coffin that may be culturally associated with the people of Kodiak Island."[19] (See the Appendix.) As mentioned earlier, this argument seemed irrelevant to Alaska Natives.

The irony of this position, however, was that it did not hold up under scrutiny. Dora Aga, the matriarch of Larsen Bay who was a young woman when Hrdlička excavated at Larsen Bay, had long maintained that Hrdlička not only took "old" remains but those of members of the Waselie family who had died during the influenza epidemic of 1918. In his 1990 letter to Sockbeson, Secretary Adams mentioned a burial "associated with a coffin" in discussing the material the Institution was prepared to transfer; mention of a burial "associated with a coffin" seems to support Dora Aga's claim.

The argument that Hrdlička had permission to dig up burials in Larsen Bay also does not hold up well. According to Dora Aga,[20] not only did no one give permission but there was no one with the authority to grant permission to dig up burials.

The Smithsonian attempted to prove, through scientific logic, that the remains held were not those of ancestors of current Larsen Bay residents. Two studies were commissioned, which from the perception of the Larsen Bay Tribal Council and its legal counsel were an attempt to validate this point (Dumond 1990; Scott 1990). While these studies certainly have value for adding to the body of literature on Kodiak Island's indigenous people, they seemed to be more inconclusive than proof of the Smithsonian's hypothesis.

From the purely scientific position, it was sometimes assumed that the people of Larsen Bay simply did not understand the concept of "scientific value" and would be opposed to any scientific research involving archaeology. This was decidedly not the case. Even as efforts were underway for the repatriation, the tribal and city governments of Larsen Bay authorized archaeological excavations by Amy Steffian of the University of Michigan (Steffian 1992:127). Also during this time period Aron Crowell, then with the Smithsonian, conducted an archaeological survey of Uyak Bay, which was not opposed by the Larsen Bay leadership. In fact, when the engine of the Smithsonian-owned boat developed serious problems, the boat was berthed in Larsen Bay and village residents offered assistance. Thus, the Larsen Bay repatriation effort was never one that was anti-science or anti-archaeology.

Extreme Positions

Both sides of the repatriation controversy had supporters that could be described as extremists. Evidence of these positions could be seen in the rhetoric espoused by some Native American people that all archaeologists should be executed and in the arrogance of some archaeologists and physical anthropologists who displayed an attitude that they somehow possessed a divine right to excavate skeletons of indigenous people and that they "owned" them after excavation. The very idea that Native American people have legal rights under the American legal system that might have impact on their access and control of skeletal collections provoked great anger in them.

Aleš Hrdlička

The personality of Hrdlička is still a factor when the topic of human remains is discussed, both on Kodiak Island and elsewhere in Alaska. His years of collecting skeletal remains in Alaska during the 1920s and 1930s helped build a well-known reputation, both among scientists and among Alaska Native peoples (Spencer 1979:609–19).

The work of Hrdlička in Alaska is well documented, mostly by his own published written accounts. His archaeological excavation techniques were considered poor, even by the standards of his time (Jordan 1987:8; Scott 1990:2, 1992:150). He apparently preferred to set himself apart from archaeologists, whom he felt were not concerned enough with gathering skeletons, in favor of an identity as a physical anthropologist (Hrdlička 1919:23).

While Hrdlička has been called a "borderline racist," his published accounts reveal that his racism went beyond "borderline."[21] In reading these accounts, it becomes clear that in his zeal to achieve his stated goal of collecting skeletal remains he routinely stepped over the line between archaeology and grave robbing. His words need no commentary:

> But just as the parts were all gathered, I saw below (the grave was on a slope) an old woman who appeared to be provoked at something and was talking rather loudly. On sending the Indian who accompanied me down to see what the trouble was, I learned that the old woman claimed the bones to be those of her long departed husband. (Hrdlička 1930a:139, describing a July 29, 1929, experience in a Yup'ik village on the lower Yukon River)

> The bones are mostly still in good condition . . . we gather some drier grass and moss, pack on the

spot, get all into the boat, strike off as far as possible from the shore so none could see what is carried . . . The old Indian and his crone nevertheless stand on the bank and look at us. They know already. (Hrdlička 1943:56, describing a July 3, 1926 experience on the Yukon River)

Some of the burials are quite recent. Open three older ones. In two the remains are too fresh yet, but secure a good female skeleton, which I pack in a practically new heavy pail, thrown out probably on the occasion of the last funeral. Then back, farther out, to avoid notice, through swamps and over moss, and with a recurring wind-driven drizzle against which my umbrella is but a weak protection. (Hrdlička 1930b:76, describing a July 10, 1926, experience on the Yukon River)

Conclusions

As I attended the burial ceremony in Larsen Bay in the fall of 1991, I felt a sense of relief, just as many others did. I had never imagined that so much would be made out of what seemed to begin as a simple issue. Because of a failure to recognize the differing world views, both sides drew battle lines, and it became a "win-lose" situation.

The scenario became a contest that took place in the American political and legal arenas. Two very significant events occurred that placed Larsen Bay on the winning side. One was the decision of the Native American Rights Fund, a national legal rights advocacy organization, to take on Larsen Bay as a test case in the ever-escalating issue of Native American repatriation. This action meant that Larsen Bay would have legal representation in Washington that would confront and negotiate with the Smithsonian, a service that the village could never have afforded to pay for. Before the case was resolved the legal expenses would exceed $100,000.[22]

The second event was the congressional effort to address the Native American repatriation issue. In the summer of 1988, in an ornate room off the side of the floor of the U.S. Senate, I urged Senator Inouye, chairman of the Senate Select Committee on Indian Affairs, to include a stop on Kodiak Island during his trip to Alaska. Julie Kitka, then vice president of the Alaska Federation of Natives, and I had met with Senator Inouye to invite him to tour Alaska in order to gather firsthand accounts of the social conditions affecting the lives of Alaska Natives. His acceptance of the Kodiak invitation provided him with an opportunity to meet the Larsen Bay leadership and hear firsthand of their repatriation request.

Under the political leadership of Senator Inouye,

two pieces of legislation were passed that made repatriation the law of the land. These were P.L. 101-185, the National Museum of the American Indian Act of 1989, and P.L. 101-601, the Native American Graves Protection and Repatriation Act of 1990.

The adversarial atmosphere eliminated the possibility of legitimate negotiation or compromise. Had an atmosphere of respect been established at the outset, a meaningful dialogue could have been carried out. There may have been the possibility, for example, to rebury the remains in containers or in a vault so that they could be retrieved if needed for pressing scientific research.

As the burial ceremony was nearing its conclusion, Father Peter Kreta, who had been officiating, called on me to speak. I could only compliment the residents of this small village for the empowerment they displayed in taking on one of the largest repatriations the Smithsonian would ever perform (the Larsen Bay collection was one of the largest in the Smithsonian). Furthermore, I reiterated what the local people already knew—that this was simply "unfinished business" that needed tending to. Contrary to the impressions one might gain from media accounts, it was not the most important, or the most pressing, issue the village had to deal with. Just two and a half years before, oil from the Exxon Valdez spill covered the beaches around Larsen Bay and the village became a center for cleanup activity. That was a crisis. Larsen Bay, like other villages in Alaska, continues to struggle with a myriad of social problems and political issues that heavily impact everyday life. These are all more pressing than the repatriation case. In my talk, I said something else that the village residents already knew— that we must respect our ancestors as they are still with us. I concluded by quoting the indigenous African scientist, Ali Mazri: "You cannot fulfill your dreams if you insult your ancestors" (Etuk 1989:1).

Perhaps the Larsen Bay repatriation case can help advance the process of changing anthropological research methods to be more considerate of the views of indigenous groups. Indigenous people are no longer willing to be just the "subjects" of research. In Alaska, as well as on a global level, they are demanding an active voice in the research design as well as in the participation in the actual research. Where western scientists are resisting these types of arrangements, they are being denied access. These are clear indications that bridges must be built between western science and indigenous knowledge for needed research to continue. In the Larsen Bay repatriation case, it is interesting to note that members of the field of anthropology, a discipline from which the very concept of ethnocentrism comes, seemed not to recognize the epistemology of the Alutiit or their emic view on treatment of the dead. Far from stifling research, a scien-

Gordon L. Pullar

tific system that recognizes both the western and indigenous world views, "a holistic and humane science" (Etuk 1989:7), will produce new and exciting information that will benefit all of humankind.

Acknowledgments

The original version of this paper was presented on December 3, 1992, at the American Anthropological Association meetings in San Francisco. I would like to thank Tamara Bray and Thomas Killion of the Repatriation Office of the Smithsonian's NMNH for having the foresight and the courage to coordinate a symposium on the Larsen Bay repatriation case. I recognize that it was not easy.

Assistance in writing this paper began with considerable information sharing both during and after the repatriation process. For that assistance I thank Karen Funk, governmental affairs coordinator for the Washington, D.C., law firm of Hobbs, Straus, Dean, and Wilder, who consistently supplied the latest information on what was happening with repatriation legislation and the issue in general. I thank Henry Sockbeson, attorney for the Native American Rights Fund, for his information sharing and without whose legal expertise the repatriation would not have become a reality.

I thank Don Dumond, University of Oregon; Rick Knecht, KANA; Joanne Mulcahy, Lewis and Clark College; and Margaret Rheingold, University of Washington, for reviewing the first draft of this paper and making revision suggestions.

As I often differed in viewpoints on the repatriation issue from many archaeologists and physical anthropologists, one might assume that I was seriously at odds with them. While this may have been the case in a very few incidences, it really has not been widespread. I respect and value the friendships of William Fitzhugh of the Smithsonian; William Workman, David Yesner, and Douglas Veltre, of the University of Alaska Anchorage; Richard Scott of the University of Alaska, Fairbanks; and Don Dumond of the University of Oregon, among others. I offer a special, though sadly a posthumous, thanks to Dick Jordan, who sometimes felt "caught in the middle" on the repatriation issue but always seemed to find a way to offer support when it was needed. I recognize the unique assistance of William S. Laughlin of the University of Connecticut. As a student of Hrdlička's in the 1930s, Dr. Laughlin helped excavate the skeletons in Larsen Bay and came full circle in helping secure their return. His "Hrdlička anecdotes" were often amusing and always informative. I also acknowledge the leadership displayed by Frank Talbot, the director of the National Museum of Natural History, for coming to Larsen Bay for the burial ceremony. I trust that by meeting and feasting with the Alutiiq people his life was in some way enriched.

In the village of Larsen Bay, there are numerous people to thank for support and information sharing, including Alex Panamaroff, Jr., Fred and Marina Katelnikoff, Valen Reft, and Frank and Jeannie Carlson. Most of all, however, I thank Dora Aga. Her Hrdlička (who she still calls "Hard Liquor") stories are very entertaining, to say the least. Moreover, she is to me personally a person who knows more about my family history than I do, and one who never hesitates to scold me when she thinks I require it nor fails to offer support when she knows I need it.

Notes

1. Personal interview, October 17, 1992.
2. Letter from Adrienne L. Kaeppler to Frank M. Carlson, president of the Larsen Bay Tribal Council, February 16, 1988 (Appendix).

3. Larsen Bay is one of seven extant Alutiiq communities in the Kodiak Island region and one of 18 in the Alutiiq culture area that also includes Prince William Sound, the lower Kenai Peninsula, and the southern Alaska Peninsula (Davis 1984:199). The current preferred self designation for the indigenous people of this area is Alutiiq or Aleut. The word Aleut, however, was an externally applied term used by Russian fur traders who arrived in the eighteenth century. The word, Alutiiq (pl. Alutiit), simply means Aleut in the language of the area. The word Sugcestun was once the preferred designation for the language but, while used commonly in Prince William Sound and the Kenai Peninsula, it is rarely used on Kodiak Island today. The language is now usually called Aleut or Alutiiq.

More accurate self designations for the people are seldom used anymore, although they are known by most elders. These terms included Sugpiaq which means "the real people," and identified the people as a whole from Prince William Sound to the lower Alaska Peninsula. Among the subgroups are the Chugachmiut of the Prince William Sound area, the Unegkurmiut of the lower Kenai Peninsula, and the Qikertarmiut of Kodiak Island, which means "the people of the island."

The terms Koniag or Koniagmiut were developed externally, perhaps by people who had difficulty pronouncing the word Qikertarmiut. Another theory is that the term Koniag derives from the Chain Aleut word for the Alutiit, Kanaagis (Pullar and Knecht 1990:1; Clark 1984:195). The name has, however, stuck to a certain extent, the most obvious contemporary application being in Koniag, Inc., the name of the corporation established for the Kodiak Island region pursuant to the Alaska Native Claims Settlement Act of 1971 (ANCSA).

Each local group also has a designation that identifies it as being from that particular place. The village of Larsen Bay is on a small bay of the same name that branches off the larger Uyak Bay. Thus the name Uyak is more identified with the area with the name of the people being Uyaksarmiut ("people of Uyaksaq") (Pullar and Knecht 1990:9).

The extant Alutiiq communities are the villages of Tatitlek and Chenega Bay in Prince William Sound; communities within the towns of Cordova, Valdez, and Seward in the Prince William Sound/Kenai Peninsula area; Port Graham (Paluwik) and Nanwalek (English Bay) on the Kenai Peninsula; the villages of Akhiok, Karluk, Larsen Bay, Old Harbor, Ouzinkie, and Port Lions in the Kodiak Island area; a community within the town of Kodiak; and the Alaska Peninsula villages of Chignik Lake, Chignik Lagoon, Perryville and Ivanof Bay. It is estimated that indigenous people have occupied Kodiak Island for nearly 8,000 years (Jordan 1987:4).

Ethnic identity is a sensitive topic among Alutiiq people. The term Aleut was externally applied by the Russians, first to the people of the Aleutian Islands (who identify themselves as Unangan) and then to the people of Kodiak Island and Prince William Sound. While having many cultural similarities, the two peoples are quite distinct from each other and have different languages. The Alutiiq people are biologically the southernmost extension of the Inuit, who stretch across arctic Alaska, Canada, Greenland, and portions of Siberia. The term Inuit is never used, however, and Alutiiq people often become very agitated if they are called Eskimos.

The confusion over the identity of Alutiiq people was further exacerbated by the artificial boundaries drawn by ANCSA, which divided the Alutiiq culture area into three regions, each with a separate ANCSA corporation.

4. Accounts of the event appeared in several local newspapers: Smithsonian Returns Larsen Bay Bones to Native Burial Site, by Mary Wilson, *Anchorage Times*, October 5, 1991, pp. A1, A8; At Rest, At Last, by Natalie Phillips, *Anchorage Daily News*, October 6, 1991, pp. A1, A14; and Ancestors Return to Larsen Bay, by Holly F. Reimer, *Tundra Times*, October 14, 1991, pp. 1, 18.
5. Native Americans to Get Remains: Smithsonian to Return Bones for Reburial; Some Are from Alaska, by Irvin Molotsky, *An-

chorage Daily News, September 13, 1989, p. A1; and Villagers Still Wait for Remains, by David Hulen, *Anchorage Daily News,* March 14, 1990, p. A1.

6. All photographs in this chapter were taken by Gordon L. Pullar.

7. The Kodiak Area Native Association is the tribal organization controlled by the seven tribal governments of the Kodiak Island area. KANA was formed in 1966, primarily to pursue the settlement of aboriginal land claims. With the passage of the Alaska Native Claims Settlement Act of 1971 KANA was charged with the responsibility of establishing a regional "for-profit" corporation that would be the recipient of title to land and cash from the settlement. KANA did this with the establishment of Koniag, Inc., and then turned its efforts to providing health, social, and educational services and to serve in a political advocacy role for the villages of the island.

8. Richard Jordan, while not a strong advocate for repatriation or reburial of human remains, believed that repatriation and reburial were necessary for the sake of maintaining strong working relationships with Alaska Natives so that archaeological excavations could continue on Native-owned land. In a November 14, 1988 letter to Dr. William Fitzhugh, Department of Anthropology, National Museum of Natural History, Smithsonian Institution, Jordan expressed his frustration with what he perceived as a threat to his archaeological future in Alaska by rigid Smithsonian policies. In the letter he said, "In a nutshell, the current Smithsonian policy on reburials is not working. And it is not working to the extent that the Smithsonian's very good name is being dragged through the mud in virtually every format where Native people have an opportunity to express their views."

9. Smithsonian to Give Back Village's Bones, Artifacts, by David Hulen, *Anchorage Daily News,* April 11, 1991, pp. A1, A12.

10. Kearney 1983:41.

11. Skeletons in Our Museums' Closets, by Douglas J. Preston, *Harper's,* February 1989:66–67.

12. Testimony in the proposed legislation, House Bill 436, An Act Relating to the Protection of Alaska Native Unmarked Burials.

13. Personal interview, October 17, 1992.

14. Personal interview, October 17, 1992.

15. Ancestors Return to Larsen Bay, by Holly Reimer, *Tundra Times,* October 14, 1991, pp. 1, 18.

16. Smithsonian to Give Back Village's Bones, Artifacts, by David Hulen, *Anchorage Daily News,* April 11, 1991, pp. A1, A12.

17. Letter from Donald J. Ortner, Chair, Department of Anthropology, NMNH, Smithsonian Institution, to Gordon L. Pullar, Kodiak Area Native Association, May 30, 1989 (Appendix).

18. Letter from Adrienne L. Kaeppler to Frank M. Carlson, president of the Larsen Bay Tribal Council, February 16, 1988 (Appendix).

19. Letter from Robert McC. Adams, Secretary, Smithsonian Institution, to Henry Sockbeson, Native American Rights Fund lawyer who represented the Larsen Bay Tribal Council, April 27, 1990 (Appendix).

20. Personal interview, July 18, 1989.

21. Smithsonian to Give Back Village's Bones, Artifacts, by David Hulen, *Anchorage Daily News,* April 11, 1991, p. A12.

22. Mary Wilson, *Anchorage Times,* October 5, 1991, pp. A1, A8. It should also be mentioned that the Smithsonian spent tens of thousands of dollars on staff time and contracted studies to resist the repatriation request.

References Cited

Bellah, Robert N., Richard Madsen, William M. Sullivan, Ann Swidler, and Steven M. Tipton

1985   *Habits of the Heart: Individualism and Commitment in American Life.* New York: Harper and Row.

Bieder, Robert E.

1990   Brief Historical Survey of the Expropriation of American Indian Remains. Report commissioned by the Native American Rights Fund.

Clark, Donald W.

1984   Pacific Eskimo: Historical Ethnography. In *Handbook of North American Indians,* vol. 5, Arctic, D. Damas, ed., pp. 185–97. Washington, D.C.: Smithsonian Institution.

Davis, Nancy Yaw

1984   Contemporary Pacific Eskimo. In *Handbook of North American Indians,* vol. 5, Arctic, D. Damas, ed., pp. 198–204. Washington, D.C.: Smithsonian Institution.

Deloria, Vine Jr.

1989   A Simple Question of Humanity: The Moral Dimensions of the Reburial Issue. *NARF Legal Review* 14(4):1–12. Boulder, Colorado: Native American Rights Fund.

Dumond, Don E.

1990   The Uyak Site (Kod-145) in Southwestern Alaskan Prehistory. A Report for the Department of Anthropology, U.S. National Museum of Natural History, Smithsonian Institution.

Etuk, Boniface

1989   Reflections for Projection, Starting from the Known: A Framework for Building Indigenous Science. Paper prepared for the Indigenous Science Conference, University of Calgary, Alberta.

Hall, Edward T.

1976   *Beyond Culture.* New York: Anchor Books/ Doubleday.

Harper, Kenn

1986   *Give Me My Father's Body: The Life of Minik, The New York Eskimo.* Frobisher Bay, Northwest Territories, Canada: Blacklead Books.

Highwater, Jamake

1981   *The Primal Mind.* New York: Penguin Group.

Hrdlička, Aleš

1919   *Physical Anthropology, Its Scope and Aims; Its History and Present Status in the United States.* Philadelphia: The Wistar Institute of Anatomy and Biology.

1930a   The Ancient and Modern Inhabitants of the Yukon. In *Explorations and Field-Work of the Smithsonian Institution in 1929,* pp. 137–46. Washington, D.C.: Smithsonian Institution.

1930b   *Anthropological Survey in Alaska.* Washington, D.C.: U.S. Government Printing Office.

1943   *Alaska Diary 1926–1931.* Lancaster, Pa.: Jaques Cattell Press.

1944   *The Anthropology of Kodiak Island.* Philadelphia: The Wistar Institute of Anatomy and Biology.

Jordan, Richard H.
1987 The Kodiak Archaeological Project: 1987 Report of Activities. Unpublished manuscript.

Kearney, Michael
1983 *World View.* Novato, California: Chandler and Sharp Publishers.

Kodiak Area Native Association
1988 *KANA Kasitaq.* Newsletter for the Kodiak Area Native Association, November.

Meighan, C.
1990 Editorial Comment. *ACPAC Newsletter.* The American Committee for Preservation of Archaeological Collections, Fullerton, California. January.

Miraglia, Rita A.
1992 The Importance of Native Involvement in Decisions Effecting Cultural Resources. Paper presented at the Alaska Anthropological Association meeting, Fairbanks.

Oleksa, Michael J. (ed.)
1987 *Alaska Missionary Spirituality.* New York: Paulist Press.

Pullar, Gordon L.
1989 The Hrdlička Legacy and Koniag Spirits. Paper presented at the Circum-Pacific Prehistory Conference, Seattle.
1990 The Kodiak Island Archaeological Project. In *Preservation on the Reservation: Native Americans, Native American Lands and Archaeology,* Anthony J. Klesert and Alan S. Downer, eds., pp. 269–74. Navajo Nation Papers in Anthropology Number 26. Navajo Nation Archaeology Department and Navajo Nation Historic Preservation Department.

Pullar, Gordon L., and Richard H. Jordan
1986 The Kodiak Archaeological Project, 1983–86: Perspectives from the President of the Native Association and the Principal Investigator. Paper presented at the Fifth Inuit Studies Conference, McGill University, Montreal.

Pullar, Gordon L., and Philomena Knecht
1990 Continuous Occupation of Larsen Bay / Uyak Bay by Qikertarmiut. Report prepared for the Native American Rights Fund. Unpublished manuscript.

Schultz, Adolph H.
1945 *Biographical Memoir of Aleš Hrdlička 1869–1943.* Biographical Memoirs, vol. 23. Washington, D.C.: National Academy of Sciences.

Scott, G. Richard
1990 Continuity or Replacement at the Uyak Site, Kodiak Island, Alaska: A Physical Anthropological Analysis of Population Relationships. Report prepared for the Department of Anthropology, Smithsonian Institution.
1992 Affinities of Prehistoric and Modern Kodiak Islanders and the Question of Kachemak-Koniag Biological Continuity. *Arctic Anthropology* 29(2):150–66.

Spencer, Frank
1979 Aleš Hrdlička, M.D., 1869–1943: A Chronicle of the Life and Work of an American Physical Anthropologist, 2 vols. Ph.D. Dissertation, Department of Anthropology, University of Michigan, Ann Arbor.

Steffian, Amy F.
1992 Archaeological Coal in the Gulf of Alaska: A View From Kodiak Island. *Arctic Anthropology* 29(2):111–29.

Suzuki, David, and Peter Knudson
1992 *Wisdom of the Elders: Honoring Sacred Native Visions of Nature.* New York: Bantam.

U.S. Government Printing Office
1989 Report of the Alaska Federation of Natives on the Status of Alaska Natives: A Call for Action. Hearing before the Select Committee on Indian Affairs, United States Senate. U.S. Government Printing Office, Washington, D.C.

Washburn, Wilcomb E.
1990 Museums and Repatriation of Objects in Their Collections. In *Change and Continuity,* Barbara Isaac, ed., pp. 15–18. Cambridge: Peabody Museum Press.

4

A MOST PECULIAR MAN

The Life and Times of Aleš Hrdlička

If the student is to make anthropology . . . his life vocation, he must also possess certain qualifications . . . he should possess those mental qualities which will enable him to follow his work with undimmed enthusiasm and vigor under smaller material compensations and perhaps other advantages than those of his friends who have . . . chosen other vocations; for anthropology is not an industrial necessity. The compensations for this lie in the high grade of his work. He deals intimately with the highest of organisms, he contributes to the knowledge of what is most worth while. His studies of human evolution and antiquity, of the developing child and youth, of the infinite variation of full-blown manhood and womanhood, of the laws that control all this, and of the means by which these laws may consciously and effectively be directed for future advance of humanity—all these will provide him with mental food of such an order that he will easily forget the regrets of not having chosen a more remunerative vocation. (Aleš Hrdlička 1920:37–38)

You interest me very much, Mr. Holmes. I had hardly expected so dolichocephalic a skull or such well-marked supra-orbital development. Would you have any objection to my running my finger along your parietal fissure? A cast of your skull, sir, until the original is available, would be an ornament to any anthropological museum. It is not my intention to be fulsome, but I confess that I covet your skull. (Dr. James Mortimer to Sherlock Holmes, in *The Hound of the Baskervilles* by Sir Arthur Conan Doyle)

Few curators have left as tangible a mark on the halls of science at the Smithsonian as Aleš Hrdlička (fig. 4.1). During his career he served as a major catalyst in transforming the field of physical anthropology at the Smithsonian, in the United States, and around the world from its obscure origins to an internationally recognized discipline dealing with many of the most profound questions of this century—human origins, evolution and variation, health and morbidity, growth and development, and ethnicity. At the Smithsonian Hrdlička presided over expansion of the field from his single cluttered office and lone position to a highly visible and productive subdivision of anthropology with four curators, support staff, laboratory facilities, library, and unparalleled collections that attracted graduate students and scientists from all over the world. Fifty years after his death, Hrdlička's collection of publications and reprints are still stored in boxes that line the walls of the Anthropology Department's seminar room from floor to ceiling. Just beyond the seminar room are two corridors that are lined with gray-green drawers stacked 14 levels high and filled with human skeletal remains. Additional collections are housed in individual offices, in two staircase corridors leading up to the attic, and in the upper rotunda

Figure 4.1. Portrait of Aleš Hrdlička in his Smithsonian office. (Courtesy of the National Anthropological Archives, Smithsonian Institution)

beneath the museum's dome. Prior to recent repatriations, the Anthropology Department housed approximately 32,000 "cataloged records" of human remains from all over the world, although the actual number of "individuals" in the collection is different since each catalog record may include the remains of more than one individual. Of the number, 14,300 records are for Native Americans from the lower 48 states and 3,500 are from Alaska. Approximately 75 percent of this "collection" was acquired by Hrdlička either personally through his own expeditions or through intermediaries and correspondents. To house this extraordinary collection, Hrdlička arranged for the museum to construct drawers and shelves that were specially designed to house crania and skeletons.

Hrdlička collected skulls and bones with a passion. With the penchant of a nineteenth-century natural historian for accumulating type collections, he and his collaborators ranged the globe to recover "representative samples" of human skeletal material from as many different cultures and time periods as possible. The passion was in naming and describing the material, with the belief that each individual contribution to knowledge would eventually lead to a brilliant synthesis. Hrdlička seemed to have seen himself as an inspired soldier of science with a duty to recover as much information as possible. He preferred large series of human remains to single individuals because larger collections offered more control over individual variation. He bemoaned the loss of "specimens" to unscrupulous collectors with the pathos of an orni-

thologist seeing the last of a bird species disappearing into the pot. The collection that resulted was Hrdlička's pride, a great scientific assemblage salvaged from the ravages of time, the indiscriminate disturbances of vandals, and environmental perturbations.

Times have changed, however, and this unassailable scientific monument to one man's collecting zeal is under attack. Changing political and social mores have invaded the previously sacrosanct halls of the academy. Under repatriation legislation much of the collection stands to be dismantled. The future of the collection, which took the "bone doctor" some 40 years to amass and involved travels to remote parts of the world, along with much energy, expense, diplomacy, and effort, seems uncertain.

Hrdlička: The Early Years

> Yet here, the first and alone of the family of seven, born with insatiate yearning to travel, see, smell, hear, feel with his own senses, and endeavor to find, gather, penetrate. With longing to know this mother earth as intimately as possible . . . to go and learn and get ever nearer the essentials, the vast secrets of it all. (Hrdlička 1943:7)

Biographies of Aleš Hrdlička (1869–1943) include works by Montagu (1944), Prokopec (1971), Schultz (1945), Spencer (1979), and Stewart (1940). Hrdlička was born in 1869 in the town of Humpolec in southern Bohemia. As a child he embraced a nineteenth-century love of natural history, encouraged by tutors and schooling. After arriving in America in 1882 at the age of 13, he worked in factories by day and attended school by night.

Hrdlička always prided himself on his medical degree, which he believed was a necessary prerequisite for a career in physical anthropology. He graduated from the New York Eclectic Medical College in 1892, first among his fellow-students, and then acquired additional medical training at the New York Homeopathic College. In 1894 he began a career in medical research among the insane at an asylum in Middletown, New York. Two years later, following a year of anthropological and medical study in Europe, Hrdlička accepted an associate in anthropology position at the newly formed Pathological Institute at the New York State Hospital. There, he was able to apply his European-gained insights and skills to initiate a systematic study of human physical variation. The study originated with data collected on mental patients at the state hospital. Hrdlička realized that in order to make sense of this data he needed to be able to define "normal" physical types with which he could then compare to "abnormal" samples. Thus began Hrdlička's interest in human skeletal remains. His early publications dealt extensively with studies of white American physical attributes and skeletal remains (e.g., Hrdlička 1898, 1932a). They also established white male Americans of European descent as the baseline norm for comparing human variability, revealing the inherent racist assumptions that permeated the fledgling field of anthropology (Gould 1981).

Although Hrdlička's private life remains for the most part obscured by the distance he maintained between his personal and professional domains, it is known that on his return from Europe in 1896 he married a former student, Marie Strickler-Dieudonnée, to whom he was devoted (Spencer 1979:54–64). When she died in 1918, Hrdlička had her remains cremated and enshrined in an urn at his home. He married again in 1920. Both marriages were childless.

Hrdlička: Anthropologist, Collector, and Curator

Hrdlička first participated in anthropological fieldwork in 1898 as a member of the American Museum of Natural History's expedition to Mexico and the American Southwest. Franz Boas described the young Hrdlička as "evidently possessed of an incredible capacity for work, and of a wonderful energy" (Prokopec 1992). The field experience was a turning point in Hrdlička's life. After it, his work gradually changed from the study of comparative anatomy to that of human populations.

In 1903 Hrdlička came to Washington as an assistant curator to set up a physical anthropology division in the U.S. Museum of Natural History. He became curator in 1910 and retired in 1941, after serving the Smithsonian for 38 years in acquiring and maintaining collections to rival those anywhere in the world. He described most of the collections now housed at the museum in a series of seven volumes entitled *Catalogues of Human Crania in the U.S. National Museum*. Over his lifetime, Hrdlička authored some 400 publications, including 20 books (Schultz 1945; Stewart 1940:21–36).

During his time at the Smithsonian, Hrdlička travelled extensively. His research on human origins in the New World (Hrdlička 1902, 1907) led him to undertake ten field expeditions between 1926 and 1938 to Alaska, the Aleutians, and the Commander Islands in search of ancient migration routes. In addition, he made trips to virtually every other continent on the globe (Table 4.1). Wherever he travelled, he examined famous skeletal material and fossil localities. He acquired human skeletal material, particularly crania, whenever he could. When he visited other institutions and museums, he carefully and systematically measured the human remains in their collections.

Hrdlička played a central role in the establishment of the American Association of Physical Anthropologists, serving as its first president and as editor of the first 23 volumes of the *American Journal of Physical Anthropology*. He served as first secretary of the National Science Foundation, president of the anthropology section of the American Association for the Advancement of Science, and president of the Washington Academy of Science. He was a member of the National Academy of Sciences. Hrdlička received numerous awards, including the Huxley Memorial Medal of the Royal Institute of Anthropology of Great Britain and Ireland and honorary doctorates from universities in Prague and Brno. One of the U.S. Liberty ships built during World War II bore the name Aleš Hrdlička.

A tireless and indefatigable worker, he referred to the enforced period of hospitalization following his first heart attack in 1939 as "the first vacation of my life" (Hrdlička 1942:20). A second heart attack in September 1943 claimed his life at the age of 75. Hrdlička's death came within a year of that of Franz Boas. With the passing of these two individuals, the formative era of American anthropology came to a close.

As a final irony, Hrdlička arranged to have his body cremated and his ashes placed in an urn that, along with his death mask, beloved calipers, and measuring devices, were displayed in his one-time office for many years. "It was ironic for Hrdlička to desecrate his own skeleton, since he obviously thought a great deal of the human framework as a research tool. It would have been a wonderful gesture, and quite a personal touch from this most impersonal of men, to have had himself filed away in the 25,000-skull boneyard of mostly unknowns that he built up from practically nothing."[1]

Hrdlička, the Man

Hrdlička was a proud, formidable man with a central European formality that he seldom relaxed. He never disguised his Czech origin, always insisting that his name should be written in its original form. He was an abrupt and disconcerting man, ceremonious and idiosyncratic, "entirely unconventional in many ways" (Stewart 1975:31). Throughout his professional career at the Smithsonian, he always dressed in a formal European manner, in a black suit with a high celluloid collar and a black clip-on tie. He disliked accepting social invitations from colleagues and preferred to keep his business and social lives separate (Stewart 1975:29).

His enthusiasm was indefatigable, his energy boundless, and his discipline unbending. He was a relentless worker who demanded the same of his associ-

Stephen Loring and Miroslav Prokopec

Table 4.1. The Life and Travels of Aleš Hrdlička

Date	Event
1869	Born in Humpolec, Czechoslovakia
1882	Emigrated to United States
1896	Medical and anthropological training in Europe; visits to France, Germany, Switzerland, Austria, Belgium, England
1898	Medical and anthropometric fieldwork in Mexico
1899	Medical and anthropometric fieldwork in Mexico
1900–1905	Fieldwork among the Indians of the American Southwest and Mexico
1903	Starts work at the Smithsonian Institution
1906	Examines early human remains in Florida
1908	Medical research among western American Indian tribes
1909	Anthropological research and collecting in Egypt; travel and collections research in Turkey, Greece, Italy, Hungary, Poland, Germany, and Russia
1910	Attends the International Congress of Americanists in Argentina; makes large skeletal collections in Peru; visits Mexico
1912	Travel to Europe, western Russia, Siberia, and Mongolia to examine early human remains
1913	Travel to the Caribbean; collects archaeological remains in Peru
1915	Fieldwork with Sioux and Chippewa in Minnesota
1916	Studies early human remains in Florida
1917	Anthropometric research among Native Americans in North Dakota, Minnesota, and Tennessee
1918	Anthropometric research among the Seminole in Florida
1920	Travel and research in Japan, Korea, China, and Hawaii
1922	Travel to Brazil to participate in conferences; travel to Europe to examine early sites and Pleistocene human remains
1923	Director of the American School of Prehistoric Studies in Europe
1925	Anthropometric and human palaeontological research in India, Ceylon, Java, Australia, South Africa, and Europe
1926	Anthropometric and archaeological research in Alaska
1927	Delivers the Huxley Memorial Lecture to the Royal Anthropological Society of Great Britain; travels to fossil localities and does collections research in Europe
1929–30	Fieldwork in Alaska
1931	First visit to Kodiak Island, Alaska
1932, 1934–36	Archaeological fieldwork at the Uyak Site, Larsen Bay, and Kodiak Island
1936–38	Archaeological fieldwork in the Aleutian Islands and on the Commander Islands (Russia)
1939	Travel to England, Russia, and Siberia
1943	Died in Washington, D.C.

ates and students. At home he claimed to sleep on boards, or on the floor, to be fit for expedition life (Schultz 1945:314). His tenure at the Smithsonian coincided with the Great Depression. To ensure that financial resources would be available for research and travel, Hrdlička regularly returned a portion of his salary to a private fund for financing fieldwork. He was generous with the resources at his disposal, personally contributing to the research of a number of individuals, always with the admonishment to return with more skulls. His private contributions, both financial and intellectual, figured significantly in the founding of the *American Journal of Physical Anthropology* in 1918.

Among Hrdlička's peculiarities was an aversion to women. According to a writer in the *Washington Star,* Hrdlička was "abrupt and disconcerting in his often gruff remarks, especially to women. He never did understand them. He objected to their smoking, wearing make-up, and working anywhere but in the home 'Where they belong.' He could not bear the thought of women in science. He even avoided looking at them, and at scientific meetings he shunned the rare species of female scientist as if they had a communicable disease. He walked out of one such mixed meeting that dealt with the sexual habits of monkeys, considering it an improper topic to discuss with women present."[2]

As concerned as he was with heredity and eugenics, Hrdlička studied his own ancestry and was pleased (relieved?) to find no serious illness or mental disorders in his early relatives (Prokopec 1992). This convinced him he was "normal." This concept must be understood in the way an anthropologist and a physician in the hospital for the insane understood it. He believed that his judgment, based on his observations and relying on his senses once all the available facts had been taken into account, must be "normal," must correspond to reality, and must be close to absolute truth. Once he made a decision, he never felt it necessary to revise it, even if new facts or evidence had accumulated to contradict it. A newspaper reporter once asked Hrdlička to name some of his more important works. He replied "I consider all my works important; otherwise I would not do them" (Prokopec 1992).

Hrdlička, the Scientist

Hrdlička's scientific interests were manyfold, but a constant trajectory is apparent through his career—from early descriptive and comparative studies to studies of human evolution. He pursued his research with perseverance and concentration, always economizing on time. According to his rigid daily schedule, he dictated four pages and measured a minimum number of skulls for his *Catalogues of Crania*. His handwriting, which is easily recognizable, shows that he also cataloged a large part of the skeletal specimens himself.

Interest in Human Variation and Craniometrics

While working as a research intern at the Hospital for the Insane in New York and later as an associate at the Pathological Institute, Hrdlička became interested in the differences between normal and pathological individuals. He applied scientific standards of description and nomenclature in identifying and characterizing separate groups within the population of the institutionalized insane. He saw in anthropological methodology a way of addressing problems in clinical medicine, identifying ailments, and synthesizing treatment procedures. Hrdlička applied his European training in anthropological methods of human measurement to a detailed study of "abnormals" who were housed in institutions in New York State.

The idea of creating comparable standards for healthy normal men, women, and children led him to a study of anatomical material in museum and institutional collections. The opportunity to participate in the American Museum of Natural History's expedition to Mexico, ostensibly to collect data on human variation, was the beginning of a lifelong commitment to physical and medical anthropological research and to studying human variation on a global scale.

The procedures and methodology of physical anthropology are by their very nature invasive, disruptive, and poorly understood by subject populations whose previous relationships with Euro-American males have been in the context of state-sanctioned colonial enterprises. Hrdlička never lingered long enough at any site to establish community, or even individual, relationships with his informants or subjects. In his avarice for data, his dealings with native people invariably consisted of taking measurements and photographs and running off to the next community and the next set of "subjects."

In the course of his life, Hrdlička was able to quantify the normal physical and physiological standards for American Indians, Eskimos, Caucasians, and Afro-American peoples. Although he had a prodigious publication record and conducted original research, he never broke free of the colonial, sexist, and racial underpinnings of nineteenth-century anthropology that seriously compromise our perceptions of his scholarship and humanity today. Yet there is little deceit in Hrdlička's work. His blinders, biases, and assumptions are readily apparent, as evidenced in the following quote: "It is quite a different thing to measure among the pliant, trusting savage, and then among the semi-civilized, suspicious, scattered free laborers and servants of a big city" (Hrdlička 1928:15, quoted in Blakey 1988:18).

Studies of Racial Differences

An underlying concern of American physical anthropology in the first half of the twentieth century had been with the biological significance of race and the scientific defense of race as an explanation of social inequality (Blakey 1988; Gould 1981). The recognition of racial variations in human skeletons was one of Hrdlička's sustained interests, and he participated actively in scientific discussions of the race concept. He fought against what he perceived to be an erroneous direction in race research, especially the eugenics movement and "scientific" racism proposed by the Nazis.[3] In his book *The Old Americans*, Hrdlička used his anthropometric techniques to determine a measure of normalcy, the "sub-type of the white people" (Blakey 1988:15), and to firmly place the Euro-American Caucasian at the apex of human evolution, the standard by which all other human groups should be measured.

Studies into the Origins of North American Indians

During his travels in Europe and Asia, Hrdlička had an opportunity to closely examine the fossil record of human evolution, a subject in which he was keenly interested. After joining the Smithsonian in 1903, he continued his studies of physical variation among

Stephen Loring and Miroslav Prokopec

American Indian populations. He also began his life-long interest in the debate over the antiquity of humans in the Americas. Hrdlička ardently supported the argument against a long antiquity in New World occupations. In order to counter spurious claims, he conducted detailed metrical studies that showed that human remains believed to be of great antiquity were morphologically within the range of recent American Indians. In addition, Hrdlička demanded good contextual data (cultural, geological, biological) for proof of human antiquity in the New World. His experience with Pleistocene faunal remains in Alaska (Hrdlička 1943:249) made him especially skeptical of spurious associations. During his travels, Hrdlička had managed to visit many important localities where human fossils had been recovered, especially in Europe and the Middle East, and he knew what good Pleistocene archaeological sites should look like and what kinds of data had to accompany and underlie claims of antiquity. Although Hrdlička has frequently been criticized for his conservative stance in the debate (Wilmsen 1965), his critiques of bogus associations and inherent flaws in the data helped to establish the rigorous standards for proof that eventually, with the discovery of the Folsom site and Blackwater Draw in the 1920s, confirmed the presence of humans in the Americas during the Pleistocene.

Hrdlička's Travels in Alaska: 1926–1938

There is therefore, except for the nature-blind, but little real lonesomeness in Alaska, and enough to call one to it year after year; not as a settler—it is not, in the main, yet a white man's country—but as a privileged visitor. (Hrdlička 1943:7)

It was in Alaska that Hrdlička earned his sobriquet "skull doctor" from the natives in the Yukon (Hrdlička 1943:223). The Aleut had their own name for him, "ashaalixnamaataax," which can be translated as "the dead man's daddy" (Laughlin in press, and personal communication).

Hrdlička was 57 years old when, in 1926, he made his first trip to Alaska to seek evidence of the route by which the first hunters, the original "old Americans," invaded the continent. He chose the Yukon River as the most probable prehistoric route over the "land-bridge" between Asia and America to the inland territories.

The possibility of fieldwork in Alaska was a siren call that Hrdlička could not resist. It was he who, almost singlehandedly, reestablished an institutional focus on Alaska at the Smithsonian. He oversaw the hiring of Henry B. Collins and T. Dale Stewart, both of whom subsequently conducted important anthropological research in Alaska. In 1926 and 1929 Hrdlička travelled on the Yukon River and its tributaries. Ostensibly searching for archaeological and skeletal material to address the question of the peopling of the New World, he also collected measurements and photographs and made plaster face casts of living Indians and Eskimos throughout the course of his journey (and on all his subsequent trips to Alaska).

It would be a poor guest who never returned favors for hospitality received. In Hrdlička's case, his medical skills and services were in demand everywhere (Hrdlička 1943:94, 167, 245; Gruber 1943): "the natives were glad to let him measure and photograph them in return for his help in any sickness or injury (Hrdlička n.d.). In a rare show of humor, Hrdlička proposed charging one old "sourdough" he treated on the Yukon "a dozen skulls, or a few skeletons" for payment of his services (Hrdlička 1943:292).

In the field, Hrdlička had to balance his collecting ardor with the concerns of Alaskan natives who did not share his scientific zeal. The popular representation of Hrdlička draws upon the image of an insensitive scientist, a reputation not unexpected given the nature of his research; the barriers of language, culture, and class; and the frenetic pace of his fieldwork. Yet his diary attests to frequent occasions where the uncomfortableness and concern of local natives precluded his collecting activities (1930a:139; 1943:43, 197–198, 235) and where native knowledge and help were solicited and procured (1943:58, 235, 250; 1945:267, 409, 416), even to the point of helping to exhume skeletons (1943:65, 73–76, 115–118, 129, 219, 312, 321–322, 334; 1945:368) and to selling or giving human remains to him (1943:233–234; 1945:323). Although they are never clearly defined, Hrdlička had personal guidelines for collecting burials that were "too recent" (1943:215, 218, 361; 1945:255). He maintains that "though the work was sometimes of a rather delicate nature, [it was accomplished] without incurring the ill will of any person . . . due to the fact that the objects of the study and collecting were frankly explained in every case to whites and natives alike through lectures or individually, and that all recent burials were strictly respected" (Hrdlička 1930a:139).

His Yukon River research and subsequent investigations of the Kuskokwim River region convinced Hrdlička that many of the older, pre-Russian contact sites had been lost to erosion. As a result, he shifted his attention to Alaska's island archipelago where stable coastlines might be expected to contain earlier materials. In 1931, while working in the Bristol Bay area, he visited Kodiak Island where he was shown the Uyak site, along with others. The Uyak site on Larsen Bay seemed ideal for excavating: the soil was not frozen, the site was accessible and looked very promising, and accommodations and hospitality were extended by the local cannery superintendent.

He spent four summer field seasons (1932, 1934, 1935, and 1936) excavating at Uyak with the assistance of volunteer crews (fig. 4.2). His research on Kodiak Island is reported in a number of annual reports (Hrdlička 1932b, 1933, 1935, 1936, 1937, 1941a, and 1941b) and in two monographs on ethnohistory and archaeology (Hrdlička 1944a, Heizer 1956). The results of the work on Kodiak led to the "recovery through excavation of many skeletal remains, and *incidently* also much of the material culture" (Hrdlička 1944a:3, emphasis added).

Following his work on Kodiak, Hrdlička shifted his attention to the Aleutian and Commander Islands (1936–1938) where he sought answers to Aleut cultural origins and routes of Asiatic-American immigration (Hrdlička 1945).

Among the general conclusions of Hrdlička's research in Alaska are his recognition and definition of a variety of Native Alaskan Eskimo and Indian physical types (based both on observations and measurements of living people and on analyses of skeletal collections); the revelation that Alaska had a much longer and more complex prehistory than had been previously realized; and new insights about the movement and distributions of different prehistoric populations and their cultural origins (Hrdlička 1930b, 1943, 1944a, and 1945).

Investigations at Larsen Bay

There never was a finer and more remunerative comparable site than this at Uyak, and within modest limits and means, and barring the rains and the gnats, there never were more favorable conditions for excavations. (Hrdlička 1945:213)

Alerted to the potential significance of the Uyak Bay site (also called the Jones Site and "Our Site") by U.S. Fisheries Bureau personnel, Hrdlička made a reconnoiter of the area a high priority of his 1931 Alaska field season. He was not the first to excavate at the site; digging there had long been a popular activity pursued by cannery employees and local villagers (Hrdlička 1944a:136). The fortuitous, albeit momentous, discovery of a human skull with artificial ivory eyes in an exposed midden profile was the event that captured Hrdlička's interest and set in motion the phenomenal "excavations" of the next four years (fig. 4.3).

Throughout his sojourn at Larsen Bay, Hrdlička worked closely with Gordon and Laura Jones, the superintendent and his wife of the Alaska Packers Association cannery at Larsen Bay. The Joneses greatly facilitated the Smithsonian research. Along with providing the implied local consent, they made the cannery's resources available and oversaw logistical constraints. In Laura Jones, Hrdlička found an enthusiastic supporter who labored ceaselessly on his behalf. Due to her efforts, Hrdlička acquired a large number of additional specimens, both artifacts and human remains, from local fishermen and trappers. In addition, she donated her personal collection of skeletons and artifacts to the Smithsonian and she became smitten by the passion to dig. Her letters are almost ghoulish in their enthusiasm for obtaining more skeletons for Hrdlička. This enthusiasm led her to exhume the graves of recently deceased cannery employees, "chinamen," to provide the good doctor with additional specimens from sites in the vicinity. Her candor and enthusiasm are revealed in a letter, dated September 14, 1931, to Hrdlička: "Packed ten skeletons and some extra bones. Two to a box as you did . . . I so want to send you all I possibly can. By the way—think I've located ten more Chinamen but it's hard digging and will have to leave them until next year. In box number 13 there was evidently a Chinaman of note for he was buried in brocade, had a 'pig tail' and a lovely white jade bracelet. I kept the bracelet (naturally) and sent you the 'pig tail' . . . Still hope you will be able to come back here next year and instruct me further in this 'bone business' as Gordon calls it" (Jones correspondence in Hrdlička n.d.).

According to Hrdlička (1944a:274, 324), the "nearby natives" had no tradition concerning the site locality. A careful reading of his narrative, however, reveals that for some local villagers the site remained significant as both a place of gardens and a place for burial.

To Hrdlička (1944a:141), "the chief object of these excavations was to secure the skeletal materials which the site evidently contained; at the same time, however, throughout the work all reasonable care was given to the cultural side of the project, every specimen that showed any human work was carefully examined, and where worth while preserved for the National Collections." It is impossible to condone Hrdlička's excavation strategy even in light of his day. He made neither plan maps nor profile drawings and, as a consequence, it is not surprising that the features he unearthed, including burials, storage pits, stone lined hearths, and houses, in the absence of documentation proved a "constant puzzle" (Hrdlička 1944a:179). The difficulty of cutting through the surface vegetation led Hrdlička, for expediency's sake, to cut a face from the top to the bottom of a midden and proceed systematically to undercut the face with a pick (Hrdlička 1944a:170) (fig. 4.4). He found note taking to be "quite impracticable, and would have confused rather than simplified matters" (Hrdlička 1944a:141). The

Stephen Loring and Miroslav Prokopec

Figure 4.2. Field crew of 1935 at Uyak site, posing with skeletons. (Courtesy of the National Anthropological Archives, Smithsonian Institution)

loss of an entire season's fieldnotes was summarily dismissed as "unfortunate," since the notes were "largely a repetition" of the preceding field season and of little consequence (Hrdlička 1944a:204).

In the name of expediency, with a conciliatory nod to archaeological procedures, he did make a rudimentary concession to separating his collection into color-coded stratigraphic units, specifically upper (black), middle (red) and lower (blue). Given the extent of the site and the varying depths of the cultural deposits (see Speaker, this volume), this notorious field technique severely compromised the potential use of both skeletal and cultural collections. Yet the scale of Hrdlička's excavations, the sheer volume of earth removed, and the quantities of materials recovered remain unsurpassed in the annals of Alaskan archaeology.

After working at the Uyak site, and before the outbreak of World War II, Hrdlička shifted his focus to the Aleutian Islands in his determination to identify the conduit for the movement of ancient peoples between continents. The Aleutian work, more reconnaissance than excavation, never approached the scale of the work at Uyak Bay. In many respects, the

work at Kodiak was Hrdlička's swan song. It represented the end of the single, most focused, and intensive period of research he undertook.

For many of us who work in the north, our interactions with native colleagues and informants contribute a tremendous amount of insight into our understanding of local peoples, both past and present, the land, and its resources. Hrdlička avidly combed the ethnohistoric and "discovery" literature for insights on the native inhabitants of Kodiak Island. Yet he apparently avoided any involvement with local native families and any possibility of discussions with them that might have proved fruitful. One of Hrdlička's students at Larsen Bay, Robert Heizer, who later went on to write an archaeological summary of the excavations, identified the outstanding anthropological need for the area as recording "what remnants of traditional ethnology are still recoverable" (Heizer 1956:5).

For Hrdlička, most of the people of Larsen Bay remained nearly invisible. A few appear as biological examples of "Koniag types" in his descriptions of the physical anthropology of the people (1944a:361–

Figure 4.3. Hrdlička standing beside the first skeleton discovered in 1932. (Courtesy of the National Anthropological Archives, Smithsonian Institution)

Figure 4.4. Hrdlička leaning against the exposed midden deposits at "Our Point," the Uyak site, 1932. (Courtesy of the National Anthropological Archives, Smithsonian Institution)

Figure 4.5. Kodiak Island natives, a group of girls (above) and a man (below), photographed as anthropological subjects by Aleš Hrdlička, 1932. These formal scientific views are about the only evidence of Hrdlička's interaction with Kodiak Island natives. (Courtesy of the National Anthropological Archives, Smithsonian Institution)

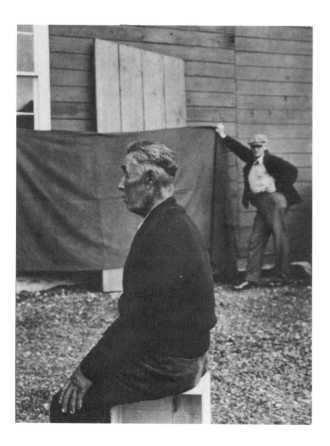

Figure 4.6. Hrdlička's own mug shot. (Courtesy of the National Anthropological Archives, Smithsonian Institution)

365), but these people are nameless and their voices silent (fig. 4.5). Despite his anthropological training, Hrdlička never lost the racist assumptions grounded in his cultural background and in his science. He never formally recognized the help and assistance he received from native Alaskans, although white informants are conspicuously acknowledged. At the beginning of the 1934 field season, Hrdlička lamented (1944a:219): "The fine banks before us, remunerative as they are in spots, are largely soulless and can give but little more than an inkling of the old life and its riches." How much more might have been illuminated and how much enmity might have been avoided had Hrdlička been more sensitive to the knowledge and interests of the people on whose land he trespassed. The world was a different place then (fig. 4.6).

The Journey of the Bones

Throughout his journeys in Alaska, Hrdlička regularly encountered cemeteries and burial localities that had been disturbed, invariably by white settlers and transient visitors, before his arrival (Hrdlička

1943:10, 55, 56, 102, 107, 127). He always lamented the loss to science, never once voicing concern as to the feelings of the descendants of this desecration. Of course, he never compared this peculiarly western custom of gathering skulls as souvenirs with his own scientific pursuits, which he held to be above such recriminations, even when knowingly at odds with local villagers. As he put it, "strange how scientific work sanctions everything" (Hrdlička 1943:56).

The human remains recovered by Hrdlička and his crew, as well as those brought to him by Laura Jones and other area residents and fishermen, were carefully marked as to their "provenance," packed in excelsior and shavings, crated, and shipped to Washington. At the Smithsonian, they were cleaned, conserved, and cataloged.

Basic metric analyses were conducted and sex and age were determined. Descriptions and measurements were taken according to internationally defined methods. Pathological findings were also noted. The results were compared with other population groups, resulting in an especially vivid picture of the people who once lived at the site in terms of their health and nutritional state, stature, body and muscle development, and demography. The skeletal collec-

Stephen Loring and Miroslav Prokopec

tion from the Uyak site, by dint of both its size and its antiquity was one of the two most studied human skeletal collections at the Smithsonian. As many as forty researchers each year came to conduct research on the Uyak collection. While a complete bibliography is not possible, some inkling of the scope and potential of this collection can be indicated. Hrdlička himself published extensively on the Kodiak Island collections (1941a, 1941b, 1944a, 1944b). Scott (this volume) examines a variety of physical attributes in order to assess the significance of skeletal attributes potentially reflecting cultural continuity. The question of population origins and cultural affinities have also been addressed through comparative studies of cranial variation (Ossenberg 1977; Zegura 1971, 1975). Edynak (1976) has used the long bones from the Uyak assemblage to study growth and development. Turner (1983) has used his analysis of teeth from Asia and the Americas to develop theories of human migration and ethnic identity. Murillo (1991), Costa (1977, 1980a, 1980b), Dahlberg (1962), and St. Hoyme (1980) have examined the dentition from the Uyak remains for indications of diet, health, and stress. Ortner and Utermohle (1981) have studied the pathological traces of diseases apparent on bones and, not incidently, the Uyak skeletal collections have also served as a valuable source of comparative data for forensic cases. For a detailed discussion of the current debate on the reasons and justification for the collection of human remains see Ubelaker and Grant (1989) and Ucko (1992).

An iron wheelbarrow used by Hrdlička's party and abandoned at the site remains as mute testimony to the activity that once took place on the shores of Larsen Bay. Today, the site is covered with luxurious vegetation, much as it was when Hrdlička first arrived. The stunning locality, with its vista of the mountain-rimmed bay, greets the visitor and resident alike. Scattered about the knoll are a few shallow pits made by local villagers searching for artifacts. The occasional human bone can be found laying on the surface.

The reburial ceremony for the human remains from the Uyak site took place October 5, 1991. About seventy people were present. The remains were reburied on top of an elevation not far from the site where the bones were excavated between 1931 and 1938. The reburial site is marked by a 12-foot-tall white Orthodox wooden cross. The contours of a pit about 50 × 10 feet in size are still visible. The journey of the bones is complete. They have returned to their original resting place.

The Man and His Times

Hrdlička entered the profession of anthropology at a time when speculation reigned and knowledge was unsystematized. He shared with his contemporary Franz Boas a perception of science that was grounded in the accumulation of facts. Hrdlička had, as one biographer put it, "a healthy aversion to unsupported hypotheses and rash speculation" (Schultz 1945:312). His universe had little room for conjecture.

Hrdlička made substantial contributions to the methodology of physical anthropology. He introduced internationally accepted anthropometric methods to America and developed several anthropometric instruments and procedures of his own design. His contributions include his works on the methodology of anthropometry, his participation in the debate over the peopling of the Americas and the development and origins of modern humans, the compilation of his seven *Catalogues of Crania,* and his unswerving encouragement of and support for physical anthropology in many countries.

The discipline of physical anthropology in America owes to Hrdlička much of the breadth that defines it. He must also be acknowledged for having the vision and energy to have amassed the biological anthropological collections at the National Museum of Natural History, one of the premier collections in the world. His legacy also includes a fund he left at the Smithsonian which has facilitated the work of researchers from around the world who have needed access to the Smithsonian collections.

Hrdlička maintained a lifelong interest in the development of anthropology as a discipline in his native Czechoslovakia. A fervent nationalist, he prepared materials for President Wilson on the history of Slavonic nations in 1918, helped exiled representatives of the Czechoslovak government meet U.S. government representatives, and prepared a memo to President Roosevelt when Czechoslovakia was endangered by Nazi Germany in 1938. In his native country, he is remembered for both the moral and material support he gave to individual researchers and to Charles University in Prague.

As a researcher who sought to chronicle and describe human cultural and physical variety as another facet of the natural world, Hrdlička was the last of a tradition of nineteenth-century scholarship in anthropology at the Smithsonian. He was committed to detailing and describing skeletal variation, but cared little for synthesis. For Hrdlička, even the interpretive significance and value of statistics for ordering his carefully described world was suspect: "having very little knowledge of mathematics Hrdlička was quite unprepared to understand the development of modern statistical methods, and is known to have declared that 'statistics would be the ruin of physical anthropology'" (Montagu 1944:115). Nor did Hrdlička ever appreciate the significance of genetics and the fundamental contribution it would make to many of the problems he sought to address. The fundamental equation of physical anthropology with natural history and the sociopolitical biases involved, particularly as applied to the concept of race, is one of Hrdlička's legacies and has been critiqued by Blakey (1988).

During his lifetime Hrdlička was unequivocally the most influential man in his field. Within the discipline, especially the subfield of physical anthropology, he acted like an overbearing European patriarch. As Montagu (1944:116) puts it, "in his manner Hrdlička tended towards the delivery of ex cathedra judgments in a somewhat pontifical style. Hrdlička had done so much for physical anthropology and, for the greater part of his life, had stood so long as the guardian angel over it, that he came to develop something of a proprietary interest over the field. This manner often amused his listeners, and irritated some, without, however, serving to diminish their respect for him personally or for his very real achievements." Despite his appearance as an imperious, quite often arrogant, self-aggrandizing figure, and a curmudgeon to boot, he was often spoken of highly. It seems as though his gruff, socially constrained manner was a mask he wore against a rapidly changing world that he sought to understand (Stewart 1975).

We doubt that Hrdlička could have ever imagined the repatriation of the skeletal collections he devoted his life to accumulating. He would have found it difficult to acknowledge a higher principle than the one that had guided his collecting: a nineteenth-century belief in the pending omnipotence of science. He lived in a pragmatic and optimistic era in which science was perceived as the way to resolve the physical and social ills that plagued humanity. With his materialist philosophy, he believed that knowledge accumulated from the sum of its parts, that science was a method for accumulating data, and that data accumulation was a worthy goal in and of itself; eventually, it would reach an unspecified critical mass and configure itself into the truth. Today, the flaws in Hrdlička's uncritical, atheoretical vision of science are obvious, as are his biases and prejudices. It is important, however, not to divorce the spirit of the times from the spirit of the man. Because of his resolute determination and thoroughness, Hrdlička was able to measure most of the cranial material, including that from Larsen Bay, that he had collected himself or had examined in various collections throughout the world. All of this information he published in his *Catalogues of Crania*. To a certain extent, this may mitigate the unprecedented loss of the original material, but the Larsen Bay repatriation still deprives the scientific community of the use of this material in future research initiatives; to what end—perhaps—time will tell.

Acknowledgments

Miroslav Prokopec would like to thank Douglas Ubelaker, the Smithsonian Institution's Office of Fellowships and Grants, and the Department of Anthropology at NMNH for facilitating his studies at the Smithsonian, and T. Dale Stewart, Lucille St. Hoyme, and Kate Cartwright for their insight and information. Both authors acknowledge the considerable energy, efficiency, and knowledge of the staff at the Smithsonian Institution Archives and the National Anthropological Archives (with a tip of the hat to Gail Yiotis who is convinced Hrdlička's ghost still stalks the museum halls). David Hunt, Tamara Bray, Nancy Benco, and Joan Gero all provided editorial assistance and comments. The deficiencies that remain are bred in part from the idiosyncracies of the authors and the problems inherent in bridging disciplines and continents.

Notes

1. "'The Skull Doctor': Head Hunter Larger Than Life," by John Sherwood, *The Washington Star,* January 10, 1977: C-1.
2. "'The Skull Doctor': Head Hunter Larger Than Life," by John Sherwood, *The Washington Star,* January 10, 1977: C-1.
3. This information was noted in Hrdlička's obituary, published in *Time* magazine, September 13, 1943.

References Cited

Blakey, Michael
1988   Skull Doctors: Intrinsic Social and Political Bias in the History of American Physical Anthropology. *Critique of Anthropology* 7(2):7–35.

Costa, Raymond L.
1977   Dental Pathology and Related Factors in Archaeological Eskimo Samples from Point Hope and King Island, Alaska. Ph.D. dissertation, University of Pennsylvania, Philadelphia.
1980a   Incidence of Caries and Abscesses in Archaeological Eskimo Skeletal Samples from Point Hope and King Island, Alaska. *American Journal of Physical Anthropology* 52:501–514.
1980b   Age, Sex, and Antemortem Loss of Teeth in Prehistoric Eskimo Samples from Point Hope and Kodiak Island, Alaska. *American Journal of Physical Anthropology* 53:579–87.

Dahlberg, A. A.
1962   Preliminary Report of the Dentition Study of Two Isolates of Kodiak Island. *Arctic Anthropology* 1:115–16.

Edynak, Gloria Jean
1976   Long Bone Growth in Western Eskimo and Aleut Skeletons. *American Journal of Physical Anthropology* 45:569–74.

Field, H.
1971   Adress [sic] for Hrdlička Congress, volume. In *Anthropological Congress Dedicated to Aleš Hrdlička*, edited by Vladimír V. Novotný, pp. 55–56. Academia: Praha.

Gould, Stephen J.
1981   *The Mismeasure of Man.* New York: W. W. Norton.

Gruber, Ruth
1943   With an Umbrella in Alaska, Hunting Skulls. *New York Herald Tibune Weekly Book Review,* 18 July 1943, p. 7.

Heizer, Robert F.
1956   Archaeology of the Uyak Site, Kodiak Island, Alaska. *University of California Anthropological Records* 17(1).

Hrdlička, Aleš
n.d.   Correspondence and newspaper clippings. Hrdlička Papers. National Anthropological Archives, Smithsonian Institution, Washington, D.C.
1898   Dimensions of the Normal Pituitary Fossa or Sella Turcica in the White and the Negro Races. *Archives of Neurology and Psychopathology* 1(4):679–98.
1902   The Crania of Trenton, New Jersey, and Their Bearing upon the Antiquity of Man in that Region. *Bulletin of the American Museum of Natural History* 16:23–62.
1907   Skeletal Remains Suggesting or Attributed to Early Man in North America. *Bulletin of the Bureau of American Ethnology* 33:1–113.
1920   *Anthropometry.* Philadelphia: Wistar Institute.
1928   The Full-Blood American Negro. *American Journal of Physical Anthropology* 12:15–30.
1930a   The Ancient and Modern Inhabitants of the Yukon. In *Exploration and Field-Work of the Smithsonian Institution in 1929.* Washington, pp. 137–146.
1930b   Anthropological Survey in Alaska. *Annual Report of the Bureau of American Ethnology,* 1928–1929:21–374.
1932a   The Principal Dimensions, Absolute and Relative, of the Humerus in the White Race. *American Journal of Physical Anthropology* 16:431–50.
1932b   Anthropological Work in Alaska. *Explorations and Field-Work of the Smithsonian Institution in 1931.* Washington, D.C., pp. 91–102.
1933   Anthropological Explorations on Kodiak Island, Alaska. *Explorations and Field-Work of the Smithsonian Institution in 1932.* Washington, pp. 41–44.
1935   Archaeological Excavations on Kodiak Island, Alaska. *Explorations and Field-Work of the Smithsonian Institution in 1934.* Washington, pp. 47–52.
1936   Archaeological Expedition to Kodiak Island, Alaska. *Explorations and Field-Work of the Smithsonian Institution in 1935.* Washington, pp. 47–53.
1937   Archaeological Explorations on Kodiak and the Aleutian Islands. *Explorations and Field-Work of the Smithsonian Institution in 1936.* Washington, pp. 57–62.
1941a   Disease and Artifacts on Skulls and Bones from Kodiak Island. *Smithsonian Institution Miscellaneous Collections* 101(4).
1941b   Artifacts on Human and Seal Skulls and Bones from Kodiak Island. *American Journal of Physical Anthropology* 28:411–418.
1942   An Anthropologist in Modern Russia. *Science Monthly* 55:19–28.

1943   *Alaska Diary, 1926–1931.* Lancaster, Pa.: Jacques Cattell Press.
1944a   *The Anthropology of Kodiak Island.* Philadelphia: Wistar Institute.
1944b   Catalogue of Human Crania in the United States National Museum: Non-Eskimo People of the Northwest Coast, Alaska and Siberia. *Proceedings of the United States National Museum* 94:1–172.
1945   *The Aleutian and Commander Islands and Their Inhabitants.* Philadelphia: Wistar Institute.

Laughlin, William S.
in   Aleš Hrdlička's Legacy to Alaskan Anthropology:
press   Rectification, Research, and Reburial. In *The First Twenty Years, The Alaskan Anthropological Association,* David Yesner, ed.

Montagu, M. F. Ashley
1944   Aleš Hrdlička, 1869–1943. *American Anthropologist* 46(1):113–17.

Murillo, Saul
1991   The Kodiak Islander Dentition. Paper prepared for the Repatriation Office, National Museum of Natural History, Smithsonian Institution, Washington, D.C.

Ortner, Donald J., and C. J. Utermohle
1981   Polyarticular Inflammatory Arthritis in a Pre-Columbian Skeleton from Kodiak Island, Alaska. *American Journal of Physical Anthropology* 56:23–31.

Ossenberg, N. S.
1977   Congruence of Distance Matrices Based on Cranial Discrete Traits, Cranial Measurements and Linguistic-eographic Criteria in Five Alaskan Populations. *American Journal of Physical Anthropology* 47:93–98.

Prokopec, Miroslav
1971   Dr. Aleš Hrdlička—A Scientist and a Man. In *Anthropological Congress Dedicated to Aleš Hrdlička,* edited by Vladimír V. Novotný, pp. 57–61. Academia: Praha.
1992   Defeats and Victories: Chapters from the Life of Dr. Aleš Hrdlička (1869–1943). Paper on file with the Arctic Studies Center and the Repatriation Office, National Museum of Natural History, Smithsonian Institution.

St. Hoyme, Lucille
1980   Incidence of Caries and Abscesses in Archaeological Eskimo Skeletal Samples from Pt. Hope and Kodiak Island, Alaska. *American Journal of Physical Anthropology* 52:501–14.

Schultz, Adolph H.
1945   Aleš Hrdlička, 1869–1943. *National Academy of Sciences Biographical Memoirs* 23:305–38.

Spencer, Frank
1979   Aleš Hrdlička, M.D., 1869–1943: A Chronicle of the Life and Work of an American Physical Anthropologist. Ph.D dissertation, University of Michigan, Ann Arbor.

Stewart, T. Dale
1940   The Life and Writings of Dr. Aleš Hrdlička (1869–1939). *American Journal of Physical Anthropology* 26:3–40.
1975   Oral History Project Interviews with T. Dale Stewart. Archives and special collections of the Smithsonian Institution, Washington, D.C.

Turner, C. G. II
1983   Dental Evidence for the Peopling of the Americas. In *Early Man in the New World,* R. Shutler, ed., pp. 147–57. Beverly Hills: Sage.

Ubelaker, Douglas H., and Lauryn Guttenplan Grant
1989   Human Skeletal Remains: Preservation or Reburial? *Yearbook of Physical Anthropology* 32: 249–87.

Ucko, Peter (ed.)
1992   *World Archaeological Bulletin No 6.* [Issue devoted to a critical discussion on the collection of human remains.]

Wilmsen, E. N.
1965   An Outline of Early Man Studies in the United States. *American Antiquity* 31:172–192.

Zegura, S. L.
1971   A Multivariate Analysis of the Inter and Intrapopulation Variation Exhibited by Eskimo Crania. Ph.D dissertation, University of Wisconsin, Madison.
1975   Taxonomic Congruence in Eskimoid Populations. *American Journal of Physical Anthropology* 43:271–84.

Part 2

The Uyak Site and Evidence
for Cultural Continuity

Don E. Dumond

5

THE UYAK SITE IN PREHISTORY

Based on his work in the 1930s, Aleš Hrdlička concluded that the Uyak site (now 49-KOD-145) contained evidence for the replacement of an earlier
population by a later one that was cranially and culturally distinct. In 1990, in connection with the request
from people of Larsen Bay for the return of the Uyak
collection to Kodiak Island, the Department of Anthropology in the Smithsonian's National Museum of
Natural History (NMNH) asked me to assess the question of the occupational and cultural continuity at the
site from an archaeological viewpoint. Although I had
spent thirty years on the archaeology and prehistory
of the nearby Alaska Peninsula, I had never had a real
reason to focus closely on the later prehistory of Kodiak Island, particularly on the well-known Uyak site,
a site that some prehistorians have wanted to ignore
because of uncertainties created by Hrdlička's field
methods. I agreed to this request with the mutual understanding that I would report the results in whatever direction they might lie.

This chapter summarizes those results. I consider
the Uyak site within the context of Kodiak archaeology and then turn to its position within the prehistory
of southwestern and south-central Alaska. Although
much of the material that follows is presented in a different and expanded form elsewhere (Dumond
1991), this chapter addresses certain matters that I
have not previously discussed.

The Kodiak Archipelago

The tightly clustered Kodiak group of islands consists
of the main island, Kodiak; the smaller island of
Afognak; and several lesser islands and islets. These
are referred to as Kodiak or Kodiak Island in the rest
of this chapter. The group is located at the northwestern edge of the Gulf of Alaska, separated from
the Alaska Peninsula of the mainland by Shelikof
Strait. When Russian fur hunters arrived in the last
half of the eighteenth century, they found it inhabited by the Koniag who, along with their relatives to
the east as far as Prince William Sound, were the most
southeasterly of the Eskimo-speaking peoples of
Alaska.

In contrast to the arctic-trending coast of the mainland from the southern Bering Sea northward, Kodiak's climate is at the extreme of the temperate but
stormy north Pacific maritime zone. It experiences
heavy annual rainfall (ca. 200 cm), cool, overcast summers, and snowy winters, but its coastline remains
open throughout the year—with sea ice that occurs
only at the heads of bays where freshwater streams reduce salinity. The interiors of the major islands are
mountainous and the coastlines are abrupt and heavily indented. Vegetation is predominantly low, with
some stands of poplars and scrubby birch; spruce,
apparently an immigrant during the past millen-

nium, is largely confined to the northern half of the group.

Terrestial fauna include the Alaska brown bear, red fox, land otters, weasels, ground squirrels, and voles. Caribou are absent. In contrast to the restricted range of land fauna, there are numerous sea mammals. Harbor seals, porpoises, northern or Steller sea lions, and sea otters are widespread. Migratory fur seals and species of large whales are found along the migration pathways that skirt the southeastern or outer coast. Marine fish are found in the relatively shallow seas of that coast. Colonies of shore birds and several species of shellfish make their homes in the fjords.

Runs of pink, silver, and dog or chum salmon are common in the short, swift streams along the coast while the commercially important sockeye or red salmon spawn only in drainages that include the lakes required for the juvenile portion of the life cycle. As a result, sockeye runs are not widespread and are found most notably in the Karluk and Ayakulik river systems and lake complexes of southwestern Kodiak Island. (For geographical summaries, see also D. Clark 1984:185–86 and Heizer 1956:1–4.)

It is not surprising that throughout historic and known prehistoric times the people of Kodiak have concentrated on littoral and marine resources. It is less clear, however, how reliant the inhabitants of the Uyak site were on these resources. Although Uyak Bay and its connecting bays are home to resident sea mammals such as the seal and harbor porpoise, are visited by the occasional whale, and have shores favored by birds and shellfish, the area is located at a considerable distance from the rich sea mammal grounds of the southeastern coast. Furthermore, although the bay's tributary streams have relatively small migrations of salmon, such as pink, they do not have runs of the more predictable sockeye salmon.

The Uyak Site and the Archaeology of Kodiak Island

Hrdlička worked at the Uyak site, also known as "Our Point" or "Jones Point," from 1931 to 1936. By his account, three acres of residential area, midden, and cemetery were mined for bones and artifacts; this work produced hundreds of whole and fragmentary human remains. The breakneck speed of excavation was accomplished by massive undercutting and forced sloughing. Crude stratigraphic control was maintained by recording three strata. The distinctive uppermost stratum was set apart from the lower two by the presence of substantial rubble presumably derived from the extensive use of sweat baths.

Hrdlička described the human remains found in these strata as belonging to two dissimilar and unrelated populations: the lower two strata yielded the long-headed Pre-Koniag and the uppermost stratum the shorter-headed Koniag. He referred to the latter, whom he suggested had replaced the former, as "Koniag" because he believed they represented the direct ancestors of the historic Kodiak natives.[1] There was no evidence, however, that the Uyak site itself had actually been occupied into the historic period (Hrdlička 1944a).

Twenty years later, Robert Heizer (1956), who had been a member of Hrdlička's field crew for two seasons, described the artifacts recovered in the excavations. Using the information available, he divided the material culture into two parts. The first included objects from the lower two strata, which Hrdlička had called Pre-Koniag, and the second contained objects from the topmost, rubble-filled stratum, which Hrdlička had identified as Koniag. Heizer saw some recognizable changes in artifact types and frequencies between the two cultural units, although nearly two-thirds of the types he found were present in both units (Heizer 1956:84–93). Although the excavation techniques had certainly not maximized artifact recovery, the very quantity of fill removed and the number of specimens recovered (more than 5,000 artifacts) suggest that all major cultural deposits were sampled.

Heizer's two-stage cultural formulation floated more or less in limbo until the 1960s when Donald W. Clark, in a campaign sponsored by the University of Wisconsin, defined a 6,000-year multistage sequence for Kodiak Island. Clark assigned Heizer's lower cultural unit to the later phase of what he termed the "Kachemak tradition," which was thought to span the first millennium a.d.[2] He incorporated Heizer's upper unit into the earlier part of a "Koniag phase" (Table 5.1). Although the Koniag phase was divided into two subgroups based on the presence or absence of pottery, Clark concluded that both represented the prehistoric forerunners of the historically known Koniag people (D. Clark 1966). Clark was unable to document archaeologically the precise transition from his late Kachemak tradition to the two variants of the archaeological Koniag phase,[3] but he was able to devise a model for the development of archaeological Koniag culture after about a.d. 1000. The model drew on the earlier Kachemak tradition components present on Kodiak, but it also recognized the apparent importation of important elements from both the Bering Sea and the northern Northwest Coast. At the same time, although Clark thought that the Koniag archaeological phase in both its ceramic and nonceramic aspects represented the direct ancestors of historic Kodiak islanders who were contacted by the Russians, he was again largely unable to document archaeologically the specific transition from prehistoric to historic times (D. Clark 1974a, 1974b). In later work he explored aspects of early historic Kodiak, pointing out

Don E. Dumond

Table 5.1. The Kodiak Island Sequence of D. W. Clark

Date	Cultural unit	Clark's component		Uyak site
	Historic Koniag			
1763				
	Archaeological Koniag Phase	Ceramic Koniag	Aceramic Koniag	Upper Stratum
1100				
		Three Saints		Middle Stratum
a.d.	Kachemak			
b.c.	Tradition			Lower Stratum
		Old Koniag		
?1500				
		Ocean Bay II		
2500	Ocean Bay Tradition			
		Ocean Bay I		
4000				

Source: Clark 1966.

that the distributions of native settlements, based on a survey made by Yurii Lisianski (1814) 22 years after the first Russian colonization, showed that historic Koniag habitation was centered on the southeast or Pacific coastal side of Kodiak, with few settlements on the northwest or Shelikof Strait coast of the islands (D. Clark 1987).

More recently, transitions from the late Kachemak tradition to the archaeological Koniag phase and from the archaeological Koniag to the historic Koniag phase have been documented for the site of Karluk at the mouth of the salmon-rich Karluk lake and river system on the coast of Shelikof Strait, about 30 km west of the Uyak site. This has been done through excavations conducted by Richard Jordan and Richard Knecht in the 1980s (Jordan and Knecht 1988; Knecht and Jordan 1985).

Jordan and Knecht explored house and midden remains at two sites (KAR-1 and KAR-31) at Karluk that represented the period from the beginning of the Christian era to the arrival of the Russians, when a Russian station was established at the river mouth, where it remained one of the few historic-period settlements of Europeans and natives on the northwest side of Kodiak. From careful work in stratified middens and houses, Jordan and Knecht defined and dated horizon markers that punctuated the transition from Kachemak through a "Transitional Koniag" to archaeological Koniag (Table 5.2). Most saliently, cul-

tural traits for the Transitional period included thick, gravel-tempered pottery, medially ridged slate dart points, and composite harpoon valves with scarfed bases. In full-blown archaeological Koniag there were base-faceted slate endblades, pebbles or small slate tablets incised with figurine forms, multiroom rather than single-room houses, and splitting adzes. As the Koniag phase developed, harpoon valves with open sockets replaced those with scarfed bases. Strikingly, pottery, the first few sherds of which occurred early, did not increase in frequency through time, but remained rare in all levels. This low frequency of pottery at Karluk was surprising; elsewhere in southern Kodiak prehistoric Koniag phase ceramics appear in quantity. Based on their work, Jordan and Knecht (1988) concluded that the full-blown archaeological Koniag phase appeared only after about a.d. 1350; in addition, they demonstrated the continuity of occupation into the historic period at Karluk (Knecht and Jordan 1985).

Because of the cultural and occupational continuity at Karluk, Jordan and Knecht rejected the idea that cultural imports were integral to the development of archaeological Koniag culture and, instead, emphasized in situ development. They underscored this notion of continuous development on Kodiak by hypothesizing that the island was responsible for the development of much of late prehistoric Eskimo culture as it is known farther north (Jordan and Knecht 1988).

The Uyak Site in Light of the Karluk Excavations

Although the integrity of preserved information from the Uyak site is poor, it is possible, because of the mass of material recovered there, to identify some horizon markers documented at Karluk (see Table 5.3).

The major Kachemak tradition markers are present in considerable number, with many of them appearing in Heizer's upper unit as well as lower unit (Dumond 1991:table 104). Although at first thought this might be attributed to physical mixture of deposits, two items diagnostic of later times appear only in the upper cultural stratum. These are incised slate tablets, which are found only in small number (Table 5.3), and an undecorated stone lamp with a broad, flat edge (7 examples; see D. Clark 1974b:114,161; Dumond 1991:table 2.8). The lamp is an artifact not easily missed nor misassigned even in Hrdlička's speedy excavation. Along with the presence in both units of many types that have been shown—at Karluk and elsewhere—to be common both to the Kachemak tradition and later cultural stages, this evidence can reasonably be taken to indicate a definite measure of continuity within the Uyak site deposits, despite the mixture that must be present.

Table 5.2. Stratigraphic Appearance of Diagnostic Koniag Markers at Karluk

Cultural unit	Excavation unit	C-14 date[a]	Marker artifact
Late Kachemak	KAR-31: Layer 6–7	a.d. 970 ± 60 (Beta-15691)	Pottery (1 sherd)
	Layer 5		Pottery (4 sherds)
	Layer 3		Pottery (8 sherds) Medially ridged slate points
Transitional Koniag	KAR-1: Floor 10	a.d. 1210 ± 80 (Beta-15016)	Medially ridged slate points Scarfed-base harpoon valves Base-faceted end blade
	Lower Midden		
Early Archaeological Koniag	Floor 9 and Upper Midden		Medially ridged slate points Base-faceted end blade Scarfed-base harpoon valves Incised tablets
	Floor 8	a.d. 1470 ± 80 (Beta-15015)	Base-faceted end blades Incised tablets Multi-roomed house Scarfed-based harpoon valves
	Floor 7		
Late Archaeological Koniag	Floors 6–1	a.d. 1660 ± 60 (Beta-15014)	Splitting adze
			Base-facted end blades Open-socketed harpoon valves Pottery (1 pot)

Source: Jordan and Knecht 1988.
[a] Uncalibrated dates.

Table 5.3. Some Koniag Phase Diagnostics at the Uyak Site[a]

Artifact	Uyak provenience[b]	
	Lower two strata	Upper stratum
Splitting adze	2	2
Incised slate tablets	0	2
Base-faceted end blades	3	1
Medially ridged slate points	15	3
Scarfed-base harpoon valve	65	7
Open-socketed harpoon valve	23	9

[a] Artifacts declared diagnostic by Jordan and Knecht (1988); some additional traits thought diagnostic by D. W. Clark (1974b), but not recovered in quantity at Karluk, are omitted here. See also Dumond 1991: Table 2.8.
[b] Provenience based on Heizer 1956.

The clearest markers of the archaeological Koniag phase according to Jordan and Knecht (1988), however, are almost entirely absent from the Uyak site. These include triangular slate endblades with faceted bases, incised slate tablets, and splitting adzes. Furthermore, there are relatively few open-socketed harpoon valves of the late type in comparison with the earlier type with scarfed bases. Although pottery was absent throughout, this is thought—as at Karluk—to be an areal, rather than a temporal, phenomenon. Overall, the evidence suggests that the Uyak site was abandoned relatively early. Despite Hrdlička's conclusion that his Koniag cranial type represented the direct ancestors of the historic Koniag, the Uyak archaeological evidence strongly suggests that the midden area was abandoned not long after about a.d. 1450—more than 300 years before the arrival of the first Russians, the event commonly recognized as the beginning of the historic period.

Don E. Dumond

Is this inference of early abandonment reasonable in terms of other evidence? The 1987 and 1988 excavations by Bryn Mawr College on the remaining fringes of the Uyak site demonstrated that surviving house pits, which had been thought on the basis of an earlier survey to represent both Kachemak and archaeological Koniag periods, were confined to the Kachemak tradition dating to before about a.d. 1000 (Steffian in press). The 1987 Bureau of Indian Affairs excavation of the remains of a single house at the head of Larsen Bay indicated abandonment sometime in the fifteenth century (Crozier 1989), at about the time the Uyak site midden areas excavated by Hrdlička apparently ceased to be used.

Fairly extensive surface surveys on the shores of the complex composed of Uyak, Larsen, Zacher, and Spiridon bays, are also relevant to the question. Of 66 sites thought to represent either Kachemak or archaeological Koniag occupations (Crowell 1986), only one (KOD-325) yielded Russian-period artifacts, and that site is suspected to have been established by Russians, rather than natives. Two others (KOD-160, KOD-339) were rumored by local people to have produced a few possibly early historic materials. Nevertheless, there is currently no indisputable evidence that any part of the Uyak Bay complex was occupied by Kodiak natives at the beginning of the Russian period, a finding that is consistent with historic evidence (Lisianski 1814) that indicates a paucity of settlement in the area 22 years after the Russians arrived.

In 1805 Captain Lisianski of the Russian Navy conducted a survey of settlements along the Kodiak coast. His results are recorded in the chart used by D. Clark (1987) in the study of Kodiak population distribution mentioned earlier. The chart shows only a single settlement in the Uyak Bay complex. That site, Ooiatsk, was at the extreme north side of the outer bay, on the tip of the peninsula that separates Uyak Bay from Spiridon Bay to the northeast (Lisianski 1814:facing p. 169). This is the approximate location of site KOD-339, where Crowell (1986:30) reported finding a thin midden with slate fragments in an area of recent disturbance. Although there were rumors that Russian-period beads and gun parts had been found at this site, he was unable to conduct interviews to confirm them.

An 1849 map in the atlas of Teben'kov (1981:50, Map 22) also identifies a single site on Uyak Bay. This was reportedly a tannery, which was located on the western side of the outer bay, opposite the site mentioned above. This site is the approximate location of KOD-325, the historic-period site that Crowell (1986:25) had presumed to be Russian rather than native. This is also the approximate location of a settlement named Ooiak, which was reported in the

1880 United States census (Petroff 1884:29) and said to be populated by 76 Kodiak natives. Again, this was the only settlement recorded in the Uyak Bay complex for that year.

In 1888 the Arctic Packing Company constructed the first Larsen Bay cannery on the northern shore across the bay from the present cannery and near a site mapped as "ruins of old Aleut village" (possibly a prehistoric site recorded by Crowell 1986). The early cannery was used for three years to pack sockeye salmon taken not from Uyak Bay but from the migratory stock of the Karluk river system (Bean 1891:184, and plate 83; Moser 1899:159), a run that by 1890 produced annual catches in excess of 3 million fish (Rich and Ball 1931:666, table 14). During its last season of operation in 1890, the cannery was apparently the site listed as "Uyak" in the 1890 United States census. The recorded population of 246 included only nine native men and six native females, the remainder being foreigners to Kodiak. It must have been this native group that constituted what was referred to in the 1890 census as "the only native settlement on this large bay [i.e., Uyak], containing less than 20 people" (Porter 1893:79).

Because of the absence of commercially important red or sockeye salmon in the Uyak Bay complex nearby (Bean 1891:184), the fish cannery was only marginally successful and in 1896 the machinery was removed from the defunct cannery. Nevertheless, the following year two other canneries were opened, one by the Pacific Steam Whaling Company and the other by the Hume Brothers & Hume, on the western shore of outer Uyak Bay. These canneries also handled sockeye taken along the coast near Karluk and at other locations around Kodiak (Moser 1899:158–159). Thus, the locations of settlements reported in the Uyak Bay complex in the late nineteenth century can only be described as fluctuating. It is not surprising, then, that an individual said to have been born in Larsen Bay in 1890 was listed in a genealogy compiled for the settlement of Karluk in the 1960s, where he was shown as an immigrant to that site (Taylor 1966, genealogical chart, section 3).

By the end of the nineteenth century there was no functioning cannery in Larsen Bay. It was only in 1911, when declining sockeye runs forced a change to fishing for previously less desirable pink salmon, that catches were reported from the Uyak Bay complex itself. And it was 1922 before canneries—the first of them floating rather than land-based—began to process Uyak salmon on location (Rich and Ball 1931:673, table 19). The present land-based cannery and settlement on Larsen Bay were evidently established even later, only a few years before Hrdlička arrived to make it his local headquarters (Hrdlička

1944a:135–136). Although one cannot say categorically that there was no settlement continuity anywhere in Uyak Bay from prehistoric times to the Russian period and after, one must certainly conclude that there is no clear evidence of settlement continuity around the Uyak site and Larsen Bay from the time of the site's abandonment to the arrival of Russian fur hunters, or between that time and the establishment of the present community known as Larsen Bay.

Furthermore, if the situation evident in Karluk is a reasonable guide, the twentieth-century population at Larsen Bay could have originated anywhere in the Kodiak Island group. In the 1960s, no more than one-third of the native inhabitants of Karluk could count forbearers for as much as three ascending generations who lived at that same location; the remaining two-thirds traced their great-grandparental ancestors to ten other settlements or settlement areas (Taylor 1966, table 7). Nevertheless, despite evidence for a lack of settlement stability by individual families, the fish-rich settlement at Karluk appears to be the nearest to the Uyak site in which occupational continuity from prehistoric to historic times can be documented.

Kodiak Prehistory in Broader Context

On the Bering Sea slope of the Alaska Peninsula west of Kodiak, the earliest examples of Transitional Koniag marker artifacts appear in quantity with the beginning of the Brooks River Camp phase (a.d. 1050 ± 50 to 1450 ± 50; Dumond 1981:153–164) in the Naknek River drainage. These artifacts include thick, gravel-tempered pottery, medially ridged slate dart blades, and splitting adzes. Also appearing at this time are the first triangular endblades of ground slate with faceted bases (which at Karluk are said to be developed Koniag), the northern-style coldtrap entrance on the subterranean one-room Naknek drainage houses, and deposits of rubble, apparently from extensive sweat bathing. (Various sequences are summarized in Table 5.4.)

The Brooks River Camp phase seems to have begun abruptly. This is based on the two earliest radiocarbon determinations for the phase—a.d. 1070 ± 65 (SI-2075) and 1106 ± 100 (I-1635)—and on the latest date of the preceding Brooks River Falls phase—a.d. 975 ± 120 (I-520) (Dumond 1981:147–152). The Brooks River Camp phase marks a decisive enough change from the Brooks River Falls phase that it is suspected to have involved at least some influx of new people (Dumond 1988b). An even earlier and equally abrupt appearance of Brooks River Camp phase pottery and medially ridged slate dart points has been reported from the Bering Sea coast at Izembek Lagoon

Table 5.4. Some Temporal Relationships

a.d.[a]	Alaska Peninsula		Kodiak Island
	Naknek Region	Shelikof Strait	
1800	Historic		Historic
1700		(inadequate sample)	Late Archaeological Koniag
1600	Brooks River Bluffs phase		
1500			Early Archaeological Koniag
1400			
1300	Brooks River Camp phase	Kukak Mound phase	Transitional Koniag
1200			
1100			
1000			
900		Kukak Beach phase	
800	Brooks River Fall phase		
700			Late Kachemak Tradition
600			
500		Takli Cottonwood phase	
400	Brooks River Weir phase		
300			

[a] Uncalibrated dates.

at the tip of the peninsula, where charcoal from an anomalous house with a whalebone framework was dated at a.d. 945 ± 105 (SI-916; McCartney 1974).

The end of the Brooks River Camp phase is determined on the basis of the earliest dates for the succeeding Brooks River Bluffs phase, a.d. 1470 ± 90 (I-523]) and 1500 ± 60 (Y-932), a cultural unit that bears an obvious relationship to the earlier phase, although it is cleanly separated from it stratigraphically by a 10-cm-thick layer of volcanic ash. Early Bluffs phase ceramics are indistinguishable in paste composition from those of the Brooks River Camp phase, although the forms differ and the pottery is much less plentiful. Barbed, medially ridged dart blades no longer appear and the Bluffs phase projectile point assemblage is dominated by ground slate triangular endblades, with the facet at the base becoming a longitudinal groove as time goes on. A few incised pebbles appear in this phase, and sweat bathing is evidenced not only by rubble but by structures actually used for the purpose (Dumond 1981:165–174). In

Don E. Dumond

all, the Bluffs phase displays particularly close artifactual correspondences to the developed archaeological Koniag phase of Karluk.

On the Pacific coast of the Alaska Peninsula the early part of the local sequence is very similar to that of Kodiak Island. On Takli Island and at Kukak Bay the earliest recorded occupation is strongly reminiscent of the earliest phase described by D. Clark (1966) for Kodiak and is in place by about 4000 b.c. (G. Clark 1977:27–30). This develops later in ways suggestive of Kodiak, while during these early times there is no appreciable evidence of contact with residents of the Bering Sea side of the peninsula, even though some of these neighbors lived and fished no more than 80 km away.

The Pacific coastal culture of the peninsula began to diverge from that of Kodiak during the Takli Cottonwood phase (a.d. 300–600; G. Clark 1977:38–40), although sharing numerous ground slate and chipped implement forms with the contemporary late Kachemak tradition. The Cottonwood assemblage included fiber-tempered pottery of the type then in use in the Naknek region of the Bering Sea coast to the west. Through the rest of the first millennium a.d., the coastal culture, called the Kukak Beach phase, continued to grow more similar in artifact inventory to that of the Norton-derived Brooks River Falls phase of the Bering Sea slope of the peninsula (G. Clark 1977:40–47).

Sometime around the end of the first millennium the Kukak Beach phase disappears. It is followed by the Kukak Mound phase that is essentially identical to the Brooks River Camp phase of the Bering Sea slope. Both of them include the Transitional Koniag marker traits. At this time the single-room house with the northern-style coldtrap entrance also appears on the Pacific coast (G. Clark 1977:47–49, 60), although there is no evidence that it spread any further to the southeast.

The evidence now available suggests that the Transitional Koniag identified by Jordan and Knecht on Kodiak postdates the beginning of the Brooks River Camp phase of the peninsula (see Table 5.4). The radiocarbon determinations are summarized in Table 5.5.

As indicated above, a date of a.d. 1050 ± 50 is reasonable for the beginning of the Brooks River Camp phase; when corrected for fluctuations in radioactive atmospheric carbon, the date calibrates to almost a century later, somewhat after A.D. 1100. Although my feeling is that the Kukak Mound phase of the Pacific coast is not significantly later than the Camp phase of the Bering Sea, there is no direct evidence to support this. The only two Kukak Mound phase radiocarbon

Table 5.5. Radiocarbon Determinations Referred to in the Text

Provenience, phase	C-14 age (before A.D. 1950)	Uncalibrated date (a.d.) (1950 minus C-14 age)	Calibrated date (A.D.)[a]
Naknek Drainage			
Late Brooks River Falls	975 ± 120 (I-520)	975 ± 120	1024 ± 122
Early Brooks River Camp	880 ± 65 (SI-2075)	1070 ± 65	1185 ± 68
	845 ± 100 (I-1635)	1105 ± 100	1210 ± 102
Early Brooks River Bluffs	480 ± 90 (I-523)	1470 ± 90	1430 ± 95
	450 ± 60 (Y-932)	1500 ± 60	1433 ± 64
Izembek Lagoon			
House 1	1005 ± 105 (SI-916)	945 ± 105	1011 ± 113[b]
Kukak Bay			
Kukak Mound	775 ± 95 (I-505)	1175 ± 95	1260 ± 98
	775 ± 110 (I-1636)	1175 ± 110	1260 ± 112
Karluk			
Late Kachemak	980 ± 60 (Beta-15691)	970 ± 60	1022 ± 64
Trans. Koniag	740 ± 80 (Beta-15016)	1210 ± 80	1273 ± 83
Early Koniag	480 ± 80 (Beta-15015)	1470 ± 80	1430 ± 83

[a] Calibrated dates based on Stuiver and Baker 1986.
[b] Possible midpoints at A.D. 1002, 1001, and 1017 are pooled here as A.D. 1011. This is considerably later than the corrected data reported by McCartney (1974: Table 1) on the basis of an earlier calibration.

dates are a.d. 1175 ± 95 [I-105] and 1175 ± 110 [I-1636], which puts the beginning of the phase to about a.d. 1100, which is comparable to about A.D. 1175 in the corrected calendar.

On Kodiak, the latest actual radiocarbon date from the Karluk levels assigned to the Kachemak tradition is a.d. 970 ± 60, and the earliest date from Transitional Koniag is a.d. 1210 ± 80 (Jordan and Knecht 1988; also see Table 5.2 in this chapter). There are either two or three undated cultural levels between the two levels that produced these dates. All of these intervening levels are assigned to the late Kachemak tradition, although they do include a few traits that are diagnostic of the later Transitional Koniag. Thus, one may conclude that the fully Transitional aspect of the archaeological Koniag phase probably does not begin before a.d. 1130 (i.e., 80 years before a.d. 1210), or A.D. 1190 in the corrected calendar. Given the nature of radiocarbon determinations, it is equally likely that it began a century or more later.

The radiocarbon evidence alone, however, is not conclusive. Analysis of variance suggests that the spread of the six calibrated radiocarbon dates relevant to Brooks River Camp, Kukak Mound, Transitional Koniag, and Izembek Lagoon (Table 5.5) could be expected to occur well over 10 percent of the time when dating a single entity ($F = 1.60$; d.f. $5/\infty$). Furthermore, the Izembek date appears to be more appropriate to the Brooks River Falls phase and late Kachemak tradition, which are evidently partly contemporaneous, than to later phases. This discrepancy may indicate some problem with the date, perhaps resulting from the reuse of old driftwood at the treeless tip of the Alaska Peninsula. The elimination of the Izembek Lagoon date increases the possibility that the remaining dates are contemporaneous.

What seems compelling, however, is the linkage of archaeological evidence with those radiocarbon dates. First, there is the appearance of diagnostic Brooks River Camp phase traits, both pottery and medially ridged dart heads, at Karluk before the end of the late Kachemak tradition (see Table 5.2). The appearance of scattered pottery in sites of the late Kachemak tradition confirms a report by D. Clark (1974b:127) of a comparable occurrence at the site of Crag Point farther north on Kodiak. Second, there is evidence of a northern source for some of the Transitional Koniag and Koniag traits that appear on the Alaska Peninsula. Although the place of origin of the medially ridged slate dart heads is not entirely clear, they are found north of the Alaska Peninsula on the southern Bering Sea in undated contexts; given the apparent lateness of their appearance at Karluk, they may turn out to have originated in that region (Dumond 1991:96). The triangular, base-faceted endblades and the thick gravel-tempered ceramics, how-

ever, are found well to the north of the Alaska Peninsula and even north of the Bering Sea during periods that clearly precede the beginning of the Brooks River Camp phase (Dumond 1991:96). It can scarcely be coincidental that they appear on the peninsula at the same time as the house with northern-style coldtrap entrance—that is, one that enters the house floor from below, replacing an earlier, Norton-style sloping passageway that enters the house at floor level.

At this point, it can reasonably be affirmed that certain innovations basic to the formation of the archaeological Koniag phase were of northern or Bering Sea origin. This agrees with the spirit of D. Clark's (1974b) conclusions published two decades ago.

Some Non-Archaeological Evidence

Forty-five years ago, a study of Eskimo ceremonialism led Margaret Lantis (1947:118) to conclude that in the context of the North Pacific:

> The [historic] Koniag were culturally . . . Eskimo-like. They, like the Aleuts, had class differences, specific similarities to Northwest Coast whale cult, and several ritual details from that area . . . Even so, they were not quite so far removed from the west Alaskan culture-center as were the Aleuts. The only explanation for this is that the Koniag were intrusive on the Pacific coast. They were so clearly a part of southwest Alaska that they could not have come from very far north but that they came from the Nushegak [sic] region or even the Kuskokwim is not preposterous.

This position accords well with the linguistic evidence. The Koniag were the only Eskimo-speaking people of North America who lived on lands adjacent to coasts that do not regularly freeze fast in winter (see, for example, the distribution in Krauss 1975). This sets them apart as geographically marginal to their linguistic relatives and hints that in their southern location they were intrusive. This impression is strengthened by internal Eskimoan linguistic relationships, which are shown schematically in Fig. 5.1.

As the schematic map indicates, the center of gravity of the Eskimoan branch of the Eskimo-Aleut linguistic stock appears clearly to be around the Bering Strait, with half of the known and separable languages located in Siberia, where they manifest the deepest mutual cleavages (Woodbury 1984). The Pacific Yupik or Alutiiq are located on the margin, where they are attached most closely to Central Alaskan Yupik. Given the time-depth for the Eskimo-Aleut and Eskimoan groups that is now suggested by linguists (e.g., Bergsland 1986:132; Woodbury 1984:61), expansion of early Eskimo speakers from the Bering Strait center of gravity could not have occurred be-

Don E. Dumond

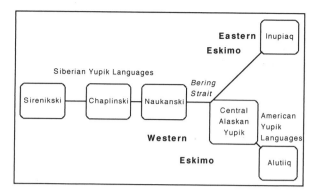

Figure 5.1. Schematic map of Eskimoan languages (after Dumond 1988) showing the relationships of the single eastern language, spoken from north Alaska to Greenland, and the five western (Yupik) languages. Pacific Coast Yupik, now more commonly called Alutiiq, was the native language of Kodiak Island when the Russians arrived.

fore the beginning of the Christian era, and was probably no earlier than the middle of the first millennium A.D.

Based on other linguistic evidence, Leer (1991) postulates the former existence in the northern Northwest Coast of a language area group that he has designated as NNWC. This group is composed of the once-adjacent but unrelated (or very distantly related) Aleut, Eyak, and Haida languages, which are notable for their mechanisms of syntactic number-marking. This continuum of languages in mutual contact was intruded upon and disrupted first by Tlingit, which in time did come to share a few number-marking features of the continuum, and later by Eskimo Alutiiq. According to Leer (1991:192):

> Alutiiq (also called Pacific Gulf Yupik, the Eskimo language of the Koniag and Chugach) shares none of the distinctive NNWC features, whereas Aleut . . . exhibits some of the most typologically unusual among them. This would seem to indicate that the linguistic ancestors of the Alutiiq were totally outside the NNWC culture area . . . [T]he final implication is that not Alutiiq but some other NNWC-type language was originally spoken on Kodiak Island.

Leer estimates the time depth within Alutiiq to be less than 1,000 years and within Kodiak Alutiiq specifically to be no more than 500 years (Leer 1991:191).

Thus, the linguistic evidence seems to indicate that Alutiiq, the Eskimo language of Kodiak Island and nearby regions, arrived on the Pacific coast within the past millennium. My own conclusion is that this, above all other evidence discussed above, implies not only contact with people from the north but also a significant migration of Bering Sea or other northerners

to Kodiak Island around A.D. 1000. It is also clear that population replacement was not complete, from both the specific archaeological evidence at Karluk and from other more general indications of technological continuity underlying stylistic change.

Concluding Discussion

In this chapter I have summarized the archaeological evidence for a significant degree of continuity between the two prehistoric cultural or ethnic divisions previously defined for the Uyak site. In assessing the occurrence there of artifacts marking the transition from the late Kachemak tradition to the archaeological Koniag phase, I concluded that the occupation at the Uyak site ended by about a.d. 1450 and, furthermore, that evidence for continued occupation in the vicinity of the site from the time of its abandonment until the arrival of the Russians at least 300 years later is inconclusive. While not contesting evidence of the unbroken continuation of occupation at nearby Karluk, I nevertheless presented evidence suggesting that during the time that Karluk was occupied there was a population influx to Kodiak Island from the mainland to the northwest.

Previous arguments against a population movement that could have extended a form of Bering Sea speech to Kodiak Island around the end of the first millennium A.D. have rested heavily on the assumption that Kodiak was densely populated at that time. In cases where this evidence has been presented quantitatively rather than impressionistically, (e.g., Jordan and Knecht 1988), the comparisons made between the number of surface-indicated house remains presumed to date to the Kachemak tradition and those thought to date to the archaeological Koniag period have been flawed. They have failed to consider that the quantity of visible surface remains, whether or not correctly dated from surface appearances, is a function of the length, as well as of the contemporary extent, of occupation. In the present case, the fact that the late Kachemak tradition, as conceived, is twice as long as the archaeological Koniag period, was ignored. I have elsewhere expressed my reservations with regard to the resulting projections (e.g., Dumond 1988a) and have put forward alternate proposals, including tentative suggestions of possible donor populations as well as accompanying social mechanisms (Dumond 1991:97–103).

Given the present state of knowledge of Kodiak prehistory, however, such discussions are beside the point. The primary question is whether the sum of evidence is sufficient to justify the conclusion that a population influx occurred, and I have attempted to summarize that evidence. Only later is one compelled to account for the occurrence with a causal explanation. Such an accounting must remain unaccomplished here, although it beckons to be addressed.

My present conclusions, therefore, can be summarized as follows:

1. There was apparently some significant cultural continuity between the lower and upper levels of the Uyak site.

2. The development of the archaeological Koniag culture involved both in situ elements *and* the introduction of important elements from outside the immediate region, in particular from the Bering Sea and farther north in Alaska. In view of the ethnographic and linguistic evidence, I presume that these introductions coincided with an actual migratory movement of people who brought Eskimoan speech to Kodiak. Thus, although there was clearly a measure of continuity on Kodiak as a whole from Kachemak to archaeological Koniag times, this continuity was no more than partial.

3. There is currently no archaeological evidence from the Uyak Bay complex, including Larsen Bay, to demonstrate continuity of residence between the time of the abandonment of the Uyak site and the arrival of Russians a number of centuries later, or between then and the establishment of the modern community of Larsen Bay.

Notes

1. It has sometimes been suggested that Hrdlička defined the strata of the Uyak site on the basis of the cranial form of the humans interred rather than by soil layers (e.g., de Laguna 1956:260). In his defense, it should be recognized that the ranges of measurements of individuals of Pre-Koniag and Koniag overlap, so that some short-headed individuals are classed as Pre-Koniag and some longer-headed individuals are classed as Koniag (Hrdlička 1944b), evidently on stratigraphic rather than morphological grounds. This suggests that site stratigraphy and head form were determined with relative independence (see Dumond 1991:62–63).

2. Except as otherwise indicated, the dating convention follows that of the sources most cited, which use radiocarbon determinations that are uncorrected for fluctuations in atmospheric carbon; dates are calculated by subtracting laboratory ages from 1950. These uncorrected dates are identified here by the use of lower case b.c. and a.d. Tree-ring corrected dates, based on the calibration of Stuiver and Baker (1986) are shown as B.C. or A.D.

3. The charge given me by the NMNH was to assess continuity at the Uyak site, which I interpreted as precluding an unquestioning acceptance of the artifacts from Hrdlička's "Koniag" stratum (and contemporary sites) as those of the direct ancestors of the historic Koniag. In this chapter, therefore, I refer to such prehistoric archaeological assemblages as "archaeological Koniag" in order to hold open the question of their relationship to the culture of the Kodiak native people of the Russian period and later. As used here, then, "archaeological Koniag" may or may not be "prehistoric Koniag."

References Cited

Bean, Tarleton H.
1891　Report on the Salmon and Salmon Rivers of Alaska. *Bulletin of the U.S. Fish Commission,* vol. 9, for 1889, pp. 165–209. Washington.

Bergsland, Knut
1986　Comparative Eskimo-Aleut Phonology and Lexicon. *Suomalais-Ugrilaisen Seuran Aikakauskirja [journal de la Societè Finno-Ougrienne]* 80:65–137.

Clark, Donald W.
1966　Perspectives in the Prehistory of Kodiak Island, Alaska. *American Antiquity* 31(3):358–71.
1974a　Contributions to the Later Prehistory of Kodiak Island, Alaska. *National Museum of Man, Archaeological Survey of Canada Paper* 20. Ottawa: National Museums of Canada.
1974b　Koniag Prehistory. *Universität Tübingen, Institut für Urgeschichte, Tübinger Monographien zur Urgeschichte* 1. Stuttgart: W. Kohlhammer.
1984　Pacific Eskimo: Historical Ethnography. In *Handbook of North American Indians,* vol. 5, Arctic, D. Damas, ed., pp. 185–97. Washington, D.C.: Smithsonian Institution Press.
1987　On a Misty Day You Can See Back to 1805: Ethnohistory and Historical Archaeology on the Southeastern Side of Kodiak Island. *Anthropological Papers of the University of Alaska* 21:105–32.

Clark, Gerald H.
1977　Archaeology on the Alaska Peninsula: The Coast of Shelikof Strait, 1963–1965. *University of Oregon Anthropological Papers* 13.

Crowell, Aron
1986　An Archeological Survey of Uyak Bay, Kodiak Island, Alaska. Report on file with the Alaska Heritage Resource Surveys, Anchorage.

Crozier, S. Neal
1989　Excavation of a Late Prehistoric Dwelling Structure on Kodiak Island, Alaska. *Arctic Anthropology* 26(2): 78–95.

de Laguna, Frederica
1956　*Chugach Prehistory.* Seattle: University of Washington Press

Dumond, Don E.
1981　Archaeology on the Alaska Peninsula: The Naknek Region, 1960–1975. *University of Oregon Anthropological Papers* 21.
1988a　The Alaska Peninsula as Superhighway: A Comment. In *The Late Prehistoric Development of Alaska's Native People,* R. D. Shaw, R. K. Harritt, D. E. Dumond, eds., pp. 379–88. Aurora: Alaska Anthropological Association Monograph Series 4.
1988b　Trends and Traditions in Alaskan Prehistory: A New Look at an Old View of the Neo-Eskimo. In *The Late Prehistoric Development of Alaska's Native People,* R. D. Shaw, R. K. Harritt, and D. E. Dumond, eds., pp. 17–

26. Aurora: Alaska Anthropological Association Monograph Series 4.

1991 The Uyak Site in Regional Prehistory: The Cultural Evidence. In *The Uyak Site on Kodiak Island: Its Place in Alaskan Prehistory*, D. E. Dumond and G. R. Scott, pp. 57–114. University of Oregon Anthropological Papers 44.

Heizer, Robert F.
1956 Archaeology of the Uyak Site, Kodiak Island, Alaska. *University of California Anthropological Records* 17(1).

Hrdlička, Aleš
1944a *The Anthropology of Kodiak Island*. Philadelphia: Wistar Institute of Anatomy and Biology.
1944b *Catalog of Human Crania in the United States National Museum Collections: Non-Eskimo People of the Northwest Coast, Alaska, and Siberia*. Proceedings of the United States National Museum 94:1–172.

Jordan, Richard H., and Richard A. Knecht
1988 Archaeological Research on Western Kodiak Island, Alaska: The Development of Koniag Culture. In *The Late Prehistoric Development of Alaska's Native People*, R. D. Shaw, R. K. Harritt, D. E. Dumond, eds., pp. 225–306. Aurora: Alaska Anthropological Association Monograph Series 4.

Knecht, Richard A., and Richard H. Jordan
1985 Nunakakhnak: A Historic Period Koniag Village in Karluk, Kodiak Island, Alaska. *Arctic Anthropology* 22(2):17–35.

Krauss, Michael E.
1975 *Native Peoples and Languages of Alaska* (map). Fairbanks: University of Alaska, Native Language Center.

Lantis, Margaret
1947 *Alaskan Eskimo Ceremonialism*. Monographs of the American Ethnological Society 11. New York: J. J. Augustin.

Leer, Jeff
1991 Evidence for a Northern Northwest Coast Language Area: Promiscuous Number Marking and Periphrastic Possessive Constructions in Haida, Eyak, and Aleut. *International Journal of American Linguistics* 37(2):158–93.

Lisianski, Urey [Yurii]
1814 *A Voyage Round the World in the Years 1803, 4, 5, & 6*. London: John Booth.

McCartney, A. P.
1974 Prehistoric Cultural Integration Along the Alaska Peninsula. *Anthropological Papers of the University of Alaska* 16(1):59–84.

Moser, Jefferson F.
1899 The Salmon and Salmon Fisheries of Alaska. *Bulletin of the U.S. Fish Commission*, vol. 18 for 1898, pp. 1–178. Washington: Government Printing Office.

Petroff, Ivan
1884 *Report on the Population, Industries, and Resources of Alaska*. Washington: Department of the Interior, Census Office.

Porter, Robert P.
1893 *Report on Population and Resources of Alaska at the Eleventh Census*. Washington: Department of the Interior, Census Office.

Rich, Willis H., and Edward M. Ball
1931 Statistical Review of the Alaska Salmon Fisheries, Part II: Chignik to Resurrection Bay. *Bulletin of the United States Bureau of Fisheries*, vol. 46, 1930, pp. 643–712. Washington: U.S. Department of Commerce.

Steffian, Amy F.
in press Fifty years after Hrdlička: Further Investigations at the Uyak Site, Kodiak Island, Alaska. In *Contributions to the Anthropology of Southcentral and Southwestern Alaska*, R. H. Jordan, F. de Laguna, and A. F. Steffian, eds. Anthropological Papers of the University of Alaska 24(1–2).

Stuiver, Minze, and Bernd Becker
1986 High-Precision Decadal Calibration of the Radiocarbon Time Scale, A.D. 1950–2500 B.C. *Radiocarbon* 28(2B):863–910.

Taylor, Kenneth I.
1966 A Demographic Study of Karluk, Kodiak Island, Alaska, 1962–1964. *Arctic Anthropology* 3(2):211–43.

Teben'kov, M. D.
1981 *Atlas of the Northwest Coasts of America*, R. Pierce, transl. Kingston, Ontario: Limestone Press. [Orig. pub. 1852].

Woodbury, Anthony C.
1984 Eskimo and Aleut Languages. In *Handbook of North American Indians*, vol. 5, Arctic, D. Damas, ed., pp. 49–63. Washington, D.C.: Smithsonian Institution.

6

THE RED, BLACK, AND BLUE

Context and Mortuary Data at Larsen Bay, Kodiak Island

How misleading must all partial excavation be; yet a large amount of work in archaeology is of just such a nature. (Aleš Hrdlička 1944a:194)

Recent events have brought about an intensive reexamination of Aleš Hrdlička's excavations at the Uyak site (KOD-145) on the northwest coast of Kodiak Island, Alaska. Hrdlička was one of the leading American physical anthropologists of his time and served as a curator in the Smithsonian Institution from 1903 until his death in 1943. After an initial reconnaissance in 1931, Hrdlička began excavations at Larsen Bay in 1932 and continued to work there until 1936.

Rarely has a single episode of early twentieth-century research been so thoroughly reevaluated from so many different angles. This attention from various scholars and Native Alaskans provides new insights into the processes involved in the interpretation of anthropological data. It has also led to a critical review of our knowledge of the Kachemak and Koniag periods of Alaskan prehistory. As is to be expected, much of the reinterpretation is based on data collected since the 1930s, but some of the new perspectives have been generated through the reevaluation of Hrdlička's own data (e.g., Urcid, this volume).

This chapter will serve to orient the reader unfamiliar with Hrdlička's work at Larsen Bay. I will begin by summarizing Hrdlička's main conclusions about the nature and significance of the Uyak site. In considering the validity of his interpretations, it is useful

to have some understanding of his methods and reasoning. Given the impact and influence of Hrdlička's ideas on Kodiak archaeology, it is worth probing the historical record for further insights into his work rather than simply dismissing it altogether.

Perhaps Hrdlička's most contentious idea was that the human remains at the site derive from two distinct and unrelated populations (Hrdlička 1944a:394; Collins 1945). He referred to the earlier group as "Pre-Koniag" and the later population as "Koniag." The latter group was considered to be ancestral to the Alutiiq. There has been much debate over the relationship between these two populations, and the issue is far from resolved. It was this question that became the focal point of the Larsen Bay repatriation case.

Along with his conclusions about the presence of two biologically different populations at the site, Hrdlička presented a scenario of a violent and sudden overtaking of one group by the other. He saw signs of warfare, massacres, and conflagration in the archaeological record that he attributed to Koniag expansion and population replacement (Hrdlička 1944a:323).

The most notorious of his assertions related to the question of cannibalism among the Pre-Koniag. Hrdlička became convinced of extensive cannibalism at Uyak after his first few days of work there in 1931 (Hrdlička 1932:102). This conviction may have been reinforced by his belief that there was a large off-site cemetery where the majority of the site's inhabitants were buried. Given this, he regarded the remains he found in the residential sectors of the site as evidence of unusual practices (Hrdlička 1932, 1944a).

Details given in Hrdlička's writings indicate that his interpretations were based on little more than casual observations and were heavily dependent on his own preconceived notions of what he would find. The pattern of his commentary in field notes, preliminary reports (especially Hrdlička 1932, 1933a, 1935), and his final report (Hrdlička 1944a) demonstrate that Hrdlička formed many of his conclusions early on in his work and subsequently made little attempt to gather supporting data or test his ideas.

Uyak Site

The Uyak site is located on a point of land at the mouth of Uyak Bay within the larger Larsen Bay on the northwest coast of Kodiak Island, opposite the Alaska Peninsula. The region around Uyak Bay has been intensively surveyed in recent years (Crowell 1986:figs. 4 and 5). Approximately 60 sites have been mapped around the bay. All are littoral and many are located at the mouths of streams, a pattern probably related to fishing considerations, specifically the salmon runs. The Uyak site has been classified as a medium-sized village (21 to 50 structures) in the regional settlement hierarchy. There are four other similarly sized villages in the region. The Uyak site remains the most extensively excavated site on Uyak Bay (Jordan and Knecht 1988:fig. 4; Dumond 1991).

The location and size of the site suggests that it housed a large, semipermanent population at the center of a regional catchment area. It is possible that the population wintered at Larsen Bay, dispersing to smaller camps and villages around the bay area in the spring and summer in order to exploit locally abundant seasonal resources such as salmon, marine mammals, shellfish, and waterfowl (Erlandson et al. 1992). Mollusk data from recent excavations at Uyak show that the harvesting of shellfish occurred in both the summer and winter, indicating that at least part of the population inhabited this village year round (Todd 1988).

The Uyak site extends some 300 m along the shore of Larsen Bay (Steffian 1992). Behind the permanent rocky point are massive cultural deposits that were the focal point of Hrdlička's work in the western portion of the site. Midden deposits reached 5 m at their greatest depth, suggesting a high population density and/or a long period of occupation. Lacking careful stratigraphic analysis for much of the site, it is not possible to determine how much of the habitation area was actually used contemporaneously.

Hrdlička excavated approximately 40 to 50 features, most of which were interpreted as house pits, although a few were identified as communal structures and sweat baths. Many of these features were visible on the surface while others were buried within midden deposits. Certainly not all of the features were contemporary, given that some were deeply buried (Heizer 1956:fig. 8), and it is unclear as to whether even all of the surface features were associated with the Koniag period, as initially presumed. Despite years of work at the site, there is little data on features aside from that reported by Heizer (1956:17–25). Recent excavations in the eastern portion of the site have located 16 residential structures that have, fortunately, been much more carefully recorded (Steffian 1992).

Though the site was not mapped to scale by Hrdlička prior to his excavations, the descriptions and photographs demonstrate that many of the surface features were found within relatively close proximity of one another. These features appear to have been of variable size, with the largest being perhaps as much as 9 or 10 m wide and 1 to 3 m deep. Few of these features were formally recorded. Many were found to be house pits upon excavation. The two largest depressions were interpreted as *kazims,* which are large communal buildings. This assessment seems to have been based primarily on their size as no other specialized or distinctive features, such as benches, were noted (Heizer 1956:17–18). Commonly associated with the house pits were slab-lined fire pits and horizontal slate slabs. These latter elements were sometimes interpreted as benches or walkways.

Burials were found in various contexts, including middens, beneath house floors, in colluvial deposits within abandoned structures, and in sterile deposits below the earliest occupation levels. The most recent burials were intrusively located within the uppermost cultural deposits and, indeed, the area has been used as a cemetery within living memory (Pullar, this volume). The location of these more recent burials has implications for the interpretation of the cultural affiliation of the "Koniag" remains, as will be discussed further below. The date of the occupational abandonment of the site has not been determined, though present evidence suggests it may have occurred prior to the full development of the Koniag tradition.

The dating of the portion of the site excavated by Hrdlička remains controversial and has not been resolved. The lack of reliable provenience data for the artifacts prevents detailed stratigraphic comparison. Steffian's work demonstrates that the eastern half of the site was occupied during the Late Kachemak period, which dates from A.D. 560 to 900 (1050 to 1390 B.P.; Steffian 1992). No radiocarbon assays have been obtained from the western portion of the site, making the artifact assemblage the only guide to chronology in this sector.

Heizer's artifact analysis, published in 1956, relied on Hrdlička's division of the site's occupation into two temporal periods, Pre-Koniag (Kachemak) and Koniag. The artifact sequences associated with the Kachemak and Koniag periods have been more completely documented and refined since Heizer's time by Clark (1970, 1974). More recently, work at two sites near Old Karluk, approximately 30 km west of Larsen Bay (Jordan and Knecht 1988), has demonstrated the co-occurrence of artifact types previously considered diagnostic of one or the other of the two traditions.

These recent studies have two important implications for interpreting the culture history of the Uyak site. First, they suggest that the transition from the Kachemak to Koniag tradition was gradual rather than abrupt, with the latter developing in situ out of the former. Second, they raise questions about the extent and nature of the Koniag occupation at the Uyak site. Given Heizer's analyses, it may be most parsimonious to interpret the Uyak site assemblages as indicative of complete or partial abandonment of the site at the time of Terminal Kachemak/Transitional Koniag (ca. 740 B.P.; Jordan and Knecht 1988), as suggested by Dumond (1991:104–106; this volume).

Excavation and Methodology

Hrdlička's work at the Uyak site evolved out of his long-term interests in Alaskan populations. In the early 1930s, little was known of the biological populations or archaeology of Alaska. Hrdlička was interested in addressing various questions about the peopling of the New World and the relationships between the different ethnic groups of Alaska. In the summer of 1931, Hrdlička made a brief reconnaissance trip to Larsen Bay. After a few days of exploratory excavation, he became convinced that the archaeological site he had discovered at Uyak Bay was one of the oldest in Alaska (Hrdlička 1932).

At no point did Hrdlička coherently articulate the hypotheses, assumptions, research goals, or methods of his work at Uyak. During the 1920s and 1930s, the prevailing research orientation in American archaeology was cultural historical, emphasizing the identification and elucidation of past events and cultural sequences. Many archaeologists also sought links between archaeological cultures and modern groups (Willey and Sabloff 1974:114). The broad goals of such cultural historical investigations were most likely what Hrdlička had in mind when he planned his work at the Uyak site.

Prior to beginning excavations at Uyak, Hrdlička had already formulated some very definite opinions about the prehistory of southern Alaska. These included the belief that the Alaska Peninsula and Kodiak Island had been major routes in the peopling of the Americas, that the ancient inhabitants of Uyak were related to both Eskimo and Northwest Coast peoples, and that the Uyak site was very old (Hrdlička 1932).

In similar fashion, Hrdlička had arrived at various conclusions about the history of the Uyak site only days after the start of his first field season there. These included his explanation for the morphological differences between skulls from the upper and lower components of the site, his ideas about the practice of cannibalism there, and his pessimistic view of the stratigraphic record, which he dismissed as too complex to try to make sense of (Hrdlička 1933a:44; 1944a:141, 149). He based his conclusions on his own powers of observation, which he apparently regarded as extremely reliable and in little need of testing or verification (Hrdlička 1944a:236, 319, 336–37). The methodology he employed relied on a simplistic understanding of stratigraphy and an unshakable confidence in his own knowledge and abilities as a scientist.

In modern archaeological practice, careful attention to features, burial practices, artifact distribution, and refuse disposal often provides valuable insights into daily life and culture history. Similarly, the control of stratigraphic relationships are recognized as critical to the analysis of diachronic change. The growing awareness of these issues in American archaeology over the past several decades has dramatically altered the methodological concerns and strategies of fieldwork. While such methods and concerns were already a part of American archaeology by the 1930s, it was still not uncommon for archaeologists to conduct excavations with little or no spatial control (Willey and Sabloff 1974:89–98).

Hrdlička, although known as a meticulous physical anthropologist, approached the archaeological excavation of the Uyak site with the primary intent of recovering as many skeletal remains as possible (Hrdlička 1941:1, 1944a:3, 141). He made no systematic attempt to record archaeological information at the site, and his field records are limited to anecdotal notes, sketch maps, and rudimentary profile drawings. The stratigraphic and contextual information that Hrdlička did record related almost exclusively to burials. Generally speaking, he did not feel there was any need to scrutinize the archaeological data too carefully, an attitude summarized in a letter written to Robert Heizer on January 12, 1933 (Letter from Aleš Hrdlička to Robert F. Heizer, 12 Jan 1933; Robert F. Heizer file; Correspondence 1903–1943; Aleš Hrdlička Papers; National Anthropological Archives; Na-

Figure 6.1. Photograph of Hrdlička's main excavations, June 1932. A study of photographs helped to identify features, excavation areas, and burial locations, and a comparison with later photos (e.g., fig. 6.2) allowed for estimates of the rate and direction of the 1932 excavations. (Courtesy of the National Anthropological Archives, Smithsonian Institution)

tional Museum of Natural History; Washington, D.C.): "Should excavation show definite strata of burials it is of importance to indicate with each skeleton from which stratum it has come. But under ordinary conditions no extreme details are necessary."

Hrdlička began his excavations on the narrow prominent point of land that he alternately referred to as "Jones Point" and "Our Point." From initial excavations on the promontory, Hrdlička's crews moved south, into the main deposits of the site (fig. 6.1). In this manner they removed a substantial portion of the site in only five seasons. Using Heizer's map (1956, fig. 3) and a revised scale based on aerial photographs of the site, it was estimated that 3200 m² of site midden (0.79 acres) was removed by Hrdlička between 1931 and 1936. Based on other photographs from Hrdlička's work, it appears that these midden deposits were up to 5 m deep in the center. The sheer volume of midden moved confirms that Hrdlička's main intention was to recover as many skeletons as possible. Concern for other types of data were obviously of secondary importance.

Stratigraphy

The deep midden deposits at the Uyak site are the result of several centuries of high density occupation. The residential structures and domestic features found at the site incorporated large amounts of stone, wood, and even bone. Most features were at least partially subterranean. Around the structures were middens containing tremendous quantities of clam and mussel shell, burned slate, fish, whale, and other animal bones, wood, and refuse. The thickness and extent of the deposits indicate intensive use over a long period of time.

Hrdlička divided the midden deposits into three strata. He referred to these as the black, red, and blue levels. Artifacts and skeletons were marked with colored pencils to indicate the stratum from which the item had been removed. Only rarely was any more precise provenience information recorded. De Laguna (1956:259) has succinctly summarized the problems resulting from the lack of spatial and vertical control at the site, noting Hrdlička's general failure "to record the provenience of specimens by the usual method of . . . grid and depth coordinates." Once again, Hrdlička had decided upon a strategy early in the first field season, and he maintained this approach throughout the rest of the project.

The upper, or black, layer in Hrdlička's system was defined by large amounts of fire-burned slate rubble (Hrdlička 1944a:203). Hrdlička attributed these deposits to sweat baths, an activity once thought to have been practiced exclusively by the Koniag.[1] The rubble in the upper layers of Uyak is similar to the refuse rock noted at KAR-029, which Crozier (1989:81) associates with cooking activities. Heizer regarded the black stratum as a readily recognizable and coherent unit (1956:7–8), and various photographs of the site stratigraphy show definite deposits of rubble. This uppermost stratum represents the "Koniag" occupation as defined by Hrdlička. Again, Hrdlička regarded the Koniag as a distinct population that had moved into the region and displaced the earlier inhabitants.

The blue stratum referred to the lowest deposits, which was typically 2 to 3 ft above the sterile zone. Aside from relative position, the blue stratum was not marked by any definable characteristics. Hrdlička (1944a:176) observed that the bones removed from this stratum were often brown or grey-brown in color. While Heizer (1956:12) agreed with this observation, he did not feel that it constituted a sufficient stratigraphic marker in and of itself. The intermediate red stratum was simply the zone below the rubble and above the blue stratum. Hrdlička considered the red and blue strata to be associated with the "Pre-Koniag" occupation, referring to the "blue" remains as the first inhabitants of the site.

The black, red, and blue distinctions were not rigorously defined or implemented as stratigraphic units. Their main function was to provide a relative vertical context for the human remains recovered. In practice, the recording of the stratigraphic position of the human remains was sometimes based on Hrdlička's judgment of whether a skull was morphologically "Pre-Koniag" or "Koniag" rather than actual relative depth (Heizer 1956:88). De Laguna (1956:259–60) also observed that "some especially well made" artifacts had been marked twice, first with black and then with red. This phenomenon reflects Hrdlička's conviction that all of the more finely crafted artifacts were made by the Kachemak people. When such items were found in the upper layers, he simply presumed that they had originally derived from the earlier context. The re-marking of artifacts was probably done after excavation.

In contrast to Hrdlička's three strata, the evidence from photos and profiles made by Heizer and others indicate that the stratigraphy was, in fact, tremendously complex. Early in 1932 Hrdlička described this complexity: "Stratification, more or less, everywhere, but almost hopeless, changes from place to place, not of chronological nature" (1944a:162). With this brief statement Hrdlička dismissed the stratigraphic record as useless, failing to realize the potential value of the information that could have been obtained through careful recording techniques.

Photographs of the gross stratigraphy of the site (e.g., Hrdlička 1944a:fig. 100) show that there was general horizontal deposition across large areas. But there were obviously many small-scale formation processes that had affected different parts of the site. The effects were undoubtedly numerous and difficult to sort out, and it is unlikely that many of Hrdlička's contemporaries would have made the effort to sort through the stratigraphic complexity of the site. Processes that likely affected the site stratigraphy included differential depositional events, feature construction, compaction, slumping, redeposition, erosion, and possibly even seismic activity. Some of these processes were in fact recognized by Hrdlička (e.g., 1944a:203, 208–11, 227, 338) but none of them were explicitly considered. While Hrdlička did at times note the sometimes dramatic effects of these processes on features and stratigraphy, he characteristically failed to associate them with potential disturbance of human remains.

In his discussions of the condition of the human remains, Hrdlička made selective observations that fit his hypotheses about such activities as warfare and cannibalism. He gave little or no consideration to any number of cultural or natural processes that might have accounted for them. Burials 5 and 6 at Rolling Bay, a Koniag site on the southeast coast of Kodiak, clearly illustrate the sort of erosional processes that could lead to partial preservation and mixing of discrete burials (Clark 1974:144). Careful attention to burial context also leads to alternate explanations for missing anatomical elements, as demonstrated by Simon and Steffian's work (this volume).

Collections

As previously discussed, the primary goal of the excavations at the Uyak site was to recover human remains to address research questions about the settlement of Alaska and the New World. At the end of five seasons of work, Hrdlička had removed several hundred burials. Exact numbers of individuals represented could never be determined due to the large numbers of isolated bones and partial remains, but 756 catalog numbers were assigned when the assemblage was accessioned into the collections of the U.S. National Museum.

In addition to human remains, Hrdlička also col-

Stuart Speaker

Figure 6.2. Photograph taken in August 1932, showing the state of excavations in the main portion of the site at the end of the season. On the right is a discard pile, which shows the types of artifacts that were not shipped to the Smithsonian. (Courtesy of the National Anthropological Archives, Smithsonian Institution)

lected artifacts encountered in his excavations. The most thorough discussion of the artifacts from the Uyak site is found in Heizer's report (1956). It is clear from Hrdlička's comments and photographs that many artifacts were left at the site. These were primarily the oversized or less elaborated items, such as crude lamps, slate slabs, and whale bone objects (fig. 6.2). A large number of smaller artifacts were also undoubtedly overlooked as a result of the excavation methods, which did not involve screening.

The archaeological assemblage from the Uyak site included examples of almost all known artifact types from Kodiak Island. Large numbers of utilitarian items were recovered, including slate knives and points; bone harpoon heads, sockets, fish hooks, and shanks; and stone mauls, wedges, adzes, and lamps. Decayed wood, matting, and basketry fragments were also common in the midden deposits (Hrdlička 1944a).

Some non-utilitarian items were also recovered, including ivory carvings of human and animal forms, labrets, and a pair of ivory eyes inset in the eye sockets of a human skull. No pottery was found, although it is known from other Koniag phase sites (Clark

1974:115ff) and from some Late Kachemak contexts (Jordan and Knecht 1988; Dumond 1991:table 2.6), but it is not by any means ubiquitous at Koniag sites.

The excavations also produced a sizeable faunal collection, which included fox, dog, bear, otter, seal, porpoise, mollusks, and a variety of bird bones. Several species identified had not been previously documented in Alaska.

Field Records

Hrdlička's (1944a) major publication on the site, *The Anthropology of Kodiak Island,* is primarily a transcript of his field diaries. It seems that he intended this to be more an autobiographical account than a site record. The most detailed sections of the volume are a synthesis of the ethnohistoric record and the physical anthropological analysis. Only rudimentary summations of the site and artifacts are provided. The unstructured and unscientific format of the volume indicates that Hrdlička never made any attempt at systematic record keeping at the site. For many years students of Kodiak Island archaeology shied away from

Figure 6.3. Burial information written on a clam shell indicating Hrdlička's haphazard approach to record keeping at the site. The note reads: "4 knives and a slate spear point, marked deep = from Annex, beneath pavement." (Courtesy of the Repatriation Office, National Museum of Natural History, Smithsonian Institution)

dealing with the Uyak site due to the very confused nature of the site's documentation. Given some of his recording techniques (fig. 6.3), it is not hard to see why.

In an effort to determine what, if any, useful archaeological data could be culled from Hrdlička's field records, I examined the archival documentation from the 1932 field season as a test case. The records utilized are found in the National Anthropological Archives and the Department of Anthropology, National Museum of Natural History, both of the Smithsonian Institution. The 1932 field records examined include: (1) a field diary giving a daily account of the work and notable discoveries (included in Hrdlička 1944a); (2) photographs, primarily of burials, though a few other features were documented as well; and (3) a collection of loose notes written on scraps of paper in the field that served as packing slips for the skeletal remains.

Hrdlička's interest in the human remains at Uyak compelled him to record the burials in a fairly comprehensive manner, often noting depths below surface and relationships to other features and burials. The skeletal remains were not cataloged in the field, making it difficult to match individual burials with the notes Hrdlička did take. In some cases, however, the 1932 records are detailed enough to permit the correlation of specific burials with specific field descriptions.

The skeletal remains from the 1932 season were given 137 catalog numbers, of which 102 represented discrete individuals. The other 35 catalog numbers were assigned to "lots" of bones, which consisted of either isolated remains or mixed postcranial elements from multiple burials. A total of 115 of the catalog numbers can be matched to specific references in Hrdlička's text, including virtually all of the crania and complete skeletons. Because the skeletal data is organized by catalog number rather than by burial event, it is necessary to discuss the data in this manner.

By cross referencing the field diary, photographs, and packing notes, it is possible to obtain some insight into the excavation activities. The information is fairly consistent between the different sources, reinforcing the impression that considerable care was taken in the recovery and recording of burials. This is echoed in the comments of two of Hrdlička's field assistants who noted that "no effort is made to locate any material more closely than this [by stratum], except when it is related to a burial, in which case it is so segregated [i.e. funerary objects were separated from other artifacts]" (MacRae and Bohannon 1934:2).

Patterns in the Data

The compilation of data from the different sources has yielded vertical provenience information, expressed in the form of depth below surface and height above sterile, for 77 sets of remains. While not ideal, these measurements are at least relatively comparable as the sterile deposit appears to have been level across the site, giving a relatively horizontal baseline for the vertical measurements. In addition, 10 other sets of cataloged remains have partial vertical provenience, either depth from surface or height from sterile.

These data allow an analysis of the relationship between stratigraphy and the morphological characteristics of the skulls as defined by Hrdlička. Fig. 6.4 shows a graph of the depth below surface and height above sterile of 47 sets of skeletal remains that were designated as either Koniag or Pre-Koniag in Hrdlička's catalog of cranial measurements (1944b; some other designations not listed in 1944b are from the catalog cards). The graph indicates that there were no remains identified as Koniag recovered below a depth of 1.5 m. Furthermore, all of the Pre-Koniag remains from the red stratum were from below 0.8 m (although some were at sterile), and all the Pre-Koniag remains in the blue stratum were lower than 1.5 m below the surface but not higher than 0.25 m above sterile.

These findings reveal some regularity in the designation of stratigraphic position of the burials in 1932, lending a degree of confidence to patterns derived from raw stratigraphic distinctions. This is not to argue that the remains in any given stratum are neces-

Stuart Speaker

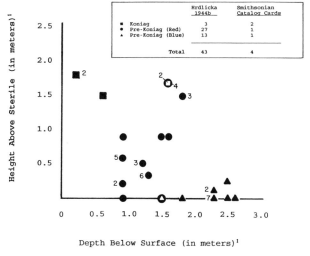

	Hrdlicka 1944b	Smithsonian Catalog Cards
■ Koniag	3	2
● Pre-Koniag (Red)	27	1
▲ Pre-Koniag (Blue)	13	1
Total	43	4

[1] Depths and heights converted from english to metric measurements

Figure 6.4. Graph of vertical proveniences of skulls and skeletons, showing depth below surface and height above sterile. Numbers next to symbols represent more than one individual at a given depth and height. Hrdlička's original depths and heights have been converted to metric measurements. (Illustration by Stuart Speaker)

sarily contemporaneous. Such an assumption would be unwarranted even in a well-controlled excavation in the absence of a detailed analysis.

The pattern seen in the graph suggests that Hrdlička did in fact use stratigraphic position for separating the remains of the "Koniag" (black) and "Pre-Koniag" (blue) groups. As noted above, Heizer said that the black stratum was, in fact, well defined and consistently recognizable and, as such, may actually be of temporal significance. In addition, Hrdlička appears to have consistently used the blue designation for remains that were not only very close to the lowest cultural levels but were also below 1.5 m from the surface, which is of relative temporal importance (i.e., earlier than the red or black levels).

The situation for the red stratum remains ambiguous. This stratigraphic designation seems to have been used to identify not only remains from the middle levels of the deposits but also those recovered from the lower levels that did not appear to Hrdlička to have the right morphological characteristics to be part of the Pre-Koniag, or "blue," skeletal series (Hrdlička 1944a:202–203). Given this situation, future tests of the validity of suggested morphological distinctions between Koniag and Pre-Koniag populations might best be undertaken with skeletal remains from the black and blue strata only, excluding remains from the red zone. The same might be said for comparisons of the artifact assemblages.

Combining information from field records, site

photographs, and aerial photographs, it was possible to identify the horizontal provenience of 120 of the 137 sets of human remains excavated during the 1932 field season. This, in turn, allowed for a partial reconstruction of the 1932 excavation area, which encompassed an estimated 282 m[2] (fig. 6.5). Some 102 of the catalog numbers associated with the plotted burials represent discrete individuals, while the remainder consist of mixed postcranial elements.[2] While the map is not to scale, it is an improvement over the sketch maps provided by Heizer (1956), and I feel that the spatial relationships between features are accurately represented. Because the locations of the features are not precise, they cannot be subjected to quantitative spatial analyses, but the map *does* preserve the horizontal relationships between burials and known features described in Hrdlička (1944a).

Mortuary Patterns

The available data indicate that the Koniag burials were generally found at shallow depths and may well have been interred after the site had been abandoned (fig. 6.6). A few comments found in some of the field records indicate that the possibility of intrusive burials was recognized (MacRae and Bohannon 1934:13; Hrdlička 1936:52, 1944a:324). MacRae and Bohannon report finding a coffin burial with nails at a depth of 5 ft (1.5 m), demonstrating that at least some postabandonment Koniag[3] burials were placed in deep pits. This burial practice (i.e., deep interment) may reflect the influence of the Russian culture and would account for the occasional Koniag burial at a meter below the surface.

Based on work at other sites, shallow burial pits seem to have been common during both the Kachemak and Koniag periods (Workman 1991:5). It has been suggested that convenient surface depressions were often utilized for burial purposes (Simon and Steffian, this volume). Burial pits excavated in well-documented Kachemak and Koniag contexts, for example, have been found at depths of 0.40 m to 0.59 m below surface (Simon and Steffian, this volume; Clark 1974; de Laguna 1934). Heizer (1956:17) noted that shallow flexed burials were common in abandoned house fill. Hrdlička (1936:52; 1944a:175) mentioned this as well, noting that several human skeletons were found on the surface of house pit depressions.

The use of shallow burials has two implications for the interpretation of the data from Hrdlička's excavations. First, burials would have been regularly exposed to the effects of subsidence and compaction, root and burrow damage, and cultural activities. Such

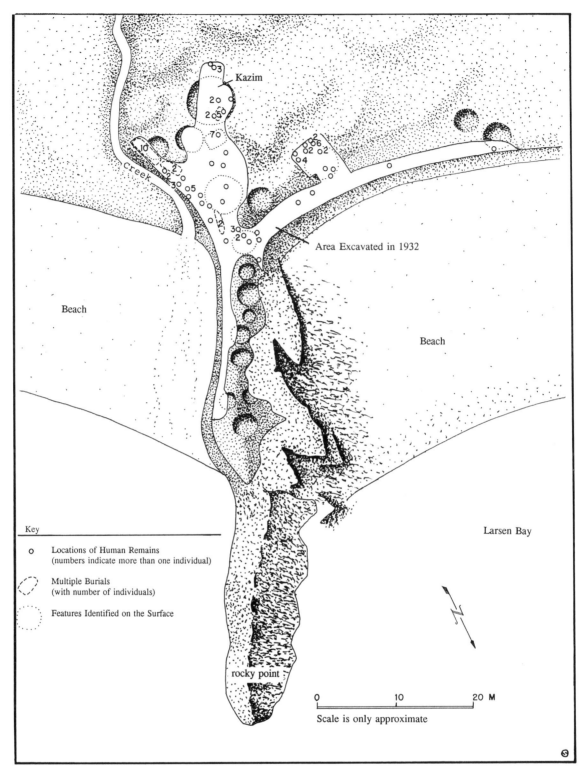

Figure 6.5. The Uyak site, showing burials excavated in the 1932 season. Map was compiled from aerial photographs; scale is approximate. (Illustration by Stuart Speaker)

Figure 6.6. Photograph of two burials identified by Hrdlička as Koniag, illustrating the very shallow depth of some of the burials found at the Uyak site. (Courtesy of the National Anthropological Archives, Smithsonian Institution)

disturbances would impact shallow remains more dramatically than deeply buried remains. This may, in part, explain the numerous incomplete and disarticulated burials recovered at the Uyak site by Hrdlička, which he frequently cited as evidence of cannibalism. These kinds of disturbances have been amply documented at Rolling Bay (Clark 1974:144) and KAR-029 on Larsen Bay (Yesner 1989). Indeed, such postdepositional disturbance was even described by Hrdlička himself (1935:50): "Koniag . . . excavations account for many disturbed burials, missing parts of skeletons, and scattered bones and skulls." In other instances, however, Hrdlička cited such partial skeletons as evidence of purposeful dismemberment.

The second implication is that most or all of the brachycephalic "Koniag" burials postdate the actual occupation of the site. Hrdlička appears to have discarded this notion in favor of hypotheses about massacres, population replacement, and other dramatic activities. By Koniag times, however, the Uyak site may have, in fact, become a cemetery for a population residing in a separate habitation area. The use of abandoned dwellings as burial locations has been documented at Rolling Bay and Kiavak 418 (Clark

1974:143–48). Although Hrdlička recognized that at least some of the Koniag burials were intrusive after the abandonment of the site, he believed that the site "became extinct before or during the very beginnings of the Russian times" (Hrdlička 1944a:140; see also 1936:52).

Isolated Skulls

Isolated skulls are an important element of the mortuary assemblage from the Uyak site. In considering the pattern of isolated skulls at different Kachemak sites, Workman (1991:7–8) has suggested that they may have been curated for use in ancestor veneration rituals, as was the case in the past among some Eskimo groups. He has argued against the idea that they were related to warfare due to the fact that both males and females are represented. The Uyak site remains (see Table 6.1) seem to offer limited confirmation of Workman's hypothesis in so far as the individuals do not seem to represent the victims of war. Only 1 of the 7 Pre-Koniag isolated skulls is male, although all 4 of the Koniag isolated skulls are male. Of the total sample of 12 isolated skulls (including one lacking temporal designation), 10 individuals are over 20 years of age and 7 are relatively mature (over 30 years of age).

The results of Clark's (1974:143–47) excavations at the Koniag sites of Rolling Bay and Kiavak 418, which yielded two isolated skulls and three other problematic skulls (poorly preserved or possibly from disturbed burials), would suggest that the practice continued into Koniag times. Seven of the combined total of 16 individuals (isolated skulls and skeletons lacking skulls) on Table 6.1 are Koniag, pointing to strong continuity in the practice of curating skulls from the Kachemak to the Koniag period on Kodiak Island.

Conclusions

The preceding analysis demonstrates that there are data to be gleaned from Hrdlička's excavations and records. The analysis has proved particularly valuable in reevaluating the critical question of the stratigraphic relations among the burials. Although the data presented here are in no way precise in the modern sense, they allow—perhaps for the first time—a look into the actual significance of Hrdlička's stratigraphic designations. One conclusion that can be drawn from this study is that Hrdlička did implement his strata designations in such a way that they can be interpreted as indicative of relative vertical provenience. The chronological significance of these strata over the larger site is open to question due to differential depositional processes, but within a discrete area (e.g., the 1932 excavations) the chronological nature of the stratigraphy may be more confidently assumed. The data from the subset of the burials excavated in 1932 may be useful for researchers concerned with controlling chronology at the site in a more careful manner than Hrdlička. This in-depth examination of Hrdlička's stratigraphic methodology provides Alaskan archaeologists with some data with which to form their own opinions about his data.

In the end, the best we can do is work with the existing data, although most or all of the conclusions drawn from them need to be reconsidered. This distinction between data and interpretation is an impor-

Table 6.1. Data on Isolated Skulls and Skeletons Lacking Skulls from 1932 Field Season[a]

SI catalog number	Sex[b]	Age[b]	Depth below surface[c]	Height above Sterile[c]	Designation[d]	Notes
Isolated skulls with some or full vertical provenience:						
366657	M	50–60	0.2	1.8	Koniag	
367210	F	45–50	0.77		Pre-Koniag (red)	
366618	M	(Adult)	1.15	0.5		Fragmentary and burned
366666	F	13–19	1.23		Pre-Koniag (blue)	
367206	M	45–50	1.77	1.28	Pre-Koniag (red)	
367207	F	45–50	1.77	1.28	Pre-Koniag (red)	
366620	F	30+	2.28	0.1	Pre-Koniag (blue)	
Isolated skulls lacking vertical provenience:						
366711	M	30–40			Koniag	In kazim
367209	M	(Young adult)			Koniag	
366601	M	30–40			Koniag	Possibly 0.05 m below surface
367229	F	14–15			Pre-Koniag (red)	
366631	F	18–20			Pre-Koniag (red)	Listed as superficial but of intermediary type
Skeletons lacking skulls:						
366704	M	18–20	0.61	1.53	Koniag	
366646	M	30–35	0.62		Koniag	
366643	M	35–45			Koniag	
366686	M	30–40			Pre-Koniag	

[a] Isolated mandibles and anatomical elements from multiple burials are not included in table.
[b] Sex and age columns use data compiled during the repatriation documentation.
[c] In meters.
[d] Designations given in Hrdlička 1944b or found on catalog card.

Stuart Speaker

tant one to make. Hrdlička's interpretations have been very contentious and may have overshadowed the data in many ways. One need not accept Hrdlička's conclusions to find uses for his data, however.

While I reject most of Hrdlička's premature conclusions, I do think that there may still be some data of lasting value to be garnered from his work. I would argue, for example, that there is evidence in Hrdlička's own notes that the Koniag burials were most likely placed at the Uyak site after the settlement had been abandoned.

The burials at Uyak were the most carefully documented portion of Hrdlička's work and have received the most attention over the years. The information obtained through osteological analyses by Hrdlička and others may in some way be enhanced by this exploration of Hrdlička's provenience data. It is fair to say that Hrdlička did not recognize the potential of the provenience data he could have collected. Although the conclusions he drew from his data are now being challenged, it is still possible to gain insights into the prehistory of Kodiak Island from his efforts.

In conclusion, the Uyak site presents a wide range of interpretive problems for modern archaeologists and physical anthropologists. Most of these difficulties stem directly from the poor quality of the data collection at the time of excavation. The diverse site records greatly complicate the matter of sorting out reliable from unreliable information. A complete reconstruction of the site will never be possible simply because so many of the pertinent details were never recorded. Working through Hrdlička's disjointed reports and scraps of notes thus becomes truly an exercise in salvage archaeology.

Acknowledgments

Stephen Loring of the Smithsonian's National Museum of Natural History made the initial suggestion that this project might be fruitful and introduced me to the various records available. The staff of the National Anthropological Archives, especially Gail Yiotis, was very helpful in making the Hrdlička collection accessible to me. An early version of this paper was presented at the 91st Annual Meeting of the American Anthropological Association, San Francisco, and Tamara Bray and Donald Clark read and provided helpful comments on that paper.

Notes

1. Similar slate rubble has been found in the Kachemak occupation levels at Karluk (Jordan and Knecht 1988).

2. Of the 137 catalog numbers, 125 were matched to specific references in the Hrdlička 1944a text, and 120 of these were mapped in horizontal location. A total of 102 of the matched catalog numbers represent discrete individuals, either isolated skulls, full skeletons, or postcrania without skulls. A total of 23 of the matched catalog numbers contained the mixed remains from multiple burials, which were not segregated into individual catalog numbers. Some 77 of the matched individuals have vertical measurements from both the surface and from the sterile deposit, and an additional 20 have one of the vertical measurements.

3. MacRae and Bohannon refer to this individual as "Aleut," which is the term they consistently apply to the Koniag remains. The terms were apparently used interchangeably during the fieldwork.

References Cited

Clark, Donald W.
1970 The Late Kachemak Tradition at Three Saints and Crag Point, Kodiak Island, Alaska. *Arctic Anthropology* 6(2):73–111.
1974 *Koniag Prehistory*. Tubingen Monongraphien zur Urgeschicte, Band 1. Stuttgart: W. Kohlhammer.

Collins, Henry B.
1945 Review of the "Anthropology of Kodiak Island" and "The Aleutian and Commander Islands and Their Inhabitants." *American Journal of Physical Anthropology* 3:355–61.

Crowell, Aron
1986 An Archaeological Survey of Uyak Bay, Kodiak Island, Alaska. Report on file at Alaska Heritage Resource Surveys, Anchorage, Alaska.

Crozier, S. Neal
1989 Excavation at a Late Prehistoric Dwelling Structure on Kodiak Island, Alaska. *Arctic Anthropology* 26(2): 78–95.

de Laguna, Frederica
1934 *The Archaeology of Cook Inlet, Alaska*. Philadelphia: University Museum, University of Pennsylvania.
1956 *Chugach Prehistory: The Archaeology of Prince William Sound, Alaska*. Publications in Anthropology No. 13, University of Washington, Seattle.

Dumond, Don E.
1991 The Uyak Site in Regional Prehistory: The Cultural Evidence. In *The Uyak Site on Kodiak Island: Its Place in Alaskan Prehistory*, by D. E. Dumond and G. R. Scott, pp. 57–114. University of Oregon Anthropological Papers No. 44, Eugene.

Erlandson, J., A. Crowell, C. Wooley, and J. Haggarty
1992 Spatial and Temporal Patterns of Alutiiq Paleodemography. *Arctic Anthropology* 29(2):42–62.

Heizer, Robert
1956 *Archaeology of the Uyak Site, Kodiak Island, Alaska*. University of California Anthropological Records, vol. 17:1.

Hrdlička, Aleš
1932 Anthropological Work in Alaska. *Explorations and Field-Work of the Smithsonian Institution in 1931*:91–102. Washington, D.C.: Smithsonian Institution.

1933a Anthropological Explorations on Kodiak Island, Alaska. *Explorations and Field-Work of the Smithsonian Institution in 1932*:41–44. Washington, D.C.: Smithsonian Institution.

1933b Letter from A. Hrdlička to R. F. Heizer, 12 Jan 1933; Robert F. Heizer file; Correspondence 1903–1943; A. Hrdlička Papers; National Anthropological Archives, National Museum of Natural History, Washington, D.C.

1935 Archeological Excavations on Kodiak Island, Alaska. *Explorations and Field-Work of the Smithsonian Institution in 1934*:47–52. Washington, D.C.: Smithsonian Institution.

1936 Archeological Expedition to Kodiak Island, Alaska. *Explorations and Field-Work of the Smithsonian Institution in 1935*:47–52. Washington, D.C.: Smithsonian Institution.

1941 Diseases of and Artifacts on Skulls and Bones from Kodiak Island. In *Smithsonian Miscellaneous Collections,* vol. 101, No. 4 (Publication 3640). Smithsonian Institution, Washington, D.C.

1944a *The Anthropology of Kodiak Island.* Philadelphia: The Wistar Institute of Anatomy and Biology.

1944b Catalogue of Human Crania in the United States National Museum Collections: Non-Eskimo People of the Northwest Coast, Alaska, and Siberia. *Proceedings of the United States National Museum* 94:1–172. Washington, D.C.: Smithsonian Institution.

Jordan, Richard H., and Richard A. Knecht
1988 Archaeological Research in Western Kodiak Island, Alaska: The Development of Koniag Culture. In *The Late Prehistoric Development of Alaska's Native People,* R. D. Shaw, R. K. Harritt, and D. E. Dumond, eds., pp. 225–306. Aurora: Alaska Anthropological Association Monograph Series No. 4.

MacRae, T. W. R., and C. T. R. Bohannon
1934 Smithsonian Institution U.S. National Museum Expedition to Kodiak Island, Alaska, Led by Dr. Aleš Hrdlička 1934; Personal Notes. Manuscript in Aleš Hrdlička Papers, National Anthropological Archives, Smithsonian Institution, Washington, D.C.

Steffian, Amy
in Fifty Years after Hrdlička: Further Investigation at
press the Uyak Site, Kodiak Island, Alaska. In *Contributions to the Anthropology of South Central and Southwestern Alaska,* R. H. Jordan, F. de Laguna, and A. F. Steffian, eds., Anthropological Papers of the University of Alaska No. 24(1–2).

1992 Archaeological Coal in the Gulf of Alaska: A View from Kodiak Island. *Arctic Anthropology* 29(2):111–29.

Todd, Nancy E.
1988 A Quantitative Study of Shellfish Remains from the Uyak Site, Kodiak Island. Senior Thesis, Bryn Mawr College, Bryn Mawr.

Willey, Gordon, and Jeremy Sabloff
1974 *A History of American Archaeology.* San Francisco: W. H. Freeman.

Workman, William
1991 Life and Death in a First Millennium A.D. Gulf of Alaska Culture: The Kachemak Tradition Ceremonial Complex. Paper presented at the 18th Annual Meeting of the Alaska Anthropological Association, Anchorage.

Yesner, David R.
1989 Osteological Remains from Larsen Bay, Kodiak Island, Alaska. *Arctic Anthropology* 26(2):96–106.

G. Richard Scott

7

TEETH AND PREHISTORY ON KODIAK ISLAND

For the past 150 years physical anthropologists have utilized a wide range of biological markers to make inferences about group origins and relationships. As a result of the new federal law on the repatriation of Native American remains, with its stipulation for establishing biological and cultural affiliation between claimants and a given collection of skeletal remains, the assessment of relationships is no longer purely a scholarly pursuit but one with significant pragmatic ramifications for Native Americans and anthropologists alike.

Although repatriation issues should be resolved using all possible lines of evidence to demonstrate the presence or absence of affiliation between prehistoric, protohistoric, and living populations, this study focuses on one line of evidence—the biological system of dentition. Teeth have the potential to play an important role in questions of repatriation because they are not only well represented in archaeological collections but they are also directly observable in living individuals. For the most part, other methods of assessing affinity are limited either to skeletal remains (craniometry, nonmetric skeletal traits) or to living populations (blood groups and other simple genetic markers, dermatoglyphics, anthropometry). Because of the availability of a myriad of genetically mediated metric and morphological variables, dental comparisons between past and present populations can be crucial in determining the likelihood of ancestral-descendant links. While repatriation of the skeletal

collection from the Uyak site on Kodiak Island is a *fait accompli,* a comparative dental analysis of past and present Kodiak Island populations provides additional insights into the question of biological continuity and helps to determine the contribution that dentition can make in linking prehistoric and modern populations.

Most physical anthropology studies of Kodiak Island populations have been based on data collected during the course of two major projects. The first was Aleš Hrdlička's large-scale excavations at the Uyak site near Larsen Bay conducted between 1931 and 1936 (Hrdlička 1944). This work led to the recovery of several thousand artifacts and more than 1,000 human skeletons. Hrdlička and many others studied the Uyak Bay skeletal collection to assess the internal relationships of skeletal samples from three different levels (blue, red, and black) at the site and to evaluate their external affinities. Hrdlička associated his blue and red levels (blue being the deeper level) with Pre-Koniag or Kachemak groups and his black level with the Koniag peoples.

The second project was the multidisciplinary Aleut-Konyag Prehistory and Ecology Project directed in the early 1960s by W. S. Laughlin and W. G. Reeder of the University of Wisconsin. In addition to collecting archaeological and ecological data, team members conducted demographic, genetic, anthropometric, dermatoglyphic, and physiological studies among the living Koniag populations. Among the members of the team were Albert and Thelma Dahlberg who collected dental impressions and made permanent plaster casts of about 300 Native American residents from four island villages. This dental series has been the focus of several problem-oriented studies (Dahlberg 1962, 1963; Turner 1967, 1969; Nichol 1984; Nichol and Turner 1986).

Materials and Methods

For my comparative study, I used the prehistoric Kodiak Island skeletons from the Uyak collection, which was housed in the Smithsonian before its repatriation. Observations were recorded for one or more dental variables on 449 individuals (Uyak blue, n = 121; Uyak red, n = 217; Uyak black, n = 111). The dental casts collected by the Dalbergs serve as the comparative sample of living Kodiak Islanders. In this sample, one or more observations were made on 269 individuals from four villages on the island (Old Harbor, n = 128; Akhiok, n = 57; Karluk, n = 57; Kaguyak, n = 27).

For the prehistoric sample, 27 morphological variables were observed (Scott 1991). A number of these were root traits that were not observable on the casts of the modern sample. For the modern sample, observations were limited to the following 14 crown traits (see Table 7.1): winging (UI1); shoveling (UI1); the canine tubercle (UC); tuberculated premolars or odontomes (UP1, UP2, LP1, LP2); Carabelli's trait (UM1); the hypocone (UM2); bifurcated hypocone (UM2); cusp 5 or metaconule (UM1); multiple lingual cusps (LP2); hypoconulid (LM2); cusp 6 (LM1); cusp 7 (LM1); the protostylid (LM1); and deflecting wrinkle (LM1), where U and L = upper and lower; I, C, P, and M = incisor, canine, premolar, molar; and 1, 2 = first and second. The standards I used to make observations on these traits (except for the bifurcated hypocone) are derived from the Arizona State University dental anthropology scoring system (Turner et al. 1991).

Several questions were posed in the analysis: (1) Do crown trait frequencies vary significantly among the living Koniag samples? (2) Do crown trait frequencies differ significantly between living Kodiak Islanders and either the Kachemak (Uyak blue plus red) or prehistoric Koniag (Uyak black)? and (3) To what extent has European gene flow had an impact on the crown trait frequencies of the living Koniag? According to Denniston (1966) and Majumder et al. (1988), genetic data from the living populations of Kodiak Island show relatively high frequencies of the Rh negative allele (r), A^2, and K. Because these genes are commonly absent in Eskimo and Indian populations, there appears to be a fairly high level of European admixture on the island. After addressing these questions, I conducted a biological distance analysis based on a method developed by Harpending and Jenkins (1973) to assess the within- and between-group variation of past and present Kodiak Island populations relative to other Native American groups.

Results

In the prehistoric Kodiak Island samples, only two of the 22 crown and root traits that could be assessed by chi-square tests showed a significant difference in frequency between the Uyak blue, red, and black components. These were the canine tubercle and Carabelli's trait (Scott 1991). In a comparable analysis of 14 crown traits from living Kodiak Islanders, none of the variables showed a significant intervillage difference (Table 7.1).

Crown trait frequencies were also compared in the Kachemak, prehistoric Koniag, and modern Koniag samples (Table 7.2). Three (incisor shoveling, Carabelli's trait, and hypoconulid) of fourteen traits differed significantly in the Kachemak and modern Koniag samples while two traits (winging and hypoconulid) showed significant differences in the prehistoric Koniag and modern Koniag samples.

In a comparison of crown trait frequencies in the prehistoric Koniag, living Koniag, and European samples (Table 7.3), five of the 12 traits observed placed the living Koniag sample in an intermediate position between the other two. This position was predicted by European admixture, if indeed the prehistoric Koniag are ancestral to the modern island population. In four traits (shoveling, hypoconulid, cusp 6, and protostylid) the frequencies in the modern Koniag sample were depressed in the direction of the European sample while in the other case (cusp 7) the frequency was slightly elevated in the direction of the European group. Of the seven remaining traits, three (winging, hypocone, and cusp 5) showed little variation among the three samples, suggesting that sampling error could explain the lack of intermediacy, and two (canine tubercle and Carabelli's trait) were similar in the prehistoric and living Koniag samples, with the European sample as an outlier. The last two traits (lower premolar multiple lingual cusps and the deflecting wrinkle) have much lower and higher frequencies, respectively, than would be expected given a high level of European admixture.

The relationships between the Kodiak Island populations and those from a broader geographical area were also assessed. Crown trait frequencies from six Kodiak Island samples (three prehistoric and three modern) and seven prehistoric and protohistoric

G. Richard Scott

Table 7.1. Crown Trait Frequencies for Four Modern Koniag Samples (Total frequencies except where noted by breakpoints; sample sizes in parentheses)

Trait	Village				Total	X^{2a}	Prob.
	Old Harbor	Akhiok	Karluk	Kaguyak			
Winging UI1	.238	.171	.146	.000	.189	1.86	NS[b]
	(105)	(41)	(41)	(14)	(201)		
Shoveling UI1						0.26	NS
(2–7)	.843	.844	.907	.786	.852		
(3–7)	.444	.444	.488	.571	.462		
	(108)	(45)	(43)	(14)	(210)		
Canine tubercle UC	.455	.633	.417	.555	.492	3.57	NS
	(55)	(30)	(36)	(9)	(130)		
Tuberculated premolars	.029	.018	.069	.098	.044		
	(204)	(110)	(116)	(51)	(481)		
Carabelli's trait UM1						3.13	NS
(1–7)	.590	.457	.575	.389	.539		
(2–7)	.390	.261	.350	.111	.328		
	(100)	(46)	(40)	(18)	(204)		
Hypocone UM1						0.97	NS
(2–5)	.698	.600	.609	.571	.643		
	(53)	(25)	(23)	(14)	(115)		
Bifurcated hypocone UM2	.219	.238	.143	.000	.189	0.47	NS
	(32)	(21)	(14)	(7)	(74)		
Cusp 5 UM1	.156	.177	.222	.000	.156	1.50	NS
	(77)	(28)	(27)	(15)	(147)		
Multiple lingual cusps LP2						1.97	NS
(2–7)	.309	.314	.195	.227	.271		
	(68)	(35)	(41)	(22)	(166)		
Hypoconulid (5-cusped LM2)	.667	.600	.667	.571	.639	0.29	NS
	(42)	(20)	(21)	(14)	(97)		
Cusp 6 LM1	.313	.226	.421	.308	.307	2.16	NS
	(64)	(31)	(19)	(13)	(127)		
Cusp 7 LM1 total	.188	.139	.083	.286	.168	1.58	NS
(minus 1A)	.043	.028	.000	.000	.028		
	(69)	(36)	(24)	(14)	(143)		
Protostylid LM1	.246	.229	.080	.077	.197	3.18	NS
	(69)	(36)	(25)	(13)	(142)		
Deflecting wrinkle LM1	.657	.619	.462	.714	.618	1.52	NS
	(35)	(21)	(13)	(7)	(76)		

[a] Chi-square values were computed for three large samples (Kaguyak was not included so d.f. equals 2). Chi-square values were not calculated for tuberculated premolars, which are based on total tooth count for all upper and lower premolars.
[b] Not significant.

Table 7.2. Comparison of Crown Trait Frequencies between Kachemak, Prehistoric Koniag, and Living Koniag Samples (Sample sizes in parentheses)

Trait	Kachemak	Prehistoric Koniag	Modern Koniag	X^2 Kachemak-Prehistoric Koniag	Prob.	X^2 Prehistoric Koniag-Modern Koniag	Prob.
Winging UI1	.125 (136)	.063 (64)	.189 (201)	2.44	NS[a]	5.76	<.05
Shoveling UI1							
(2–7)	.885	.926	.852	4.98	<.05	0.33	NS
(3–7)	.635 (52)	.519 (27)	.462 (210)				
Canine tubercle UC	.614 (70)	.545 (44)	.492 (130)	2.77	NS	0.35	NS
Tuberculated premolars (all)	.031 (314)	.025 (157)	.053 (481)	0.68	NS	1.08	NS
Carabelli's trait UM1							
(1–7)	.362	.667	.539	5.62	<.05	0.27	NS
(2–7)	.169 (59)	.394 (33)	.328 (204)				
Hypocone UM2							
(2–5)	.667 (96)	.725 (51)	.643 (115)	0.68	NS	2.41	NS
Bifurcated hypocone UM2	.187 (75)	.238 (42)	.189 (74)	0.002	NS	0.38	NS
Cusp 5 UM1	.170 (53)	.132 (38)	.156 (147)	0.05	NS	0.38	NS
Multiple lingual cusps LP2 (2–7)	.266 (79)	.395 (38)	.271 (166)	0.008	NS	2.25	NS
Hypoconulid (5-cusped LM2)	.865 (89)	.826 (46)	.639 (97)	12.58	<.01	5.13	<.05
Cusp 6 LM1	.393 (84)	.368 (38)	.307 (127)	1.63	NS	0.51	NS
Cusp 7 LM1							
(1A–5)	.178	.182	.168	1.23	NS	0.05	NS
(1–5)	.056 (107)	.023 (44)	.028 (143)				
Protostylid LM1							
(2–6)	1.78 (73)	.286 (35)	.197 (142)	0.11	NS	1.32	NS
Deflecting wrinkle LM1	.596 (52)	.444 (27)	.618 (76)	0.07	NS	2.51	NS

[a] Not significant.

Table 7.3. Comparison of Crown Trait Frequencies in Prehistoric Koniag, Living Koniag, and Europeans

Trait	Prehistoric Koniag	Living Koniag	European[a]	Living Koniag Intermediate[b]
Winging UI1	.063	.189	.103	N
Shoveling UI1 (3–7)	.926	.852	.046	Y
Canine tubercle UC	.545	.492	.720	N
Carabelli's trait UMI (2–7)	.375	.328	.503	N
Hypocone UM2	.765	.643	.732	N
Cusp 5 UM1	.132	.156	.130	N
Multiple lingual cusps LP2	.395	.271	.580	N
Hypoconulid LM2	.826	.639	.262	Y
Cusp 6 LM1	.368	.307	.076	Y
Cusp 7 LM1 (1–5)	.023	.028	.059	Y
Protostylid LM1	.286	.197	.131	Y
Deflecting wrinkle	.444	.618	.195	N

[a]Mean frequency for Europeans from Scott (1973), Turner (1984), and Turner and Markowitz (1990).

[b]European admixture on Kodiak Island results in living Koniag trait frequencies intermediate between prehistoric Koniag and Europeans.

northern populations were compared. With the exception of the St. Lawrence Island Eskimo sample, the data for the northern populations are based on the observations of Turner (1985).

Two points should be made about the symmetrical relationship matrix derived from this analysis (Table 7.4). The first is that, unlike most distance matrices, the Harpending and Jenkins (1973) method computes distance values that can be either positive or negative, with the highest positive value indicating greatest similarity and the highest negative value indicating greatest dissimilarity. The second is that the trace of the matrix (the values in the matrix diagonal)

shows the degree of divergence of each group from the mean trait frequencies (i.e., estimate of common ancestral frequencies) of all other groups in the sample array. The highest trace value indicates the greatest divergence and the smallest trace value shows the least average divergence from a presumed common ancestor.

With a focus on the modern (Old Harbor, Akhiok, and Karluk) and prehistoric (Uyak blue, red, and black) Kodiak Island samples in the matrix, the following conclusions can be drawn: (1) the modern Koniag samples are more similar to one another than to any of the prehistoric samples; (2) of the three prehis-

Table 7.4. Symmetrical Relationship Matrix Based on 10 Crown Traits Showing Distance Values between Living Koniag, Kachemak (Uyak Blue and Red), Prehistoric Koniag (Uyak Black), and Other Prehistoric Northern Populations (Samples 7–12 from Turner 1985)

	(1)	(2)	(3)	(4)	(5)	(6)	(7)	(8)	(9)	(10)	(11)	(12)	(13)
(1) Old Harbor	**70**	75	54	−6	−5	28	−40	−20	−36	−46	−47	−27	0
(2) Akhiok	75	**104**	72	−6	13	29	−40	−10	−51	−64	−70	−41	−9
(3) Karluk	54	72	**88**	−6	13	36	−41	−24	−46	−55	−54	−45	8
(4) Uyak Blue	−6	−6	−6	**26**	−3	16	−12	4	7	−2	−5	−3	−11
(5) Uyak Red	−5	13	13	−3	**32**	−3	25	5	−15	−29	−23	−24	14
(6) Uyak Black	28	29	36	16	−3	**50**	−26	−37	−15	−22	−28	−32	4
(7) Eskimo	−40	−40	−41	−12	25	−26	**74**	1	6	13	19	−4	24
(8) Aleut	−20	−10	−24	4	5	−37	1	**50**	11	2	3	26	−12
(9) N. Maritime	−36	−51	−46	7	−15	−15	6	11	**38**	45	45	30	−19
(10) C. Maritime	−46	−64	−55	−2	−29	−22	13	2	45	**88**	78	40	−48
(11) Gulf of Georgia	−47	−70	−54	−5	−23	−28	19	3	45	78	**82**	38	−39
(12) Athapaskan	−27	−41	−45	−3	−24	−32	−4	26	30	40	38	**51**	−8
(13) St. Lawrence I.	0	−9	8	−11	14	4	24	−12	−19	−48	−39	−8	**93**

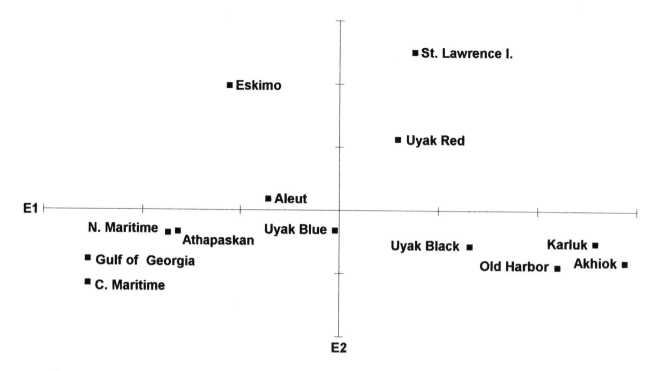

Figure 7.1. Plot of first two eigenvectors based on dental morphological variation showing relative relationships of three living and three prehistoric Kodiak Island samples to other native North American populations. (Illustration by G. Richard Scott)

toric samples, Uyak black is most similar to the modern Koniag series; (3) while Uyak red shows positive values relative to two living Koniag samples, Uyak blue shows identical negative values vis-à-vis all three modern Koniag groups; (4) Uyak blue is most similar to Uyak black, but it also shows positive values with Northern Maritime and Aleut groups; at the same time, Uyak red is most similar to Eskimos, St. Lawrence Islanders, and two living Koniag groups. Additionally, Uyak blue generally shows a closer similarity to Northwest Coast Indians than to Eskimos while Uyak red and black shows more similarity to Eskimos and living Koniag groups than to Northwest Coast Indians. The matrix trace shows that the Akhiok and St. Lawrence Island Eskimo samples are the most highly divergent in this array while the Uyak blue and red samples are the least divergent. Uyak blue, which has small positive and negative distance values relative to Eskimos, Aleuts, and Northwest Coast Indians, most closely approximates a hypothetical common ancestor for the groups in this array. The relationships between the groups are illustrated in fig. 7.1. The first two eigenvectors, which account for 69.4 percent of the total variance, were plotted to provide a two-dimensional representation of these relative distance values (see Harpending and Jenkins 1973 for more information about the statistical method used here).

Discussion

The question of population continuity on Kodiak Island has been hotly debated by archaeologists and physical anthropologists since the time Hrdlička unearthed the Uyak skeletal collection. Basing his conclusions primarily on craniometric data and general skull morphology, Hrdlička (1944) argued that the Pre-Koniag were distinctly different from, and not ancestral to, either the prehistoric or modern Koniag. Most subsequent craniometric analyses (Brennan and Howells, n.d.; Utermohle and Merbs, 1979; Utermohle 1984, 1988), using more sophisticated measures of biological distance, generally supported Hrdlička's claim of a lack of continuity between the Pre-Koniag and Koniag. Interestingly, these analyses generally found the Pre-Koniag to be more similar to southwest Alaskan Eskimos and the Koniag more similar to Aleuts and/or Northwest Coast Indians (Brennan and Howells, n.d.; Utermohle 1988; Heathcote 1986; Zegura 1978).

In contrast to the results from craniometric analyses, studies of nonmetric cranial traits, crown and root traits, and post-cranial measurements suggest there was continuity between the Pre-Koniag and Koniag (Ossenberg 1989; Turner 1988; Scott 1991, 1992). In terms of external relationships, Ossenberg

G. Richard Scott

(1989) believes that the three prehistoric Kodiak Island samples are closely related to southwest Alaskan Eskimo populations. Using dental evidence, Turner (1988) suggests a link between Kodiak Island and Northwest Coast Indian population, although in one analysis he finds the lowest mean measures of divergence for a combined Kodiak sample are with Point Barrow and Point Hope Eskimos. Although the early Kodiak Island sample shows some ties to the Northwest Coast, my previous assessment of dental morphological data led me to conclude that both the Pre-Koniag and prehistoric Koniag samples fell largely within the Eskimo-Aleut biological sphere (Scott 1991, 1992).

Despite a relatively high level of European gene flow on Kodiak Island (Denniston 1966), the genetic distance analysis shows that the modern Koniag are most similar to Yupik Eskimo and Aleut groups and, furthermore, that all three groups are about equally distant from living Na-Dene speaking populations in Alaska and Canada (Scott 1991). In addition, European admixture, while evident in the dental traits, does not obscure the relationship between the prehistoric Koniag (Uyak black) and the modern Koniag as I had originally surmised (Scott 1991). Although the earlier populations of Kodiak Island (Uyak blue and red) had some cosmopolitan elements, particularly from the Aleutians and Northwest Coast, the prehistoric Koniag show more definitive ties to the living inhabitants of the island.

Despite the influx of disparate groups—both Native American and European—to Kodiak Island over the past two millennia, dental morphological data support the position that the population history of the island is best characterized by biological continuity over this time span. This conclusion does not, however, contradict the archaeologically derived model of Dumond (1991), which proposes a significant migratory influx of peoples from the Alaska Peninsula to Kodiak shortly after A.D. 1000. It should be emphasized that almost all researchers (Hrdlička excluded), using different types of evidence, have concluded that the Pre-Koniag skeletons at the Uyak site were related most closely to southwest Alaskan Eskimos (presumed Yupik speakers). It is the external affinities of the Koniag sample from Uyak, not the Pre-Koniag, that has generated a number of different interpretations. If cranial deformation among the Koniag (essentially absent in the Pre-Koniag) has affected patterns of relationship derived through craniometry (Scott 1991, 1992) and if the results of analyses of dental and nonmetric cranial traits are correct, one can suggest that a migration from the Alaska Peninsula during Koniag times would involve elements not that distantly removed, temporally, spatially, and genetically, from the Pre-Koniag themselves.

If the Norse in Greenland had survived for 1,000 years in isolation and if Greenland had just been resettled by modern Norwegians, one would find it difficult to detect, using skeletal and dental data, the new wave of Norwegian migration to the island. On the other hand, the cultural and linguistic differences that had accumulated over the past millennium would likely be very evident. This may explain in part why archaeologists, linguists, and physical anthropologists, who focus on variables that change at significantly different rates, have failed to reach full agreement on Kodiak Island's population history from the past 2,000 years. If the Kachemak and Koniag peoples were both derived from a southwest Alaskan "proto-Yupik" Eskimo population, their common ancestry might obscure their separate migrations to the island. Thus, the interpretation of biological continuity should be viewed in a broad, rather than in a narrow, sense.

Acknowledgments

I extend my gratitude to Albert A. Dahlberg and Christy G. Turner II who made possible my observations on the large collection of living Koniag dental casts. My earlier work on the Uyak skeletal collection was facilitated through the kind offices of Donald Ortner, Department of Anthropology, Smithsonian Institution.

References Cited

Brennan, M. J., and W. W. Howells
n.d.   A Craniometric and Linguistic Grouping of Selected North American and Asian Peoples. Unpublished manuscript, Department of Anthropology, Peabody Museum, Harvard University.

Dahlberg, A. A.
1962   Preliminary Report of the Dentition Study of Two Isolates of Kodiak Island. *Arctic Anthropology* 1:115–16.
1963   Analysis of the American Indian Dentition. In *Dental Anthropology*, D. R. Brothwell, ed., pp. 149–77. New York: Pergamon Press.

Denniston, C.
1966   The Blood Groups of Three Konyag Isolates. *Arctic Anthropology* 3:195–205.

Dumond, D. E.
1991   The Uyak Site in Regional Prehistory: The Cultural Evidence. In *The Uyak Site on Kodiak Island: Its Place in Alaskan Prehistory*. University of Oregon Anthropological Papers No. 44, Eugene.

Harpending, H. C., and T. Jenkins
1973   Genetic Distance among Southern African Populations. In *Methods and Theories in Anthropological Genetics*, M. H. Crawford and P. L. Workman, eds.,

pp. 177–99. Albuquerque: University of New Mexico Press.

Heathcote, G. M.
1986   *Exploratory Human Craniometry of Recent Eskaleutian Regional Groups from the Western Arctic and Subarctic of North America.* BAR International Series 301, Oxford.

Hrdlička, A.
1944   *The Anthropology of Kodiak Island.* Philadelphia: Wistar Institute.

Majumder, P. P., W. S. Laughlin, and R. E. Ferrell
1988   Genetic Variation in the Aleuts of the Pribilof Islands and the Eskimos of Kodiak Island. *American Journal of Physical Anthropology* 76:481–88.

Nichol, C. R.
1984   Genetic Analysis of Metric and Nonmetric Dental Variation in Living Kodiak Island Eskimos. *American Journal of Physical Anthropology* 63:198–99 (abstract).

Nichol, C. R., and C. G. Turner
1986   Intra- and Interobserver Concordance in Classifying Dental Morphology. *American Journal of Physical Anthropology* 69:299–315.

Ossenberg, N. S.
1989   Nonmetric Traits of the Skull Reveal Affinities between People of Northeast Asia and Northwest North America. Paper presented at the Circum-Pacific Prehistory Conference, Seattle.

Scott, G. R.
1973   Dental Morphology: A Genetic Study of American White Families and Variation in Living Southwest Indians. Unpublished Ph.D. dissertation, Department of Anthropology, Arizona State University, Tempe.
1991   Continuity or Replacement at the Uyak Site: A Physical Anthropological Analysis of Population Relationships. In *The Uyak Site on Kodiak Island: Its Place in Alaskan Prehistory.* University of Oregon Anthropological Papers No. 44, Eugene.
1992   Affinities of Prehistoric and Modern Kodiak Islanders and the Question of Kachemak-Koniag Biological Continuity. *Arctic Anthropology* 29:150–66.

Turner, C. G.
1967   Dental Genetics and Microevolution in Prehistoric and Living Koniag Eskimo. *Journal of Dental Research* 46 (part 1):911–17.
1969   Microevolutionary Interpretations from the Dentition. *American Journal of Physical Anthropology* 30:421–26.

1984   Advances in the Dental Search for Native American Origins. *Anthropogenetica* 8:23–78.
1985   Dental Evidence for the Peopling of the Americas. *National Geographic Society Research Reports* 19:573–96.
1988   A New View of Alaskan Population Structure at about Historic Contact. In *The Late Prehistoric Development of Alaska's Native Peoples,* R. D. Shaw, R. K. Harritt, and D. E. Dumond, eds., pp. 27–36. Aurora: Alaska Anthropological Association Monograph Series 4.

Turner C. G., and M. A. Markowitz
1990   Dental Discontinuity between Late Pleistocene and Recent Nubians. Peopling of the Eurafrican-South Asian Triangle I. *Homo* 41:32–41.

Turner C. G., C. R. Nichol, and G. R. Scott
1991   The Arizona State University Dental Anthropology System: Scoring Procedures for Key Morphological Traits of the Permanent Dentition. In *Advances in Dental Anthropology,* M. A. Kelley and C. S. Larsen, eds., pp. 13–31. New York: Alan R. Liss.

Utermohle, C. J.
1984   From Barrow Eastward: Cranial Variation of the Eastern Eskimo. Unpublished Ph.D. dissertation, Department of Anthropology, Arizona State University, Tempe.
1988   The Origin of the Inupiat: The Position of the Birnirk Culture in Eskimo Prehistory. In *The Late Prehistoric Development of Alaska's Native People,* R. D. Shaw, R. K. Harritt, and D. E. Dumond, eds., pp. 37–46. Aurora: Alaska Anthropological Association Monograph No. 4.

Utermohle, C. J., and C. F. Merbs
1979   Population Affinities of Thule Culture Eskimos in Northwest Hudson Bay. In *Thule Eskimo Culture: An Anthropological Retrospective,* A. P. McCartney, ed. pp. 435–77. National Museum of Man Mercury Series, Archaeological Survey of Canada Papers No. 88.

Zegura, S. L.
1978   The Eskimo Population System: Linguistic Framework and Skeletal Remains. In *Eskimos of Northwestern Alaska,* P. L. Jamison, S. L. Zegura, and F. A. Milan, eds., pp. 8–30. Stroudsburg: Dowden, Hutchinson and Ross.

8

CANNIBALISM OR COMPLEX MORTUARY BEHAVIOR?

An Analysis of Patterned Variability in the Treatment
of Human Remains from the Kachemak Tradition
of Kodiak Island

Over the past 60 years the Uyak site has figured centrally in three major anthropological debates in the Gulf of Alaska: the origins and cultural evolution of the Pacific Eskimo; the social context of prehistoric mortuary practices; and, most recently, the rights of indigenous people to participate in decisions regarding the collection and curation of human remains. To a large extent these issues have grown out of the conspicuous quantities of human skeletal material collected from the Uyak site by Aleš Hrdlička (1944) and the questionable methods by which they were removed.

Although subsequent investigators have recognized the inadequacies of Hrdlička's field methods (de Laguna 1956:260; Heizer 1956; Clark 1974:170; Jordan and Knecht 1988:226), his skeletal collections and interpretations continue to figure prominently in evaluations of culture history and population biology. In part, this reflects the fact that the Uyak skeletal collection was one of the largest and best-preserved samples of human remains from Alaska. It also reflects the centrality of the Uyak site in the debate over the development of Koniag culture.

Fortunately, through the combined efforts of other researchers (de Laguna 1934; Heizer 1956; Clark 1966, 1970; Lobdell 1980; Yesner 1989; Simon 1992; Steffian in press), additional data have been collected so that human skeletal remains can be evaluated independently of Hrdlička's confusing collections. Although these assemblages are significantly smaller

than the Uyak collection, they provide solid empirical data with which to reexamine many earlier questions.

This chapter focuses on the social context of prehistoric mortuary practices during the Kachemak tradition on Kodiak Island. Based on the analysis of human skeletal material recovered during recent excavations, it examines variability in the treatment of human remains and addresses the long-standing idea that social violence and cannibalism were prevalent features of prehistoric life on Kodiak Island.

Violence and Cannibalism in the Kachemak Tradition

Anthropologists studying the Kachemak tradition have repeatedly noted the diverse treatment of human remains (de Laguna 1934; Heizer 1956; Clark 1970; Lobdell 1980; Jordan 1988; Jordan and Knecht 1988). Kachemak assemblages are characterized by mass burials, partial skeletons, articulated skeletal segments, isolated skeletal elements, and human bone exhibiting perimortem breakage, burning, and cultural modification. The presence of many of these characteristics in the Uyak assemblage led Hrdlička to believe that the Pre-Koniag practiced cannibalism. Since then, anthropologists have continued to interpret scattered and damaged human bone as evidence of violence and cannibalism. Unfortunately, these arguments contain little description, quantification, or critical evaluation of the distribution of these characteristics within skeletal assemblages. Furthermore, few researchers have considered the archaeological context or taphonomic history of human remains before concluding that violence and cannibalism occurred.

In part, perpetuation of the violence and cannibalism arguments reflect Hrdlička's profound and enduring influence on Kodiak anthropology. In a recent book on cannibalism, White (1992) points out that expectations of such behaviors as cannibalism often steer interpretations of archaeological data. He suggests that when ethnographic data on cannibalism exist, there is a tendency to interpret damaged human bone as evidence of cannibalism (White 1992:19). Although there is no ethnographic evidence of institutionalized cannibalism in south-central Alaska, we believe that expectations of this behavior persist as a result of Hrdlička's emphatic and widely published identification of cannibalism at the Uyak site (see Anonymous 1932a, 1932b; Hrdlička 1941a, 1941b, 1944). Similarly, widespread ethnographic documentation of intergroup violence and warfare in the North Pacific may also have strongly influenced interpretations of archaeological data (Moss and Erlandson 1992:74).

In short, the criteria used to identify these behaviors are often ambiguous, circumstantial, and rooted in cultural biases. Despite the limited analyses of Kachemak skeletal assemblages as well as the long-standing debate over the material correlates of cannibalism and the highly controversial nature of such studies, Hrdlička's claims and subsequent identifications of cannibalism have only recently come under close scrutiny (White 1992:26–27; Workman 1992; Simon 1992).

We argue that cannibalism and violence alone cannot account for the full range of behaviors associated with the Kachemak mortuary complex (see also de Laguna 1934; Clark 1970) and, furthermore, that a focus on patterned variability in the treatment of human remains is more informative in understanding prehistoric culture than the simple presence or absence of cannibalism.[1] Pattern recognition studies can provide insight into past behaviors. For example, cultural modifications evident on human bone (e.g., cutmarks) record the alterations and manipulative activities performed on bodily remains. Likewise, other types of archaeologically visible evidence, such as disposal location, type of disposal, type of mortuary facility, number of individuals in a disposal receptacle, and the quantity, quality, and source of grave furnishings, all record information on an individual's social persona (Saxe 1970:7; O'Shea 1984:36, 39–41). By identifying how different classes of mortuary data covary and by combining this information with other

sets of archaeological data, we can begin to formulate hypotheses about the social context of human remains.

Kachemak Tradition at the Crag Point and Uyak Sites

The assemblages of human skeletal material examined in this study date to the Late Kachemak tradition of Kodiak Island. Cultural materials associated with this tradition are found throughout lower Cook Inlet and the Kodiak Archipelago. They date to the first millennium A.D. (Clark 1984:139) and precede the more complexly organized Koniag tradition recorded at historic contact. Archaeologically, the Late Kachemak is characterized by numerous village sites with clusters of single-roomed semisubterranean structures within thick accumulations of midden (Jordan and Knecht 1988). Artifacts and faunal remains recovered from the middens indicate a subsistence focus on marine resources, accompanied by the use of mass capture technologies (e.g., nets) and storage. The Kachemak tradition is also characterized by the widespread use of items for personal adornment, the production of elaborate artwork, and the diverse treatment of human remains (de Laguna 1934; Clark 1984:139; Workman 1980).

The skeletal materials included in this study were recently excavated from undisturbed portions of the Crag Point and Uyak sites as part of the Kodiak Archaeological Project (Jordan and Knecht 1988). Although these sites reflect spatially, temporally, and, perhaps, functionally distinct occupations within the Kachemak tradition, there are similarities in the treatment of human remains between the two assemblages.

Crag Point Site

The Crag Point site (KOD-044; also referred to as No. 241) is located at the mouth of Anton Larsen Bay on northeastern Kodiak Island (see frontispiece). The site is in a cove sheltered by Crag Point to the northwest and many small offshore islands. These landforms protect the site from stormy weather associated with Kodiak's maritime climate but they also obstruct the view of surrounding areas. Kizhuyak Bay to the west and most of Anton Larsen Bay are not visible from the cove. At Crag Point, cultural materials are deposited on either side of a freshwater creek behind a gently sloping beach. When they were first investigated, these deposits covered an area of more than 2100 m² and were up to 2 m deep (Clark 1970:74). Tectonic activity and erosion have impacted the site, however. The abundance of artifacts and faunal remains on the beach front suggests that it was once substantially larger.

James J. K. Simon and Amy F. Steffian

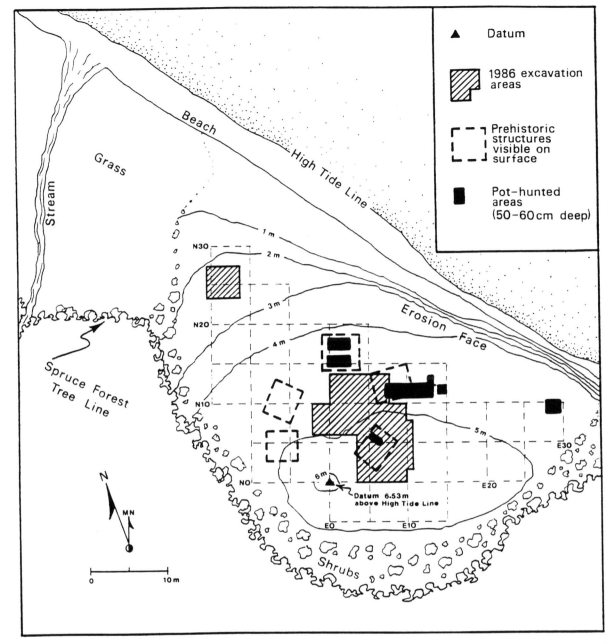

Legend:
- ▲ Datum
- 1986 excavation areas
- Prehistoric structures visible on surface
- ■ Pot-hunted areas (50-60 cm deep)

Figure 8.1. Crag Point site map. (All illustrations in this chapter were prepared by James J. K. Simon and Amy F. Steffian)

Archaeological investigations at Crag Point began in 1964 when Clark and Workman excavated a trench along the site's erosion face (Clark 1970). Additional fieldwork was conducted in 1986 (Jordan and Knecht 1988) when more than 138 m³ of deposits were excavated from the center of the site (fig. 8.1). Both the 1964 and 1986 excavations revealed a complex arrangement of structures, artifacts, and human skeletal remains surrounded by thick accumulations of shell midden. At least eight structures have been identified at Crag Point and more than 3,600 artifacts

collected. Together, the assemblages document a long history of occupation. Most of the cultural material dates to the Late Kachemak tradition, although there is also evidence of earlier and later occupations (Clark 1970; Jordan in press). The 1-sigma range of five calibrated radiocarbon dates on wood and charcoal samples from two of the site's house floors place the Kachemak occupation between 733 and 2701 B.P. (Mills 1992; Erlandson et al. 1992:table 1).

Unfortunately, limited archaeological research in Anton Larsen Bay and adjacent Kizhuyak Bay makes it difficult to place Crag Point within a local subsistence and settlement system. The presence of permanent structures and large deposits of faunal material suggests that the site was occupied repeatedly. Although the length and season of occupation are unknown, the artifact assemblages provide some clues to site function. While they include a wide range of hunting and fishing equipment, utilitarian tools, and items of personal adornment, they are dominated by net sinkers and fishing equipment. It appears that the site may have functioned as a base for specialized fishing or hunting activities. Whatever their function, smaller sites like Crag Point are distinct from larger, more prominently located sites like the Uyak site (e.g., Erlandson et al. 1992).

Uyak Site

The Uyak site (KOD-145) is located in the modern village of Larsen Bay on the southwestern coast of Kodiak Island. Cultural materials are deposited on and adjacent to a rocky point at the entrance to Larsen Bay. This point, and gently sloping beaches on either side, overlook larger Uyak Bay (fig. 8.2). On a clear day the Alaska Peninsula is visible to the northwest, some 45 km across Shelikof Strait. In comparison to Crag Point, the Uyak site is large; when Hrdlička (1944:141) began his investigations, the site covered more than 3.24 ha. Today, cultural deposits run 300 m along the shore and in places extend more than 80 m inland.

Although Hrdlička's excavation was one of the largest in Alaska, he left a substantial portion of the Uyak site unexcavated (Crowell 1986). During the summers of 1987 and 1988, a new excavation was undertaken in the eastern area of the site in order to study Kachemak economic and social organization at the village level (Steffian in press). More than 4,400 artifacts were recovered and 16 structures were identified from an estimated 401 m³ of excavation. The excavation revealed a cluster of single-roomed houses, storage structures, burials, and other features that are roughly contemporaneous. Like Crag Point, these features were surrounded by a dense deposit of shell midden. The history of site formation as preserved in the site's stratigraphy, an analysis of the artifact assemblage, and the results of radiocarbon dating indicate that the eastern area of the site was part of a sizable Kachemak village, occupied at least semipermanently over several hundred years. The 1-sigma range of five corrected radiocarbon dates on charcoal and wood samples from house floors place this occupation between 959 B.P. and 1306 B.P. (Mills 1992; Steffian in press).

The Uyak artifact assemblage suggests that a wide range of productive activities occurred at the site. Many hunting implements, utilitarian tools, and a large number of items for personal adornment were manufactured. In contrast with Crag Point, however, there was little evidence of fishing equipment. Instead, the Uyak assemblage is dominated by hunting equipment and chipped stone tools. In addition, it contains a large proportion of raw materials that are not locally available, and there is abundant evidence that these materials were worked into finished products at the site (Steffian 1992).

In the Uyak Bay region, the Uyak site is one of at least five large villages located at the entrances of smaller adjoining bays (Jordan and Knecht 1988). With their excellent views of the surrounding areas, these settlements provided their inhabitants with the ability to monitor the movements of both sea mammals and other people in Uyak Bay. The large sites consist of many structures and are distinct from the smaller and more secluded sites situated along inner bays (Crozier 1989). In the Uyak Bay region, there were at least 30 of these smaller sites, many of them located at the mouths of salmon streams. Although issues related to settlement seasonality are still being studied, it appears that the larger village sites, like the Uyak site, were used for winter population aggregation and that the smaller sites served as seasonal bases for the procurement of salmon and other resources (see Erlandson et al. 1992). Whatever the case, the location, size, structure, and contents (Fitzhugh 1992) of the Uyak site suggest that this village was occupied for a large part of the annual cycle.

Study of the Skeletal Material

Previous analyses of human skeletal collections from the Kachemak tradition have generally failed to quantify or describe the archaeological context of human remains, the cultural modification of human bone, and the composition of human skeletal assemblages in a manner suitable for intrasite and intersite comparison. In an attempt to avoid this problem, our study combines methods from physical anthropology, zooarchaeology, and taphonomy to produce a comprehensive and systematic review of the human skeletal data.

The study examines the social context of mortuary behavior by assessing the archaeological and taphonomic context of human bone, as well as the covarying relationships between biological characteristics, the distribution of cultural bone modification, and the type of disposal. This approach produces biological and archaeological data that, when integrated, are best described as mortuary data. Only when bio-

James J. K. Simon and Amy F. Steffian

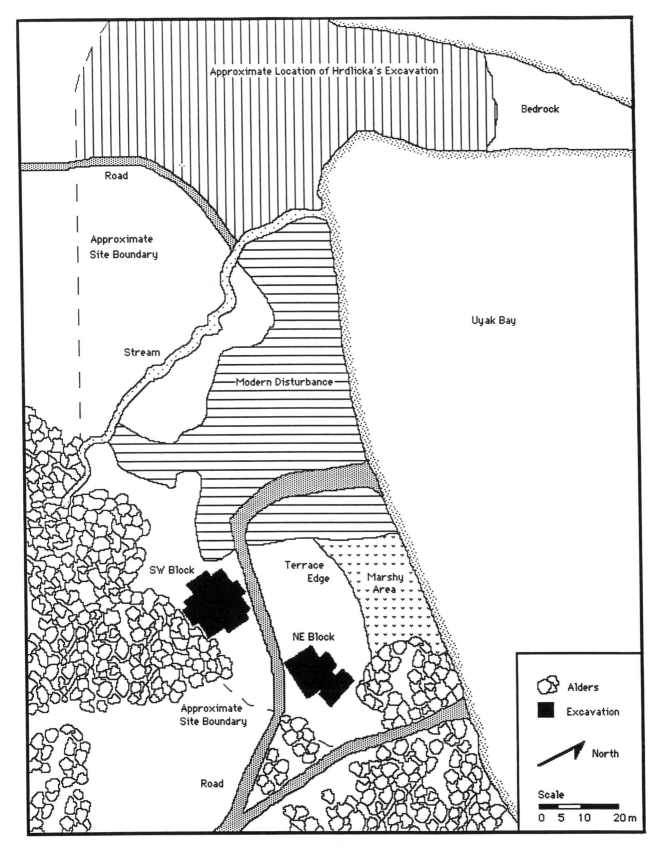

Figure 8.2. Uyak site map.

logical data are evaluated within an anthropological framework can the cultural context of the mortuary behavior be investigated.

Assemblage Composition

For this study, skeletal element identification and sex and age estimations were based on methods outlined in Todd (1920), Schour and Massler (1941), McKern and Stewart (1957), Johnston (1962), Phenice (1967), Gilbert and McKern (1973), Ubelaker (1978), Brothwell (1981), Merbs (1983), Lovejoy et al. (1985), and Bass (1987). A specimen was considered identifiable if it could be minimally assigned to an element category. These specimens are quantified as the number of identified specimens (NISP). Unidentified specimens were generally small unconjoined bone fragments resulting from post-depositional breakage. These are quantified as the number of unidentified specimens (NUSP). Nonhuman skeletal remains and a few specimens of questionable taxa were excluded from analysis.

Reports on Kachemak human skeletal material generally fail to present summaries of assemblage composition suitable for intrasite and intersite comparison. Instead, they present the number of individuals found in a site without an inventory of skeletal elements (but see Yesner 1989). To evaluate assemblage composition between archaeological contexts, skeletal element representation must be quantified and standardized so that comparisons are possible. This is particularly important for Kachemak sites where burials commonly lack skeletal elements and human bones are frequently scattered. In these circumstances, the minimum number of individuals (MNI) provides an inaccurate representation of skeletal abundance. Although the human body is frequently used as the unit of analysis in mortuary studies, it is important to account for missing bones and to quantify the proportion of each element. The archaeological context of Kachemak human remains suggests that anatomical parts may be a more significant cultural unit than the entire body. This approach is similar to that taken in faunal analysis, which focuses on body part rather than on whole individual due to economic considerations (e.g., Binford 1978, 1984).

In this study, the human skeletal assemblages from Uyak and Crag Point are summarized using the standardized minimum number of elements (SMNE), a modified version of Binford's (1984) minimal animal units (MAU). SMNE only portrays the proportion of various bones in an assemblage and does not consider the effects of "riders" or economic utility as in faunal analyses (e.g., Metcalfe and Jones 1988). The first step

in producing SMNE values is to outline standard anatomical or bone categories (e.g., radius, femur, mandible). The skeletal assemblage is then summarized by determining the minimum number of elements (MNE) needed to account for the total number of bones found in each category. These measurements are standardized by dividing MNE by the constant number of bones found in a living individual for each bone category (e.g., 1 mandible, 2 radii, 5 lumbar vertebrae). This produces a second column of measurements (SMNE), which indicates the minimum number of anatomical units needed to account for the assemblage. To compare human skeletal frequencies from different archaeological contexts (Schiffer 1987:3–4, 13), SMNE is determined separately for each burial or disposal unit, then standardized again to describe the proportion of each bone category in the skeletal subassemblage. This is accomplished by adding all values in the SMNE column to produce a Total SMNE, and then dividing each SMNE value by the Total SMNE and multiplying by 100 percent. This procedure is identical to that used in calculating %MAU in faunal studies (e.g., Bunn and Kroll 1986:434–35); %SMNE and %MAU are distinct analytical units, however. The %SMNEs are measurements that facilitate comparison between burials, types of burials, and site assemblages because they demonstrate the relative contribution of each bone category to the assemblage. To simplify comparison, %SMNE values are plotted in a graphic form to illustrate the differences between types of disposal.

The SMNE and %SMNE measurements are influenced by: (1) the proportion of an individual or individuals introduced into an archaeological context, which is directly related to treatment of the dead, (2) the effects of differential preservation and disturbance, and (3) the methods of archaeological sampling and recovery. Plotting %SMNE values from burials where any number of complete individuals were interred, preserved, and recovered results in a perfectly rectangular plot. In this analysis %SMNE values for the ideal situation are equal to 4.762 percent for each bone category. This ideal situation is the standard by which skeletal assemblage composition is evaluated for each type of disposal. Any %SMNE values that fall below 4.762 percent indicate that skeletal elements of a particular category are missing from a subassemblage. Values greater than 4.762 percent reflect bone categories that contribute a relatively greater proportion of skeletal elements to the overall subassemblage because other categories are lacking bones. Therefore, the crucial values to examine in investigations of assemblage composition are those that fall below the ideal example.[2]

James J. K. Simon and Amy F. Steffian

Identification of Bone Modification

To identify bone modification, each specimen was viewed under a stereomicroscope using harsh incandescent illumination (250 watts) and magnification powers ranging from 10X to 70X. Observations were made twice to insure consistent identification. To avoid interobserver error, bone modification discovered by laboratory assistants was classified by Simon.

Cutmarks and chopping marks were identified using methods outlined by Bunn (1981), Potts and Shipman (1981), and Shipman and Rose (1984). In general, cutmarks are characterized by elongated grooves with V-shaped cross-sections and by fine, parallel striations in the main groove (Potts and Shipman 1981:577). When distinct, elongated V-shaped grooves occur at the sites of major muscle attachment and, when different specimens exhibit similar grooves, it is likely that these grooves are cutmarks. During our investigation, however, parallel striations were rarely observed because of limited magnification. Chopping marks were characterized by grooves with V-shaped cross-sections, generally perpendicular to the axis of the bone and associated with small fragments of bone crushed inward at the bottom of the groove (Potts and Shipman 1981:577).

In this study, we distinguished between two classes of cutmarks: disarticulation cutmarks and defleshing or skinning cutmarks. Disarticulation cutmarks occurred on bone articulation surfaces and in adjacent areas where muscles, tendons, and ligaments were severed to separate bones. In contrast, defleshing cutmarks occurred at major muscle attachments or in places where they would have been used to remove tissue.

Three categories of fractures were used to describe broken bone within the skeletal assemblages: recent or postdepositional breakage, perimortem fracture, and fracture of indeterminate origin. The character of the broken surface relative to the external and internal bone surfaces is the best method of determining the time of fracture (Lyman and O'Brien 1987). Recent fractures are characterized by bone surfaces that have a different color, texture, and patina than the original unbroken bone surfaces (White 1992:133). In addition, recent bone damage lacks dirt or matrix on the broken surface, loose bone fragments are often present, and shaft fractures appear stepped or perpendicular (Shipman 1981:104–106).

Perimortem breakage is the alteration of fresh bone at or around the time of death (Turner 1983). Fresh bone fractures are oriented with the bone structure resulting in slender fragments that are almost always longer than they are wide. Perimortem breakage is characterized by smooth, fine-textured fracture surfaces that form acute and obtuse angles with the bone's outer cortical surface and long axis (see Johnson 1983 and references therein). Perimortem breakage was recorded during our study but, because it can result from either cultural, biological, or geological processes, it was considered ambiguous evidence of human activity in the absence of additional evidence.

Mortuary Data

Crag Point Assemblage

The assemblage of human remains from Crag Point contains 1,192 identified specimens (NISP) and 72 unidentified fragments (NUSP) from three distinct archaeological contexts: a multiple burial with the remains of at least five individuals found within a pile of slate slabs; a burial with incomplete but largely articulated remains of one individual found on the floor of the semisubterranean house; and 417 human bone fragments found scattered across the site. The burials and scattered remains are described in Simon 1992,[3] but the data are summarized here to facilitate a comparison between the Crag Point and Uyak sites.

CRAG POINT BURIAL A   The single burial of a young adult, probably male and between the ages of 21 and 35, was excavated from the northwest corner of a single-roomed semisubterranean house (Floor 3-B, fig. 8.3). A total of 129 identified remains were recovered (NUSP = 1), representing 10.8 percent of the total identified human skeletal assemblage at the site. The individual was lying directly on the house floor in a flexed position on the left hip with chest down and head turned to the right. No artifacts were associated with the grave.

Like many Kachemak burials, this interment was disturbed by subsequent digging, a common characteristic of Late Kachemak midden sites (Jordan and Knecht 1988). As a result, a variety of bones were removed or lost from the grave. The remains were well-preserved, suggesting that differential preservation cannot account for the missing elements. The posture of the skeleton indicates the area of disturbance coincided with the expected location of the missing elements. Table 8.1 and fig. 8.4 summarize the skeletal element composition of this burial and illustrate which elements are missing. In general, the plot is rectangular, which, when coupled with the articulated nature of the remains, suggests that one complete individual was interred. The bones show no signs of cultural or carnivore bone modification.

CRAG POINT BURIAL B   A slate-slab burial containing a minimum of five individuals was found below house

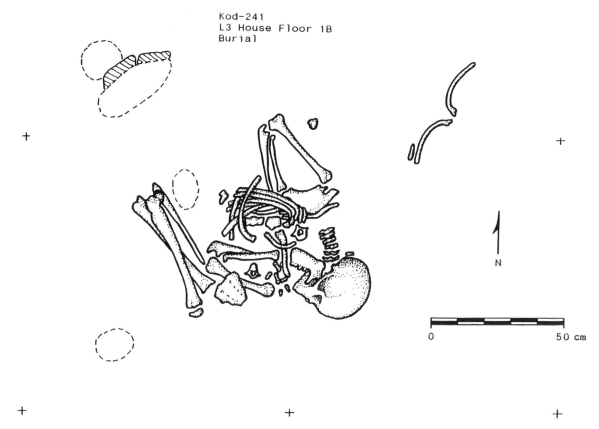

N

0   50 cm

Figure 8.3. Plan view of Crag Point Burial A: single interment.

floor 3-B, approximately 50 cm west of the single burial (fig. 8.5). A total of 687 identified remains (NUSP = 30) were recovered, representing 57.6 percent of the total identified Crag Point assemblage. It is not known whether this feature was associated with the adjacent house or whether it was contemporary with the occupation of the structure. The remains were both covered and partially underlain by slate slabs, suggesting a "cairn-like" mortuary feature. Most of the elements were disarticulated, although several groups of bones occurred as skeletal units (i.e., several lower arms, hands, and groups of vertebrae). No grave goods were found in this facility.

The burial contained a single child, one adult male, one adult female, and two adults of unknown sex. The child was between 2.5 and 3.5 years old at death based on dental development and long bone growth. The adult female was between 35 and 55 years old based on dental attrition and degenerative changes of the pelvis, and the adult male was from 18 to 21 years old based on pubic symphysis morphology. It was not possible to determine the sex of the two remaining adults.

The assemblage composition of the burial (Table 8.2 and fig. 8.4) suggests that complete individuals are not represented because various major skeletal elements are missing. Either complete individuals were not introduced into this feature or differential preservation, disturbance, and/or exhumation activities skewed the assemblage composition. Because of the irregular %SMNE plot and the disarticulated nature of the skeletal remains, we expected that some bones would exhibit modification; however, we found neither cultural nor carnivore bone modification.

Differential preservation is an unlikely explanation for the missing elements in the multiple burial. Small epiphyses from the child and small cancellous bones and thin bones (i.e., scapulae) from the adults were all well preserved (see Gordon and Buikstra 1981). Likewise, unintentional burial disturbance is an unlikely cause of the disarticulated and incomplete skeletons because the remains were covered and partially underlain by undisturbed stone slabs. Within this feature, the spatial organization of remains is patterned. The child's remains were restricted to one area of the feature (see fig. 8.5) in contrast to those of the four adults, which were more scattered. The most dispersed remains were those of two individuals found just below the concentrated remains of the child. It appears that, when the child was interred,

James J. K. Simon and Amy F. Steffian

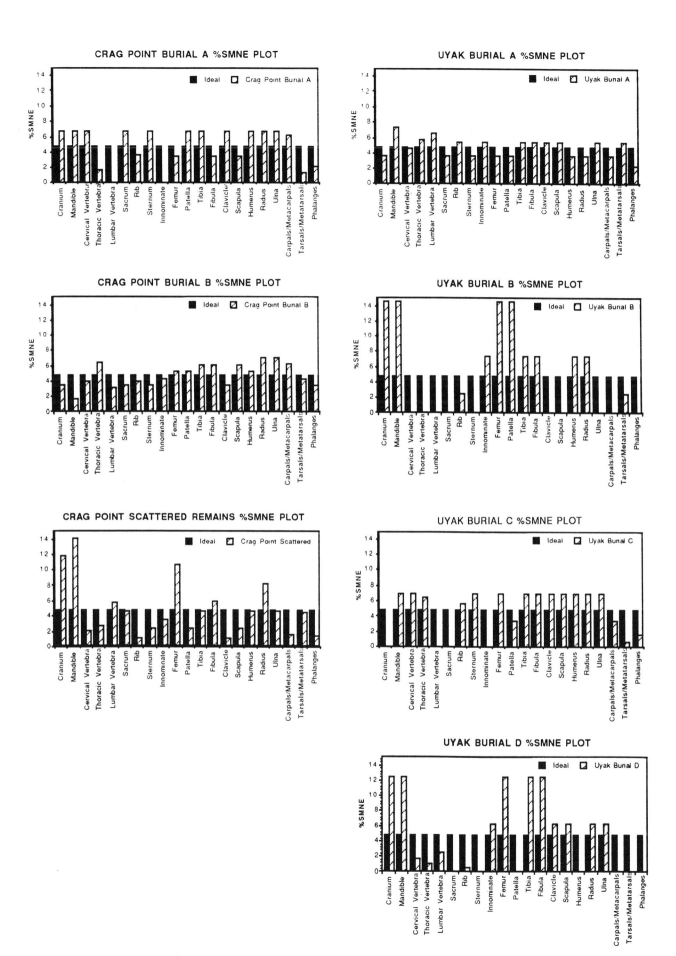

Figure 8.4. %SMNE plots for the Crag Point and Uyak human skeletal assemblages.

Table 8.1. Crag Point Burial A Assemblage Composition

Element	MNE	No. per individual	SMNE	%SMNE
Cranium	1	1	1.000	6.782
Mandible	1	1	1.000	6.782
Cervical Vertebra	7	7	1.000	6.782
Thoracic Vertebra	3	12	0.250	1.696
Lumbar Vertebra	0	5	0.000	0.000
Sacrum	1	1	1.000	6.782
Rib	13	24	0.542	3.676
Sternum	1	1	1.000	6.782
Innominate	0	2	0.000	0.000
Femur	1	2	0.500	3.391
Patella	2	2	1.000	6.782
Tibia	2	2	1.000	6.782
Fibula	1	2	0.500	3.391
Clavicle	2	2	1.000	6.782
Scapula	1	2	0.500	3.391
Humerus	2	2	1.000	6.782
Radius	2	2	1.000	6.782
Ulna	2	2	1.000	6.782
Carpals/ Metacarpals	24	26	0.923	6.260
Tarsals/ Metatarsals	5	24	0.208	1.411
Phalanges (Carpal and Tarsal)	18	56	0.321	2.177
Total SMNE			14.744	99.995

the underlying adult remains were disturbed. To the southwest were the more spatially discrete remains of two additional individuals. These remains were found in relatively more articulated postures, with partial and/or complete segments of arms, legs, hands, feet, ribs, and vertebrae present. Based on these observations, we suggest that the inhumation of remains occurred periodically and that this feature is a mortuary crypt.

CRAG POINT SCATTERED REMAINS   The third category of remains at Crag Point consists of human bones scattered throughout the deposits, both on house floors and in the surrounding midden. Isolated bones or skeletal units represent 31.5 percent (NISP = 376, NUSP = 41) of the total identified Crag Point assemblage. The origin of these scattered elements is unknown (but see Hrdlička 1944:227; de Laguna 1934:167; Lobdell 1980:35). This class of material, however, contains the remains of men, women, and children, as well as all major classes of skeletal material (Table 8.3). We assume that these scattered remains do not represent unidentified burials. As illus-

trated in fig. 8.4, the scattered materials represent partial individuals and are more variable in assemblage composition than either the single or multiple burials. But because the entire site was not excavated, it is impossible to determine whether the observed variability reflects archaeological sampling or actual assemblage composition. In addition, it is possible that some of the scattered material did, in fact, result from disturbed or unidentified burials.

Cultural bone modification was found exclusively on the scattered remains. This pattern suggests that the scattered bones did not result entirely from disturbed burials (de Laguna 1934; Hrdlička 1944:227), since the burials recovered from Crag Point contained no culturally modified bones. One would expect to find some cultural modification on the remains of individuals in burials if the scattered remains resulted from disturbed interments; conversely, there should be no cutmarks on the scattered material.

Cultural modification was identified on the remains of adult females and immature individuals of unknown sex (see also Hrdlička 1944:224, 248); however, sex estimations were not possible for many of the modified bones. Of the identified remains that exhibited cultural modification, 7.7 percent (n = 29) had cutmarks, chopping marks, or drilled holes.[4] This proportion did not include cutmarked human bone that was not identifiable to element (n = 9) and bones that exhibited only perimortem breakage (n = 6). If these are counted, however, culturally modified specimens increase to 11.4 percent (n = 44) of the total assemblage of scattered human bone (see Table 8.4). Thus, the proportion of culturally modified bones in the scattered human material ranges from a minimum of 7.7 percent to a maximum of 11.4 percent. It should be noted that carnivore modification was observed on only 14 specimens from the scattered remains, representing 3.7 percent of the identified scattered assemblage.

Two categories of culturally modified human bones were recognized at Crag Point: bones exhibiting cutmarks, chopping marks, and/or perimortem breakage, and bones used as cultural objects. Although perimortem breakage alone is considered an ambiguous criterion for identifying cultural modification in this study, several specimens also exhibited evidence of cutmarks (see Table 8.4), supporting the cultural origin of this breakage. The first category of cultural bone modification, when evaluated by anatomical location, is indicative of dismemberment, skinning, and defleshing (figs. 8.6, 8.7). In addition, instances of perimortem breakage suggest that both traumatic injury and bone processing (figs. 8.6B,C,D and 8.7C) may have occurred. These behaviors are difficult to evaluate within the context of other complex mortuary treatments inasmuch as bones may

James J. K. Simon and Amy F. Steffian

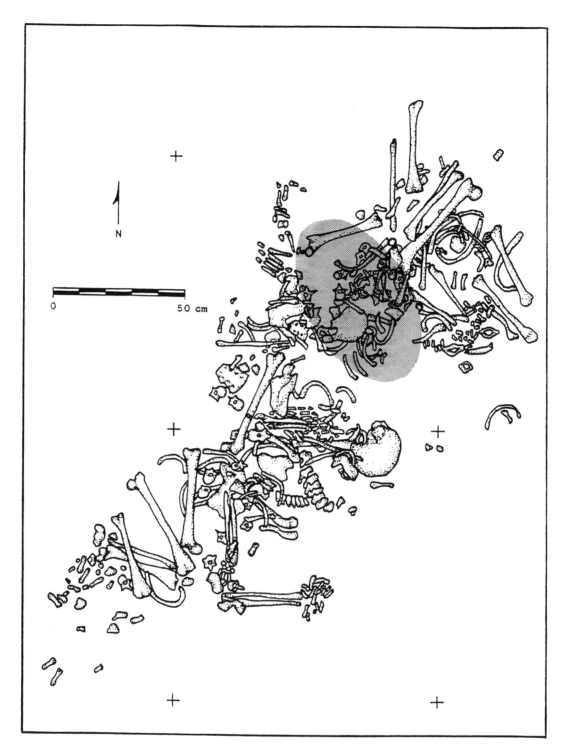

Figure 8.5. Plan view of Crag Point Burial B: mortuary crypt. The concentrated remains of the child are shown in the shaded area.

Table 8.2. Crag Point Burial B Assemblage Composition

Element	MNE	No. per individual	SMNE	%SMNE
Cranium	2	1	2.000	3.505
Mandible	1	1	1.000	1.752
Cervical Vertebra	16	7	2.286	4.006
Thoracic Vertebra	44	12	3.667	6.426
Lumbar Vertebra	9	5	1.800	3.154
Sacrum	2	1	2.000	3.505
Rib	56	24	2.333	4.089
Sternum	2	1	2.000	3.505
Innominate	5	2	2.500	4.381
Femur	6	2	3.000	5.257
Patella	6	2	3.000	5.257
Tibia	7	2	3.500	6.134
Fibula	7	2	3.500	6.134
Clavicle	4	2	2.000	3.505
Scapula	7	2	3.500	6.134
Humerus	6	2	3.000	5.257
Radius	8	2	4.000	7.010
Ulna	8	2	4.000	7.010
Carpals/ Metacarpals	93	26	3.577	6.269
Tarsals/ Metatarsals	58	24	2.417	4.236
Phalanges (Carpal and Tarsal)	111	56	1.982	3.473
Total SMNE			57.062	99.999

have been processed for ritual use. For example, ethnohistorical accounts record that the Koniag treated whaling gear with fluids derived from human corpses (Davydov in Holmberg 1985:49; Gideon 1989:60; Lisiansky 1814:174, 209). In summary, the currently available data do not support, or discount, the possibility that traumatic death occurred or that human bones were processed for consumption at Crag Point.

The second category, human bone artifacts, is represented by a single specimen. This type of cultural modification, however, is common in other Late Kachemak assemblages (see de Laguna 1934, Plate 47-15, 16; Hrdlička 1941a, Plate 2, 3, 8-2, 9, 10, 11-2; Urcid, this volume). The specimen from Crag Point consists of an innominate bone with a hole drilled just below the iliac crest (fig. 8.8), suggesting that the bone was to be tied to, or suspended from, some object (de Laguna 1934; Hrdlička 1944:227; Clark 1970, fig. 10; but see Urcid, this volume).

Uyak Assemblage

The assemblage of human remains from the recent excavations at the Uyak site consists of 546 identified specimens (NISP) and 48 unidentified fragments (NUSP) from five distinct archaeological contexts: three burials, one partial cremation, and scattered human remains.

UYAK BURIAL A   This burial was a disarticulated double interment containing the incomplete remains of two adult individuals: a female between the ages of 30 and 55 and a male between the ages of 16 and 21. This burial accounts for 57.5 percent of the total identifiable Uyak human skeletal assemblage (NISP = 314; NUSP = 8). Major skeletal elements were missing from both individuals in the interment (see fig. 8.4 and Table 8.5). Despite the absence of these elements, no cultural bone modification was observed. The absence of skeletal material, the partially articulated nature of the remaining elements, the absence of cutmarks, and the presence of maxillary teeth of the male despite the absence of his head suggest that this burial was disturbed following decomposition. It is unclear whether the interment of these two individuals was simultaneous or whether this facility represents a mortuary crypt where interment occurred periodically.

Table 8.3. Crag Point Scattered Assemblage Composition

Element	MNE	No. per individual	SMNE	%SMNE
Cranium	5	1	5.000	11.794
Mandible	6	1	6.000	14.153
Cervical Vertebra	6	7	0.857	2.022
Thoracic Vertebra	13	12	1.083	2.555
Lumbar Vertebra	12	5	2.400	5.661
Sacrum	2	1	2.000	4.718
Rib	10	24	0.417	0.983
Sternum	1	1	1.000	2.359
Innominate	3	2	1.500	3.538
Femur	9	2	4.500	10.614
Patella	2	2	1.000	2.359
Tibia	4	2	2.000	4.718
Fibula	5	2	2.500	5.897
Clavicle	1	2	0.500	1.179
Scapula	2	2	1.000	2.359
Humerus	4	2	2.000	4.718
Radius	7	2	3.500	8.256
Ulna	4	2	2.000	4.718
Carpals/ Metacarpals	18	26	0.692	1.633
Tarsals/ Metatarsals	45	24	1.875	4.423
Phalanges (Carpal and Tarsal)	32	56	0.571	1.348
Total SMNE			42.395	100.005

Table 8.4. Summary of Culturally Modified Human Remains from Crag Point

Type of modification	No. of specimens	% of scattered remains (NISP = 376)[a]
Cutmarks only	15	3.99
Cutmarks and chopping marks	2	0.53
Cutmarks and perimortem breakage	9	2.39
Drilled holes	1	0.27
Bones with perimortem breakage that conjoin with bones with cutmarks	1	0.27
Slices/shaving marks	1	0.27
Perimortem breakage only	6	1.60
Unidentified bones cutmarks only	6	1.56[b]
Unidentified bones cutmarks and perimortem breakage	1	0.26[b]
Unidentified bones perimortem breakage only	2	0.52[b]

[a] NISP = Number of Identified Specimens.
[b] Percentage of scattered remains for these classes of data were calculated by adding the unidentified specimens exhibiting cutmarks and/or perimortem breakage (n = 9) to the number of identified specimens (NISP = 376) to produce a divisor of n = 385.

No slate slabs were associated with the burial facility, but the remains of the individuals were placed in a conical pit dug into a depression caused by the collapse of structure 11, a single-roomed semisubterranean house (fig. 8.9). The facility was a large oval pit 150 cm long and 105 cm wide with its long axis oriented east-west. Stratigraphic evidence indicates that the burial postdates the collapse of the structure 11 and may postdate the occupation of this area of the village.

A large oval labret of high rank coal, which is not available on Kodiak Island (Steffian 1992; in press:fig. 12Q), was found in association with the burial. To our knowledge, this labret style is confined to the Kachemak tradition; similar labrets have not been found in later Koniag deposits. Thus, on stylistic grounds, the burial appears to date to the Kachemak tradition. The labret was found near the skull of the adult female. Seven teeth had facets on their labial/buccal surfaces, indicating that the female wore laterally placed labrets. None of the teeth associated with the adult male exhibited labret facets.

Uyak Burial B   Burial B was situated approximately 8 m southwest of Burial A. It contained the remains of a child between the ages of 6 and 9, based on dental development. The burial was poorly preserved, consisting primarily of teeth and a few bone fragments (NISP = 47, NUSP = 18), and represents only 8.6 percent of the total identifiable Uyak assemblage. Because of poor preservation, it is impossible to assess the skeletal composition and posture of this interment (see fig. 8.4 and Table 8.6). No cultural modification was observed on any of the remains.

The child was buried in a pit dug through layers of cultural debris. This pit is visible as a slight depression on the surface of the site and as a large, irregularly shaped excavation in the weathered ash at the base of the site (fig. 8.9). The base of the burial pit was roughly 2 m in diameter. Extensive deposits of shell midden suggest that this area was used repeatedly as a trash dump. Stratigraphic evidence suggests that interment took place during the period of shell midden accumulation. Therefore, it seems likely that this burial is contemporary with the Kachemak occupation of the site. Two artifacts were associated with the burial—a ground slate projectile point and a wedge of sea mammal bone.

Uyak Burial C   Burial C contains the partially disarticulated remains of a single adult individual of indeterminate sex. Despite the absence of reliable age indicators, it appears that the individual was an older adult, as suggested by dental attrition, antemortem tooth loss, and the presence of osteophytosis and osteoarthritis. The burial accounts for 21.4 percent of the total identifiable Uyak human skeletal assemblage (NISP = 117; NUSP = 6). Skeletal elements were missing from this interment (see Table 8.7 and fig. 8.4). The remaining bones were in a flexed position on the left hip with the chest down (fig. 8.10). The bones of the right leg and right arm were disarticulated and stacked on top of the left tibia, which was in anatomical position with the femur. The mandible was placed on top of this pile of long bones. Most of the teeth were not articulated, although they were found elsewhere among the remains, and the maxillary teeth were present, although the cranium was missing. These data, in addition to the lack of cultural modification on the remains, suggest that the burial was disturbed following decomposition. The articulated nature of the ribs, vertebrae, and left leg suggest that when inhumation occurred the individual was at least partially in the flesh. Like the female in Burial A, this individual exhibited labret facets on three teeth indicating that he or she wore a pair of lateral labrets.

The individual was buried in the uppermost layer of the site in a loose deposit of humus. The individual was placed in a pit dug into a depression caused by the collapse of Structure 1 (see fig. 8.11). Stratigraphic evidence indicates that the burial significantly post-

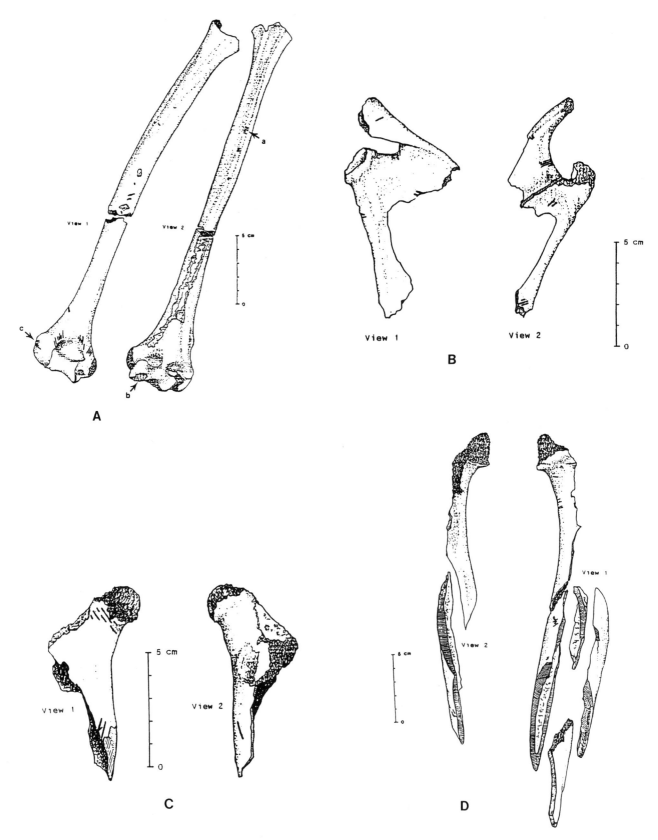

Figure 8.6. Culturally modified human bones from Crag Point. Cutmarks are indicated by black lines, perimortem breakage by crosshatching. A, Left humerus (Specimen #CS063), showing (a) disarticulation cutmarks, (b) scavenger modification; (c) defleshing cutmarks; B, Left scapula (Specimen #CS116); C, Right proximal femur (Specimen #CS120); D, Conjoining pieces of left femur (Specimen #CS122a-e).

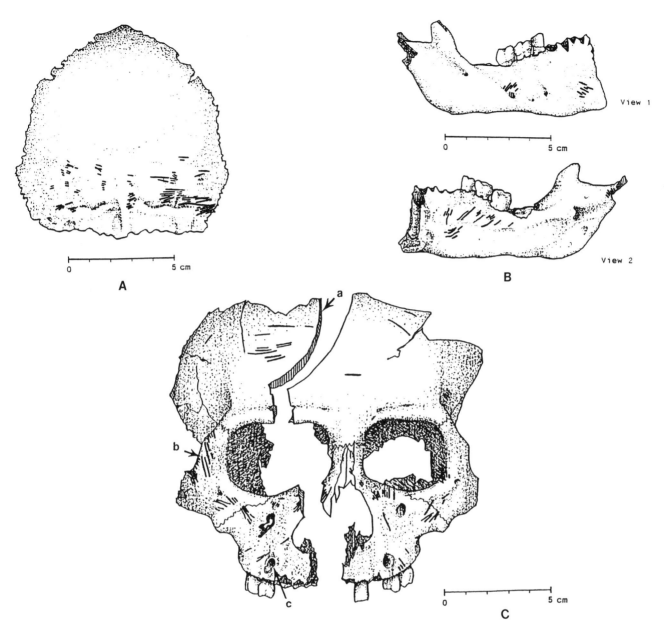

Figure 8.7. Culturally modified human bones from Crag Point. Cutmarks are indicated by black lines, perimortem breakage by crosshatching. A, Occipital (Specimen #CS137); B, Right half of a child's mandible (CS#199a); C, Facila portion of a cranium (Specimen #CS075a), showing (a) perimortem breakage, (b) defleshing cutmarks, and (c) peri-apical osteitis at the left and right first premolars.

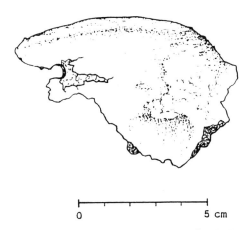

Figure 8.8. Ilium fragment (Specimen #CS136) with drilled hole just below iliac crest.

dates the occupation of Structure 1 and, quite possibly, the occupation of this area of the site. Artifacts associated with this burial, however, suggest that it dates to the Kachemak tradition. Grave furnishings include an antler toggling harpoon, an antler leister prong, a piece of worked antler, a coal bead, a coal bead preform, and a fragment of a slate ulu. Interestingly, five of these six artifacts are made of raw materials (e.g., high rank coal and caribou antler) that were not available on Kodiak Island. Although none of these items is diagnostic of the Kachemak tradition, a comparison with other artifacts in the recent collection from the Uyak site indicates that each is identical to other specimens from the Kachemak deposits. On typological grounds, it appears that this is a Late Kachemak burial.

UYAK BURIAL D   This burial is a partial cremation containing the remains of an older adult, as implied by the presence of osteoarthritis and extensive osteophytosis. Mandibular morphology suggests that this individual was male. Without additional indicators of sex and age, however, this identification remains speculative. Burial D is classified as a partial cremation based on the results of experimental studies by Buikstra and Swegle (1989).

The partial cremation represents 11.7 percent of the total identifiable Uyak human assemblage (NISP = 64, NUSP = 16). Many bones are missing from this individual (see fig. 8.4 and Table 8.8). Although no cultural bone modification was observed on these remains, perimortem breakage and other types of extensive bone modification indicative of carnivore activity were present on 22 percent (n = 14) of the identified specimens. The occurrence of this bone modification suggests that the remains were exposed on the surface before they were covered by the shell

midden. Burning and carnivore activity are reasonable explanations for the missing remains. No grave furnishings were recovered with these remains.

In contrast to the Uyak burials described above, this individual was found at the base of cultural deposits beneath a thick accumulation of shell midden. The body was burned in a slight depression, 200 cm long by 90 cm wide by 12 cm deep, at the entrance to a semisubterranean house (structure 6; fig. 8.11). The burned area was characterized by a thin reddish layer of weathered ash flecked with charcoal and by the presence of small concentrations of carbonized wood. The area was less than 2 m long and 1 m wide and well-contained. Upright slate slabs were found on two sides of the mortuary facility.

UYAK SCATTERED REMAINS   Scattered human remains were uncommon in the eastern portion of the Uyak site. The weathered proximal portion of a left femur with fused proximal epiphyses was recovered from the uppermost layer of the site. No cultural modification was apparent on this element, although poor preservation and weathering make this difficult

Table 8.5. Uyak Burial A Assemblage Composition

Element	MNE	No. per individual	SMNE	%SMNE
Cranium	1	1	1.000	3.660
Mandible	2	1	2.000	7.319
Cervical Vertebra	9	7	1.286	4.705
Thoracic Vertebra	19	12	1.583	5.794
Lumbar Vertebra	9	5	1.800	6.587
Sacrum	1	1	1.000	3.660
Rib	35	24	1.458	5.337
Sternum	1	1	1.000	3.660
Innominate	3	2	1.500	5.489
Femur	2	2	1.000	3.660
Patella	2	2	1.000	3.660
Tibia	3	2	1.500	5.489
Fibula	3	2	1.500	5.489
Clavicle	3	2	1.500	5.489
Scapula	3	2	1.500	5.489
Humerus	2	2	1.000	3.660
Radius	2	2	1.000	3.660
Ulna	3	2	1.500	5.489
Carpals/ Metacarpals	27	26	1.038	3.800
Tarsals/ Metatarsals	36	24	1.500	5.489
Phalanges (Carpal and Tarsal)	37	56	0.661	2.418
Total SMNE			27.326	100.003

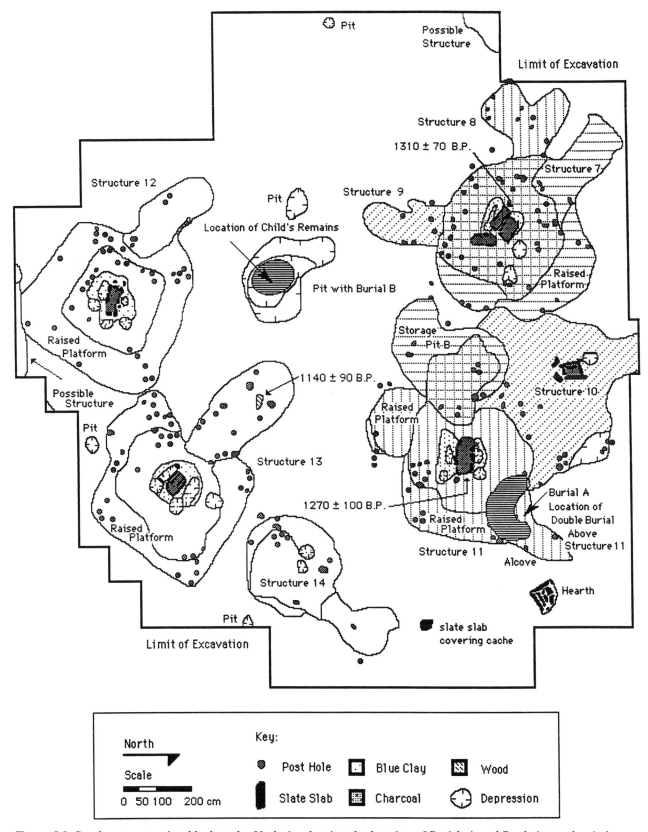

Figure 8.9. Southwest excavation block at the Uyak site showing the location of Burials A and B relative to the site's structures.

Table 8.6. Uyak Burial B Assemblage Composition

Element	MNE	No. per individual	SMNE	%SMNE
Cranium	1	1	1.000	14.633
Mandible	1	1	1.000	14.633
Cervical Vertebra	0	7	0.000	0.000
Thoracic Vertebra	0	12	0.000	0.000
Lumbar Vertebra	0	5	0.000	0.000
Sacrum	0	1	0.000	0.000
Rib	4	24	0.167	2.444
Sternum	0	1	0.000	0.000
Innominate	1	2	0.500	7.316
Femur	2	2	1.000	14.633
Patella	2	2	1.000	14.633
Tibia	1	2	0.500	7.316
Fibula	1	2	0.500	7.316
Clavicle	0	2	0.000	0.000
Scapula	0	2	0.000	0.000
Humerus	1	2	0.500	7.316
Radius	1	2	0.500	7.316
Ulna	0	2	0.000	0.000
Carpals/ Metacarpals	0	26	0.000	0.000
Tarsals/ Metatarsals	4	24	0.167	2.444
Phalanges (Carpal and Tarsal)	0	56	0.000	0.000
Total SMNE			6.834	100.000

to assess. In addition, three human teeth, two deciduous molars and one permanent tooth, were recovered from scattered contexts at the site. In comparison with Crag Point, the paucity of scattered remains at the Uyak site is remarkable; only 0.7 percent (NISP = 4, NUSP = 0) of the Uyak human skeletal assemblage consists of scattered remains.

Discussion

Studies of mortuary variability are based on the principles that the specific mortuary treatment provided an individual is related to his or her social standing in life and that the "mortuary treatment accorded any given individual will be related systematically to the treatment received by other members of the society" (O'Shea 1984:35–36). These principles provide the link by which archaeological remains can be used to study a society's program for the disposal of the dead in order to better understand the structure of that society. Because mortuary behavior is part of an operating cultural system, it also reflects other aspects of

that system (e.g., social and economic organization). Thus, by identifying patterns in mortuary behavior it is possible to uncover other aspects of past cultural systems.

In the following section, we formulate hypotheses about Kachemak social and economic organization based on the mortuary data. As an initial step, we isolate and describe patterns in the data to identify aspects of Kachemak mortuary behavior, bearing in mind that generalizations about mortuary behavior must be evaluated in terms of potential confounding variables, such as diachronic variation and sampling bias (Peebles 1971; O'Shea 1984). Because the mortuary data considered here may have accumulated over 2,000 years, temporal variation in the treatment of the dead may obscure patterning that reflects the operation of Kachemak mortuary systems at a single point in time. In addition, because the datasets are small and solely from village contexts, the full range of mortuary behavior may not be represented. If Kachemak people practiced some form of burial disposal outside their villages (e.g., ridge-top cairn burial, mummifica-

Table 8.7. Uyak Burial C Assemblage Composition

Element	MNE	No. per individual	SMNE	%SMNE
Cranium	0	1	0.000	0.000
Mandible	1	1	1.000	7.121
Cervical Vertebra	7	7	1.000	7.121
Thoracic Vertebra	11	12	0.917	6.528
Lumbar Vertebra	0	5	0.000	0.000
Sacrum	0	1	0.000	0.000
Rib	19	24	0.792	5.638
Sternum	1	1	1.000	7.121
Innominate	0	2	0.000	0.000
Femur	2	2	1.000	7.121
Patella	1	2	0.500	3.561
Tibia	2	2	1.000	7.121
Fibula	2	2	1.000	7.121
Clavicle	2	2	1.000	7.121
Scapula	2	2	1.000	7.121
Humerus	2	2	1.000	7.121
Radius	2	2	1.000	7.121
Ulna	2	2	1.000	7.121
Carpals/ Metacarpals	13	26	0.500	3.561
Tarsals/ Metatarsals	2	24	0.083	0.593
Phalanges (Carpal and Tarsal)	14	56	0.250	1.780
Total SMNE			14.042	99.992

James J. K. Simon and Amy F. Steffian

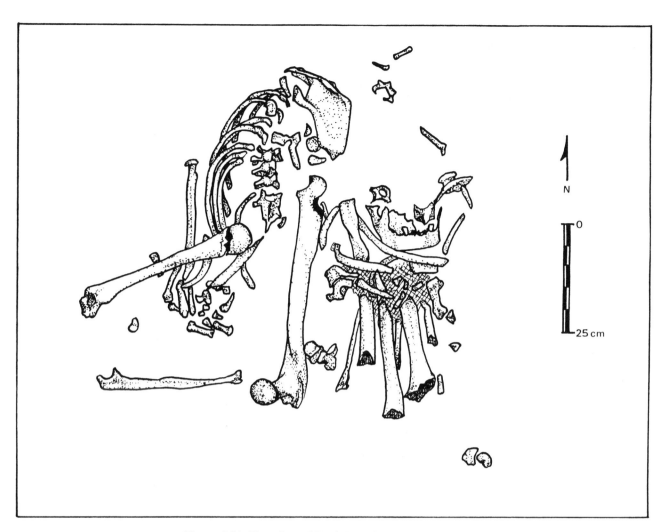

Figure 8.10. Plan view of Uyak Burial C: single interment.

tion and cave burial, or burial at sea), this type of mortuary practice would not be represented in our sample. Despite these potential complications, patterns observed in the assemblages provide valuable insights into the organization of Kachemak society.

In the following discussion, we summarize the general patterns observed in the Uyak and Crag Point mortuary assemblages to assess the long-standing arguments for Kachemak cannibalism and social violence and to provide a foundation for formulating ideas about the organization of Kachemak society. We hope that both the patterns and the ideas we formulate from them will be taken as working hypotheses that need to be carefully scrutinized as additional data are collected.

Mortuary Patterns

1. Together, the Crag Point and Uyak assemblages illustrate that human remains were buried in resi-

dential areas (see also Clark 1984:140; Heizer 1956; Workman 1992). Within these areas, disposal occurred in a wide range of contexts, including structure floors, depressions formed by collapsed structures, and areas used for dumping refuse. Neither inhumations nor scattered remains appear to occur in spatially segregated portions of the village (e.g., formal cemeteries). Furthermore, it appears that living areas continued to be occupied after the disposal of human remains. At both sites, this is evidenced by the deposition of midden over both burial facilities and scattered elements.

2. In a previous study, Workman (1992:20) reports that Kachemak burial facilities were not labor-intensive features. This generalization is supported by our research. In the eastern portion of the Uyak site graves were located to take advantage of existing depressions in the site's living area. Although these facilities were not elaborate, interrupted and mixed strata attest to their construction. Similarly, at Crag Point an

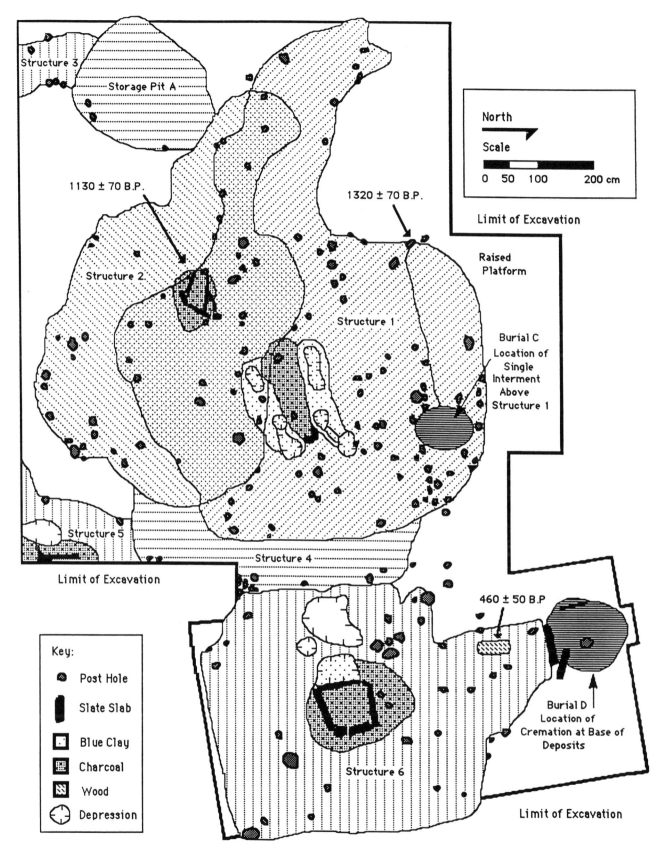

Figure 8.11. Northeast excavation block at the Uyak site showing the location of Burials C and D relative to the site's structures.

Table 8.8. Uyak Burial D Assemblage Composition

Element	MNE	No. per individual	SMNE	%SMNE
Cranium	1	1	1.000	12.550
Mandible	1	1	1.000	12.550
Cervical Vertebra	1	7	0.143	1.793
Thoracic Vertebra	1	12	0.083	1.046
Lumbar Vertebra	1	5	0.200	2.510
Sacrum	0	1	0.000	0.000
Rib	1	24	0.042	0.523
Sternum	0	1	0.000	0.000
Innominate	1	2	0.500	6.275
Femur	2	2	1.000	12.550
Patella	0	2	0.000	0.000
Tibia	2	2	1.000	12.550
Fibula	2	2	1.000	12.550
Clavicle	1	2	0.500	6.275
Scapula	1	2	0.500	6.275
Humerus	0	2	0.000	0.000
Radius	1	2	0.500	6.275
Ulna	1	2	0.500	6.275
Carpals/ Metacarpals	0	26	0.000	0.000
Tarsals/ Metatarsals	0	24	0.000	0.000
Phalanges (Carpal and Tarsal)	0	56	0.000	0.000
Total SMNE			7.968	99.997

existing structure was used for a single burial and a simple pile of slate slabs housed a multiple interment.

3. At both sites, individuals were typically found in flexed positions both in single and multiple burials (see also Hrdlička 1944:202, 228, 250; Heizer 1956; Clark 1968, 1970; Lobdell 1980).

4. Multiple burials contain the remains of men, women, and children, and some appear to be mortuary crypts to which individuals were periodically added (see Hrdlička 1944; Heizer 1956). The multiple burial at Crag Point appears to have been a mortuary crypt based on the patterns of skeletal disarticulation. Hrdlička recorded similar features in the western area of the Uyak site, many of which, like the Crag Point facility, were associated with piles of stone slabs (e.g., Hrdlička 1944:148, 179, 250). It must be emphasized, however, that not all multiple burials are associated with stone facilities and not all of them necessarily functioned as crypts.

5. Burials at both sites contained incomplete and partially disarticulated bones and evidence of intentional intrusion. Disturbance often coincided with the expected location of missing elements. The lack of cutmarks and the partially disarticulated nature of buried remains suggest that disturbance occurred after the bodies had decomposed so that bones could be moved without tool-assisted disarticulation. Disturbance was intentional, as suggested by the absence of major skeletal elements, stacking of portions of remaining bones into piles, and the presence of undisturbed stone slabs covering a disturbed burial. In addition, the articulated condition of some major skeletal segments (e.g., vertebrae and ribs, arms, legs, hands, and feet) suggests that primary inhumation, rather than secondary burial of disarticulated bones, was practiced (cf. Hrdlička 1944:170, 230).

6. The scattered remains of men, women, and children commonly occur in Kachemak sites (see also de Laguna 1934; Hrdlička 1944; Heizer 1956; Clark 1970; Lobdell 1980). Cultural modification of bone associated exclusively with these remains suggest that they are not solely the result of disturbed burials (cf. de Laguna 1934; Lobdell 1980). The complete absence of cultural modification on buried remains at both Crag Point and Uyak, despite the incomplete and partially disarticulated nature of many burials, suggests that burials and culturally modified scattered bones represent mutually exclusive and independent mortuary behaviors.

7. Two categories of culturally modified human bones are found in Kachemak sites: those representing the manufacture of cultural objects from human bone, and those representing the processing of human remains. Although only one specimen from the Crag Point assemblage was modified for use as a cultural object, archaeologists have documented other occurrences of human bone artifacts in Kachemak sites. The modifications generally consist of drilled holes in the sphenoid bone or maxilla of crania, the ascending ramus of mandibles, the ilium of innominates, and in the neck of scapulae (e.g., de Laguna 1934:46–47, Plate 47-15, 16; Hrdlička 1941a, Plate 2, 3, 8-2, 9, 10, 11-2; 1941b, 1944:267; Heizer 1956:14; Clark 1970:88; Lobdell 1980:31; Urcid, this volume). As noted earlier, the drilled holes suggest that human bones were tied to or suspended from some object. Finally, the types of bones modified into cultural objects are frequently the types of bones missing from burials.

8. The presence and location of cutmarks suggest that some human remains were systematically disarticulated and defleshed. In addition, the occurrence of perimortem breakage suggests that some of the recently defleshed bones were processed. Although cutmarks and perimortem breakage were not observed in the assemblage from the eastern area of the Uyak site, they have been observed in other assemblages of Kachemak remains (e.g., de Laguna 1934:43–44, 46–48; Hrdlička 1944; Lobdell 1980:18–19, 26).

Although there are many similarities in the Crag Point and Uyak mortuary data, there are also some notable differences. As discussed above, these differences may simply be the result of sampling error, or they may reflect regional or temporal variations in mortuary behavior or functional differences in site use. Whatever the answer, they may be significant dimensions of Kachemak mortuary behavior that, when combined with additional observations, may eventually reveal more discrete patterns in the treatment of the dead.

1. Although burials at both sites occurred in habitation areas, the specific location of facilities varied. At Crag Point, an individual was buried on one of the site's house floors. At Uyak, by contrast, burials did not occur within any structures. Two Uyak burials were placed in pits dug into depressions formed by the collapse of the site's structures. Similar depressions at Crag Point were not utilized to dispose of the dead.

2. Cremation was apparently conducted at the Uyak site and is reported from other Kachemak sites (e.g., Hrdlička 1944:228; Heizer 1956), but it does not appear to have been practiced at Crag Point. Distinctions between burned human bone and cremation, however, have not been addressed in previous accounts of Kodiak cremation.

3. Grave furnishings were recovered from three of the four Uyak burials, but none were recovered from the Crag Point burials. This may indicate that grave offerings became more common towards the end of the Kachemak tradition (cf. Hrdlička 1944:228).

4. Scattered remains formed a large proportion of the skeletal assemblage from Crag Point (31.5 percent of NISP) but were rare in the eastern area of the Uyak site (0.7 percent of NISP).

5. In these two recently excavated assemblages, culturally modified human bones were present only in the Crag Point assemblage and occurred at that site only among scattered remains.

Conclusions

Based on the patterned variability in mortuary data identified at Crag Point and Uyak, we argue that cannibalism and violence cannot account for the full range of behaviors associated with the Kachemak mortuary complex. Previous studies have suggested that cannibalism and/or social violence (e.g., warfare) were prevalent features of Kachemak society. The main evidence used in these interpretations consists of disarticulated and incomplete burials, scattered human bones, and damaged human bone.

Our study found, however, that disarticulated and incomplete burials apparently resulted from the intentional opening of burials to remove bones from already-decomposed individuals. There is no evidence that the burials represent the remains of "cannibalistic feasts." Scattered human remains, which consist of both culturally modified and unmodified bones, may have come from burials that were either intentionally or unintentionally disturbed. Intentional disturbance has been suggested to have been a common feature of Kachemak mortuary behavior. Unintentional disturbance was also probably common at Kachemak village sites where house building and other cultural activities, as well as natural depositional processes (i.e., tectonic activity, erosion, and animal scavenging), would have disturbed underlying deposits (Jordan and Knecht 1988). Only culturally modified scattered bones remain as potential evidence of cannibalism and social violence.

We have seen that two types of culturally modified bones are found at Kachemak sites: those that have been worked into cultural objects and those that represent the dismemberment, defleshing, and processing of an individual around the time of death. Human bone artifacts may or may not relate to the mutilated remains, given the absence of detailed descriptions of the co-occurrence of artifactual manipulation and dismemberment and defleshing cutmarks. Thus, after reevaluating the evidence used to suggest that cannibalism and violence characterized the Late Kachemak tradition, we are left with one small subset of data that may or may not support this interpretation —that is, a maximum of 44 culturally modified specimens representing 2.4 percent of the total assemblage of identified and unidentified specimens from the Uyak and Crag Point sites. We do not believe that this evidence, which could represent a range of other behaviors (e.g., ritual processing or medical examination; see Hrdlička 1941b; Laughlin 1980:96), suggests that cannibalism and/or social violence were prevalent during the Late Kachemak tradition.

Putting aside the issue of Kachemak cannibalism, we also attempt in this conclusion to integrate the mortuary behavior within a larger cultural context using available independent data. The following discussion is presented as a set of hypotheses to be tested and critically evaluated as additional data become available.

Previous ethnological studies of mortuary behavior have suggested that, if "a permanent, specialized, bounded disposal area for the exclusive disposal of a group's dead exists, then it is likely that this represents a corporate group who has rights over the use and/or control of crucial but restricted resources" (Goldstein 1976:61 in O'Shea 1984:13; see also Saxe 1970). Based on this hypothesis, we suggest that mor-

James J. K. Simon and Amy F. Steffian

tuary crypts, where individuals were periodically deposited and from which bones were removed, represent this kind of specialized disposal facility. Furthermore, we suggest that corporate groups used these crypts, removed bones from burials, and used human bones as cultural objects to ritualize their claim to particular territories by identifying with their ancestors and, in turn, with traditionally used village sites and resources.

But what aspects of the natural and cultural landscape might have produced territorial behavior? Anthropologists have often assumed that high levels of environmental productivity in the Gulf of Alaska created economic stability for prehistoric foraging societies (e.g., Jordan 1988, 1989). An ongoing analysis of the spatial and temporal distribution of resources in Uyak Bay, however, suggests that there is significant variation in the availability and accessibility of critical sources of food and raw material (see also Yesner 1990). For example, variation in the timing and productivity of salmon runs, seasonal occurrences of paralytic shellfish poisoning, severe and unpredictable winter weather, frequent tectonic activity, and interregional variation in the distribution of resources (Erlandson et al. 1992) are some of the factors that affected the reliability of resources and, hence, the subsistence strategies of Kodiak foragers.

Moreover, there is evidence of widespread nutritional stress in the Crag Point and Uyak skeletal assemblages (Steffian and Simon 1993). The presence of stress-related Harris lines, along with the structure of resource availability, suggest that high levels of environmental productivity did not produce or ensure complete economic stability (Lobdell 1988:55; Yesner 1990:2). The potential for economic difficulties is particularly apparent in light of increasing population density.

If population growth occurred during the Late Kachemak, as suggested by Jordan and Knecht (1988), competition over access to variable resources may have increased as well (see also Erlandson et al. 1992). One method of ensuring access to resources would be the establishment of harvesting areas specific to individual corporate groups (e.g., extended families, individual villages, or both). For example, in Uyak Bay, salmon spawn in many local streams during the summer. Although the location of these salmon runs is constant, timing and productivity vary within each stream. Thus, to consistently incorporate salmon into a subsistence economy, it is necessary to maintain access to fishing areas. In the face of population growth, territoriality may have emerged to ensure control of economically important resources, such as salmon and/or foraging areas that contained a range of critical resources (see Yesner 1992).

This idea is supported by settlement pattern data

from Uyak Bay where large, at least semipermanently occupied villages, like the Uyak site, are situated at the mouths of bays, and smaller, perhaps more task-specific sites are located inside these bays. In Uyak Bay, large settlements may have been located to claim or ensure access to particular foraging areas. Placing primary villages at the mouths of bays may have enabled the inhabitants to control the use of resources inside the bay.

Finally, it is also possible that population growth and competition for resources led to some forms of social conflict within this system. Although the mortuary data presented here suggest that social violence was not as prevalent a feature of Kachemak society as previously assumed, there are contexts within the economic and social system where violence may have occurred. As recently discussed by Moss and Erlandson (1992), an increase in social conflict seems to accompany the development of complex forms of social and political organization in many of the late prehistoric coastal foraging societies of the North Pacific. In fact, the human remains from Crag Point which exhibit cutmarks and perimortem breakage could represent violent encounters. Violence, however, is at one end of the spectrum of behaviors that may be associated with increasing sedentism, territoriality, and ultimately the emergence of greater organizational complexity.

Acknowledgments

This research reflects a great deal of support from many individuals, communities, and institutions. We are especially grateful to the people of Ouzinkie and Larsen Bay for allowing us to study their ancestry. Financial support for the Crag Point and Uyak excavations came from the Kodiak Area Native Association, the University of Michigan Museum of Anthropology, and a National Science Foundation grant awarded to Richard H. Jordan. Funding for laboratory analysis was provided by the 1990, 1991, and 1992 Geist Fund of the University of Alaska Museum. We would also like to thank the University of Alaska, Fairbanks, Department of Anthropology for providing space for this study, and Tamara Bray and Tom Killion for inviting us to participate in the symposium. Sincere thanks to Sharron McClellan for laboratory assistance, Carol Gelvin-Reymiller for producing figs. 8.1, 8.3, 8.5, 8.6, 8.7, and 8.9, and G. Richard Scott for his assistance in tooth identifications. Thanks are also extended to Jane Buikstra and Don Clark for their comments and support. Finally, as students of Dick Jordan we would like to acknowledge his influence on our research. His support and intense passion for Kodiak archaeology contributed substantially to our research.

Notes

1. Even if cannibalism occurred, it is necessary to understand its social context, as there are many cultural manifestations of this behavior (see White 1992).

2. The figure of 4.762 percent reflects the number of bone categories. In other words, a different number of categories would produce a different standard.

3. Recent reevaluation of the Crag Point assemblage identified a numerical error in the published total number of identified specimens (NISP) and the relative contribution of each disposal category to the total assemblage (%NISP). The corrected total and percentages appear in this paper.

4. These values were previously published in Simon (1992) as "7.8 percent to 11.5 percent" due to a numerical error in the reporting of NISPs.

References Cited

Anonymous
1932a Dr. Hrdlička Finds Proof of Cannibalism. *El Palacio* 32:81–82.
1932b Cannibal Remains on Alaskan Island. *Science* 5(1933):9–10.

Bass, William M.
1987 *Human Osteology: A Laboratory and Field Manual.* Special Publication No. 2. Columbia: Missouri Archaeological Society.

Binford, Lewis R.
1978 *Nunamiut Ethnoarchaeology.* New York: Academic Press.
1984 *Faunal Remains from Klasies River Mouth.* New York: Academic Press.

Brothwell, D. R.
1981 *Digging Up Bones.* Ithaca: Cornell University Press.

Buikstra, Jane E., and Mark Swegle
1989 Bone Modification Due to Burning: Experimental Evidence. In *Bone Modification,* R. Bonnichsen and M. H. Sorg, eds., pp. 247–58. Orono, Maine: Center for the Study of the First Americans.

Bunn, Henry T.
1981 Archaeological Evidence for Meat-Eating by Plio-Pleistocene Hominids from Koobi Fora and Olduvai Gorge. *Nature* 291:574–77.

Bunn, Henry T., and Ellen M. Kroll
1986 Systematic Butchery by Plio/Pleistocene Hominids at Olduvai Gorge, Tanzania. *Current Anthropology* 27(5):431–52.

Clark, Donald W.
1966 Perspectives in the Prehistory of Kodiak Island, Alaska. *American Antiquity* 33(1):358–71.
1968 Koniag Prehistory. Ph.D. Dissertation, Department of Anthropology, University of Wisconsin, Madison. Ann Arbor.
1970 The Late Kachemak Tradition at Three Saints and Crag Point, Kodiak Island, Alaska. *Arctic Anthropology* 6(2):73–111.
1974 *Contributions to the Later Prehistory of Kodiak Island, Alaska.* Archaeological Survey of Canada, Mercury Series Paper 20. Ottawa: National Museum of Man.
1984 Prehistory of the Pacific Eskimo Region. In *Handbook of North American Indians,* vol. 5, Arctic, David Damas, ed., pp. 136–48. Washington, D.C.: Smithsonian Institution.

Crowell, Aron
1986 An Archaeological Survey of Uyak Bay, Kodiak Island, Alaska. Manuscript on file with the Alaska Office of History and Archaeology, Anchorage.

Crozier, S. Neal
1989 Excavation at a Late Prehistoric Dwelling Structure on Kodiak Island. *Arctic Anthropology* 26(2):78–95.

de Laguna, Frederica
1934 *The Archaeology of Cook Inlet.* Philadelphia: The University Museum, University of Pennsylvania.
1956 *Chugach Prehistory: The Archaeology of Prince William Sound, Alaska.* University of Washington Publications in Anthropology, Vol. 13. Seattle: University of Washington Press.

Erlandson, Jon, Aron Crowell, Christopher Wooley, and James Haggarty
1992 Spatial and Temporal Patterns in Alutiiq Paleodemography. *Arctic Anthropology* 29(2):42–62.

Fitzhugh, Ben
1992 Clams and the Kachemak: Evidence for Seasonal Shellfish Use on Kodiak Island. Paper presented at the First International Conference of Arctic Social Sciences, Lavalle University, Ste-Foy, Quebec.

Gideon, Hieromonk
1989 *The Round the World Voyage of Hieromonk Gideon 1803-1809,* Lydia T. Black, transl. and Richard A. Pierce, ed. Kingston, Ontario: The Limestone Press.

Gilbert, B. Miles, and Thomas W. McKern
1973 A Method for Aging the Female Os Pubis. *American Journal of Physical Anthropology* 38:31–38.

Goldstein, L.
1976 Spatial Structure and Social Organization: Regional Manifestations of Mississippian Society. Ph.D. Dissertation, Department of Anthropology, Northwestern University, Chicago. University Microfilms, Ann Arbor.

Gordon, C., and J. Buikstra
1981 Soil pH, Bone Preservation, and Sampling Bias at Mortuary Sites. *American Antiquity* 46:566–70.

Heizer, Robert F.
1956 *Archaeology of the Uyak Site Kodiak Island, Alaska.* Berkeley: University of California Anthropological Records 17(1).

Holmberg, Heinrich Johan
1985 *Holmberg's Ethnographic Sketches* [originally published as *Ethnographische skizzen ueber die volker des russischen Amerika, Acta Scientiarum Fennicae, 1855–1863*]. Fairbanks: University of Alaska Press.

Hrdlička, Aleš
1941a *Diseases of and Artifacts on Skulls and Bones from Kodiak Island.* Smithsonian Miscellaneous Collection 101(4). Washington, D.C.: Smithsonian Institution Press.
1941b Artifacts on Human and Seal Skulls from Kodiak Island. *American Journal of Physical Anthropology* 28(4): 411–21.

1944   *The Anthropology of Kodiak Island.* Philadelphia: Wistar Institute of Anatomy and Biology.

Johnson, Eileen
1983   A Framework for Interpretation in Bone Technology. In *Carnivores, Human Scavengers & Predators: A Question of Bone Technology,* Genevieve M. LeMoine and A. Scott MacEachem, eds., pp. 219–40. Proceedings of the Fifteenth Annual Conference, Archaeological Association, University of Calgary, Calgary.

Johnston, F. E.
1962   Growth of the Long Bones of Infants and Young Children at Indian Knoll. *American Journal of Physical Anthropology* 20:249–54.

Jordan, Richard H.
1988   Kodiak Island's Kachemak Tradition: Violence and Village Life in a Land of Plenty. Paper presented at the 15th Annual Meeting of the Alaska Anthropological Association, Fairbanks.
1989   Qasqiluteng: Feasting and Ceremonialism Among the Traditional Koniag of Kodiak Island. Ms. on file, Department of Anthropology, University of Alaska, Fairbanks.
in press   A Maritime Paleoarctic Assemblage from Crag Point, Kodiak Island, Alaska. In *Contributions to the Anthropology of Southcentral and Southwestern Alaska,* Richard H. Jordan, Frederica de Laguna, and Amy F. Steffian, eds. Anthropological Papers of the University of Alaska 24(1-2).

Jordan, Richard H., and Richard A. Knecht
1988   Archaeological Research on Western Kodiak Island, Alaska: The Development of Koniag Culture. In *The Late Prehistoric Development of Alaska's Native People,* Robert Shaw, Roger Harritt, and Don Dumond, eds., pp. 225–306. Alaska Anthropological Association Monograph Series No. 4, Anchorage.

Laughlin, William S.
1980   *Aleuts: Survivors of the Bering Land Bridge.* New York: Holt, Rinehart and Winston.

Lisiansky, U.
1814   *A Voyage Round the World in the Years 1803, 4, 5, and 6; Performed by the Order of His Imperial Majesty Alexander the First, Emperor of Russia, in the Ship Neva.* Reprinted in 1968. Ridgewood, New Jersey: The Gregg Press.

Lobdell, John E.
1980   Prehistoric Human Populations and Resource Utilization in Kachemak Bay, Gulf of Alaska. Ph.D. dissertation, Department of Anthropology, University of Tennessee, Knoxville.
1988   Harris Lines: Markers of Nutritional Stress in Late Prehistoric and Contact Period Eskimo Post Cranial Remains. In *The Late Prehistoric Development of Alaska's Native People,* Robert D. Shaw, Roger K. Harritt, and Don E. Dumond, eds., pp. 47–55. Alaska Anthropological Association Monograph Series No. 4, Anchorage.

Lovejoy, C. Owen, Richard S. Meindl, Robert P. Mensforth, and T. J. Barton
1985   Multifactorial Determination of Skeletal Age at Death: A New Method with Blind Tests of Accuracy. *American Journal of Physical Anthropology* 68:1–14.

Lyman, R. L., and M. J. O'Brien
1987   Plowzone Zooarchaeology: Fragmentation and Identifiability. *Journal of Field Archaeology* 14:493–98.

McKern, Thomas W., and T. D. Stewart
1957   *Skeletal Age Changes in Young American Males, Analyzed from the Standpoint of Identification.* Army Headquarters Quarter Master Research and Development Command, Technical Report EP-45, Natick, Massachusetts.

Merbs, Charles F.
1983   *Patterns of Activity-Induced Pathology in a Canadian Inuit Population.* National Museum of Man, Mercury Series, Archaeological Survey of Canada Paper No. 119. National Museum of Man, Ottawa.

Metcalfe, Duncan, and Kevin T. Jones
1988   A Reconsideration of Animal Body-Part Utility Indices. *American Antiquity* 53(3):486–504.

Mills, Robin O.
1992   Radiocarbon Calibration of Archaeological Dates from the Central Gulf of Alaska. Masters Thesis, Department of Anthropology, University of Alaska, Fairbanks.

Moss, Madonna L., and Jon M. Erlandson
1992   Forts, Refuge Rocks, and Defensive Sites: The Antiquity of Warfare Along the North Pacific Coast of North America. *Arctic Anthropology* 29(2):73–90.

O'Shea, John M.
1984   *Mortuary Analysis.* New York: Academic Press.

Peebles, C.
1971   Moundville and Surrounding Sites: Some Structural Considerations of Mortuary Practices. In *Approaches to the Social Dimensions of Mortuary Practices,* J. A. Brown, ed., pp. 69–91. Washington, D.C.: Memoirs of the Society for American Archaeology.

Phenice, T. W.
1967   A Newly Developed Visual Method of Sexing the Os Pubis. *American Journal of Physical Anthropology* 30:297–302.

Potts, Richard, and Pat Shipman
1981   Marks Made by Stone Tools on Bones from Olduvai Gorge, Tanzania. *Nature* 291:577–80.

Saxe, Arthur A.
1970   Social Dimensions of Mortuary Practices. Ph.D. dissertation, Department of Anthropology, University of Michigan, Ann Arbor.

Schiffer, Michael B.
1987   *Formation Processes of the Archaeological Record.* Albuquerque: University of New Mexico Press.

Schour, I., and M. Massler
1941 The Development of the Human Dentition. *Journal of the American Dental Association* 28:1153–60.

Shipman, Pat
1981 *Life History of a Fossil: An Introduction to Taphonomy and Paleoecology*. Cambridge: Harvard University Press.

Shipman, Pat, and Jennie Rose
1984 Cutmark Mimics on Modern and Fossil Bovid Bones. *Current Anthropology* 25(1):116–17.

Simon, James J. K.
1992 Mortuary Practices of the Late Kachemak Tradition in Southcentral Alaska: A Perspective from the Crag Point Site, Kodiak Island. *Arctic Anthropology* 29(2):130–49.

Steffian, Amy F.
1992 Archaeological Coal in the Gulf of Alaska: A View from Kodiak Island. *Arctic Anthropology* 29(2):111–29.
in press Fifty Years after Hrdlička: Further Excavation at the Uyak Site Kodiak Island, Alaska. In *Contributions to the Anthropology of Southcentral and Southwestern Alaska*, Richard H. Jordan, Frederica de Laguna, and Amy Steffian, eds. Anthropological Papers of the University of Alaska 24(1–2).

Steffian, Amy F., and James J. K. Simon
1993 Nutritional Stress among Prehistoric Foragers of the Central Alaskan Gulf. Paper presented at the 20th Annual Meeting of the Alaska Anthropological Association, Anchorage.

Todd, T. Wingate
1920 Age Changes in the Pubic Bone: I. The Male White Pubis. *American Journal of Physical Anthropology* 3:285–334.

Turner, Christy G.
1983 Taphonomic Reconstructions of Human Violence and Cannibalism Based on Mass Burials in the American Southwest. In *Carnivores, Human Scavengers & Predators: A Question of Bone Technology*, Genevieve M. LeMoine and A. Scott MacEachem, eds., pp. 219–40. Proceedings of the Fifteenth Annual Conference, Archaeological Association of the University of Calgary, Calgary, Alberta.

Ubelaker, D. H.
1978 *Human Skeletal Remains: Excavation, Analysis, Interpretation*. Washington, D.C.: Taraxacum.

White, Tim D.
1992 *Prehistoric Cannibalism at Mancos 5MTUMR-2346*. Princeton: Princeton University Press.

Workman, William
1980 Continuity and Change in the Prehistoric Record from Southern Alaska. In *Alaska Native Culture and History*, Y. Kotani and W. B. Workman, eds., pp. 49–102. Senri Ethnological Studies 4. National Museum of Ethnology, Osaka.
1992 Life and Death in a First Millennium A.D. Gulf of Alaska Culture: The Kachemak Tradition Ceremonial Complex. In *Ancient Images, Ancient Thought: The Archaeology of Ideology*. S. Goldsmith, S. Garvie, D. Selin, and J. Smith, eds., pp. 19–25. Proceedings of the 23d Annual Chacmool Conference, Calgary Archaeological Association, University of Calgary, Alberta.

Yesner, David R.
1989 Osteological Remains from Larsen Bay, Kodiak Island, Alaska. *Arctic Anthropology* 26(2):96–106.
1990 Evolution of Subsistence in the Kachemak Tradition: Evaluating the Maritime Stability Model. Paper presented at the International Conference on Archaeological Zoology, Washington, D.C.

9

CANNIBALISM AND CURATED SKULLS

Bone Ritualism on Kodiak Island

In the summer of 1991, the National Museum of Natural History (NMNH) returned 756 lots of human skeletal remains recovered from the Uyak site to the community of Larsen Bay. Their inventory and deaccession provided the opportunity to reassess previous interpretations of prehistoric ritual behavior at the site. In this chapter, I use the osteological data generated during the deaccession process to reexamine the issue of cannibalism at the Uyak site and to draw some conclusions about Kachemak ritual activities in the first millennium A.D. The study focuses on specific types of modifications found on the human bones.

Cannibalism at Kodiak Island?

Aleš Hrdlička excavated at the Uyak site between 1931 and 1936. During his first field season, he formulated the notion that most of the burials at the site were the result of violent deaths or represented the aftermath of cannibalistic, or anthropophagous, activities (1944:150, 228, 350–51). Hrdlička based his interpretations on observations of partial interments, disarticulated burials, and scattered anatomical elements.

The link Hrdlička made between the particular characteristics of the Uyak site burials and cannibalism ultimately rested on his assumption that all human societies treat their dead in the same way. Because of his own cultural biases, he assumed that, in

general, cemeteries would naturally be located apart from residential areas. Thus, the human remains Hrdlička found in the excavated portions of the Uyak site, which consisted primarily of house floors and features associated with domestic activities, appeared anomalous in light of his preconceived notions. This contextual evidence, together with the partial and disarticulated nature of the burials, seemed sufficient to him to support his ideas about "massacres" and "cannibalistic feasts" (Hrdlička 1944:149, 155, 293). No attempt was later made to determine whether the osteological data supported his conclusions.

Hrdlička's ideas were frequently accepted as fact by later scholars (i.e., Heizer 1956:12, 14; Clark 1974:149; Jordan 1988; Workman 1992), although none of them actually examined the human remains recovered from the site. To adequately evaluate Hrdlička's assumptions about cannibalism at the Uyak site, it is necessary to examine the premises on which his interpretations were based, analyze the nature of the archaeological deposits at the site, and study in detail the osteological evidence itself.

Behavioral and Archaeological Correlates of Anthropophagy

Hrdlička assumed that the partial and disarticulated burials he uncovered at the Uyak site were the result of dismemberment and that dismemberment was a prelude to cannibalism. There are, however, many other cultural and natural processes that can alter the relationships of the anatomical elements of a skeleton. Furthermore, it is often difficult to identify deliberate dismemberment of the human body in the archaeological record. The perimortem separation of body parts does not always or necessarily leave traces on bony tissue. Consider, for example, the dismemberment of alleged heretics by torture devices during the Spanish inquisition.

If dismemberment had occurred and cutting tools were involved, cutmarks on specific anatomical landmarks might be construed as evidence of such activity. But even if it could be established that dismemberment was practiced and cutting tools were used, this alone would still not constitute sufficient evidence for cannibalism. The intentional cutting of joints and the separation of bones could be done, for instance, in conjunction with specific mortuary practices. The body of an individual might, for example, be disassembled to permit it to fit into a small grave or repository, or position it in a prescribed manner (Stewart 1992:81). There are other types of cultural behavior that result in dismemberment but have no relation to cannibalism, such as the preparation of shrunken heads among the Jivaro of Ecuador.

Finally, it should be noted that cannibalism does not necessarily involve alterations to bony tissue. The extraction of specific organs or tissue for ritual purposes could be accomplished without cutting, breaking, or smashing any bones. Among the Bimin-Kukusmin of Papua, New Guinea, for example, in the idealized practice of anthropophagy, female lineage agnates are required to eat small morsels of flesh from the lower portion of the stomach of the deceased (Porter 1983:16).

Formation Processes at the Uyak Site

The general context in which human remains were found at the Uyak site must also be considered in evaluating Hrdlička's conclusions. A basic understanding of the archaeology of the site suggests several alternative hypotheses that could also account for the presence of disarticulated burials and isolated anatomical parts.

As Heizer (1956) described, the Uyak site comprised a relatively large settlement with several occupational phases. The depth of cultural deposits, which measured up to 6 m in some sectors, indicated that the site was occupied for a substantial period of time. On the surface were circular depressions that were identified as house pits associated with hearths and trash pits.

Given the presence of domestic features and the long period of habitation, there is little doubt that lat-

er occupations would have impacted upon earlier ones. If inhabitants had buried their dead beneath dwellings or within the residential zone, as the archaeological evidence suggests, the presence of partial interments and scattered remains, which Hrdlička relied on to support his cannibalism hypothesis, could easily be explained in terms of site formation processes. These processes include a variety of human, animal, and environmental disturbances, any of which could have contributed to the postmortem disarticulation of skeletons.

The impact of site formation processes on burials at the Uyak site can be assessed by redefining Heizer's descriptive burial typology within the context of likely taphonomic processes (Table 9.1).[1] Undisturbed primary burials appear at Uyak as anatomically complete and articulated skeletons (fig. 9.1a). On the other hand, primary burials that have been disturbed by natural processes or accidental human disturbance can be subdivided into three types. Type A consists of partially disturbed, anatomically complete skeletons (fig. 9.1b). Type B refers to partially disturbed, anatomically incomplete skeletons, in which missing elements may have been removed for use in other behavioral contexts or for reburial (fig. 9.1c). In Heizer's scheme, partially distributed Types A and B fall under Incomplete Discrete burials. Type C consists of anatomically complete but totally disturbed interments; this type would likely come under Heizer's category of secondary burials (fig. 9.1e).

Heizer would have probably also included dissociated anatomical elements removed from partially disturbed burials and reinterred in his category of Secondary burials. In the redefined typology, these are classified as secondary burials Type A (fig. 9.1d).

Table 9.1. Comparison of Heizer's (1956) Classification of Burial Types at the Uyak Site with Redefined Burial Typology Incorporating Taphonomic Processes

Heizer typology	Taphonomically based typology
Complete Discrete	Undisturbed Primary Burial
Incomplete Discrete	Partially Disturbed Primary Burial Types A and B
Secondary	Completely Disturbed Primary Burial (Type C), or Secondary Burial Types A and B
Mass Burial	Multiple Burials (coeval or sequential)
Dissociated Bones	Disturbed Primary Burial Types A and C, or Secondary Burial Type A

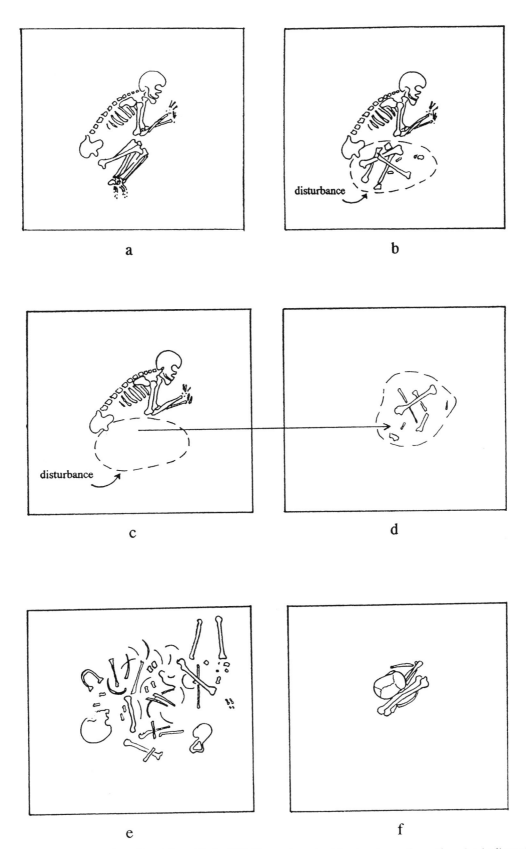

Figure 9.1. Redefined categories of burials at Uyak. (All illustrations in this chapter, unless otherwise indicated, are by Javier Urcid)

These are distinguished from Type B, secondary burials or disarticulated skeletons that result from ritual exhumation and subsequent reinterment; these burials, which may or may not be anatomically complete or carefully arranged, represent true secondary burials (fig. 9.1f).

In general, the concept of mass burial assumes coeval interments. The mass burials classified as such by Heizer at Uyak involved between 6 and 20 individuals. Although they could represent simultaneous deaths that necessitated communal graves, the burial features identified at Uyak could also represent successive burials interred next to each other at different times. Such contiguous, successive interments would likely lead to disturbance of previous burials. Finally, Heizer's category of Dissociated Bones could correspond to the redefined disturbed primary burial, Type A or C, or secondary burial, Type A.

In light of the redefined categories, it would appear that customary treatment of the dead at the Uyak site involved placing primary burials within domestic contexts. Many individuals may have been buried contiguously but not contemporaneously. Site formation processes would then account for four of the five categories defined by Heizer. While coeval interments may have occurred, true secondary burials and cremations do not seem to have been part of the mortuary repertoire of the inhabitants of the Uyak site.

Osteological Data

If the inhabitants of the Uyak site deliberately dismembered individuals with cutting implements for purposes of cannibalism, one would expect to find cutmarks on joints or on muscle, tendon, or ligament attachments. If skulls and long bones were broken to gain access to other body tissues, one might also expect to find certain types of modifications. If this practice was habitual, there would be patterning in the placement of cuts and/or specific types of bone breakages, as well as a high incidence of such features.

An examination of several hundred skeletons in the osteological assemblage from the Uyak site revealed only two instances of cutmarks on post-cranial bones. Both examples presumably came from isolated contexts at the site. In one case, cutmarks were located on the two first ribs of an adult individual (No. P0363703) recovered from the middle stratum of the site. The marks, which ran along the anterior border of the necks of the bones and were symmetrically located on each rib (fig. 9.2), occurred only on the superior surface of the bone and had no relation to muscle or tendon attachments. In the other example, cutmarks were located on the right inferior surface of

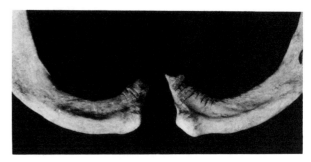

Figure 9.2. Cuts in an antimeric pair of first ribs (Cat. No. P0363703). (Courtesy of the Repatriation Office, National Museum of Natural History, Smithsonian Institution)

an isolated first cervical vertebra (No. P0363694). The vertical and horizontal provenience of this bone is unknown. In another case in which decapitation might be suspected based on the presence of a single, presumably dissociated cranium, mandible, and first three vertebrae (No. P0366602), there were no cutmarks on the third cervical vertebra. Therefore, something you might expect to reflect decapitation based on anatomical representation does not based on the lack of cutmarks.

Most of the broken bones from Uyak lacked epiphyses. In several cases, carnivore tooth marks were found in the vicinity of the breakages. While there was a variety of fracture types, there was no evidence of percussion pits or anvil scars that would indicate purposeful breakage to extract marrow.

An incomplete cranium of a male aged 35 to 45 years old (No. P0366618) illustrates the speculative nature of Hrdlička's claims of cannibalism. A field note in Hrdlička's handwriting accompanying this skull offers the following assessment:

Jones Point; Male skeleton; prob[able] cannibalism;
Skull all smashed; many parts missing;
East pit ab[ou]t 4' deep.

A careful examination of the broken edges of the cranium indicated that natural erosion, rather than purposeful human action, was responsible for the breakage (fig. 9.3).

In summary, neither the archaeological nor osteological evidence support Hrdlička's contention that the inhabitants of Uyak dismembered bodies to engage in cannibalistic practices. Rather, complex mortuary behaviors combined with site formation and taphonomic processes seem to better account for the specific characteristics of the burials excavated at the Uyak site.

Javier Urcid

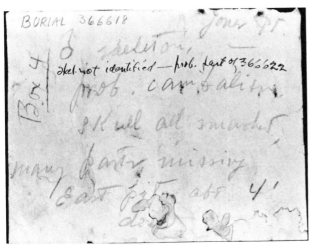

Figure 9.3. Field note and broken cranium P0366618. (Courtesy of the Repatriation Office, National Museum of Natural History, Smithsonian Institution)

Bone Ritualism during the Kachemak Tradition

Various types of bone modifications, including premortem, perimortem, and postmortem alterations, have been reported for the remains from the Uyak site. Hrdlička described several different types of treatments, including unintentional reshaping of the head resulting from the use of cradleboards, the possible practice of tooth ablation,[2] and two purported cases of trephination[3] (Hrdlička 1940, 1941a). He also noted the use of human bone in the manufacture of utilitarian and ritual objects (Hrdlička 1941a, 1941b).

In the remainder of this chapter, I focus exclusively on modifications that involve drilled perforations, cutmarks unrelated to dismemberment, inlay, polish-

ing, and painting. Examples of similar types of bone modification from other Kachemak tradition sites are discussed when the data shed further light on the ritual significance of such bone alterations.

Modified Bones from the Uyak Site

Hrdlička's goal at the Uyak site was to recover as large a collection of human skeletal remains as possible. This, combined with the short field seasons, bad weather, and small labor force, led him to essentially ignore the complex stratigraphy and contextual relationships between features, artifacts, and burials at the site in the interests of moving quickly. To maintain some semblance of vertical control, Hrdlička devised a simplistic tripartite system of relative depths using color codes to organize excavated material (see Speaker, this volume). Although inherently imprecise, this scheme has long served as the framework for identifying and dating archaeological cultures on Kodiak Island (Table 9.2).

Despite Heizer's attempts to reconstruct the archaeological context of some of the Uyak materials, none of the burials he discusses can be related to specific catalog numbers[4] or sets of human remains (fig. 9.4). In the same way, except for the burials excavated in 1932 (see Speaker, this volume), none of the skeletons can be assigned proveniences within the site or related to one another. This overall lack of spatial and chronological control imposes definite limits to what can be said about the significance of the modified bones found at the site.

The modified bones from the Uyak site were studied with a stereoscopic microscope. Through magnification, it was possible to identify a number of previously unreported alterations and to suggest how various modifications were likely made. Each modified bone in the Uyak site collection is discussed individually; the order of presentation follows the year of excavation.

BURIAL P0363622   This burial, recovered in 1931 from the eroding northern edge of the site approx-

Table 9.2.   Hrdlička's Tripartite Stratigraphic Scheme in Relation to Archaeological Cultures and Absolute Dates

Horizon	Position	Culture	Absolute date
Black	Upper	Aleut/Koniag	A.D. 13–1500
Red	Middle	Koniag/Pre-Koniag	A.D. 1100
Blue	Lower	Pre-Koniag	1300 B.C.

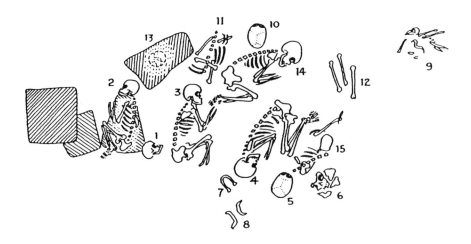

1. Dissociated skull (male?)
2. Female burial
3. Male burial
4. Male (?) burial
5. Skull lacking mandible
6. Crushed skull
7. Mandible
8. Mandible, broken at symphysis

9. Eagle and smaller bird skeleton
10. Skull (part of no. 11?)
11. Disturbed male skeleton
12. Dissociated arm bones
13. Skull crushed under slate slab
14. Adult male burial with hole in skull
15. Incomplete skeleton (part of 5 or 6?)

Figure 9.4. Burial feature reconstituted by Heizer. The catalog numbers of the skeletons are unknown (After Heizer 1956:fig. 4 © University of California Press, used by permission).

imately 1.5 m below the surface in the red stratum, consisted of a complete and intact cranium and mandible belonging to a male aged 20 to 25 years of age. The skull was found resting on its right side (see Hrdlička 1944:137–38, figs. 38–40). Because the skull was pulled from an eroding profile, it is unclear if it had any associated postcranial remains. A unique feature of the cranium was its artificial ivory eyes (see Hrdlička 1941a, plate 11-1). The ivory eyes had been inlaid by filling in the eye sockets with a perishable substance, though all traces of this substance were apparently removed by Hrdlička in the field (Hrdlička 1941a:10).

In addition to the inlaid eyes, the skull had been further modified by drilling two circular perforations on each of the greater wings of the sphenoid. The hole on the right side was 3.5 mm in diameter. Although the upper edge of the perforation was chipped off, the remaining portion had a smooth texture, suggesting it had been abraded, possibly through use of a suspension cord. In addition, a small portion of the beveled spheno-frontal suture adjacent to the perforation was broken, perhaps as a result of

the pulling forces of suspension. The perforation on the left side was 4 mm in diameter. The external border of this hole had a ridge with exfoliations and presented no evidence of wear.

Because of the completeness of the cranium and the location of the holes, it is possible to say that they had been drilled from the exterior surface. There was a slight asymmetry in the placement of the holes; the right one was more anteriorly placed on the temporal surface of the wing and closer to the spheno-frontal suture than its counterpart. In addition to the perforations, the cranium exhibited cuts on the frontal bone and on both zygomatic processes. The mandible was not drilled, cut, or polished (fig. 9.5).

BURIAL P0366697 The burial, which was found in 1932 in the blue stratum, some 2 m below the surface, contained the modified and seemingly isolated skull of a male individual aged 35 to 45 years. The skull was found near a "mass" burial (Nos. P0366696–P0366699) that contained at least eleven individuals (Table 9.3). Its proximity to these burials suggests that it may have had associated postcranial remains and

Javier Urcid

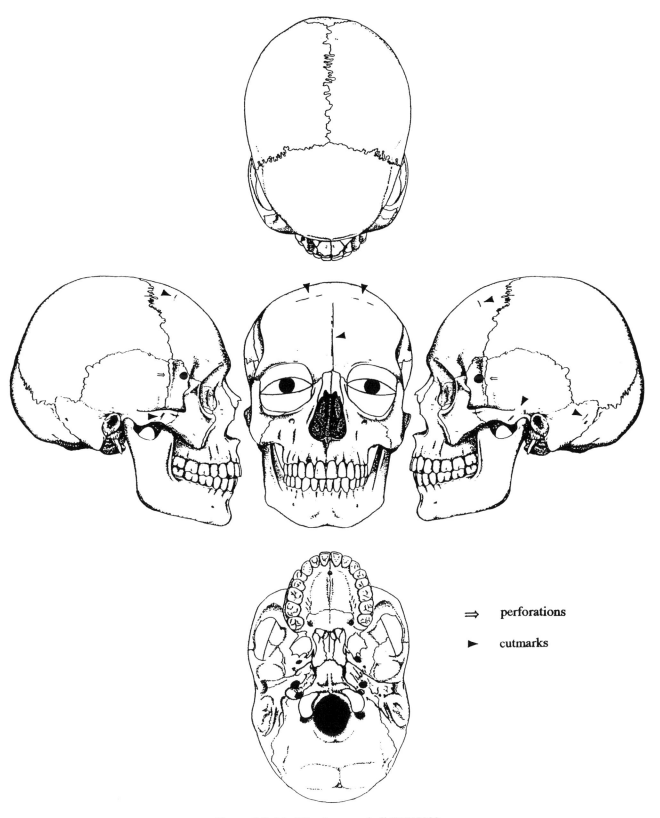

$\Rightarrow$ perforations

$\blacktriangleright$ cutmarks

Figure 9.5. Modifications to skull P0363622.

Table 9.3. Composition of Multiple Burials P0366696 to P0366699

Burial no.	MNI[a]	Anatomical element	Age	Sex
366696	1	cranium/mandible	27–33	female
366697	1	cranium/mandible	35–45	male
366698	5	mandibles only	30–40	male
			30–40	male
			50+	female
			35–40	female
			6–7	?
36699	11	postcrania only	adult	?
			adult	?
			adult	?
			adult	?
			adult	?
			adult	?
			adult	?
			adult	?
			adult	?
			child	?
			child	?

[a] MNI = Minimum number of individuals.

was not a dissociated element or accoutrement of another burial.

While the mandible was complete and intact, the cranium was fragmented, though most of the pieces were present. The fact that the two anatomical elements articulate is supported by correspondences in the temporo-mandibular joints, dental occlusion, and patterns of tooth wear.

The mandible is perforated through the symphysis menti just below the alveolus. The aperture was produced by two drilling episodes. The first began from the anterior surface of the bone and the other started on the posterior side. The holes had similar diameters (7 mm) with the anterior deeper than the posterior (7.5 and 3 mm, respectively). At the point where the two perforations met, their slightly unequal courses are evinced by overlapping thin and partial shelves.

The cranium exhibited cutmarks on the frontal bone, left parietal bone, left temporal bone, and right zygomatic process. Some areas of the vault had distinctive striations, apparently caused by some type of abrasive material (fig. 9.6).

BURIAL P0379244   This burial, which was excavated during the 1934 field season, consisted of the mandible of a probable male aged 14 years old (see Hrdlička 1941a:5 and plate 2, fig. 1). The mandible was located near the complete skeleton of another male individu-

al, about 2 m below the surface in the red level.[5] This skeleton was found in a flexed position lying on its left side, with the head resting on a slate slab and facing east. According to a loose field note that accompanied the modified mandible, it was found near the pelvis of this individual, "a short distance above the burial" (Heizer 1956:13). MacRae and Bohannan (1934:13), who excavated the burial, described the mandible as an ornament or fetish in their field notes.

Both ascending rami of the mandible contained artificial perforations 6.5 mm in diameter. The holes were drilled from the exterior to the interior surface, as evidenced by the smooth lateral edges of the holes and splinters around the medial rims. A third, unfinished perforation was located on the anterior surface of the mandible's body, closer to the right side of the symphysis menti, midway between the alveolar line and the mental protuberance. The unfinished perforation was 6 mm in maximum diameter and 8 mm deep. The hole was slightly conical and the base concave. Cutmarks were also observed on the lateral surface of the posterior border of the right ramus and the right coronoid process. Traces of red pigment were discernible over portions of the lateral surface of the right ascending ramus and the right side of the body of the bone. The surfaces of the mandible had a polished appearance, which suggest extensive handling in antiquity (fig. 9.7).

BURIAL P0374674   This burial, excavated in 1935, consists of the complete cranium and mandible of a male aged 40 to 50 years old. The skull was found in a multiple burial with at least 12 other individuals.[6] The depth of the multiple burial feature places it intermediate between the blue and red levels. The skull was associated with three other crania, which were, according to Hrdlička (1944:267, fig. 151), "nicely arranged at right angles."

The cranium had three circular perforations in the sphenoid bone. Two of the holes were found on the right greater wing. Each measured 5 mm in diameter. One was located on the temporal surface of the wing, near the spheno-frontal suture; the other was situated slightly below, cutting through the superior spheno-temporal suture (see Hrdlička 1941a: plate 1, fig. 2). The third hole was found on the left greater wing. It was 6 mm wide and was asymmetrically located with respect to the holes on the opposite side, being situated approximately in the center of the temporal surface. The mandible was also perforated, with one hole in each ascending ramus. Both holes were approximately 5 mm in diameter. There was a slight asymmetry in their relative location (fig. 9.8).

In addition, the cranium and mandible both exhibited cutmarks. On the cranium, the marks occurred on the frontal bone, the right and left zygoma-

Javier Urcid

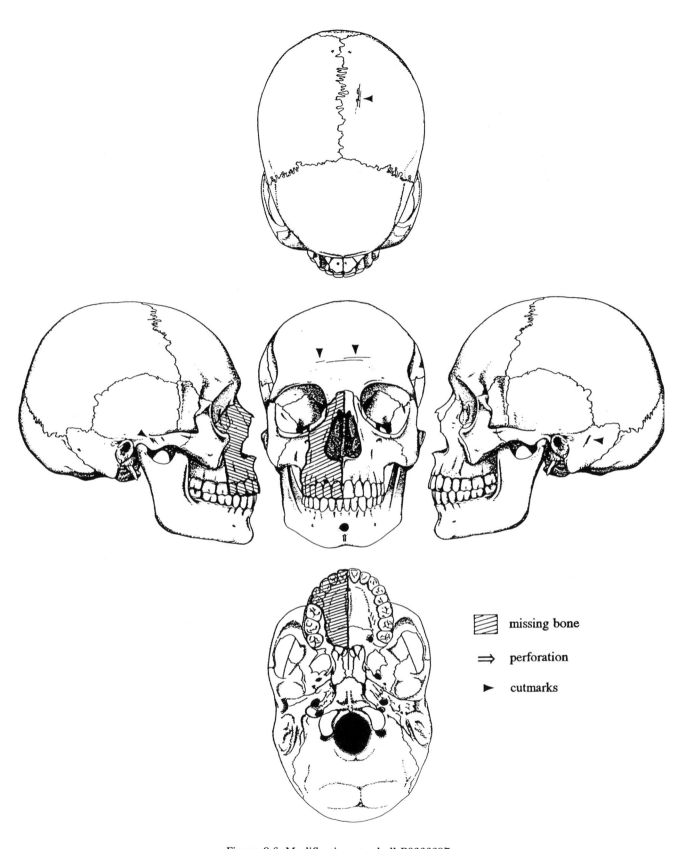

missing bone

$\Rightarrow$ perforation

► cutmarks

Figure 9.6. Modifications to skull P0366697.

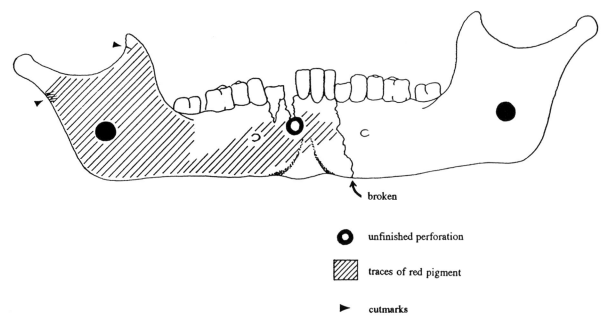

broken

⊙   unfinished perforation

▨   traces of red pigment

▶   cutmarks

Figure 9.7. Mandible P0379244.

tics, the nasal bones, the parietals, the temporals, both zygomatic processes, and at the base of the occipital. The marks on the mandible appeared on the lateral surface of the anterior border of the right ramus. A small portion of the inferior border of the left zygomatic bone was abraded and polished.

BURIAL P0379250 This burial, excavated in 1935, included one dissociated skull fragment consisting of the left greater wing of a sphenoid from an adult individual (see Hrdlička 1941a:5 and plate 3, fig. 1, left). The temporal surface of the skull fragment exhibited a single perforation 6 mm in diameter. The upper edge of the perforation was beveled, a wear pattern possibly resulting from suspension. The perforation had been drilled from the exterior to the interior surface. As Hrdlička (1941a:5) noted, it was probably the cranium and not just a loose sphenoid fragment that had originally been drilled. The sphenoid fragment was found in the upper level of the site (black level), but Hrdlička believed that it had been displaced from lower levels.

BURIAL P0374555 This burial was excavated in 1935, but nothing is known of its context. The burial included the incomplete skeleton of a female 19 to 21 years of age (fig. 9.9A). The right innominate had a circular perforation located approximately in the center of the ilium near the iliac crest. The perforation was 9 mm in diameter. The left innominate was not present.

BURIAL P0374558 This burial, excavated in 1935 from the lowest levels of the site (blue stratum), contained the incomplete skeleton of a female adult (fig. 9.9B). The cranium, which was nearly complete but warped by postmortem pressure, had two perforations located on either of the greater wings of the sphenoid. Both holes were 5 mm in diameter and their borders exhibited wear on the upper portions. The external lower edge of the left hole was splintered. The pattern of wear observed again suggests suspension.

The skull had cutmarks on both the frontal and right zygomatic bones. The left zygomatic bone was not present. The nasal bones, zygomatic processes, and condyles of the foramen magnum were present but did not show evidence of cutmarks (as in the cranium in Burial P0374674). The mandible was present but was not drilled and showed no evidence of cutmarks (fig. 9.10).

Perforations occurred in some postcranial elements of the skeleton, including both scapulae[7] and the right innominate (the left innominate was not present). The nearly complete right scapula had a hole 7 mm in diameter on the neck of the glenoid cavity. A second smaller hole (4.5 mm) was drilled below the first one, close to the lateral border. The incomplete left scapula had two perforations placed near the same landmarks as on the right scapula. The hole on the glenoid cavity neck was 7 mm in diameter. Bone splinters present around the edge of the hole on the dorsal surface indicate that the perforation

110   *Javier Urcid*

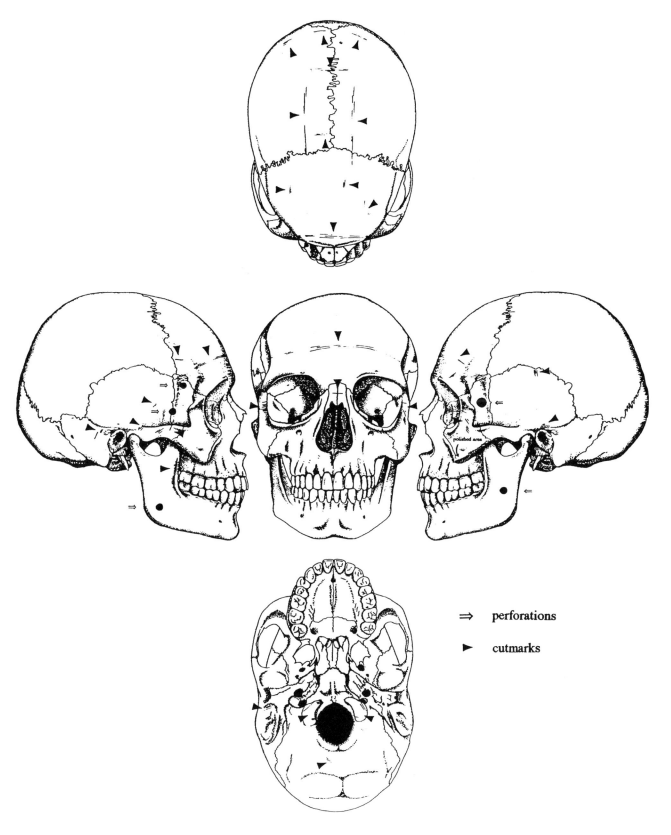

$\Rightarrow$ perforations

$\blacktriangleright$ cutmarks

Figure 9.8. Modifications to skull P0374674.

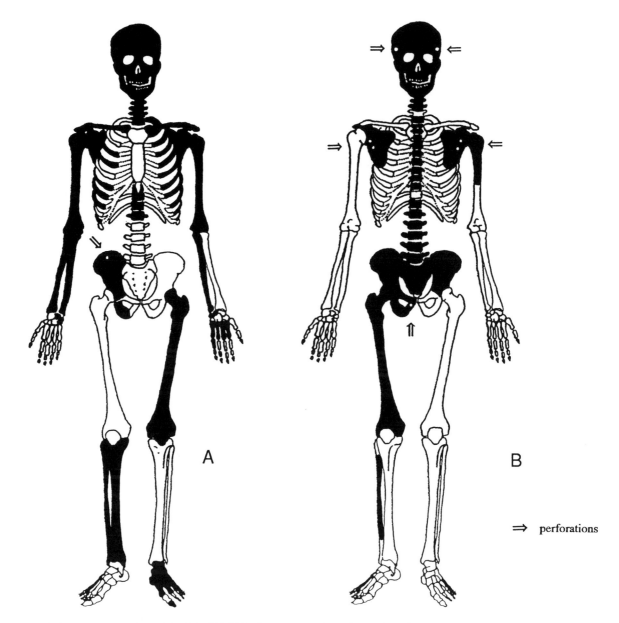

Figure 9.9. A, Homunculus of burial P0374555. B, Homunculus of burial P0374558. (Shaded elements indicate bones present.)

⇒ perforations

was made from the costal side. The lower perforation, initiated from the dorsal surface, was not finished. Its medial edge was broken, possibly an accident during the drilling episode. From what remains of the lateral rim, it was possible to determine that the hole was originally 4.5 mm in diameter and its base was concave. The perforation on the right innominate was about 8 mm wide and located approximately in the center of the pubis body.

BURIAL P0374582   This burial, which was excavated in 1935 from the deepest component of the site (blue level), consisted of the antimeric pair of innominates from an adult individual, probably a male. Both ele-

ments are incomplete, and the pubis body and the ischial tuberosity are missing. A large portion of the ilium from the right innominate was also missing. Each bone had two perforations located on the upper part of the iliac plate near the crest. Since most of the right ilium was missing, the perforations on it were incomplete, though enough of the holes remained to determine that their original diameter was approximately 5 mm. In the left innominate, the anterior perforation was 4.5 mm wide and the posterior hole was 5 mm in diameter.

BURIAL P0374721   This burial, found in 1935 in the upper level of the site (black stratum), included a dis-

Javier Urcid

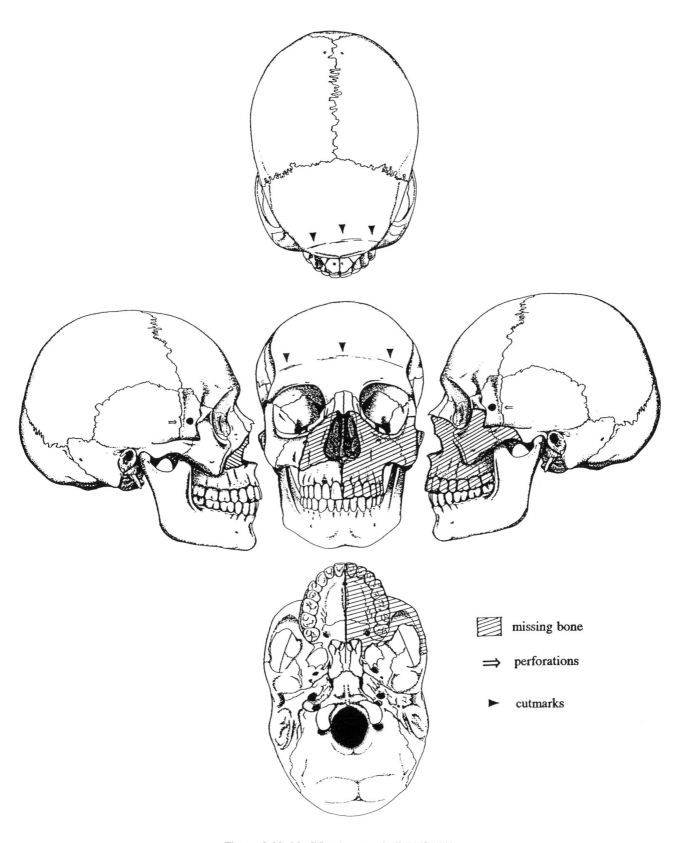

	missing bone
⇒	perforations
►	cutmarks

Figure 9.10. Modifications to skull P0374558.

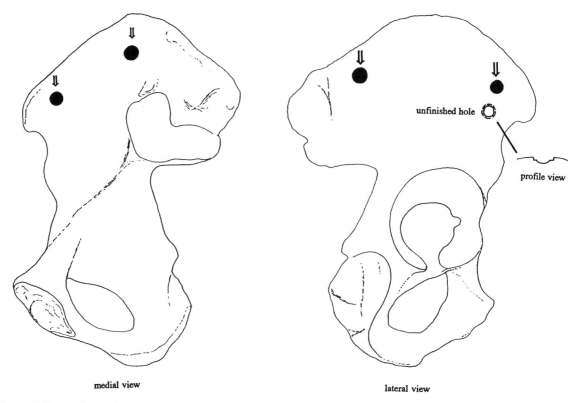

unfinished hole

profile view

medial view

lateral view

Figure 9.11. Medial and lateral views of the right innominate P0379248 with profile of mark left by the unfinished perforation.

sociated left innominate minus the pubis.[8] The bone belonged to a male individual, probably 30 to 40 years of age. The innominate exhibited two perforations on the ilium, both of which were located close to the iliac crest. The larger hole, 10.5 mm in diameter, was situated near the midline and the smaller, 9 mm in diameter, was placed closer to the anterior portion of the bone. The rims of both holes on the lateral surface were neatly delineated while the edges of the perforations on the medial surface were irregular and had small splinters, suggesting that the holes had been drilled from the exterior surface.

BURIAL P0379248   This burial, excavated in 1935 from the intermediate layers (red level), contained the complete right innominate of a male individual 21 to 25 years of age. The bone exhibited two complete perforations on the ilium, close to the iliac crest (see Hrdlička 1941a: plate 3, fig. 2, right). The anterior hole was 6 mm in diameter, and the posterior one was 5.5 mm. A third, yet unfinished, perforation was located just below the hole on the anterior portion, but on the lateral surface of the ilium. The unfinished perforation was marked by a concentric ring 1 mm deep and 4 mm in maximum diameter. Such a mark indicates the use of a thin, hollow drill (fig. 9.11). As evidenced by the pattern of bone splinters at the

edges of the hole, all three perforations were initiated from the lateral surface. It seems, however, that the complete perforation on the anterior portion was later redrilled from the medial to the lateral surface.

BURIAL P0379249   This burial, also excavated in 1935 and recovered from the red level, consisted of a dissociated, incomplete right scapula of an adult individual. The scapula had two perforations (see Hrdlička 1941a: plate 2, fig. 2). A complete hole was drilled through the body of the spine about 3 cm from the medial border of the bone. Splinters on the lower rim indicate that the hole was initiated from the upper surface of the spine. The other perforation, located along the medial border about 3 cm below the glenoid fossa, terminated before it reached the costal surface. It was 5 mm in diameter and 4 mm deep, and had a rather conical cross-section and a rounded bottom. What Hrdlička (1941a: 5) interpreted as the "hacking off" of the acromion process in this scapula was actually the neighboring edge of an *os acromiale,* a discontinuous trait resulting from an ununited ossification center.

BURIAL P0379251   This burial, found in 1935 near the transition between the red and the black levels, consisted of an isolated, nearly complete ilium of a child between 6 and 8 years of age. The age estimate is based primarily on the size of the bone, which was compared with better-represented immature skeletons from the same collection that had been aged by tooth development. The unfused ilium had one perforation located near the anterior iliac crests (see Hrdlička 1941a: plate 3, fig. 1, right). Along the edge of the missing central portion of the bone, traces of another perforation were found, but so little of the perimeter remained that the original size of the hole could not be estimated.

BURIAL P0377701   This burial, recovered during either the 1936 or the 1937 field season from the intermediate layers (red level), was apparently found in association with several other burials, according to a loose field note.[9] The burial contained the partial postcranial remains of a male individual over the age of 25. The left innominate was not present, and the right one lacked the pubis. The associated right femur appears to fit the socket of the right innominate. The latter bone had four circular perforations that were paired and arranged vertically on the ilium (see Hrdlička 1941a:plate 3, fig. 2, left). The set of perforations on the posterior aspect of the bone was located above the auricular surface. The upper hole was 7.5 mm in diameter and the lower was 9 mm. The set of anterior perforations was located near the iliac spine. The upper hole was 8.5 mm in diameter and the lower one was 9 mm. Bone splinters on the medial edges indicate that they were drilled from the exterior to the interior side.

Discussion of Modified Bones from the Kachemak Tradition

The number of known modified bones from the Uyak site nearly doubled as a result of the inventorying and deaccessioning procedures involved in the repatriation of the skeletal remains to Larsen Bay (see Tables 9.4 and 9.5). The modified bones in the collection represent a minimum of 13 individuals. Their ages range from 7 to 60 years, although only three subadults are present. While both genders are represented, males predominate.

The spatial distribution of the modified bones at the site can be only suggested in general terms based on the year in which the burial was collected. Over half of the modified bones were found in 1935 when large portions of the east, west, and south sectors of the site were excavated. The lack of vertical and horizontal control at the site further limits an understanding of the context of burials and the associations between modified bones and other human burials, artifacts, and architectural features.

While we know that four modified bones came from the lowest (blue) level, six from the intermediate (red) level, and three from the upper (black) stratum, these relative depths tell us little about actual temporal distribution and the continuity or discontinuity in the practice of bone modification. Hrdlička's tripartite system was an arbitrary device that was unrelated to the site's cultural stratigraphy. The color levels not only assume homogeneous vertical and horizontal development of deposits but they also ignore topographic differences and postdepositional distur-

Table 9.4.   Summary of Contextual Data for Modified Bones from the Uyak Site (Arranged by relative vertical provenience)

Burial no.	Date	Stratum	Burial context	Anatomical representation	Sex	Age
366697	1932	blue	multiple/disturbed (11)	cranium/mandible	M	35–45
374558/92	1935	blue	single burial	cranium/mandible/postcranium	F	48–59
374582	1935	blue	disturbed single burial	innominates (both)	M?	Adult
374674[a]	1935	blue/red	multiple/disturbed (12)	cranium/mandible	M	40–50
379244[a]	1934	red	associated with single burial	mandible	M?	14
363622[b]	1931	red	unknown	cranium/mandible	M	20–25
377701[a]	1936/37	red	disturbed burial	innominate (one)	M	25+
379248[a]	1935	red	disturbed burial?	innominate (one)	M	21–25
379249[a]	1935	red	unknown	scapula (one)	?	Adult
379251[a]	1935	red/black	disturbed burial?	innominate (one)	?	6–8
374721	1935	black	disturbed burial	innominate (one)	M	30–40
379250[a]	1935	black	isolated/disturbed burial	cranium (fragment)	?	Adult
374555	1935	?	single burial?	cranium/mandible/postcranium	F	17–20

[a] Published by Hrdlička.
[b] Only the inlaid eyes published.

Table 9.5. Summary of Treatment of Modified Bones from the Uyak Site (Arranged by relative vertical provenience)

Burial no.	Modified bone(s)	Type of modification	Total no. of holes	Finished holes	Unfinished holes	Minimum diameter	Maximum diameter
366697	mandible	drilling/cuts	1	1		—	7.0
374558/92	sphenoid/scapulae/pubis	drilling	7	6	1	4.5	8.0
374582	innominates (left-right)	drilling	4	4		4.5	5.0
374674[a]	sphenoid/mandible	drilling/cuts	5	5		5.0	6.0
379244[a]	mandible	drilling/paint/ polishing	3	2	1	6.0	6.5
363622[b]	sphenoid	drilling/cuts/ inlays/polishing	2	2		3.5	4.0
377701[a]	innominate (right)	drilling	4	4		7.5	9.0
379248[a]	innominate (right)	drilling	3	2	1	4.0	6.0
379249[a]	scapula (right)	drilling/cut off piece	2	1	1	5.5	9.0
379251[a]	innominate (right)	drilling	2	2		6.0	6.0
374721	innominate (left)	drilling	2	2		9.0	10.5
379250[a]	sphenoid (left)	drilling	1	1		—	6.0
374555	innominate (right)	drilling	1	1		—	9.0

[a] Published by Hrdlička.
[b] Only the inlaid eyes published.

bances. The inability to link stratigraphic layers from separate areas of the site leaves open the possibility that modified bones assigned to different vertical units may actually have been used or discarded during the same period.

Based on the available information, it seems that the majority of modified bones recovered at the site were found as dissociated anatomical elements. The partial skeleton in Burial P0374558 (fig. 9.9B) is an important exception. While the original position of this set of human remains is unknown, the bones do seem to belong to a single individual, as attested by matches between certain joints and similarities in bone color, texture, and soil staining. Using this example, it is possible to establish a link between various perforated anatomical parts, i.e., the greater wings of sphenoid, the scapulae, and the pubic bones. Another skull (No. P0374674) with holes in both the greater wings of the sphenoid and the mandible expands the associations between drilled elements to include lower jaws. Additional links between the various perforated anatomical elements and other types of modifications can be established on the basis of another skull (No. P0363622), which had perforations on the sphenoid, cutmarks on several locations of the cranium, inlaid ivory eyes, and was polished.

The co-occurrence of drilled perforations in matching anatomical elements varies considerably. In the case of matched crania and mandibles, all combi-

nations of drilled and undrilled elements are present (see Table 9.6). In one case, both the cranium and mandible are perforated; in two other cases, the crania are perforated but the mandibles are not; in still another, the cranium is not perforated but the mandible is. Finally, in one case, neither the cranium nor the mandible are perforated, but holes are present in the right innominate of the same individual.

Despite these variations, the anatomical links established through various cross-correlations suggest that drilled perforations in sphenoids, mandibles, and pubes, as well as cutmarks, inlaid artificial eyes, and cranial polishing, are modifications associated

Table 9.6. Co-occurrence of Drilled Perforations in Matching Crania and Mandibles

Burial no.	Perforated cranium	Perforated mandible
366697	no	yes
374558	yes	no
374674	yes	yes
379244	—	yes
363622	yes	no
379250	yes	—
374555	no	no

Javier Urcid

with a single ritual complex. Thus far, there is no direct way to relate this specific set of modifications to the perforations observed in several ilia from the Uyak site, but the range in perforation diameters and the presence of holes in one pubis argue for their inclusion in the same ceremonial complex.

In terms of the physical characteristics of the modifications, it appears that all 37 known perforations were drilled into flat bones, specifically the wings of the sphenoid, the mandible, the scapulae, and the innominates. There is a tendency, most obvious in the sphenoids, towards asymmetry in the location and number of perforations. The diameters of the perforations range from 3.5 to 10.5 mm. The perforations were drilled from the inner to the outer bone surfaces, as indicated by two composite and three unfinished drillings (the mandible of skull P0366697, the innominate P0379248, the mandible P0379244, and the scapula P0379249). This suggests that the holes were usually drilled into dry anatomical elements that could be easily manipulated. Two unfinished perforations provide evidence of the type of drilling implements employed. These were thin cylindrical tools, both hollow and solid, that may have been manufactured from long bones, possibly of medium-sized birds. The drills were probably rotated with a bow drill and an abrasive medium was perhaps used in the process.

By microscopically examining the wear patterns evident in the drilled perforations, it is possible to suggest the functions of the holes. The holes in the crania indicate wear around the upper edges, which could have been produced by a cord used to suspend the skull. In a complete cranium, the eye sockets would have prevented a cord from being passed through the holes drilled in the greater wings of the sphenoid. Thus, if some of the perforations in the crania were indeed made to aid suspension, it would have been necessary to insert a cord through each of the perforations on the sphenoid, pull the two cords through the foramen magnum, and then tie the four loose ends together (fig. 9.12).

The fact that many perforations retained splinters around their perimeters suggests that some of them were not used for suspending the bones but instead may have been used to fasten the anatomical elements together. Tying the elements together would have had the effect of restricting their movement. In cases of matching crania and mandibles where perforations were not made, prominent features of the skull's architecture, such as the zygomatic arches, nasal cavity, or mandibular condyles, may have been used to fasten the elements together.

The size and location of cutmarks, which appeared on four skulls and one isolated mandible, suggest they were associated with defleshing procedures. Cut-

marks invariably occur on the upper face, on the frontal bones, in the zygomatic regions, the mastoid areas, and on the ascending rami of the mandibles. In one case, cutmarks were present on both the cranial vault and around the base of the skull. The marks on the top of the head exhibited a rectangular pattern.

Based on their characteristics, it is possible to suggest when and in what order the bone modifications were made. The cutmarks were apparently produced around the time of death. The perforations, on the other hand, were made at a point later in time as they were drilled into dried bone. Although these alterations to the bone were done at different times, all of the modifications appear to be related to a single ritual complex.

There is no reason to assume that the human remains from the Uyak site exhibit the total range of possible behaviors associated with the ritual complex suggested above. De Laguna (1934:43–44) described a primary burial feature from the Yukon Fox Farm site on Kachemak Bay containing the remains of an adult male and a child that were accompanied by two isolated adult skulls. While the crania in this burial share basic similarities with the modified skulls from Uyak, they exhibit some additional features as well. The faces of the three adults had been coated with white clay, seemingly for the purpose of building up the facial features. Such treatment was not evident in the child's skull. The orbital sockets of all four skulls were inlaid with artificial bone eyes, and the child's skull exhibited cutmarks. None of the remains from the Yukon Fox Farm site were perforated.

The evidence from the Uyak and Yukon Fox Farm sites suggests that the cutmarks observed on skulls dating to the Kachemak tradition were produced during the process of defleshing. This was apparently undertaken in order to decorate the skulls prior to burial. The evidence from Uyak Burial P0374558, which contained both modified and unmodified bones, suggest that certain decorated primary burials were exhumed, specific anatomical elements drilled, the modified and unmodified bones curated as a set, and eventual secondary burial. The two single skulls from Yukon Fox Farm suggest that a second decorating episode occurred prior to reinterment. Corroborating evidence of postmortem modification, extensive handling, and protection from weathering prior to reburial comes from the polished texture and red pigment on one mandible (No. P0379244) and one skull (No. P0363622) from the Uyak site.

The lack of contextual and chronological control for the skeletal remains from the Uyak site make it difficult to ascertain whether the frequencies of modified bones were different for various time periods. In the Uyak collection as a whole, there were a total of 756 catalog numbers. These identification numbers

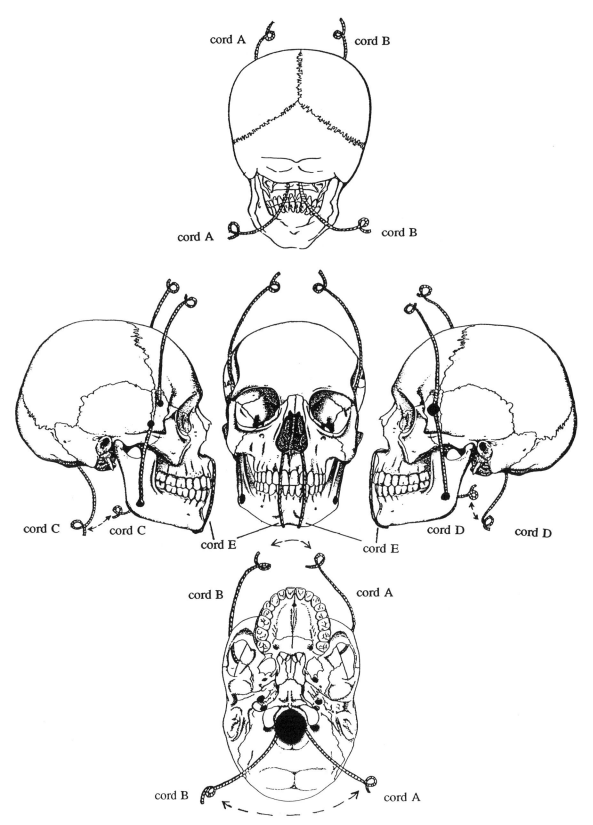

Figure 9.12. Diagram of skull P0374674 showing how cords were tied if perforations were drilled for purposes of suspension and attachment.

were assigned variously to dissociated bones, complete skeletons, and commingled lots of remains that contained up to 20 individuals. Since there was not time during the deaccessioning project to systematically organize and analyze the dissociated anatomical elements, it is only possible to offer a conservative estimate of a minimum of 400 individuals in the Kachemak assemblage. Thus, the 13 individuals with modified anatomical elements would constitute about 3 percent of the mortuary population, a low proportion even in the absence of adequate chronological controls. The figure clearly indicates that the alteration of human remains was not a particularly common practice at the Uyak site.

There have been a number of different interpretations of the modified bones from Kodiak Island, including the idea that they represent trophy heads (de Laguna 1933:743–44, Hrdlička 1944:185) or shaman's amulets or charms (Hrdlička 1941a:14); were associated with ancestor worship (Hrdlička 1941a:11); or were prepared for suspension to decorate whaling boats (Cook 1981:162). Of the four, the last is the least probable because of the carefully curated condition of many of the altered bones. Although most modified bones had been subjected to various taphonomic processes, none exhibited evidence of weathering due to exposure to the elements. If the complex mortuary practices described above were associated with trophy head taking, the small number of modified skulls at the site would suggest a low incidence of warfare. If bone ritualism was associated with ancestor worship, the small number of modified bones in the Uyak collection would indicate that only a few individuals received special treatment. Given that these individuals crosscut age and gender categories, the ritual would suggest a relatively complex social hierarchy.

Conclusions

A careful review of the material correlates of ritual anthropophagy, site formation processes, and the osteological record suggests that Hrdlička's cannibalism hypothesis is unfounded. The cutmarks noted on a few skulls from the site were not produced as a prelude to cannibalism, but rather seem to have constituted part of a prolonged and complex sequence of modifications carried out on the remains of certain individuals.

The ceremonial sequence apparently began shortly after an individual's death with the defleshing of the head,[10] followed by decoration of the skull with plaster facial features and artificial eyes. Other perishable materials may have also been utilized in the ritual decoration. The crania embellished in this way were then buried, with or without the rest of the body.

Sometime after organic decomposition, the remains were exhumed and some of the bones were drilled with holes. The perforations may have been made to suspend or attach the bones to some kind of supporting device or to physically join them. In this way, the modified bones could have served to decorate a ritual setting or could have been the focus of a ritual event themselves. It is impossible to determine whether the facial features were rebuilt at this time. In some cases, the modified bones appear to have been handled extensively, suggesting the importance of their physical presence and manipulation at ceremonial events. Presumably, the modified bones were eventually reburied.

Although various scenarios have been proposed to account for these mortuary practices, it is beyond the scope of the present study to elaborate on the symbolic significance of the modified elements. Mortuary practices and materials from other parts of the world, such as the modelled skulls from the Levant (Kenyon 1979; Rollefson 1985), Nazca trophy heads from coastal Peru, and the ancestor figures from the South Pacific (fig. 9.13), are suggestive, however. Their significance in connection with the mortuary behaviors of the peoples of Alaska during the Kachemak tradition remains to be explored.

Acknowledgments

Special thanks are extended to Carol Butler and David Hunt for their support during the Larsen Bay deaccession project. Tamara Bray, Douglas Owsley, and John Verano read a preliminary version of the paper and made important comments for its improvement. The views expressed, however, remain my sole responsibility. Jerome Edwards took the photographs for fig. 9.2 and fig 9.3. The photographs in fig. 9.13 are courtesy of John Verano (A) and Paul Taylor (B and C).

Notes

1. Heizer included cremations in his classification scheme, although only one was identified at the site. The cremated remains were those of a single adult individual. The color of the burned fragments, their texture, and the patterns of cracks indicate that it had been dry bone, rather than a corpse, that had been burned.

2. The question of whether tooth ablation was actually practiced among paleo-Arctic peoples has been debated in the literature (Cook 1981; Merbs 1968).

3. The two "trephinations" discussed by Hrdlička (1941a, Pl. 4-1 and Pl. 6) involve a depressed skull fracture in one case (No. P0379252), one of six such occurrences from the Uyak site assemblage, and two lytic lesions on the left parietal of an infant (No. P0372883) in the other.

4. The catalog numbers were assigned by the Smithsonian Institution upon accession.

5. The catalog number of this skeleton has not been determined.

6. The catalog number(s) of the skeletal remains comprising this burial feature cannot be ascertained.

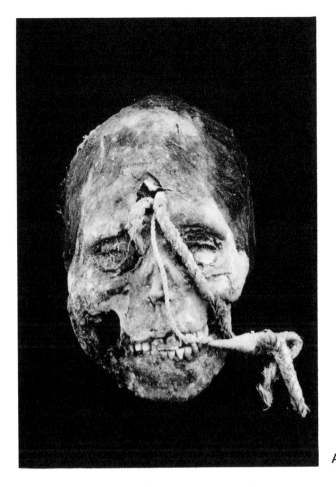

A

C

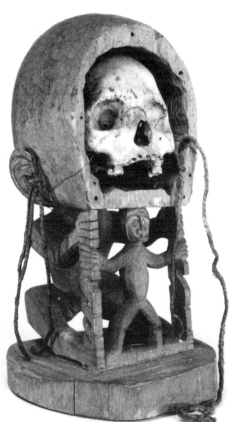

B

Figure 9.13. A, Nazca trophy head, B and C, two Javanese ancestor figures. (Photograph A courtesy of John Verano, photographs B and C courtesy of Paul Taylor)

7. The left scapula had been originally assigned to Burial P0374592, but it was determined to be the antimeric pair of the right scapula of Burial P0374558.

8. When examined in 1991, this bone was in a lot containing 69 innominates, 5 sacra, and 1 scapula.

9. The catalog numbers of these other burials are not known.

10. The cuts on the atlas (No. P0363694) described in the first part of this chapter could have been the result of the ceremonial severing of the head associated with the ritual complex under discussion. It is possible that the striations noted on one skull from the Uyak site (No. P0366697) were produced by the application of clay in the manner described for the burials from the Yukon Fox Farm site.

References Cited

Clark, Donald W.
1974   *Koniag Prehistory. Archaeological Investigations at Late Prehistoric Sites on Kodiak Island, Alaska.* Stuttgart: Verlag W. Kohlhammer.

Cook, Della C.
1981   Koniag Eskimo Tooth Ablation: Was Hrdlička Right After All? *Current Anthropology* 22(2):159–63.

de Laguna, Frederica
1933   Mummified Heads from Alaska. *American Anthropologist* 35 (4):742–44.
1934   *The Archaeology of Cook Inlet, Alaska.* Philadelphia: The University Museum, University of Pennsylvania Press.

Heizer, Robert F.
1956   Archaeology of the Uyak Site, Kodiak Island, Alaska. *Anthropological Records* 17:1. Berkeley: University of California Press.

Hrdlička, Aleš
1940   Ritual Ablation of Front Teeth in Siberia and America. *Smithsonian Miscellaneous Collections* 99(3):1–37.
1941a   Diseases of and Artifacts on Skulls and Bones from Kodiak Island. *Smithsonian Miscellaneous Collections,* vol. 101(4):1–25.
1941b   Artifacts on Human and Seal Skulls from Kodiak Island. *American Journal of Physical Anthropology* 28: 411–21.
1944   *The Anthropology of Kodiak Island.* Philadelphia: The Wistar Institute of Anatomy and Biology.

Jordan, Richard H.
1988   Kodiak Island's Kachemak Tradition: Violence and Village Life in a Land of Plenty. Paper presented at the 15th Annual Meeting of the Alaska Anthropological Association, Fairbanks.

Kenyon, M. Kathleen
1979   *Archaeology in the Holy Land.* 4th ed. London: E. Benn.

MacRae, T. W. R., and C. T. R. Bohannan
1934   Smithsonian Institution U.S. National Museum Expedition to Kodiak Island, Alaska, Led by Dr. Ales Hrdlička 1934; Personal Notes. Manuscript in Hrdlička Papers, National Anthropological Archives, Smithsonian Institution, Washington, D.C.

Merbs, C. F.
1968   Anterior Tooth Loss in Arctic Populations. *Southwestern Journal of Anthropology* 24:20–32.

Rollefson, Gary O.
1985   The 1983 Season at the Early Neolithic Site of Ain Ghazal. *National Geographic Research* 1 (1):44–62.

Stewart, T. Dale
1992   *Archaeological Exploration of Patawomeke: The Indian Town Site (44St2) Ancestral to the One (44St1) Visited in 1608 by Captain John Smith.* Smithsonian Contributions to Anthropology, No. 36. Washington, D.C.: Smithsonian Institution Press.

Porter, F. J. Poole
1983   Cannibals, Tricksters, and Witches. Anthropophagic Images among Bimin-Kuskusmin. In *The Ethnography of Cannibalism.* Paula Brown and Donald Tuzin, eds. pp. 6–32. Society for Psychological Anthropology.

Workman, William
1992   Life and Death in a First Millennium A.D. Gulf of Alaska Culture: The Kachemak Tradition Ceremonial Complex. In *Ancient Images, Ancient Thought: The Archaeology of Ideology.* S. Goldsmith, S. Garvie, D. Selin, and J. Smith, eds. pp. 19–25. Proceedings of the 23d Annual Chacmool Conference. Calgary Archaeological Association.

10

CONTINUITY AND FUNCTION IN THE CEREMONIAL MATERIAL CULTURE OF THE KONIAG ESKIMO

This chapter attempts to define the characteristics and function of Koniag ceremonialism in the late prehistoric era and trace the development of this ceremonial complex on the basis of archaeological materials. Until recently, few researchers had focused on Koniag ceremonial life, despite the fact that an understanding of this aspect could shed light on Koniag sociopolitical organization, religion, and ethnic affiliation. Among the exceptions were Lantis (1947), who discussed Koniag rituals in a more general study of Alaskan Eskimos, and Birket-Smith (1953), who studied ceremonialism among the Chugach, a closely related group to the Koniag. Birket-Smith's treatment of Alutiiq[1] rituals, however, was based on data collected in the 1930s, long after traditional culture had disappeared from the region. A revival of interest in Koniag ceremonialism has begun recently with the work of Crowell (1992) and Jordan (1988).

Most of what is currently known about Koniag ceremonial life derives from a handful of ethnohistoric documents written during the late eighteenth and nineteenth centuries. Although not particularly insightful or complete, these reports contain enough descriptive information to allow the reconstruction of major events in the Koniag annual ceremonial round (Donta 1993). These reports also contain descriptions of material culture specifically identified as having been involved in ceremonial activities. Some of these objects, collected during the contact period, can now be found in museums in Europe and the United States. These objects provide additional insights into the nature of Koniag ceremonial life.

Recent archaeological research in the Kodiak area has documented a number of artifacts that correspond to these historic-period ceremonial materials. Excavations at two Koniag sites on Kodiak Island, conducted by Bryn Mawr College between 1983 and 1989, have yielded important information on the content and practice of Koniag ceremonial life during the late prehistoric era. One site, New Karluk (KAR-001), located on the western coast of Kodiak Island, consisted of a series of 11 house floors layered one on top of the other. Because of the excellent preservation conditions in these layers, ritual objects, including masks, figurines, amulets, rattles, drums, and mortuary goods, were recovered. These materials have been dated to the transitional (A.D. 1100–1300), early (A.D. 1300–1600), and late (A.D. 1600–1784) Koniag phases. Additional detail on the contexts and stratigraphy at New Karluk are described in Jordan and Knecht (1988).

The second site, KOD-026, located on Monashka Bay in the eastern part of Kodiak Island, was initially tested by Donald Clark (1974a) in the early 1960s. The excavations revealed the presence of both Kachemak and early Koniag components. Because preservation conditions were generally poor, Clark found few fragile ceremonial artifacts similar to those from New Karluk. He did, however, recover more than 150 incised stone artifacts decorated with images of anthropomorphic figures in the early Koniag component, leading him to suggest that they might be related to some unknown Koniag ritual (Clark 1964). In my own excavations at the site in 1989, I recovered another 147 incised stones. Subsequent analyses of these artifacts indicate that most of the images depict human figures dressed in ceremonial costumes and, occasionally, carrying ritual-related objects. These images thus provide additional information on early Koniag ceremonialism, which appears to be closely related to that of the late Koniag phase and the historic period.

Ethnohistorical Survey

At the time of the first sustained contact with Russian fur-traders in 1784, the Koniag were described as a densely settled, complexly organized people (Shelikov 1981). Additional information gathered over the next 20 years confirmed these initial observations and also added important detail (Merck 1980; Ioasaf in Black 1977; Davydov 1977; Gideon 1989; Lisianskii 1814). The Koniag numbered at least 8,000 people during the 1780s and may have included as many as 15,000 prior to contact. The population was organized into villages of several hundred people, led by hereditary chiefs, chiefs' assistants, shamans, and priests or "wise men." Society was divided into distinct levels based on wealth and social standing, both of which were passed on from generation to generation. Only those from noble, wealthy families were eligible to hold political positions. The rich often owned slaves who were valued both for the status they conveyed to their owners and for the labor they provided. Commoner families rarely owned slaves. Social distinctions were maintained by an elaborate system of display involving specific material correlates of wealth, such as amber and dentalium shells, as well as decorative elements, such as labrets, tattoos, earrings, special hats, and distinctive parkas.

The Koniag system of sociopolitical differentiation based on wealth and status was reflected in and supported by a ceremonial round that emphasized not only the social standing of the living but also their relationship to honored dead ancestors. Only the nobles could sponsor ceremonial feasts, occasions that offered the hosts an opportunity to demonstrate their wealth through gift distribution (Gideon 1989:46–48). Ancestors were honored in speeches in which the rights of the noble families to their positions of status were reiterated and the validity of the system as a whole was reaffirmed (Donta 1993:202). In all Koniag ceremonies, status and the power of the dead were recurrent themes, the latter being particularly impor-

tant to justifying one's social position and accompanying rights.

The Koniag ceremonial calendar consisted of two primary types of observances. The first included life crisis ceremonies and seasonal activities that were held throughout the year. The second type, which took place over several months during mid-winter, was devoted specifically to the hosting of large dancing festivals that often incorporated families from multiple villages (Davydov 1977:108; Gideon 1989:44–45).

Family celebrations of birth, first events, initiations, marriages, and deaths were held throughout the year. These often included public rituals in which status markers, such as labrets or tattoos were given to the individuals involved. The extent and duration of such events depended on the status of the family. At the death of an important individual, slaves might be ritually killed, the deceased's house or room destroyed, and a feast held to honor him or her (Merck 1980:108; Lisianskii 1814:200). In contrast, ceremonialism surrounding life crises in poor families was unelaborated and feasts were not held (Sarychev 1807:77; Davydov 1977:179).

During the spring and summer months, war raids were conducted and whales were hunted. Both types of activities were strictly regulated according to ceremonial tradition. Warfare was the responsibility of the village chief who enticed men to fight for him with gifts that varied according to social rank. The chief gained prestige through successful raids and economic strength by capturing slaves from neighboring groups (Gideon 1989:41–43). Whale hunting was restricted to the highest ranked individuals in the village who inherited this right from their ancestors. The whale hunters were members of a cult within which knowledge related to hunting was closely guarded (Lantis 1938; Heizer 1943). The power to kill whales was obtained from the mummified bodies of high-status individuals, which were kept in secret locations known only to cult members (Pinart 1873). The whalers were greatly respected for their abilities, but they were also feared for what was viewed as their unclean power derived from their association with the dead. High-status Koniags evidently were powerful in both life and death.

The winter ceremonies began with the conclusion of the fall hunting season. These festivals were initiated by a secret society consisting of the male members of the villages (Lantis 1947:27). Secret society members, acting as evil spirits, intimidated women and children. The spirits were thought to be ancestors who had either gained greater status in the supernatural world and risen to successively higher planes or had become evil (Pinart 1873). As with some Northwest Coast Indian groups, Koniag secret societies may have functioned to demonstrate family rights obtained through contacts with ancestor spirits. The bulk of the winter ceremonial season was devoted to hunting festivals and the public celebration of family events that had occurred during the year. The latter may have included the celebration of especially important political marriages and annual feasts of the dead, as reported for the Chugach (Birket-Smith 1953:112), but not specified for Kodiak. Hunting festivals among the Koniag were limited in variety compared with those in the Central Yupik area. Only a general hunting festival was held, although there are some indications that the Doll Festival may have been observed as well (see Crowell 1992). There is little or no evidence for the existence of Bladder Festivals, Messenger Feasts, or the Asking Feast in the Kodiak area, despite their popularity among Eskimos of the Bering Strait area (Nelson 1983:357–93).

During Koniag hunting festivals guests wore their best clothing and jewelry. Ceremonies consisted of a formal meal, dancing, storytelling performances, speeches honoring ancestors, and the presentation of gifts. Seating, distribution of food, and the types of gifts given were all regulated according to social rank. Festivals were held throughout the winter months for as long as the food supply lasted.

The two most important village members in organizing the Koniag ceremonial round were the shaman and the priest. The shaman was concerned with medical affairs (including fertility) and the foretelling of success (Merck 1980:107). As such, the influence of the shaman apparently was restricted to life crises events. The village priest, on the other hand, was responsible for the winter ceremonies (Lisianskii 1814:208). The priest was a highly respected religious specialist familiar with the properties of the spirit realm. He wrote most of the songs and speeches for the winter festivals. Both the shaman and the priest were believed to have supernatural abilities.

Material Culture

The ethnohistoric reports describe many of the items of material culture involved in the Alutiiq ceremonies. As an integral part of the ceremonies, material culture can be very informative as to the meaning and significance of specific rituals. Material culture is itself an important medium for ritual expression. Furthermore, material culture is a means by which to constitute ritual propositions, graphically represent sanctity, and render the ambiguous visually obvious (Conkey 1985:305).

Historic Koniag ceremonial materials can be grouped into two basic categories that parallel the division between the year-round and the winter ceremonial events. Items of a personal nature associated with life crises and, thus, the shaman, consist of anthropomorphic figurines, amulets, and mortuary goods. Sweat baths, a recurrent trait of ritual cleansing, also appear to have been important elements of seasonal or year-round ceremonies (see Table 10.1). Items employed in the winter festivals described in the ethnohistoric reports include drums, rattles, special bowls, masks, and special clothing and headdresses (see Table 10.2). Examples of such ceremonial objects were collected by Russian and other European explorers during the contact period (as in Ray 1981; Fitzhugh and Crowell 1988; Varjola 1990). These types of objects have also been recovered from late Koniag phase archaeological contexts at the sites of New Karluk and Monashka Bay.

In the rest of this chapter, I present the ethnohistoric and archaeological evidence for ceremonial items and discuss their temporal distribution. I also consult additional data from other sites in the Alutiiq area in order to assess whether these ceremonial artifacts were present prior to the Koniag phase.

Life Crises Objects

ANTHROPOMORPHIC FIGURINES Anthropomorphic figurines were reportedly used by women to promote fertility (Lisianskii 1814:178) and by shamans for the performance of specific tasks (Birket-Smith 1953:127). They were also worn on hats as protective

Table 10.1. Features and Items of Alutiiq Material Culture Described as Being Involved in Year-round Ceremonies

Ceremonial trait	References
Anthropomorphic figures, bone or wood	Lisianskii 1814:178; Birket-Smith 1953:127
Amulets, usually carved representations of birds	Holmberg 1985:46; Birket-Smith 1953:118
Mortuary procedures and goods: simple for the poor, elaborate for the rich	Shelikhov 1981:54; Merck 1980:107; Billings 1980:205; Sauer 1802:177; Ioasaf in Black 1977:86; Davydov 1977:179, 223; Gideon 1989:54; Lisianskii 1814:200; Langsdorff 1814;48; Holmberg 1985:53; Birket-Smith 1953:89
Sweatbath, using hot rocks and water to produce steam	Sauer 1802:177; Billings 1980:205; Gideon 1989:49–50; Lisianskii 1814:198, 201; Holmberg 1985:52; Birket-Smith 1953:85

Table 10.2. Features and Items of Alutiiq Material Culture Described as Being Involved in Winter Ceremonial Activities

Ceremonial trait	References
Drums (also called tambourines), wood with membrane cover, sometimes painted	Shelikhov 1981:55; Merck 1980:101; Billings 1980:206; Sauer 1802:176; Davydov 1977:107–111; Gideon 1989:43–46; Pinart 1872;23; Dall 1884:128; Birket-Smith 1953:81, 109–110, 126
Rattles, wood with puffin beaks and decorative eagle feathers	Shelikhov 1981:55; Merck 1980:101; Billings 1980:206; Sauer 1802:176; Davydov 1977:107–111; Gideon 1989:43–45; Langsdorff 1814:64; Pinart 1872:23; Dall 1884:128; Birket-Smith 1953:109, 127
Special bowls, wood, sometimes decorated with bones, teeth, crystals or beads, sometimes shaped like animals	Billings 1980:207; Gideon 1989:43; Birket-Smith 1953:59–60, 81
Masks, wood, usually painted, often with encircling hoop, wooden bangles and decorative eagle feathers	Shelikhov 1981:55; Merck 1980:101; Billings 1980:206; Sauer 1802:176; Ioasaf in Black 1977:86; Davydov 1977:109–111; Gideon 1989:45; Lisianskii 1814:210; Pinart 1872:23–24, 1873:676; Dall 1884:128; Birket-Smith 1953:94–95, 109, 113, 127
Special headdresses, including "festive hats" and "embroidered hoods," feathers in hair or inserted in a headband, sometimes including ochre	Merck 1980:101, 107; Davydov 1977:107–108; Gideon 1989:45; Lisianskii 1814:109; Holmberg 1985:37; Birket-Smith 1953:69, 114
Special parkas, sometimes birdskin, usually the "best clothing" of those involved	Merck 1980:101; Davydov 1977:107–110; Gideon 1989:40; Lisianskii 1814:208; Birket-Smith 1953:110

amulets (Ivanov 1949b:211; Black 1991:41–42). Alutiiq anthropomorphic figurines from the contact period collected by Cook (Kaeppler 1978:65), Lisianskii (1814:plate III; Ivanov 1949b:199), and others (Ivanov 1949b; Birket-Smith 1941:155) exhibit three primary forms. The first type is carved in wood, includes body parts that are often exaggerated, and frequently has human hair attached. This type most likely equates with the fertility dolls described by Lisianskii, due to the fact that this is the only Alutiiq figurine in which sexual characteristics are depicted, let alone exaggerated. It is also possible that the attached hair may have been related to life power or fertility (Ivanov 1949a:166–167; de Laguna 1987:87). While it was reported that dolls were sometimes used by childless women "to represent the wished-for infant offspring" (Lisianskii 1814:178), there are no further clues as to how the figurines helped promote fertility.

The second type of figurine is also made of wood, but in contrast to the first the face is emphasized and little attention is given to the rest of the body. Such figurines with "different looking faces" were reportedly used by shamans. Each was presumed to represent a different spirit (Birket-Smith 1953:127). The spirit figures could purportedly be made to perform beneficent or evil deeds, according to the needs of the shaman.

The third type of figurine was carved in bone or ivory and depicts a seated figure with arms folded across the chest. The individual is usually portrayed wearing status markers such as earrings, nose ornaments, and labrets. This type occurs in two sizes. The smaller was apparently worn on hats (Black 1991:41) and the larger version was kept in the home or on the person (Ivanov 1949b). Both appear to have been important for protection. Given the features of this figurine type, it is possible that it represents a protective ancestor spirit in the flexed burial position commonly used in the Alutiiq area (Ivanov 1949b:208–212).

A total of 26 human figurines, many similar in form to those in ethnographic collections, were found exclusively in the late Koniag levels at New Karluk (fig. 10.1). Three pieces are clearly of the female fertility type. One of these obviously represents a pregnant female and has hair still attached (Fitzhugh and Crowell 1988:136). Two others have genitalia depicted and a groove around the head for hair attachment (as in fig. 10.1B). A fourth, more stylized figurine also probably belongs to this category (fig. 10.1D), as may two other male pieces (fig. 10.1A). Other fertility figurines have also been found in Koniag contexts (Clark 1974b:271). Twenty of the figurines correspond to the description of shamanic spirit-helpers. The faces on the figurines are carved in precise detail, while the bodies are completely unelaborated without limbs of any kind (Fitzhugh and Crowell 1988:135; and fig. 10.1C). Many of the figurines wear large lateral labrets that distort the mouth into a V-shape. Only one example of the seated type of figurine was recovered from New Karluk. It was carved in ivory and was found near the surface of the site (Black 1991:40).

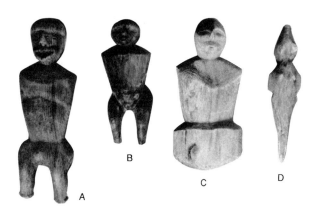

Figure 10.1. Wooden anthropomorphic figurines from New Karluk, all from late Koniag contexts: A, B, D, fertility type; C, shamanic type. (All illustrations in this chapter are by Christopher Donta)

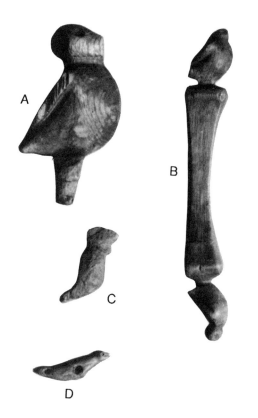

Figure 10.2. Wooden and bone bird amulets from New Karluk: A, B, D, late Koniag; C, early Koniag.

ZOOMORPHIC FIGURINES   Among the Koniag, two types of zoomorphic figurines were thought to provide supernatural power. Bird-shaped objects worn on high-status hunting hats were said to be good luck for hunting as well as in preventing accidents on the open water (Holmberg 1985:46; Birket-Smith 1953:118). Several bird amulets were acquired by Etholén (Varjola 1990:238–39) and Holmberg (Birket-Smith 1941:155, 159) during the mid-nineteenth century. Sea otters were another kind of animal rendered in amulet form that were apparently used by hunters for protection (Liapunova 1967). Both the bird and sea otter figurines were sometimes clothed in miniature sewn garments, as they were thought of as transformed human spirits who were fond of rich adornment (Black 1982:115). How this concept of human-animal transformation fits in with the status hierarchy described by Pinart (1873:677–78) is uncertain at present.

Six wooden and bone bird amulets, some including posts to insert on hats, were found in the early and late Koniag levels at New Karluk (fig. 10.2). None of the pieces were found clothed, but at least one was painted. Another wooden object at the site, though not worn as a hat ornament, depicts a part-human, part-bird figure, possibly in the process of transformation (Jordan and Knecht 1988:300).

MORTUARY GOODS   Koniag death ceremonies varied according to the social standing of the deceased, as was the case with the other life crises events. The mortuary offerings included in the grave also corresponded to the social position of the deceased. A number of different types of grave goods are described in the ethnohistoric sources. Typical grave goods included food, hunting implements, and other utilitarian items. If the deceased was especially rich, the grave furnishings might also include a kayak, armor, and ornaments. The very rich might be mummified, a process through which the individual's high social standing could be converted into spiritual power that could ultimately be used by members of the whaling cult. Pinart (1872, 1875) and Dall (1878) found evidence of mummification on Kodiak and in the Shumagin Islands during the late 1800s. The two explorers also collected mortuary items that corresponded to the ethnohistoric descriptions of Koniag burial goods. Other collections from mortuary contexts of the contact phase have also been documented (Clark 1974b:146–47; Jacobsen 1977).

Evidence for death ceremonialism at New Karluk is presently confined to the uppermost level of the site. Ten burial events were recorded, including both simple burials with few, if any, grave goods, and more elaborate burials with food, elite objects, and ceremonial paraphernalia. Though the sample from New

Christopher Donta

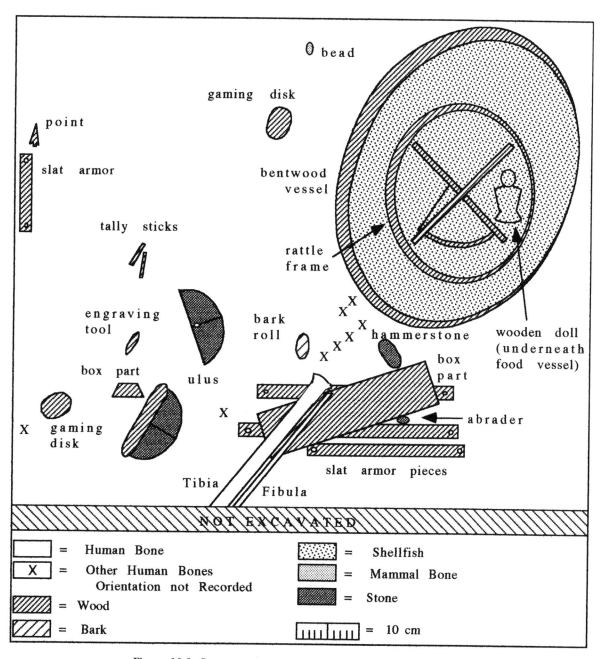

bead

gaming disk

point

slat armor

bentwood vessel

tally sticks

rattle frame

engraving tool

bark roll

hammerstone

wooden doll (underneath food vessel)

box part

ulus

box part

abrader

gaming disk

slat armor pieces

Tibia

Fibula

NOT EXCAVATED

☐ = Human Bone		▦ = Shellfish
☒ = Other Human Bones Orientation not Recorded		▨ = Mammal Bone
▧ = Wood		▨ = Stone
▨ = Bark		⊞ = 10 cm

Figure 10.3. Grave goods associated with New Karluk Burial 4.

Karluk is too small to be considered conclusive, the burial patterns at the site do appear to correspond to the ethnohistoric observations that differential treatment of the dead was accorded on the basis of status. One of the burials in particular documents the attention paid to graves of the rich. This burial contained the remains of an adult male positioned on a layer of grass matting inside the large central room of a house in the uppermost level of the New Karluk site (fig. 10.3). The body was accompanied by the remnants of a wooden slat armor suit. Alongside it was a large bentwood vessel that contained shellfish. The frame of a circular rattle had been placed on top of this vessel. A wooden figurine, various pieces of hunting equipment, several woodworking tools, some utilitarian items, and gaming pieces were also found in association with the body.

SWEAT BATHS Sweat baths were another important component of Koniag ceremonialism. They were an integral part of many events for which ritual cleansing was deemed important, including births, first events, and marriages (Sauer 1802:177; Gideon 1989:49–50; Holmberg 1985:52). In sweat lodges fire-heated rocks were splashed with water to produce steam. The prevalence of this activity and the technology involved produced large quantities of concentrated rock debris (Heizer 1956:23). Fire-cracked rock is a characteristic trait of most Koniag phase sites in the Kodiak area, including New Karluk and Monashka Bay. At the latter site, where rock debris comprised as much as a third of the soil volume of certain levels, the evidence for sweat bathing is particularly clear.

In summary, a look at the distribution of life crises traits at New Karluk and Monashka Bay indicates that artifacts related to these traits are most common in the late Koniag levels, although there is also some limited evidence from earlier contexts (see fig. 10.4). All of the ceremonial artifacts and activities described above were present in the late Koniag phase occupations. Two of these features, amulets and the sweat bath, were also recorded for the early Koniag phase. The sweat bath was apparently a part of the local culture even earlier, as fire-cracked rock debris was noted in transitional Koniag levels at both New Karluk and Monashka Bay. Better information from New Karluk mortuary contexts is needed before temporal changes in funerary patterns can be affirmed.

Additional evidence from other sites in the Alutiiq area indicates that almost all of the material traits associated with life crisis events in the Koniag phase were also present during the preceding Kachemak phase. Bone figurines with detailed faces and simplified bodies very similar to the Koniag shaman anthropomorphic pieces were found in Kachemak contexts at Uyak (Heizer 1956:198), Yukon Island (de Laguna 1975:114–16), and Palugvik (de Laguna 1956:221–23). Seated figurines described as ancestor hat amulets were recovered at Koniag sites on Afognak Island (Clark 1974a:76) and near Akhiok (Black 1991:40), and in the lower Kachemak levels at Uyak (Heizer 1956:196). There is no evidence in the published literature of fertility figurines at Kachemak sites. Bird amulets similar to those at New Karluk were found at Uyak (Heizer 1956:80), Three Saints Bay, and Kachemak Bay (de Laguna 1975:116–17).

Both elaborate and simple burials have been noted at other Koniag sites (Clark 1974b:143–47), at Kachemak sites on Kodiak (Heizer 1956:13), and in Kachemak Bay (de Laguna 1975:43). Data from the Chugach area include not only simple and elaborate burials but also numerous cave burials and evidence for mummification, both during and prior to the Koniag phase (de Laguna 1956:70–92). The sweat bath was also known during the late Kachemak phase, as attested to by rock debris from the top portions of Kachemak deposits at Crag Point (Clark 1970:74–75) and in the lower deposits at Monashka Bay, although it is not found in the same quantities as during the Koniag phase.

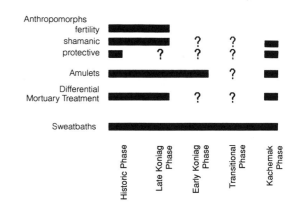

Figure 10.4. Generalized temporal distribution of life crises traits at sites in the Alutiiq area.

Winter Ceremonial Items

Koniag drums were described by Davydov (1977:107) as "animal bladders inflated and stretched round a hoop with a handle so that they are like a shuttle cock racket only bigger." The drums were used in conjunction with rattles as accompaniment to songs and dances at winter festivals. Examples of these drums were collected by Etholén (Varjola 1990:240–41) and Pinart (1872:23) from Kodiak Island during the nineteenth century. Similar drum parts, consisting of 17 detached handles and rims, have been recovered from New Karluk. These pieces were found evenly distributed between the early and late Koniag occupations of the site. Drum handles are notched and grooved at one end to accommodate the rim and lashings (fig. 10.5). No morphological changes in the forms of the drums are apparent between the earliest and latest examples from New Karluk.

Rattles used by the Koniag consisted of wooden circular frames held together by crossbeams from which dangled numerous puffin beaks. Rattles were collected by Langsdorff (1814:plate II) and Fisher (Clark 1984:193), among others. Two circular rattle frames were found at New Karluk, both in the late Koniag levels. A single puffin beak was also found in a late Koniag context at the site. In addition, rattles have been depicted on at least four incised stones from the Kodiak area, including one illustrated by Reinhardt (1981:102), one from New Karluk, and two from the 1989 excavations at Monashka Bay (fig. 10.6).

During ceremonies food was served in round or animal-shaped bowls. These were often painted and might also be "decorated with bones, crystals, beads, and the teeth of various animals" (Billings 1980:207; Gideon 1989:43; Birket-Smith 1953:81). Ceremonial bowls were collected by Etholén (Varjola 1990:81–83) and Jacobsen (Birket-Smith 1953:60–61) from both

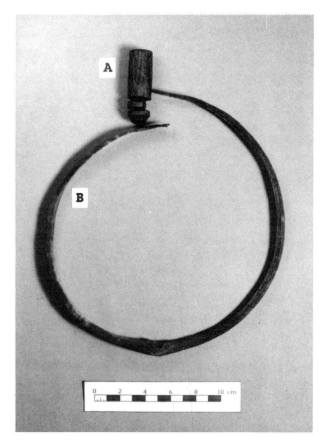

Figure 10.5. New Karluk, late Koniag contexts: A, wooden drum handle; B, wooden drum rim.

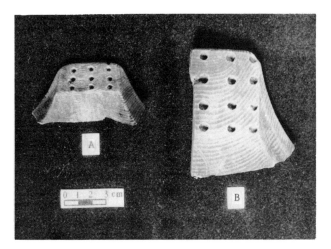

Figure 10.7. Fragments of wooden ceremonial bowls, with holes for decorative insets, from New Karluk: A, historic; B, late Koniag.

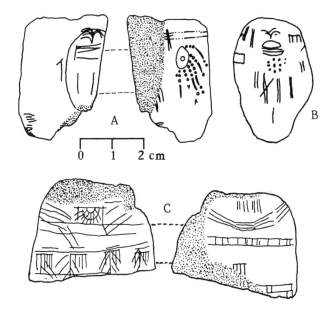

Figure 10.6. Rattle motifs on incised stones from: A, B, Monashka Bay; C, New Karluk, all from early Koniag contexts.

the Koniag and Chugach. Several of these were decorated with status items such as beads and dentalia. Two examples of decorated bowls were also found in the late Koniag levels at New Karluk, though the evidence is fragmentary (fig. 10.7). Both are rim pieces drilled with numerous holes that apparently once contained insets similar to those described by Billings (1980:207).

Koniag masks were commonly used in the winter ceremonies. These objects have been variously described in the ethnohistoric records as "strange," "outlandish," and "hideous." Koniag masks were typically carved in wood, usually painted, and often had a hoop around the outside to which were attached "variously formed appendages" (Dall 1884:129). Masks fitting this description were collected by Malaspina (Feder 1977), Voznesenskii (Lipshits 1955), Pinart (Lot-Falck 1957), among others. Most of the ethnographic specimens were painted and had attached hoops and mask bangles (Fitzhugh and Crowell 1988:50, 88). The vast majority depict human faces that are often adorned with labrets. In fact, of the more than 100 masks collected in the Alutiiq area during the contact period, only three represent nonhuman entities. This contrasts sharply with the imagery of masks in the Central Yupik area, where zoomorphic forms clearly predominate over human ones.

A large sample of masks, including 11 full-sized specimens and 30 of smaller proportions, were recovered from New Karluk. All but four of these were from the late Koniag levels of the site (figs. 10.8 and 10.9). Like the ethnographic masks from the Alutiiq area, almost all of the images portrayed are human. Only one of the 41 New Karluk masks is not anthropomorphic,

Figure 10.8. Full-sized wooden mask from New Karluk, late Koniag.

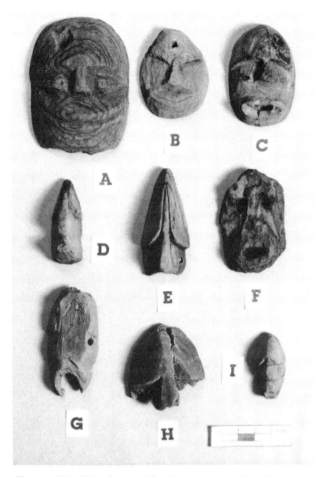

Figure 10.9. Wooden and bark masks from New Karluk, all late Koniag.

a solitary zoomorphic mask that represents an owl (Fitzhugh and Crowell 1988:135). Some of the masks portray fairly realistic human faces with labrets (as in fig. 10.8) while others depict beings with pointed heads (figs. 10.9D and 10.9E), a characteristic trait of Alutiiq evil spirits (Pinart 1873:678; Birket-Smith 1953:121). Most of these masks have attachment holes around the perimeter to which wooden bangles or hoops holding wooden bangles were once attached. More than 100 wooden bangles were found at New Karluk (fig. 10.10). The bangles are most commonly shaped like feathers, although there are also square, round, and unique types. Many of the bangles are painted, although no paint was found on the masks themselves. The mask bangles were found throughout the early and late Koniag levels of the site.

Some of the figures depicted on incised stones from Kodiak appear to be wearing masks. On either side of the head, often rising far above the face, or sometimes angled away from the face, are incised elements that are interpreted as headwear or mask parts. In most cases, these elements consist of multiple sets of paired lines, often meeting at one or both ends,

forming an object very similar in shape to the feather-shaped mask bangles described above. On several of the Monashka Bay specimens, these mask bangles are depicted as dangling from a hoop-like feature that partially surrounds the face (fig. 10.11). Mask-like elements can be seen on at least eight incised stones from New Karluk and Monashka Bay, all from early Koniag contexts.

During ceremonies, the Koniag reportedly wore their "best clothing" and donned special "festive hats" or "embroidered hoods" as part of their rich and elaborate ceremonial costumes. Status markers were worn in quantity in the ears, nose, and lips, reinforcing the differences between social ranks. Feathers were worn loosely in the hair to add to the decorations. A large collection of ceremonial clothing and hats was acquired by Voznesenskii during the 1840s (Ray 1981:98, 100; Fitzhugh and Crowell 1988:209, 220). Included among these objects were cormorant coats and parkas made of caribou and ground squirrel skins and tall conical ceremonial headdresses decorated with paint and embroidery.

Although such clothing and headwear items were

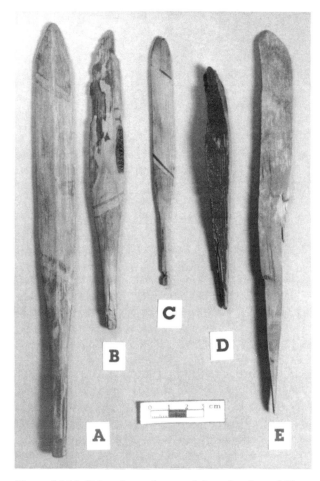

Figure 10.10. Painted wooden mask bangles shaped like feathers from New Karluk, all late Koniag.

In summary, the temporal distribution of winter festival traits at New Karluk and Monashka Bay (fig. 10.13) seems to parallel that of the life crises ceremonies. Most of the artifacts associated with Koniag winter festivals (about 80 percent) occurred in the late Koniag component of the site, despite the fact the materials from these levels constitute only about 60 percent of the total site assemblage. Bowls and rattles were entirely confined to the late Koniag phase, and the majority of mask-related artifacts (82 percent) were found in late Koniag contexts. Drum parts were found equally in early and late Koniag phases.

Evidence for the use of drums and masks has also been found in Kachemak contexts in the Alutiiq area. Although drums seem to have been made primarily out of wood, de Laguna (1975:104) recovered a bone drum handle similar to the New Karluk wood specimens from the Yukon Fox Farm site. At least two wooden masks have been fortuitously recovered from Kachemak contexts, one at Crag Point (Clark 1970:85) and one at Old Karluk. Clark's mask has heavy eyebrow ridges and a large forehead, features very much like those seen on specimens from New Karluk and many of the ethnographic examples. The Old Karluk mask is nearly identical to another from New Karluk. There is presently no evidence for the use of puffin-beak rattles or ceremonial bowls in Kachemak contexts.

Conclusions

As indicated by the ethnohistoric descriptions, Koniag society was organized, both socially and politically, along the lines of hereditary status differences. This system apparently pervaded ceremonial life as well. Descriptions of ceremonial activities are so saturated with references to status and wealth distinctions that it seems quite probable that Koniag ceremonialism functioned, to a great extent, to reinforce the existing social system. Descriptions of Koniag religious ideas follow this pattern as well, indicating that high status in life was equated with high status after death (Lisianskii 1814:199–200; Sonne 1978). High ranking ancestors became spirits capable of affecting the world of the living. Supernatural power thus became linked with real social power.

Koniag ceremonial material culture, both historic and prehistoric, also reflects the importance of status, wealth, and the power of human spirits. A number of the ceremonial artifacts described above were decorated with elements specifically identified in the ethnohistoric reports as status markers. Status is also obviously depicted on a large portion of the incised stones, which provide evidence of Koniag ceremonial costumes from the early Koniag phase. The incised

not recovered intact from New Karluk or Monashka Bay, evidence for ceremonial headdresses and clothing can be seen in images on incised stones. Headwear is the most common decorative element on both the New Karluk and Monashka Bay incised images. These elements most frequently consist of the bangles or feathers described above. Clothing is also represented on many of the incised figures, depicted by one or more elements drawn below the face and often covering a large portion of the figurine surface (fig. 10.12). Neither the shapes of the clothing items nor functional elements such as sleeves are discernable on the pieces. When clothing styles and designs are depicted, the most frequent type represented is a parka with V-neck collar. In addition to clothing and headwear, items of personal adornment indicative of status are also portrayed on a large number of the figurines. These elements include beads, earrings, labrets, and possibly tattoos. The complete picture of the rich Koniag ceremonial costume supports the association between status and ceremony described during the contact phase.

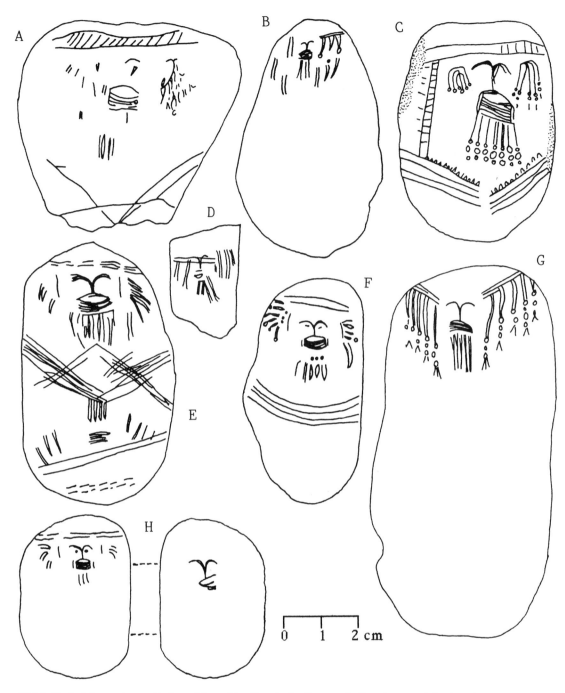

Figure 10.11. Probable mask motifs from Monashka Bay, including encircling bars and feather bangles, all early Koniag.

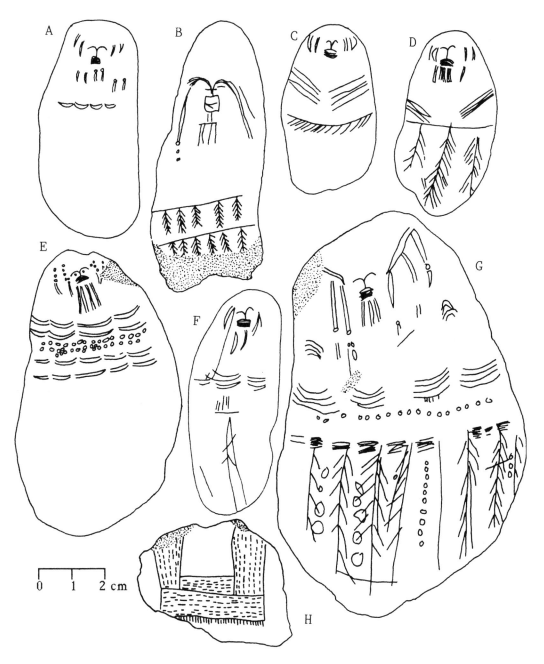

Figure 10.12. Incised images with clothing designs and status elements such as tattoos, earrings, and beads; all early Koniag from Monashka Bay.

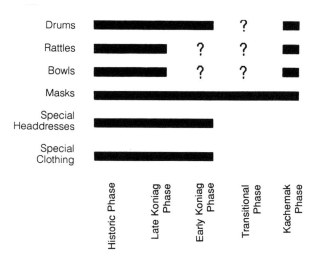

| | Drums | Rattles | Bowls | Masks | Special Headdresses | Special Clothing |

Figure 10.13. Generalized temporal distribution of winter ceremonial items at sites in the Alutiiq area.

stones indicate that special headdresses, parkas, labrets, and earrings were all worn at the ceremonies, reinforcing the awareness of status differences between village members. The images on the figurines, masks, and incised stones—whether human or spirit—are nearly all anthropomorphic, and all are concerned with status. The message of these materials is that social status existed on a continuum that extended from life into death, linking the two domains.

This conceptualization of Koniag ceremonialism rests largely on data that spans a period of about 600 years. Based on the available information, it is possible to suggest that ceremonial forms seen during the contact period had essentially been in place by at least the early Koniag phase, ca. A.D. 1300. Incised stone imagery indicates that status and ceremonialism were already closely intertwined by this time. Many other ceremonial features, including amulets, drums, masks, and the sweat bath, were already known during this period as well. Continuity in ceremonial form over the period from A.D. 1300 until well into historic times, ca. A.D. 1870s, is thus indicated.

Generalizations beyond the Koniag phase are not easy to make at the present time. Despite a fairly large sample of artifactual material, only a small number of ceremonial artifacts have been recovered from Kachemak contexts. The problem lies in determining whether the lack of ceremonial artifacts at Kachemak sites is due to an unelaborated ceremonial culture or is simply a matter of preservation bias. Until a Kachemak site of the same caliber as New Karluk is found, comparisons between the two phases will be difficult to make. Collections from Kachemak phase sites do, however, contain some ceremonial artifacts

similar to those from the Koniag phase, perhaps suggesting a degree of continuity much longer than the 600 years presently indicated.

Acknowledgments

Many individuals involved in the Bryn Mawr College archaeological project have contributed to the analyses and interpretations presented in this chapter. Richard Jordan initiated the project and was working along similar theoretical lines prior to his untimely death. Richard Knecht, the Kodiak Area Native Association, and Bryn Mawr College were critical in the completion of the 1989 fieldwork. The criticisms and support of Richard Davis, Susan Kaplan, and Alison Donta have helped this research immeasurably.

Note

1. The term Alutiiq refers to Pacific Eskimos, a group that includes the Koniag, Chugach, and Unegkurmiut.

References Cited

Billings, Joseph
1980   Voyage of Mr. Billings . . . 1789–1790–1791. In *Siberia and Northwestern America, 1788-1792. The Journal of Carl Heinrich Merck, Naturalist with the Russian Scientific Expedition Led by Captain Joseph Billings and Gavriil Sarychev.* Richard A. Pierce, ed. and Fritz Jaensch, transl. pp. 199–210. Kingston, Ontario: Limestone Press.

Birket-Smith, Kaj
1941   Early Collections from the Pacific Eskimo. Nationalmuseets Skrifter, *Etnografisk Raekke* 1:121–63. Copenhagen.
1953   *The Chugach Eskimo.* Nationalmuseets Skrifter, Etnografisk Raeeke 6. Copenhagen.

Black, Lydia T.
1977   The Konyag (the Inhabitants of the Island of Kodiak) by Iosaf [Bolotov] (1794-1799) and by Gideon (1804–1807). *Arctic Anthropology* 14(2):79–108.
1982   *Aleut Art: Unangan of the Aleutian Archipelago.* Anchorage: Aleutian/Pribilof Islands Association.
1991   *Glory Remembered: Wooden Headgear of Alaska Sea Hunters.* Juneau: Alaska State Museums.

Clark, Donald W.
1964   Incised Figurine Tablets from Kodiak, Alaska. *Arctic Anthropology* 2(1):118–34.
1970   The Late Kachemak Tradition at Three Saints and Crag Point, Kodiak Island, Alaska. *Arctic Anthropology* 6(2):73–111.
1974a   Contributions to the Later Prehistory of Kodiak Island, Alaska. *National Museum of Man Mercury Series Archaeological Survey Paper No. 20.* Ottawa.
1974b   *Koniag Prehistory: Archaeological Investigations at Late Prehistoric Sites on Kodiak Island, Alaska.* Stuttgart: Verlag W. Kohlhammer.

1984 Pacific Eskimo: Historical Ethnography. In *Handbook of North American Indians, Vol. 5, The Arctic.* David Damas, ed. pp. 185–97. Washington, D.C.: Smithsonian Institution Press.

Conkey, Margaret
1985 Ritual Communication, Social Elaboration and the Variable Trajectories of Paleolithic Material Culture. In *Prehistoric Hunter-Gatherers: The Emergence of Cultural Complexity.* T. Douglas Price and James A. Brown, eds. pp. 299–323. New York: Academic Press.

Crowell, Aron
1992 Postcontact Koniag Ceremonialism on Kodiak Island and the Alaska Peninsula: Evidence From the Fisher Collection. *Arctic Anthropology* 29(1):18–37.

Dall, William H.
1878 *On the Remains of Later Prehistoric Man Obtained from Caves in the Catherina Archipelago, Alaska Territory, and Especially from the Caves of the Aleutian Islands.* Smithsonian Contributions to Knowledge, Vol. 22.
1884 On Masks, Labrets, and Certain Aboriginal Customs. In *3rd Annual Report of the Bureau of American Ethnology,* pp. 67–151.

Davydov, G. I.
1977 *Two Voyages to Russian America, 1802-1807.* Richard A. Pierce, ed. and Colin Bearne, transl. Kingston, Ontario: Limestone Press.

Donta, Christopher
1993 *Koniag Ceremonialism: An Archaeological and Ethnographic Analysis of Sociopolitical Complexity and Ritual Among the Pacific Eskimo.* Ph.D dissertation, Department of Anthropology, Bryn Mawr College. Ann Arbor: University Microfilms.

Feder, Norman
1977 The Malaspina Collection. *American Indian Art Magazine* 2(3):40–51, 80, 82.

Fitzhugh, William W., and Aron Crowell
1988 *Crossroads of Continents: Cultures of Siberia and Alaska.* Washington, D.C.: Smithsonian Institution Press.

Gideon, H.
1989 *The Round the World Voyage of Hieromonk Gideon, 1803–1809.* Richard A. Pierce, ed. and Lydia Black, transl. Kingston, Ontario: Limestone Press.

Heizer, Robert F.
1943 Aconite Poison Whaling in Asia and American: An Aleutian Transfer to the New World. *Bureau of American Ethnology Bulletin* 133:419–68. Anthropological Papers No. 24.
1956 Archaeology of the Uyak Site Kodiak Island, Alaska. *University of California Anthropological Records* 17(1).

Holmberg, Heinrich Johan
1985 *Holmberg's Ethnographic Sketches.* Marvin W. Falk, ed. and Fritz Jaensch, transl. Fairbanks: University of Alaska Press.

Ivanov, S. V.
1949a O znachenii dvukh unikalhnykh zhenskikh statueto amerikanskikh eskimosov. *Sbornik Muzeia Antropologii i Etnographii* 11:162–70.
1949b Sidiachie chelovecheskie figurki v skulĺpture Aleutov. *Sbornik Muzeia Antropologii i Etnographii* 12:195–212.

Jacobsen, Johan Adrian
1977 *Alaskan Voyage 1881–1883.* Erna Gunther, transl. Chicago: University of Chicago Press.

Jordan, Richard H.
1988 Qasqiluteng: Feasting and Ceremonialism among the Traditional Koniag of Kodiak Island, Alaska. Paper presented at Crossroads of Continents exhibit opening, Smithsonian Institution, Washington, D.C.

Jordan, Richard H. and Richard A. Knecht
1988 Archaeological Research on Western Kodiak Island, Alaska: The Development of Koniag Culture. In *The Late Prehistoric Development of Alaska's Native People.* Robert D. Shaw, Roger K. Harritt, and Don E. Dumond, eds. pp. 356–453. Alaska Anthropological Association Monograph Series No. 4, Anchorage.

Kaeppler, Adrienne L.
1978 *Cook Voyage Artifacts in Leningrad, Berne, and Florence Museums.* Honolulu: Bishop Museum Press.

de Laguna, Frederica
1956 *Chugach Prehistory: The Archaeology of Prince William Sound, Alaska.* Seattle: University of Washington Press.
1975 *The Archaeology of Cook Inlet, Alaska.* 2d ed. Anchorage: Alaska Historical Society.
1987 Atna and Tlingit Shamanism: Witchcraft on the Northwest Coast. *Arctic Anthropology* 24(1):84–100.

Langsdorff, Georg Heinrich von
1814 *Voyages and Travels in Various Parts of the World, during the years 1803, 1804, 1805, 1806, and 1807.* Vol. 2. London: Henry Colburn.

Lantis, Margaret
1938 The Alaskan Whale Cult and Its Affinities. *American Anthropologist* 40:438–64.
1947 *Alaskan Eskimo Ceremonialism.* Seattle: University of Washington Press.

Liapunova, Rosa G.
1967 Zoomorfnaia skulptura Aleutov. *Sbornik Muzeia Antropologii i Etnographii* 24:38–54.

Lipshits, B. A.
1955 O kollektsiiakh Muzeia antropologii i etnografii, sobrannykh russkimi pute bestvennikami i issledovateliami na Aliaske i v Kalifornnii. *Sbornik Muzeia Antropologii i Etnographii* 16:358–69.

Lisianskii, Iuri
1814 *Voyage Round the World in the Years 1803, 4, 5, and 6.* London: John Booth.

Lot-Falck, Eveline
1957 Les Masques Eskimo et Aleoutes de la Collection Pinart. *Société des Américanistes Journal* 46:5–43.

Merck, Carl Heinrich
1980   *Siberia and Northwestern America, 1788–1792. The Journal of Carl Heinrich Merck, Naturalist with the Russian Scientific Expedition Led by Captain Joseph Billings and Gavriil Sarychev.* Richard A. Pierce, ed. and Fritz Jaensch, transl. Kingston, Ontario: Limestone Press.

Nelson, Edward William
1983   *The Eskimo about Bering Strait.* Washington, D.C.: Smithsonian Institution Press.

Pinart, Alphonse L.
1872   *Catalogue des Collections Rapportées de l'Amérique Russe (Aujourd'hui Territoire d'Aliaska) par Alphonse Pinart, Membre de Plusieurs Sociétes Savantes de France et des Etats-Unis, Exposeés dans l'une des galeries du Museum d'histoire naturelle de Paris (section d'Anthropologie).* Paris: J. Claye.
1873   Eskimaux et Koloche, Idees religieuses et traditions des Kaniagmioutes. *Revue d'Anthropologie* 2:673–80.
1875   *La Caverne d Aknañh, Ile d'Ounga, Archipel Shumagin, Alaska.* Paris: E. Leroux.

Ray, Dorothy Jean
1981   *Aleut and Eskimo Art: Tradition and Innovation in South Alaska.* Seattle: University of Washington.

Reinhardt, Gregory A.
1981   The Incised Stones From Kodiak, Alaska. *The Masterkey* 55:101–105.

Sarychev, Gavriil
1807   *Account of a Voyage of Discovery to the North-East of Siberia, the Frozen Ocean, and the North-East Sea. Vol. 2.* London: Richard Phillips.

Sauer, Martin
1802   *An Account of [an] . . . Expedition to the Northern Parts of Russia . . . In the Years 1785, etc. to 1794.* London: T. Cadell, Jr. and W. Davies in the Strand.

Shelikhov, Grigorii I.
1981   *Voyage to America, 1783–1785.* Richard A. Pierce, ed. and Marina Ramsay, transl. Kingston, Ontario: Limestone Press.

Sonne, Birgitte
1978   Ritual Bonds between the Living and the Dead in Yukon Eskimo Society. *Temenos* 14:127–83.

Steward, Julian H.
1942   The Direct Historical Approach to Archaeology. *American Antiquity* 4:337–343.

Varjola, Pirjo
1990   *The Etholén Collection.* Helsinki: National Museum of Finland.

Workman, William
1990   Life and Death in a First Millennium A.D. Gulf of Alaska Culture: The Kachemak Tradition Ceremonial Complex. In *Ancient Images, Ancient Thought: The Archaeology of Ideology.* A. S. Goldsmith, S. Garvie, S. Selin, and J. Smith, eds. pp. 19–25. Calgary: Archaeological Association, University of Calgary.

11

STILL A BIG STORY

The Prehistory of Kodiak Island

Aleš Hrdlička's excavation of the Uyak site has been the largest single-site dig in Alaska. His was the only archaeological project in the state where mine cars were used to dispose of the site spoil. The Smithsonian Institution project began, to paraphrase Hrdlička's words (1943:402), as a "big, new story" in the annals of Alaskan archaeology. It resulted in glowing descriptions of the past of a people who, it was said, had found an island in the sun (save for the biting gnats and mists). But Hrdlička's methods and conclusions have been faulted. Except for the recovery of a large collection of cultural material, the several seasons of excavation failed to realize their potential. The archaeology of the Uyak site thus is appropriate for an internal salvage operation.

In this chapter, I outline the place of Kodiak Island and its inhabitants in Alaskan Native history and further discuss the Uyak site. Secondarily, I comment on the work of other authors in this volume.

Archaeological Research on Kodiak Island

Since the last decades of the 1700s, explorers and travelers have documented the native peoples of Kodiak Island, making them among the better known "tribes" of North America (Black 1977; Davydov 1977; Gideon 1989; Holmberg 1985; Lisianski 1814; Merck 1980; Pinart 1873; Sarychev 1806; Sauer 1802; Shelikhov 1981). The explorers collected ethnographic speci-

mens, ranging from kayaks to hunting weapons and decorated rain parkas, from these groups. During the last half of the nineteenth century, they were joined by collectors, among them the Finnish explorer Heinrich J. Holmberg (Birket-Smith 1941), the French naturalist and traveler Alphonse L. Pinart (1873), and William J. Fisher, who collected for the Smithsonian Institution (Crowell 1992; Fitzhugh and Crowell 1988). Among the specimens they collected were objects from archaeological proveniences (Birket-Smith 1941; Crowell 1992:22).

But it was not until 1931 that the archaeology of Kodiak Island received any serious attention. In that year Aleš Hrdlička extended his arctic search for human osteological collections southward to the Gulf of Alaska, to the large midden site located next to the Alaska Packers Association cannery and the small village of Larsen Bay. Hrdlička thus became the father of Kodiak prehistory. Although his excavation methods were unscientific, he was a good synthesizer and could spin a daily tale of gnat bites and the joy of discovery, which made his final report, *The Anthropology of Kodiak Island* (1944), popular with the general public. The report was also widely consulted by frustrated archaeologists, for Hrdlička's bequest to posterity had generated interpretations that set the primary research orientation of Kodiak prehistory for the next generation of prehistorians (Clark 1993).

After the multi-season excavation campaign at the Uyak site, there was a lull in archaeological research on the island, with only a few minor projects and Heizer's (1956) publication of the Uyak artifacts as exceptions. The next "campaign" on the island was undertaken by the University of Wisconsin Aleut-Konyag Project from 1961 to 1964. The project's findings resulted in a more sharply defined archaeological sequence and added a new cultural tradition (Ocean Bay) antedating the occupation of the Uyak site (Clark 1966). Hrdlička's Pre-Koniag or Uyak site Lower Levels tradition received a broader referent, the Kachemak tradition, which was named to recognize relationships with a similar archaeological culture identified at Kachemak Bay, Outer Cook Inlet, by Frederica de Laguna (de Laguna 1934). The designation Koniag for the historic habitation of Kodiak Island was retained for the most recent tradition, which is represented in the upper levels of the Uyak site and at large midden sites elsewhere on Kodiak. This framework notwithstanding, the prehistory of Kodiak Island remained poorly known due to small samples, inadequate exploration of certain periods, poor organic preservation, and a focus limited to certain kinds of sites.

Since 1964 there have been many small-scale archaeological projects on the island. In 1971 Clark and Workman returned to excavate components of the Ocean Bay culture that earlier had been defined on the basis of a very small but highly distinctive collection (Clark 1979). In 1977 a continuing series of more or less unrelated agency surveys and excavations began, the first ones being those of the U.S. Fish and Wildlife Service (see Clark 1993; Haggarty et al. 1991; and Moss and Erlandson 1992). Other agency work has included Bureau of Indian Affairs excavation at the head of Larsen Bay (Crozier 1989; Yesner 1989) and a small-scale salvage project at the Larsen Bay settlement itself.

In 1983 major excavations began under the direction of Richard Jordan, initially from Bryn Mawr College and later from the University of Alaska, Fairbanks. The Kodiak Archaeological Project focused on excavations at Karluk (Jordan and Knecht 1986; Knecht and Jordan 1985) and Crag Point, a site that Clark and Workman (Clark 1970) had tested. Most subsequent projects on Kodiak can be traced, either directly or indirectly, to this project and its personnel. These include Crowell's 1990-1991 excavations at historic Three Saints; Steffian's work at the Uyak site (1992, in press, and this volume); Donta's work at Monashka Bay (this volume); Knecht's analysis of Karluk collections and his continuing surveys, project sponsorship, and museum-oriented work with the cultural heritage program of the Kodiak Area Native Association; Hausler-Knecht's 1988-1991 excavation of Ocean Bay components; and B. Fitzhugh's problem–

oriented area surveys that are just beginning (personal communication to D. Clark).

For orientation, the reader may consult the cultural sequence diagrams in Dumond's paper (this volume) and the discussions of regional prehistory (Dumond this volume; also Dumond and Scott 1991). Further information on Kodiak prehistory is presented in this paper and in publications by Clark (1984a, 1984b, 1992, 1993), Erlandson et al (1992), Dumond (1991), Haggarty et al. (1991), and Workman (1980).

Kodiak Island and Its Inhabitants

Survival of the Archaeological Record

Today, people might regard the magnificent expanses of beach, the rocky headlands that break the sea, and the inviting inlets on Kodiak as simply places for recreation. But in the past the beaches and coves were lined with villages, many of which had been occupied for so long that two-, three-, and four-meter-thick accumulations of shell, bone, and fire-cracked rock had built up. Since the beginning of the twentieth century, and probably earlier, most of the archaeological record has been lost to the ocean. Subsidence during the 1964 Good Friday earthquake lowered the northeastern coastline more than one meter, and the ensuing coastal erosion has been disastrous. Based on my observations in 1988-1991, the increased erosion continues today. In some coastal areas only a few remnants of sites or the rare elevated site survive, and these traces are under heavy pressure from vandalism. Nevertheless, enough of the rich record has survived so that Kodiak Island continues to be a prime attraction for the investigation of ancient maritime hunting cultures. Moreover, while the northeastern part of the island subsided in 1964, the southwestern part actually rose. Similar conditions may have occurred in the past. The coast between Afognak Island (northeastern Kodiak) and the Kenai Peninsula had drowned long before 1964. Earthquakes and tidal waves undoubtedly were part of the experience of past islanders, but it is not known if they had any disastrous effects on the inhabitants. Erosion, rather than smaller populations and natural disasters, is mainly responsible for the decreasing number of sites as one goes back in time.

A Large Island

Kodiak is located in the North Pacific only 30 km off the Pacific coast of the Alaska Peninsula at the west side of the Gulf of Alaska.

The relatively self-contained area was the home of a very populous Pacific Eskimo group or aggregate of subtribes commonly called the Koniags (not Kaniagmute) or Qikertarmiut, and recently, in reference to their contemporary acculturated status, Alutiiqs. The Koniags also occupied the adjacent coast of the Alaska Peninsula. It is estimated that they numbered nearly 10,000 at the time of European contact. A related Eskimo people lived on outer Cook Inlet and in Prince William Sound, while farther east along the coast were the Eyak and Tlingit Indians and to the northwest across the Alaska Peninsula lived the Eskimos of the southern Bering Sea region. Ethnically, and in some respects culturally, the Koniags contrast sharply with their neighbors to the west-southwest, the Aleuts, and those to the north, the interior-oriented Athapaskan Indians.

Natural Environment

The climate of Kodiak is at the harsh end of the temperate scale, with an inordinate number of rainy days punctuated by intensive cyclonic storms. Because the climate is milder than that of the Arctic region usually associated with Eskimos, there is open water during all seasons, although the bay heads that receive fresh stream water tend to freeze, including inner Uyak Bay. Winter days are characterized by temperatures that hover around freezing or drop to only a few degrees below 0°C along the outer coast, but conditions are more severe towards the heads of large bays that indent the island. Spring comes very gradually. Though low-elevation snow may melt along the outer coasts by the beginning of April, drifts linger in the spruce forests into June.

The shallow sea banks on the southeast side of the island produce abundant fish resources for local fisheries and for mammals and birds that rely on fish. They also enabled the islands to support a dense human population, especially on the outer coasts. The complex coastline further increased the linear extent of the littoral zone and availability of resources, including a range of shellfish.

The relatively high annual precipitation (around 200 cm) supplies a large number of streams, which, because of the topography, tend to be small and short. This results in a proliferation of places where salmon can spawn. Most numerous are pink salmon (*Oncorhynchus gorbuscha*) and red salmon (*O. nerka*); the latter arrive early to ascend the streams until they reach a lake where they spawn. "Pinks" and the other three species—silver salmon (*O. kisutch*), chum salmon (*O. keta*), and the relatively uncommon king salmon (*O. tshawytscha*) do not have this requirement. Although red salmon arrive at major streams as early as late April and silver salmon linger in a necrotic state at spawning grounds until December, most salmon are available primarily during the summer months. The mountainous interior of the island offered few food resources but at the southwestern end where rivers are larger, salmon fishing camps were located far up the drainages of the Karluk and Ayakulik rivers.

Forests are limited to stands of balsam poplar (*Populus tacamahaca*), black cottonwood (*P. trichocarpa*), small gnarled Kenai birch (*Betula kenaica*), and spruce (*Picea sitchensis*). The spruce is largely confined to the northern half of the island and was more restricted or absent during earlier millennia (Heusser 1960). The poplars are found mainly in stream bottoms southwest of the spruce forest. The primary source of timber for construction probably was driftwood brought in by ocean currents and conveniently debarked and trimmed by battering on stormy shores. The availability of driftwood in earlier times may be questionable, however, since most driftwood from the last century appears to stem from logging or other human activity. Conversely, the late glacial or early Holocene establishment of forests along the Northwest Coast coupled with the world-wide early Holocene rise in sea level may have fed considerable timber into the ocean to be carried northward by the Alaska coastal current.

Major environmental changes that occurred in the past were the stabilization of sea levels about 6,000 years ago and the arrival of spruce forests in the northeastern end of the island about 1,000 years ago. The lives of the maritime hunters of Kodiak could have been affected by changes in oceanic circulation and water temperatures (these await documentation) and by short-term changes in sea level caused by earthquakes. It is interesting to speculate how and when Kodiak received its very limited indigenous land fauna, mainly brown bears (*Ursus arctos*), red fox (*Vulpes vulpes*), voles (*Microtus oeconomus*), river otter (*Lutra canadensis*), weasels (*Mustela erminea*), and ground squirrels (*Citellus*), and whether any of these species were brought in by humans before the extensive introductions of non-native species during the late nineteenth and early twentieth century.

Subsistence Economy

The resources available to the prehistoric inhabitants of Kodiak varied between localities and, possibly, through time. Although faunal analyses, which are available for selected remains collected at the Uyak site, are not quantified (Kellogg 1936), there are indications that subsistence varied through time. For example, sea otter (*Enhydra lutris*) may have been utilized as food only during the Ocean Bay tradition, although the evidence may have been skewed by later ritual disposal of the remains. In general, only a small number of northern fur seal (*Callorhinus ursinus*) were taken, but just before and possibly at the time of contact in 1763 fur seal were harvested extensively (Clark 1986). Fox bones are abundant in Kachemak sites where this animal evidently was consumed for food. They are present to varying degrees at Koniag phase sites. Dog remains occur in moderate quantities in both Kachemak and Koniag deposits, and there is also some evidence that dogs might have been eaten.

During most of the prehistoric period, the commonly hunted sea mammals were porpoises, notably harbor porpoises (*Phocoena phocoena*) and especially harbor seals (*Phoca vitulina*). Northern sea lions (*Eumetopias jubata*) were taken, but it is difficult to assess their importance because the meat was probably stripped from the bones at the kill site. The same applies to brown bear. The importance of whales is also difficult to determine. Ethnographic accounts accord whales great importance in the lives of Kodiak islanders. But the caloric contribution of whale oil and meat compared with other food sources is difficult to assess for the prehistoric past. Whether other prehistoric inhabitants were whalers or simply salvaged the occasional dead or stranded whale and its bones is a matter for further investigation.

Based on ethnographic accounts and the range of fishing implements recovered from archaeological sites, sea fishing was a major occupation. Although detailed analyses have not been published, cod, sculpin, halibut, and many species of smaller fish apparently were caught.

Birds of almost every kind were utilized not only for food but also for their skin, feathers, and bills. Some 49 species have been identified from the samples Hrdlička collected at the Uyak site (Heizer 1956:26; Hrdlička 1944:477; Friedmann 1935).

Finally, shellfish were utilized in large quantities. Shell is one of the main components of the midden deposits at village and camp sites. It probably reflects subsistence more directly than other types of faunal refuse because virtually nothing is stripped away and left at the "kill site" (in this case, the littoral zone), consumption probably occurred immediately and locally (although evidence shows that whole clams were taken from Uyak Bay inland to fishing camps along Karluk River and Karluk Lake) and, finally, shell was not scavenged later. Although detailed analyses are unavailable, the main shellfish exploited were blue mussel (*Mytilus edulis*); three species of clams locally referred to as butter clams (*Saxidomus giganteus*), horse clams (possibly *Tresus* sp.), and cockles (*Clinocardium* sp.); sea urchin; the tiny periwinkle (*Littorina*) in immense numbers; and smaller amounts of chiton, barnacles, and other species. It should be noted that the waters of Kodiak are highly susceptible to infestation by the microorganism that causes paralytic seafood poisoning in humans—the so-called red tide.

Archaeological Cultures

Technological Characterization

The archaeological cultures of Kodiak (Ocean Bay, Kachemak, and Koniag) are characterized primarily by skin, stone, bone and wood, and, to a very limited extent, metal and ceramic-based technologies. These peoples were devoted to the hunting of sea mammals and fishing, to processing the catch, and to fabricating the requisite equipment. They also had to make ceremonial paraphernalia for masked ceremonies and clothing and ornaments with which to demonstrate and reinforce wealth and status. Although such technologies are almost universal, we can focus on some of the more specific aspects that highlight Kodiak technology. The material discussed below comes from collections described in Clark 1966, 1970, 1974a, 1974b, 1979; Crozier 1989; Heizer 1956, 1948; Hrdlička 1944; Jordan and Knecht 1986.

Most cutting implements, including broad knives for splitting fish and cutting meat, were ground from slate, or, in the very earliest phase, Ocean Bay I, flaked from chert. Projectile points were made of bone, chert, or ground slate, depending on the class of projectile. Following the Ocean Bay tradition very little chert was flaked on Kodiak Island, although this technology remained popular in adjacent areas. Rough stone slabs, bars, cobbles, and small boulders were used extensively for fish lines and net weights, for very large hide scrapers, and as material blanks for stone lamps and large grooved splitting adzes. The Koniags also had rare tools pounded from native copper, a material traded in from the mainland northeast of the island. Shell was used very little, although shell ornaments are known and some shell artifacts may have gone unrecognized in shell middens. Other more or less exotic materials have been recovered, especially ornaments made of marble, amber, and jet (coal). Throughout most of prehistory the islanders did not use pottery; when pottery from the Bering Sea region was eventually adopted, it was not universally accepted. Large pots were popular in the southwestern part of the island. These were introduced sufficiently early in the second millennium A.D. that their localized distribution cannot be laid to recent introduction.

Most implements probably were produced from

organic materials, such as wood, hides, furs, and feathers. The archaeological remains from these industries are biased and temporally late. As evident from ethnographic collections (e.g., those featured in the Crossroads of Continents exhibition) and in late prehistoric wet-site collections, especially those from Karluk (Jordan and Knecht 1986; Milan 1974), organic materials are common. Skin-covered boats hold paramount importance among wood and hide artifacts. Though direct archaeological evidence for boats in the form of wooden parts, especially of kayaks, goes back only a few centuries on Kodiak, there is an inferential basis for proposing their presence for several thousand years. Boats were required because of the almost exclusively coastal focus of subsistence and travel.

Prehistoric Culture Sequence

The study of Kodiak prehistory benefits from the fact that, during a span of about 7,000 years, many distinctive changes in technology and artifact styles occurred, providing landmarks in the sequence. For three decades archaeologists have divided the indigenous cultures of Kodiak Island into three successive traditions, including a notable historic period of more than two centuries duration. The prehistoric sequence is described below, emphasizing the periods best represented at the Uyak site.

Ocean Bay

The first tradition, named after a locality fronting the ocean, is marked by several technological developments that stand out both within and beyond the context of regional prehistory. The tradition begins at least 6,500 years ago (uncalibrated date). It is characterized by bifacial flaking and microblade industries, together with associated bone-working technologies by which artifacts such as barbed harpoon heads and grooved points for microblade inserts were made. These bone artifacts are best known from the recent excavations of P. Hausler-Knecht (1993) at the Rice Ridge site. The Ocean Bay microblade cores are not the same as those associated with the American Paleoarctic or Denali complexes of interior Alaska, but there remains the possibility of earlier derivation from the inhabitants of Beringia—the ancient ice-free land mass that linked Alaska and eastern Siberia. Later, during Ocean Bay, microblade production ceased, bone working techniques were copied to slate, and a ground slate industry developed. The ground slate industries of northwestern North America apparently originated from this invention by Ocean Bay people (Clark 1982). Thereafter, in Ocean Bay II, lithic fabrication was based on both chert flaking (including also basalt) and slate grinding.

There is some evidence at the end of the Ocean Bay tradition of contact with Arctic Small Tool tradition people (Hausler-Knecht, personal communications). These people lived on the shores of the Bering Sea and also had a colony at Kachemak Bay on outer Cook Inlet, but they did not become established on Kodiak or on the adjacent Pacific coast of the Alaska Peninsula.

Kachemak Tradition

The Kachemak tradition developed around 1400 b.c. (uncalibrated radiocarbon years). Its origins are poorly understood. Although there are suggestions of continuity with the Ocean Bay tradition, the evidence for discontinuity outweighs them.

TECHNOLOGY Early Kachemak is characterized by a much greater use of grooved cobble and notched pebble weights, suggesting changes in fishing techniques; the adoption of lip plugs or labrets, which may have been present earlier elsewhere, especially on the Northwest Coast; a shift in slate fabrication from the common saw-scrape-grind (polish) sequence to one with little sawing and no scraping to form a blank; and, finally, a decrease in the importance of chert flaking and an increase in slate grinding. The broad, single-edge ground slate semilunar knife or ulu—the hallmark of Eskimos—became common, although it was small and not abundant in Early Kachemak. Holes were drilled in slate blades to allow them to be hafted—a feature totally absent in Ocean Bay. During the Kachemak tradition, many implements were flaked from slate and other fissile rocks; these included large hide scrapers and other scrapers that did not require sharp cutting edges. Toggle harpoon heads made their appearance on Kodiak at this time. This is surprising considering that Ocean Bay sea mammal hunters had flourished without this implement for 3,000 years. Finally, in Late Kachemak times stone lamps became very large, weighing up to 40 kg. Carvings of whales, seals, humans, and female human breasts in the bowl or on the lamp exterior point to an association between lamps and rituals in religious beliefs.

The presence of exotic goods provides evidence for trade. One Late Kachemak house at the Uyak site, which was recently excavated by Steffian (1992), appears to have been a home workshop for producing jet (coal) ornaments, particularly labrets. The raw material probably came from the mainland. Many elements of Kachemak technology, as well as some stylistic elements, are similar to those of the Norton culture of the Bering Sea region. Nevertheless, the two traditions remained highly distinctive in their emphasis on ground slate (Kachemak) and bifacially flaked chert tools (Norton). Since contact between the two cultures occurred over a period of nearly two millennia (the full span of Norton), correspondences may have developed gradually and cumulatively (Clark 1982b). There remains a strong possibility that several elements of Norton technology originated on the Pacific Coast.

Steffian's (this volume) house floor illustrations provide the best information on Kachemak houses. Entry passages were half to fully equal to the length of the house, which was rectangular with a central hearth, often contained between slate slabs. The single rooms tend to be about 4 m² with only slight variance. In some cases, Late Kachemak houses were smaller than the poorly known Ocean Bay houses and, Late Koniag houses.

BURIAL PRACTICES The dead commonly were interred in the refuse middens of presumably still occupied settlements, keeping the deceased as members of the community. Incomplete burials and scattered human bones are common. The latter often contain cut marks or breaks or have been made into artifacts. These conditions have generated considerable discussion of a probable Kachemak mortuary complex and possible cannibalism (Workman 1992). By contrast, Ocean Bay burial practices are all but unknown.

The chapters by Simon and Steffian and Urcid (this volume) deal with two Kachemak collections—one from the Uyak site and the other from Crag Point. Neither study supports Hrdlička's interpretation of cannibalism by Kachemak tradition people. Nevertheless, given the sensational and controversial nature of the topic, interest in cannibalism is likely to remain a concern for discussion into the next century. Moreover, the variety of mortuary behaviors present is of equal interest.

The value of a detailed study of these remains is illustrated in these chapters. For example, Urcid finds that bones were perforated from both the anterior and interior surfaces (in the case of a mandible), indicating postmortem modifications on dry, no longer articulated bones, and at Crag Point cultural bone modification is found exclusively on scattered human remains, not on burials. Certain findings invite further explication: the occurrence of human bones chewed by carnivores, for instance. Under what circumstances would animals be in a position to chew corpses at an occupied or only temporarily abandoned village? The carnivores probably were dogs, less likely foxes. At Crag Point there are traces, on the bones, of dismemberment, skinning, and defleshing.

Considering the ritual danger associated with handling human remains in many societies, this finding raises questions about the circumstances of such activity, which evidently took place within the village area.

These authors suggest that taphonomic processes, such as disturbances and digging of house pits, are responsible for the scattered, isolated, and fragmented condition of skeletal material at Uyak site and in other Kachemak deposits. The condition of this material can be compared with material found in Koniag deposits at the same site and elsewhere and in midden deposits in the Aleutian Islands that were formed under conditions similar to those in the Kachemak tradition—by people who also dug their housepits into older deposits and who interred their dead in the middens and in collapsed houses. Hrdlička had personal experience excavating all three contexts and found the occurrence of human bone in the Uyak Lower or Kachemak deposits to be distinctly different. Others who have excavated in the region tend to agree. Taphonomy or site disturbance is not a sufficient explanation.

Koniag Tradition

Almost every trait that was found in Late Kachemak changed in the succeeding Koniag tradition. Early archaeological work on Kodiak pointed to very rapid change. Further archaeological explorations, however, suggest that the latter culture essentially developed out of the former during the centuries between A.D. 1000 and 1300 (Jordan and Knecht 1986). Change continued to the time of historic contact. In many cases, Koniag developments were compatible with the earlier lifeways and technology to which they were additions (or deletions), or shifts in attributes, as are discussed below for certain cases. Nevertheless, some changes have implications touching on regional social institutions and interactions and point to new population increments (migration) as a probable contributing factor.

TECHNOLOGY Ceramics appeared locally during the Kachemak-Koniag transition, but they were never adopted in all parts of Kodiak. Their distribution forcefully demonstrates the variability that existed among the Koniags, suggesting they were not a single, monolithic, and discrete tribe.

The vapor-type sweat bath appears in the Kachemak-Koniag transition. The evidence consists of massive accumulations of discarded firecracked stone. Originally, the stones had been heated and carried into a house compartment where they were sprinkled with water to produce heat and steam. This trait was shared with neighboring Athapaskan tribes of southcentral Alaska. Historically, the sweat bath had several social and ritual functions.

As in Kachemak times, slate was perforated for hafting in Koniag times. But the drilling technique changed from one producing straight, neatly prepared holes to one producing gouged, often crooked, holes. Details are discussed elsewhere (Clark 1974a). This change might mark a significant historical event inasmuch as the objective and result (a drilled hole) remained unchanged, although the new technique actually produced a worse hole.

During Koniag times adze blades, used for working wood and possibly large whale bones, became far more abundant than they had been previously. Among the types were flat planing adze blades and large, heavy, grooved splitting adzes. The latter first appear on Kodiak at this time. The reason for this apparent increased emphasis on working wood is not evident. It was about this time that spruce forests appeared at the northeast end of the island, but driftwood probably continued to supply timber and fuel. More wood would have to have been split by heavy adzes for sweat baths and considerable wood would have been used to construct the large, turfed-over houses, but for most purposes it would have sufficed to split the wood with wedges.

With some notable exceptions, like the splitting adzes, Koniag stone and bone artifacts differ from those of the Kachemak tradition mainly at the attribute level. Some of the Koniag artifacts, documented to varying degrees archaeologically and ethnographically, attract special attention. Among them are artifacts that seem to be out of place in an Eskimo culture, for example, petroglyphs, long slender ground slate whaling dart tips (and a peculiar method of whaling), and probable mummification. It is difficult, though, to compare adequately the prehistoric Koniag and Kachemak cultures. There is better preservation of Koniag organic material, especially of wooden artifacts, and there are ethnographic observations and collections for the Koniag.

HOUSES The large multifamily Koniag houses were very different from the small Late Kachemak houses. The Late Koniag semisubterranean compound house had several family chambers and a sweat bath appended to a common room (or possibly a community hall in the case of the largest structures). Pits from abandoned houses consist of large sunken rectangles with one or two smaller subrectangular pits on the outside along each wall; these are sometimes joined to the main room by a short passage (Knecht and Jordan 1985:fig. 6). The houses constitute a very important "artifact" inasmuch as they reflect adaptations to the environment, social organization, and external relationships in the adoption of particular fea-

tures, and, as has been noted, they changed through time.

As yet, few semisubterranean compound houses have been dated prior to protohistoric times. Jordan and Knecht (1986:273) report a house possibly of this type (House Floor 8) at Karluk dated between 1400 and 1500 a.d. This type of house differs from the houses of the Bering Sea region, which seldom have more than one appended room and have depressed or coldtrap-type entry passages (lacking on Kodiak), but similar architectural principles of construction may have been used in the two regions. Finally, the Koniag house is similar in plan to those of the Tanaina Indians on Cook Inlet.

Place of the Uyak Site in Prehistory

As Speaker notes in this volume, "the Larsen Bay [Uyak] site presents a wide variety of interpretive problems for modern archaeologists." One of the problems is the prehistory (or historiography) of the site, Hrdlička's summaries notwithstanding. Another is what the study of the artifact assemblage can tell us about the site's settlement and lifeways.

Because of poor provenience records and Hrdlička's selective collecting, the answer to the second question is "very little." The common, often ubiquitous, implements that stand to provide the most information on activities, activity areas, site zonation, and specialized production were most subject to Hrdlička's culling. These included the ugly hammerstones, fragments of broken adzes, fragmented slate knives, boulder chip and stone slab scrapers, more or less natural abraders, pebble fishing weights, and roughly fashioned bone wedges. Notched pebble weights normally occur by the thousands in most Kachemak tradition deposits but only 31 weights are present at Uyak (Heizer 1956:43), although judging from Hrdlička's references to "birdstones" many more must have been encountered. In the same way, simple boulder flakes often occur in such frequency at some sites that thousands might be expected at Uyak, but only 23 are recorded. This implement, however, does occur in low frequency at some sites, so it is possible that the Uyak site assemblage is simply highly peculiar for reasons that would be worth considering.

Except for recent excavations in Late Kachemak houses at the periphery of the site by Steffian (in press and this volume) and one unacceptable date obtained on wood by Heizer, the Uyak site still remains to be dated by the radiocarbon method. Potentially, this is possible by extracting small samples from bone artifacts for AMS dating but, because of the poor provenience records, individual dates would be of uncertain relevance. It would be necessary to obtain and interpret the profile of numerous dates. The immense thickness of midden deposits processed by Hrdlička may indicate a considerable antiquity for the site, but the artifact types present suggest that the deposits date mainly to the Late Kachemak tradition, with some Early Kachemak tradition and part of the Koniag phase also represented.

Dumond (this volume) notes the incomplete, truncated state of the Koniag tradition record and I will not comment further on that period here. Recent excavations by Steffian should provide an unmixed first millennium A.D., Late Kachemak assemblage to compare with the somewhat mixed assemblage described by Heizer (1956).

Certain artifacts show that the site was also settled in Early Kachemak or first millennium B.C. times, but the extent of Early Kachemak occupation is problematical. Unusually few flaked chert artifacts were recovered and these probably were imports. Elsewhere Early Kachemak people produced a few flaked chert implements and on northeastern Kodiak the industry was maintained almost at the level in which it appeared during the Ocean Bay tradition.

One Early Kachemak diagnostic trait is the grooved plummet—a cobble grooved around or sculptured at one end to leave a knob (designated as Type V by Heizer). Only 9 specimens are recorded, all from the lower levels at Uyak, compared to the same number from half a season's work by four persons at the Old Kiavak site (author's data). But many of the latter were broken and, considering that broken specimens from Uyak probably were discarded, this comparison forms a poor basis for determining the magnitude of Early Kachemak occupation. De Laguna (1934: Pl. 38) reports a certain distinctive style of toggle harpoon head from early Yukon Island (Early Kachemak) components, of which there are two examples from more extensive Uyak site excavations (Heizer 1956:63, Pl. 58 x). Artifact typology thus supports identification of an Early Kachemak occupation, but one that appears to have been of limited magnitude or of short duration.

Conversely, there is no hint of any earlier occupation of the Uyak site. Hrdlička noted an initial occupation sealed off from the overlying deposits by a layer of volcanic ash. It might be possible to identify a plausible tephra in the Early Kachemak temporal range but that would be unrewarding inasmuch as the earliest artifacts were not identified or segregated, nor is there even a list of the types of items encountered.

Koniag-Kachemak Continuity and Discontinuity

There has been a tendency, at least on my part, to view Kodiak prehistory in terms of successive traditions ending in brief periods of rapid technological change (ushering in new traditions), possibly including migration and language change. This view recognizes that change also occurred over time within traditions but does not see that as necessarily part of a trajectory leading to the next tradition. Considering the new evidence now available, I would suggest that there is more developmental continuity in the 7000-year-sequence and that change within the scope of traditions is not necessarily very different in kind or magnitude from that occurring during so-called transitions. This opens for consideration the question of Kachemak-Koniag cultural and biological continuity both on Kodiak and specifically at the Uyak Site.

In earlier periods, essentially the same relationships or boundaries held between the prehistoric cultures of Kodiak Island and those of the adjacent regions of Alaska as were described for the historic cultures of southern Alaska at the beginning of this chapter. This is a noteworthy parallel with possible cultural and biological continuity occurring in the same area.

The question of cultural and biological succession on Kodiak is a problem, generated by Hrdlička's interpretation of the Uyak Site, that has been primary to much of the later archaeology done on the island. Here it is the focus of the papers by Dumond and Scott. Hrdlička proposed that the Koniag culture and population suddenly and completely replaced their predecessors (which he termed Pre-Koniag). Various lines of reasoning also suggest that there has been linguistic change or replacement in the Pacific area resulting in a Yupik Eskimo dialect being spoken at the time of historic contact. The possibility of migration and ethnic succession on Kodiak has been of special interest, even prior to the Larsen Bay repatriation case during which it became a central issue. The arguments, pro and con, are the subject of an extensive literature (Clark 1974, 1988, 1992; Dumond 1991 and this volume; Scott 1991 and this volume; Jordan and Knecht 1986; Lantis 1947). As noted in the previous discussion, there were quantum changes in the material, social, and, possibly, political culture at the end of the Kachemak tradition and during the Koniag tradition. New trait complexes were introduced (e.g., pottery) and some trait attributes changed, although in some cases the change served no apparent purpose. There is evidence, then, that something happened in prehistory, possibly a migration of people.

There are other ways of looking at the evidence, however. The changes might have occurred through local development or randomly as the centuries elapsed. They may have been stimulated or induced through contacts with mainland peoples or through actual population interchange. The last was small-scale migration, but in the large-scale sense of population displacement and ethnic succession it was not classical "wave" migration. To understand the possible impact of small-scale migration, the Koniags and their predecessors on Kodiak should not be thought of as a single tribe but as an aggregation of village or local units (Townsend 1980). The history of one local subtribe was not necessarily that of the island group.

Normally, hypotheses of migration and replacement draw forth demands for proof. But here the case is the opposite. Prehistorians find the hypothesis of continuity on Kodiak Island difficult to reconcile with Eskimo prehistory, and here is why: ethnicity is defined foremost on the basis of language, and the Koniags were linguistically Eskimos. Accepting that continuity overweighs discontinuity or migration in Koniag genesis, the antecedents of the Koniags presumably also spoke an Eskimo language and had an Eskimoan culture. This is not an unreasonable assumption inasmuch as the Kachemak tradition, on which to a large degree the Koniag is based, shows numerous crossties with the ancestral Eskimo culture termed Norton, and the archaeological record on Kodiak does show at least a certain degree of continuity.

Difficulties start with the fact that if we assume a link between ethnicity, language, and culture, this relationship logically extends back to the beginning of the Kachemak tradition, or about 3400 years ago. For many prehistorians, early Eskimo (the Norton noted above) is seen as having developed out of the Arctic Small Tool tradition (ASTt) and, therefore, ASTt also is posited as ancestral Eskimo. Judging from their distinctive artifacts, however, there is no relationship between the Kachemak tradition and the ASTt (including the Denbigh Flint Complex), even though late ASTt and Early Kachemak overlap. Given the lack of any evident relationship between the two, it is difficult to see both ASTt and the Kachemak tradition as ancestral Eskimo. There rests the contradiction, with the very origins of Eskimos at stake, depending on the model selected.

The attribution of a particular language or ethnicity to an archaeological entity involves establishing a direct link between an identified historic community and an archaeological component. But at the Uyak site there is a gap in occupation at the critical juncture of European contact. Hrdlička thought that the site had been abandoned shortly before the arrival of the Russians on Kodiak (contact was about A.D. 1763, settlement A.D. 1784); Dumond (this volume), with whom I agree, proposes that the occupation of the site ceased some centuries earlier.

The apparent discontinuity in occupation in the Larsen Bay area may simply be a sampling problem. There are several inadequately investigated sites in the vicinity, including a midden below some recently built houses, that probably would fill this gap. The sto-

ry is different for human skeletal remains. The Uyak site apparently continued to be utilized as a graveyard for people who lived in the vicinity. Steffian (this volume) reports burials in abandoned first millennium A.D. housepits, and there are numerous references to Koniag burials in housepits in Hrdlička's publication (1944) and elsewhere (McRae and Bohannan n.d.).

Considering that local variation and ongoing change characterize the span of the Koniag phase (ca. A.D. 1100 or 1200 onward) elsewhere on Kodiak, it is not surprising that the upper level assemblage from the Uyak site does not match exactly late-prehistoric Koniag assemblages found elsewhere. And, thus while the differences commented on by Dumond support his suggestion of a gap in occupation at this particular site, it does not necessarily follow that for the area there was discontinuity between the inhabitants of the Uyak Site and the Larsen/Uyak Bay vicinity or that the latest-prehistoric inhabitants of the area were newcomers whose ancestors arrived after the Uyak site was abandoned.

Unquestionably, there was a significant cultural relationship between the southern Bering Sea and Pacific Coast regions, including Kodiak, across the Alaska Peninsula during the second millennium A.D., as adumbrated by Dumond. The overall assessment is quite clear: that in some respects the two regions became very much alike. Details related to population movements, possibly from more than one source, and *in situ* development, which also is very evident, remain a matter for discussion.

The pursuit of these details can be fascinating. Take, for instance, the perforated sea mammal humerus characteristically used in the ring-and-pin game of Arctic Eskimos. Strangely, this game is rarely mentioned in the extensive ethnographic literature and archaeological reports for areas outside of Arctic Canada and Greenland. A late prehistoric specimen was found at Point Barrow (Dekin 1987:833), and there are reports that the game was being played at Unalakleet in the present century (Carrigher 1958:116). Farther south, on Kodiak Island, three specimens were recovered from a Late Kachemak site; one from well within Kachemak deposits should antedate A.D. 1000 (Clark 1970 and unpublished data). Here, then, is a Thule Culture-Pacific Area connection plausibly linked to a hypothesized southern influx of Neoeskimos from the Bering Sea region. Although the same trait is also reported ethnographically for the Northwest Coast (Culin 1907:559; fig. 743) and the number of recovered specimens favors an Arctic origin, their earliest documented occurrence seems to be on Kodiak Island.

A point to be drawn from this digression is that much of what is Neoeskimo actually could be Pacific in origin. This places the question of a southward-moving Neoeskimo population spread to the Pacific in a somewhat different light. It would not be inappropriate to suggest the presence of multiple centers of Neoeskimoization (the commonly accepted center being Bering Strait). Through a southern center (Kodiak, Alaska Peninsula, Bristol Bay), Northwest Coast Area traits also may have been drawn into Eskimo culture. One ingredient in Kodiak prehistory and the formation of Koniag culture that must be recognized is the role of contact with early peoples of the Northwest Coast. Some traits found also on the Bering Sea side of the Alaska Peninsula point in that direction. These include splitting adzes and the vapor, or steam, sweat bath. There are additional traits common to Kodiak and the Northwest Coast to the exclusion of the Bering Sea region, for example, petroglyphs and puffin beak rattles. Puffin beak rattles, which are characteristic Northwest Coast artifacts and have also been recorded ethnographically for the Aleuts, have been recovered from a late prehistoric context at Karkuk and are portrayed, probably somewhat earlier, on an incised figurine (Reinhardt 1981; see also Donta this volume), so its earliest documented occurrence now is on Kodiak.

The evidence from physical anthropology, discussed extensively during the last four decades (see Scott this volume), provides more definitive information about questions of continuity or discontinuity in the local population. Scott finds that there is no evident biological discontinuity between the Uyak Lower Levels (Kachemak) and Upper Level (Koniag) populations, nor is there any between the Upper Level skeletal population and historic or modern Koniag Eskimos. The Uyak Site Koniags thus are descended from either the Uyak Lower Levels population *or from a similar population*. In turn, the historic Koniags descended from a population similar to the Uyak Site Koniags, possibly one in which the latter was a subset. Pertinent questions are: What area of Alaska was occupied about 1,000 years ago by a population with the Uyak Lower characteristics, and what area has been occupied since then by people having Uyak Upper and historic Koniag characteristics? Only limited early skeletal and dental series from immediately adjacent areas are available to answer these questions. Interestingly, Scott sees the Uyak Blue or lower-Lower dentition, of, I estimate, 2000 to 3000 years ago, as closely approximating a plausible common ancestor of the Eskimos, Aleuts and Indians of Alaska. For the second question, the general answer is that prior to recent European admixture the Koniag were not very different from other Eskimo populations of southwest Alaska. The net result of this analysis is that for fine-tuned interpretations of prehistory, the human dental and osteological data permit various hypothe-

ses both of population movement and of continuity in the makeup of the Koniags. Evidently, archaeologists have been asking the wrong questions of the physical data. As Scott (this volume) states, "common ancestry might obscure their [Kachemak and Koniag] separate migrations to the island. . . . biological continuity should be viewed in a broad rather than narrow sense."

He also provides a "second opinion" on proposed West Coast Indian or so-called Nadene affiliation of the inhabitants of prehistoric Uyak. Unlike Turner (1988 and elsewhere), Scott finds that the primary links are with the Eskimo universe. That is a more comfortable position from which to postulate the prehistory of Kodiak Island, but a less challenging one.

Conclusions

Cultural continuity is the key issue in Kodiak prehistory, not only at the Uyak site between the Koniag and Kachemak traditions, but also elsewhere between Kachemak and earlier Ocean Bay. Considered in terms of the simple model of continuity vs migration, the conventional model of Eskimo origins (which does not identify Kodiak Island as the center of the universe) is at risk. Testing Hrdlička's interpretation of culture history at the Uyak Site and of Kodiak then remains a viable objective within the continuity/ migration model. The reader may be dismayed that I have not firmly indicated which option is correct, a dilemma that demonstrates the point made above. The model itself likely is at fault, and a better understanding of interactions among maritime societies should afford the means to break out of this model. That is what archaeologists are attempting to achieve now.

A recent trend in south Alaskan studies takes prehistory beyond the study of artifacts and the level of historiography by looking for patterns of social, political and economic development shared between prehistoric cultures over extensive expanses of the North Pacific Coast (Moss and Erlandson 1992). There always had been suggestions, by archaeologists and ethnographers, of long standing cultural and/or biological interchange among peoples extending from the Aleutian Islands to Puget Sound. Today, such queries are being directed towards interregional trends expressing social, political and economic aspects of the various Pacific Coast ethnic groups, for instance, the rise of warfare, development of status and rank, and population increase and its concomitant effect on settlement and resource utilization (Erlandson et al. 1992). The archaeological signatures of these trends often are indirect, and extensive data are required to

Donald W. Clark

adequately test the archaeologists' hypotheses. This type of research must unfold along with continuing historiographic research if for no other reason than the fact that there remain inadequacies in the basic data base for the cultural sequence. Just as answers for diachronic questions posed by the cultural sequence are not simple, the case is equally complex synchronically.

For example, why were the inhabitants of Kodiak Island whalers, but those to the east on the northern Northwest Coast were not. The Northwest Coast people had the technological and organizational capabilities to be whalers, and they had access to the animals.

Another example of a boundary east of the Pacific Eskimo area involves the distribution of stone lamps. Lamps were used on Kodiak and in adjacent Pacific Eskimo and Aleut areas for at least 7,000 years, but there evidently was a long-standing boundary near Yakutat, south and east of which any use of such lamps on the Northwest Coast is highly uncertain (de Laguna et al. 1964 cite a few highly dubious cases). Seemingly impermeable as this boundary was to lamps, much else that was Indian and Eskimoid passed back and forth between various ethnic groups, including, probably in earliest Ocean Bay times, microblade technology, in later Ocean Bay times the saw-snap-scrape mode of working slate (Davis 1989), in Early Kachemak times labrets and much else, and in late Koniag times a ritual involving production of human figurines incised on slate pebbles (Clark 1964; Donta this volume; de Laguna et al. 1964; Ackerman 1968). Similarly, it is suspected that the production of petroglyphs on Kodiak Island was strongly stimulated by influence from the Northwest Coast where petroglyph masonry was common.

It has been implied that there were contacts between Kodiak and the Northwest Coast area of such a nature that they resulted in the transmission, between areas, of more than technology and trade items, albeit very selectively. A similar relationship evidently existed with peoples of the Aleutian Islands (Holland 1992; McCartney 1974). In some cases all three areas formed a common community, though communication between the ends of this chain must have been indirect.

The interlocking chain of discrete coastal cultures continues to stimulate a modern generation of archaeologists. And in similar vein, this volume is more than a postmortem or an inglorious end to an ambivalently viewed episode in Alaskan archaeology. While little new data are presented, old data, examined retrospectively or in context and greater detail, enhance our understanding of the Uyak site and of the prehistory of Kodiak Island.

References Cited

Ackerman, Robert
1968   *The Archaeology of the Glacier Bay Region, Southeastern Alaska.* Washington State University Laboratory of Anthropology, Report of Investigations No. 44. Pullman.

Birket-Smith, Kaj
1941   *Early Collections from the Pacific Eskimo.* Ethnological Studies, Nationalmuseets Skrifter. Ethnografisk Raekke 1:121–63. Copenhagen.

Black, Lydia (transl. and ed.)
1977   The Konyag (the Inhabitants of the Island of Kodiak) by Iosaf Bolotov (1794–1799) and by Gideon (1804–1807). *Arctic Anthropology* 14(2):79–108.

Carrigher, Sally
1958   *Moonlight at Midday.* New York: Alfred Knopf.

Clark, Donald W.
1964   Incised Figurine Tablets from Kodiak Alaska. *Arctic Anthropology* 2(1):118–34
1966   Perspectives in the Prehistory of Kodiak Island, *American Antiquity* 33(1):358–71.
1970   The Late Kachemak Tradition at Three Saints and Crag Point, Kodiak Island, Alaska. *Arctic Anthropology* 6(2):73–111.
1974a   *Koniag Prehistory.* Tubinger Monographien Zur Urgeschichte, vol. 1. Tubingen.
1974b   *Contributions to the Later Prehistory of Kodiak Island, Alaska.* National Museum of Man [Canadian Museum of Civilization] Mercury Series, Archaeological Survey of Canada Paper No. 20. Ottawa.
1979   *Ocean Bay: An Early North Pacific Maritime Culture.* National Museum of Man, Mercury Series, Archaeological Survey of Canada Paper No. 86. Ottawa.
1980   Relationships of North Pacific and American Arctic Centres of Slate Grinding. *Canadian Journal of Archaeology* 4:27–38.
1982a   An Example of Technological Change in Prehistory: The Origin of a Regional Ground Slate Industry in South-Central Coastal Alaska. *Arctic Anthropology* 19(1):103–26.
1982b   From Just Beyond the Southern Fringe: A Comparison of Norton Culture and the Contemporary Kachemak Tradition of Kodiak Island. *Arctic Anthropology* 19(2):123–32.
1984a   Pacific Eskimo: Historical Ethnography. In *Handbook of North American Indians, vol. 5, Arctic.* D. Damas, ed. pp. 185–97. Washington, D.C.: Smithsonian Institution.
1984b   Prehistory of the Pacific Eskimo Region. In *Handbook of North American Indians, vol. 5, Arctic.* D. Damas, ed. pp. 136–48. Washington, D.C.: Smithsonian Institution.
1986   Archaeological and Historical Evidence for an 18th-Century "Blip" in the Distribution of the Northern Fur Seal at Kodiak Island, Alaska. *Arctic Anthropology* 39(1):39–42.

1988   Pacific Eskimo Encoded Precontact History. In *Late Prehistoric Development of Alaska's Native People*. R. D. Shaw, R. K. Harritt, and D. E. Dumond, eds. pp. 211–23. Aurora: Monograph of the Alaska Anthropological Association No. 4.

1992   "Only a Skin Boat or Two": The Role of Migration in Kodiak Prehistory. *Arctic Anthropology* 29(1):2–17.

1993   *Archaeology on Kodiak: The Quest for Prehistory and its Implications for North Pacific Prehistory*. Anthropological Papers of the University of Alaska No. 24.

Crozier, S. Neal
1989   Excavation at a Late Prehistoric Dwelling Structure on Kodiak Island, Alaska. *Arctic Anthropology* 26(2): 78–95.

Crowell, Aron
1988   Prehistory of Alaska's Pacific Coast. In *Crossroads of Continents: Cultures of Siberia and Alaska*. W. Fitzhugh and A. Crowell, eds. pp. 130–40. Washington, D.C.: Smithsonian Institution Press.

1992   Postcontact Koniag Ceremonialism on Kodiak Island and the Alaska Peninsula: Evidence from the Fisher Collection. *Arctic Anthropology* 19(1):18–37.

Culin, Stewart
1907   *Games of the North American Indian*. Bureau of American Ethnology, 24th Annual Report, 1902–3. Washington, D.C.

Davis, Stan D., ed.
1989   *The Hidden Falls Site, Baranof Island, Alaska*. Aurora: Alaska Anthropological Association Monograph Series No. 5.

Davydov, G. I.
1977   *Two Voyages to Russian America, 1802–1807*. Richard A. Pierce, ed., and Colin Bearne, transl. Kingston, Ontario: Limestone Press.

Dekin, Albert A.
1987   Sealed in Time—When Ice Entombed an Eskimo Family. *National Geographic* 171(6):824–36.

Dumond, Don E.
1991   The Uyak Site in Regional Prehistory: The Cultural Evidence. In *The Uyak Site on Kodiak Island: Its Place in Alaskan Prehistory*. D. Dumond and R. Scott, pp. 57–114. Eugene: University of Oregon Anthropological Papers No. 44.

Dumond, Don E., and Richard Scott
1991   *The Uyak Site on Kodiak Island: Its Place in Alaskan Prehistory*. Eugene: University of Oregon Anthropological Papers No. 44.

Erlandson, Jon, Aron Crowell, Christopher Wooley, and James Haggarty
1992   Spatial and Temporal Patterns in Alutiiq Paleodemography. *Arctic Anthropology* 29(2):42–62.

Fitzhugh, William W. and Aron Crowell
1988   *Crossroads of Continents: Cultures of Siberia and Alaska*. Washington, D.C.: Smithsonian Institution Press.

Friedmann, H.
1935   Avian Bones from Prehistoric Ruins on Kodiak Island, Alaska. *Journal Washington Academy of Sciences* 24:44–51.

Gideon, Hieromonk
1989   *The Round the World Voyage of Hieromonk Gideon 1803–1809*. Richard A. Pierce, ed. and Lydia Black, transl. Kingston, Ontario: Limestone Press.

Haggerty, James C., Christopher B. Wooley, Jon M. Erlandson and Aron Crowell
1991   The 1990 Exxon Cultural Resource Program: Site Protection and Maritime Cultural Ecology in Prince William Sound and the Gulf of Alaska. Exxon Shipping Company and Exxon Company, Anchorage.

Hausler-Knecht, Philomena
1993   Early Prehistory of the Kodiak Archipelago. Paper presented at the Origins, Development, and Spread of North Pacific-Bering Sea Maritime Cultures seminar, June 3–7, Honolulu.

Heizer, Robert F.
1947   Petroglyphs from Southwestern Kodiak Island, Alaska. *Proceedings of the American Philosophical Society* 93(1):284–93

1948   Pottery from the Southern Eskimo Region. *Proceedings of the American Philosophical Society* 93(1):48–56.

1956   *Archaeology of the Uyak Site Kodiak Island, Alaska*. University of California Anthropological Records 17.

Heusser, Calvin J.
1960   *Late Pleistocene Environments of North Pacific North America*. American Geographical Society Special Publication No. 35. New York.

Holland, Kathryn M.
1992   In the Wake of Prehistoric North Pacific Sea Mammal Hunters. *Arctic Anthropology* 29(2):63–72.

Holmberg, Heinrich Johan
1985   *Holmberg's Ethnographic Sketches*. Originally published as Ethnographische skizzen ueber die volker des russischen Amerika, Acta Scientiarum Fennicae, 1855–1863. Fairbanks: University of Alaska Press.

Hrdlička, Aleš
1943   *Alaska Diary*. Lancaster, Pennsylvania: Jacques Cattell Press.

1944   *The Anthropology of Kodiak Island*. Philadelphia: The Wistar Institute of Anatomy and Biology.

Jordan, Richard H. and Richard A. Knecht
1986   Archaeological Research on Western Kodiak Island, Alaska: The Development of Koniag Culture. In *The Late Prehistoric Development of Alaska's Native People*. Robert Shaw, Roger Harritt, and Don Dumond, eds. pp. 225–306. Aurora: Alaska Anthropological Association Monograph Series No. 4.

Kellogg, R.
1936   Mammals from a Native Village Site on Kodiak Island. *Proceedings of the Biological Society, Washington* 49:37–38.

Knecht, Richard A. and Richard H. Jordan
1985   Nunakakhnak: An Historic Period Koniag Village in Karluk, Kodiak Island, Alaska. *Arctic Anthropology* 22(2):17–35.

de Laguna, Frederica
1934   *The Archaeology of Cook Inlet, Alaska.* Philadelphia: The University Museum.

de Laguna, F., F. Riddell, D. McGeein, K. Lane, J. Freed, and C. Osborne
1964   *Archaeology of the Yakutat Bay Area, Alaska.* Bureau of American Ethnology Bulletin 192. Washington, D.C.

Lantis, Margaret
1947   *Alaskan Eskimo Ceremonialism.* Monographs of the American Ethnological Society No. 11. New York: J. J. Augustin.

Lisianskii, Yurii
1814   *A Voyage Round the World in the Years 1803–1806.* London: John Booth.

McCartney, Allen P.
1974   *Prehistoric Cultural Integration along the Alaska Peninsula.* Anthropological Papers of the University of Alaska 16(1):59–84.

McRae, T. W. R. and C. T. R. Bohannan
1934   Smithsonian Institution U.S. National Museum Expedition to Kodiak Island, Alaska Led by Dr. Aleš Hrdlička 1934, Personal Field Notes. Aleš Hrdlička Papers, National Anthropological Archives, Smithsonian Institution.

Merck, C. H.
1980   *Siberia and Northwestern America 1788–1792: The Journal of Carl Heinrich Merck, Naturalist with the Russian Scientific Expedition Led by Captains Joseph Billings and Gavriil Sarychev.* R. A. Pierce, ed., and F. Jaensch, transl. Kingston, Ontario: Limestone Press.

Milan, Frederick
1974   Excavations at Karluk. In *Contributions to the Later Prehistory of Kodiak Island, Alaska,* by D. W. Clark. pp. 81–97. National Museum of Man, Mercury Series, Archaeological Survey of Canada Paper No. 20.

Moss, Madonna L., and Jon M. Erlandson
1992   Maritime Cultures of Southern Alaska: Papers in Honor of Richard H. Jordan. *Arctic Anthropology* 29(2).

Pinart, Alphonse L.
1872   *Catalog des Collections Raportées de l'Amérique Russe.* Paris: J. Claye.
1873   Eskimaux et Koloche. Idées religieuses et traditions des Kaniagmioutes. *Revue d'Anthropologie* 2:673–80 Paris: E. Leroux.

Reinhardt, Gregory A.
1981   The Incised Stones from Kodiak Island. *Masterkey* 55(2):101.

Sarychev, Gavriil
1806–7 *Account of a Voyage of Discovery to the North-east of Siberia, the Frozen Ocean and the North-east Sea.* 2 vols. Printed for R. Phillips by J. Barnard, London.

Sauer, Martin
1802   *An Account of a Geographical and Astronomical Expedition to the Northern Parts of Russia.* London: A. Strahan.

Shelikhov, Grigorii I.
1981   *A Voyage to America 1783–1786.* Richard A. Pierce, ed., and Marina Ramsay, transl. Kingston, Ontario: Limestone Press.

Simon, James J.K.
1992   Mortuary Practices of the Late Kachemak Tradition in Southcentral Alaska: A Perspective from the Crag Point Site, Kodiak Island. *Arctic Anthropology* 29(2):130–49.

Steffian, Amy F.
1992   Archaeological Coal in the Gulf of Alaska: A View from Kodiak. *Arctic Anthropology* 29(2):111–29.
in press   Fifty years after Hrdlička: Further Excavation at the Uyak Site, Kodiak Island, Alaska. In *Contributions to the Anthropology of Southcentral and Southwestern Alaska,* R. H. Jordan, F. de Laguna, and A. F. Steffian, eds. Anthropological Papers of the University of Alaska No. 24.

Townsend, Joan
1980   Ranked Societies of the Alaska Pacific Rim. In *Alaska Native Culture and History.* Y. Kotani and W. B. Workman, eds. pp. 123–56. Senri Ethnological Studies 4. National Museum of Ethnology, Osaka.

Turner, Christy G., II
1988   Ancient Peoples of the North Pacific Rim. In *Crossroads of Continents: Cultures of Siberia and Alaska.* W. Fitzhugh and A. Crowell, eds. pp. 111–16. Washington, D.C.: Smithsonian Institution Press.

Workman, William B.
1980   Continuity and Change in the Prehistoric Record from Southern Alaska. In *Alaska Native Culture and History.* Y. Kotani and W. Workman, eds. pp. 49–101, Senri Ethnological Series No. 4. National Museum of Ethnology, Osaka.
1992   Life and Death in a First Millennium A.D. Gulf of Alaska Culture: The Kachemak Tradition Ceremonial Complex. In *Ancient Images, Ancient Thought: The Archaeology of Ideology.* S. Goldsmith, S. Garvie, D. Selin, and J. Smith, eds., pp. 19–25. Proceedings of the 23d Annual Chacmool Conference. Calgary: Archaeological Association.

Yesner, David R.
1989   Osteological Remains from Larsen Bay, Kodiak Island, Alaska. *Arctic Anthropology* 26(2):96–108.

Part 3

The Lessons of Larsen Bay

12

THE CONCEPT OF CULTURAL AFFILIATION AND ITS LEGAL SIGNIFICANCE IN THE LARSEN BAY REPATRIATION

In recent legislation granting Native Americans the right to reclaim skeletal remains and specific classes of artifacts held by museums and other institutions, the decision to repatriate is tied to the demonstration of cultural affiliation. As defined in Public Law 101-601, the Native American Graves Protection and Repatriation Act (NAGPRA), cultural affiliation means "a relationship of shared group identity that can be reasonably traced historically or prehistorically between a present day Indian tribe or Native Hawaiian organization, and an identifiable earlier group." This definition, which entails the recognition of cohesive, discrete, and ethnically distinct social units in both historic and prehistoric contexts, is rooted in anthropology.

In this chapter we examine the meaning and significance of the term "cultural affiliation" from both an anthropological and a legal point of view. The problems resulting from the attempt to transfer an inexact and discipline-specific concept from one intellectual domain to another are illustrated in the case of the Larsen Bay repatriation. A review of the trajectory and outcome of this case provides some useful guidelines in charting a course for future interactions between museums and native peoples as we work towards a mutually acceptable understanding of "cultural affiliation."

Cultural Affiliation and Anthropology

The notion of culture, though differentially applied and understood, is central to anthropology. Its explanatory importance within the field may be likened to that of evolution in biology or gravity in physics. A brief glance at the literature, filled with discourse on cultural complexity, multiculturalism, cultural interaction, cultural identities, and culture conflict, to name but a few current topics, provides a sense of how large the idea looms in the consciousness of anthropologists. It is, no doubt, the polysemous and multifaceted quality of the concept of culture that has contributed to its longevity within the field and made it one of the principal vectors of intra-disciplinary growth.

To better understand what is entailed by the term *cultural affiliation*, it is useful to consider the etymology of the word *culture*. The term derives from the Latin verb *colere*, meaning to till or cultivate. In its most generic sense, culture retains this original association with the working of the land. Through time, culture acquired a more specific meaning in that it came to refer to the process of progressive refinement and breeding in the domestication of a particular crop. Wagner (1981:21) suggests that the modern sense of culture, with its connotations of elitism, derives from an elaborate metaphor that draws upon the terminology of crop breeding and improvement to refer to an image of an individual's control, refinement, and domestication of him or herself.

The anthropological appropriation of the word culture involves a further abstraction from the initial metaphorical reference in which the notion of personal refinement is transferred from the level of the individual to the collectivity or the group. E. B. Tylor is generally credited with having introduced the term in the social sciences. Equating culture with civilization, Tylor (1871:1) defined it as "that complex whole which includes knowledge, belief, art, morals, law, custom, and any other capabilities and habits acquired by man as a member of society." This all-inclusive and enumerative definition of culture, to a large extent, still accurately reflects the traditional anthropological understanding of, and approach to, culture.

The connection between the "opera house" and the anthropological sense of culture is not immediately apparent. In untangling this relationship, however, we begin to gain some insight into the significance of the term. Wagner (1981:22) writes that "the very core of our own culture, in its accepted image, is its science, art, and technology, the sum total of achievements, inventions, and discoveries that define our idea of 'civilization.'" These achievements are preserved, taught, and expanded upon in cultural institutions, like museums, libraries, and universities, in a cumulative process of refinement. It is in the context of the cultural institution, the repositories of our collective and cumulative *Culture*, that the two major senses of the term come together.

That many of the basic tenets of anthropology were formed within the hallowed halls of the museum, the most archetypical of our cultural institutions, is probably more than mere coincidence. In the museum, ethnological specimens and data are transformed, through processes of analysis, classification, and preservation, into objects of our own culture. Through their appropriation, ethnographic objects housed in the museum come to embody the concept of culture in both senses of the term: they are at once elemental to the re-presentation of cultures and constitutive of Culture with a capital C as experienced and understood by the museum-goer.

Because the idea of culture in the anthropological sense developed within the context of the museum, the notion of ethnographic cultures assumed the characteristics of a museum assemblage; that is, they were viewed as finite, discrete, and unequivocal (Wagner 1981:29). Ethnographic cultures were thought of as having peculiar styles and techniques that could be determined with great precision. As Wagner (1981:29) notes, although it might not be possible to

ascertain whether a particular living Indian was *really* Cheyenne or Arapaho, even through direct questioning, the cultural affiliation of styles and artifacts was never in doubt (Wagner 1981:29). The reification of the material component of a culture had the effect of freezing that particular group configuration in time and space, denying the emergent and interactive nature of cultures and cultural identities.

This is the legacy of the concept of cultural affiliation. The semantic history of the word culture provides some insight into how different groups of people have been constructed as cultures through the work of anthropology. Through the metaphor of culture, indigenous peoples are reduced to constellations of artifacts, styles, and techniques. As the critical and reflexive trends in anthropology continue to evolve, the image of cultures as static, bounded, and homogeneous is increasingly called into question. In parallel fashion, we see non-Western peoples challenging these constructs, as well, both in discourse and in praxis. It is paradoxical, then, that at a time when such conceptual artifices are being deconstructed by anthropologists and Native Americans alike, we find ourselves in the position of having to reaffirm such structures and categories in the context of recent legislation.

Cultural Affiliation and the Law

The notion of cultural affiliation has been incorporated into repatriation law as the operative legal standard upon which decisions to return human remains and artifacts will be based. The requirement set forth by Congress that a tribal group demonstrate cultural affiliation was intended to ensure that the claimant has a reasonable connection to the materials being requested (Congressional Report 101-877:14). A party that is able to establish a reasonable connection is entitled to seek repatriation of culturally affiliated materials from museums or other public repositories. In the event that a repatriation request is denied, the implication of the statute is that the claimant would have the right to bring suit in a court of law to compel the return of the materials in question. By making *cultural affiliation* the operative standard, the Congressional act, in effect, confers legal standing on culturally affiliated claimants.

The concept of standing is a cornerstone of U.S. constitutional law. Article III of the Constitution specifies that the power of courts to resolve disputes extends only to genuine cases and controversies. Courts do not render advisory opinions nor establish policy; such functions are the province of the legislative and executive branches of the government. For someone to bring suit, "the irreducible constitutional mini-

Tamara L. Bray and Lauryn Guttenplan Grant

mum of standing requires that plaintiffs have suffered an injury in fact, which is an invasion of a legally protected interest that is concrete and actual or imminent, rather than conjectural or hypothetical" [*Lujan v. Defenders of Wildlife*, 112 S. Ct. 2130, (1992)]. The notion of legal standing is thus seen as fundamental to the separation of powers between the different government branches.

Repatriation legislation, in recognizing cultural affiliation as a relationship that satisfies the requirement of standing, potentially expands the scope of this legal principle far beyond its traditional bounds. The ramifications of so extending the notion of standing could be significant in terms of legal precedent, depending on how far the courts are willing to go to find a sufficient nexus between the claimant and the materials. While anthropologists have been instrumental in fostering the notion of cultures as discrete and timeless entities, it must be recognized that the complexity and contingency of human social relations render the delineation of such groups, on a practical level, almost entirely arbitrary. While understanding that membership in a cultural group is not biologically inscribed but rather dependent on historical circumstance, cultural affiliation must be thought of as existing on a continuum rather than as an either-or condition. Where a claimant falls along this continuum makes the difference between having standing to sue versus having the claim dismissed. Given this, the question of the term's parameters must inevitably be addressed by the courts.

In considering the issue of standing in the context of repatriation, it is useful to divide claims into the following three categories: (1) claims brought by lineal descendants, (2) claims brought by tribal members, and (3) claims brought by other individuals or groups who assert some degree of Native American heritage. Each of these three categories of claimants is recognized in the NAGPRA legislation.

A challenge to a claimant's standing is least likely to occur in the case of an action brought by a lineal descendant. It is well settled by common law and various state court cases that lineal descendants have standing to assert a claim for the skeletal remains of their ancestors. The right of lineal descendants to initiate a lawsuit is, thus, not contingent on a demonstration of cultural affiliation. Rather, it is based on a direct familial relationship, a connection long recognized by the courts as a basis for standing.

Beyond direct lineal ties, the issue of standing becomes more complex. Does a member of a specific tribal group have standing to seek the remains of tribal ancestors? While this question has not been fully addressed by the courts, we can draw an analogy to the concept of *representational standing* for guidance. If a person bringing an action is not directly harmed,

but is within what is referred to in law as the *zone of interests,* it may be possible for him or her to establish standing [*Sierra Club v. Morton*, 405 U.S.727 (1970)]. The requisite elements for establishing representational standing include the following: (1) that the members of the group bringing action would otherwise have standing to sue in their own right; (2) that the interests the group seeks to protect are germane to the organization's purpose; and (3) that neither the claim asserted nor the relief requested requires the participation of individual members in the lawsuit. The zone of interests principle is arguably the basis for finding that a tribal person, even if not a direct lineal descendant, has standing to assert a claim over the remains and associated artifacts of another tribal member.

Legal precedent for the recognition of tribal standing may be found in the court case of *Charrier v. Bell,* in which the Tunica-Biloxi tribe sued a Louisiana pothunter over ownership rights to a mortuary assemblage recovered on private property. The court, siding with the Tunica-Biloxi, ruled that even though the tribe had not produced a perfect *chain of title* to the buried remains and artifacts, the native corporate group nonetheless represented an "accumulation of descendants of former Indians who occupied the land" and was thus a valid representative of the interests of the deceased [*Charrier v. Bell,* 496 So.2d 601 (La.App.1 Cir. 1986), cert. denied, 498 So.2d 753 (La. 1986)].

In contrast to the rights of tribal members to bring actions, the courts have dismissed suits brought by groups such as American Indians Against Desecration (AIAD) for lack of standing. In *American Indians Against Desecration, et al., v. Amrep Southwest,* Inc. [Civ. No., 86-0815C (D.C.N.M. 8/21/86) (unpublished opinion)], AIAD brought suit to prevent a developer from disturbing or moving any human remains or artifacts from a site that was scheduled for development. The District Court held that AIAD did not have standing to bring the claim because it could not demonstrate "ancestral ties to persons whose remains were excavated at the site."

With tribal standing fairly well recognized, Congress could have easily made tribal affiliation the basis of repatriation legislation. However, certain Native American advocates considered the tribal affiliation standard too restrictive, arguing that modern-day Indian peoples of any tribe have greater claim to ancestral remains than any public or private institution. Congress agreed and adopted the notion of cultural affiliation as the degree of relationship necessary to satisfy the standing requirement. Congressional reports detailing the history of the repatriation legislation (Congressional Report 101-473; Congressional Report 101-877) indicate that the formulation of cultural affiliation as the baseline relationship may have evolved out of discussions held by the Panel for a National Dialogue on Museum-Native American Relations in 1990 (Anonymous 1992).

The implications of transforming a broad anthropological concept (cultural affiliation) into an operative legal standard (standing) pose many questions for the courts. Can any Native American person, regardless of tribal origin, claim to be culturally affiliated with any Native American artifact? Can other cultural groups request the return of cultural artifacts from public institutions? Can non-indigenous peoples assert an affiliation with prehistoric remains at some generic level? If the concept of culture has no fixed boundaries, the relationship of cultural affiliation may at some point be ruled too vague or too tenuous to satisfy the constitutional requirements of standing. In such a case, a court might find the repatriation laws, on their face constitutional, to represent an unconstitutional expansion of the doctrine of standing as applied to specific facts.

To date, no court action has been brought to test the precise legal parameters of cultural affiliation. Such a case could foreseeably arise if, for example, one tribe brought an action to reclaim remains and related artifacts that were seemingly more closely associated with another tribal group. Another situation in which a court ruling might be required would be a case in which a requesting tribe occupied the land from which remains and artifacts were recovered, but the evidence of cultural continuity was weak or disputed. This latter situation is precisely what occurred in the Larsen Bay repatriation request. While that case was resolved without the need for legal action, it brought to the fore the meaning of the term cultural affiliation and the type of proof necessary to establish the required degree of connection to the disputed materials.

The Larsen Bay Repatriation

In May of 1987 the Larsen Bay Tribal Council of Kodiak Island, Alaska, passed a resolution calling for the return of the burials removed from the Uyak site by Aleš Hrdlička in the 1930s. The skeletal remains in question, totaling some 756 individually catalogued sets, were housed in the National Museum of Natural History of the Smithsonian Institution. These burials ranged in age from the early historic period to approximately 3000 B.P. (Heizer 1956).

From the earliest discussions between the Larsen Bay people and the Smithsonian Institution, the overriding issue for the anthropologists was the relationship between the claimants and the archaeological remains. This question was complicated by the fact that the archaeological evidence, in the form of patterned variability in mortuary practices and artifact assemblages, suggested a discontinuity in the culture history of the site. The available archaeological and biological information led anthropologists at the Smithsonian to question the relationship between the ancient population and the modern inhabitants.

Frustrated in their initial attempts to obtain the return of the mortuary remains, the Larsen Bay Tribal Council enlisted the aid of the Native American Rights Fund (NARF), a legal services organization. In pressing the case, NARF argued that the modern village residents were the direct lineal descendants of the Koniag people who had, according to oral tradition, always occupied Kodiak Island. To buttress the claim, NARF retained the services of two consultants to prepare a report documenting the continuous occupation of Larsen Bay (Pullar and Knecht 1990). Once the report was completed, NARF asserted that it had satisfied the statutory requirement that the requesting party establish, "by a preponderance of the evidence," its cultural affiliation with the materials in question.

As direct lineal descendants, or even tribal descendants, the people of Larsen Bay would have certainly had a legitimate claim to the remains from the Uyak site. The Smithsonian, however, believed in good faith that the available evidence was at least equivocal, if not insufficient to support the villagers' claim of cultural continuity and direct descent. Hoping to obtain an unbiased scientific opinion, the museum contracted two outside scholars who were recognized regional experts to analyze and evaluate the available biological and archaeological evidence bearing on the question (Dumond 1990; Scott 1990).

Not surprisingly, the findings and conclusions of the experts contracted by the Smithsonian differed significantly from those of NARF's anthropological consultants. The two sets of experts disagreed, not because they were acting in bad faith or deliberately trying to be contentious, but rather because the evidence used to establish membership in a culture group, like the notion of a discretely bounded cultural unit itself, is inherently arbitrary and amorphous. As given in NAGPRA, admissible evidence in the demonstration of cultural affiliation can include geographic, genealogical, biological, archaeological, anthropological, linguistic, folkloric, and historic information (Congressional Report 101-473:9). These particular domains of study are, for the most part, more interpretively oriented than empirically derived. Thus, it is unlikely that the kinds of evidence obtained from such studies would *prima facie* yield a precise and unequivocal determination of cultural affiliation.

In the end, the Smithsonian agreed to repatriate the materials requested to the people of Larsen Bay. The return of the skeletal remains and identifiable funerary objects from the Uyak site was completed in January of 1992. The Larsen Bay case, thus, never reached litigation. At least one legal commentator, however, has observed that, had the case gone to court, "the ability of the Larsen Bay Villagers to make the required showing [would have been] questionable" (Platzman 1992:528).

What is the message of the Larsen Bay experience? Perhaps foremost it is that anthropology and the law make strange bedfellows. Beyond the obvious problems of transferring theoretical concepts across intellectual and epistemological boundaries, there is the seeming incongruity of intertwining anthropology with Native American interests. Making an anthropological concept the basis for satisfying a precise legal requirement in the context of a law intended to benefit Native Americans is paradoxical. The consequences of this legal irony are illustrated in the Larsen Bay example. In this case, attorneys, native peoples, and museum officials alike turned to the anthropological experts to provide evidence of cultural affiliation. Such a reliance on anthropology was probably not what Congress intended when it drafted the legislation, nor what Indian peoples envisioned as the result of their struggle for the right to rebury ancestral remains.

The Larsen Bay case also illustrates the contingent and political nature of scientific inquiry and interpretation. The differences in the experts' assessments of cultural continuity make it clear that the meaning of scientific data is not empirically given, but rather it is constructed in relation to specific world views, goals, and interests. Science cannot be understood as a superorganic system existing apart from and outside of human society. Such a view mystifies the knowledge produced within this system, making it appear given and immutable. Science should rather be understood as embedded within a particular socioeconomic configuration and associated with a specific world view. As the ideological and political motivations of scientific inquiry and so-called facts become more transparent, it is possible to see how indigenous interpretations of culture history can be admitted as alternative ways of understanding the past.

The solution to the problem of determining cultural affiliation is to be found in dialogue. Rather than being given or imposed, an understanding of cultural affiliation must be mutually constructed. It is imperative that Native Americans, museum professionals, anthropologists, government regulators, and lawyers work together to forge a consensus on the meaning and parameters of this concept. The alternative to dialogue is costly, protracted, and adversarial litigation, an outcome that would defeat the great strides already made towards elaborating a sensible and fair resolution to the difficult questions of repatriation.

References Cited

Anonymous
1992   Report of the Panel for a National Dialogue on Museum/Native American Relations (Feb. 28, 1990). *Arizona State Law Journal* 24(1):487–500.

Congressional Report 101-473
1990   Providing for the Protection of Native American Graves and the Repatriation of Native American Remains and Cultural Patrimony. Senate Report, 101st Congress, 2d Session.

Congressional Report 101-877
1990   Providing for the Protection of Native American Graves, and for Other Purposes. House of Representatives Report, 101st Congress, 2d Session.

Dumond, D.
1991   The Uyak Site (KOD-145) in Southwestern Alaskan Prehistory. Report prepared for the Department of Anthropology, U.S. National Museum of Natural History, Smithsonian Institution, Washington, D.C.

Heizer, R.
1956   Archaeology of the Uyak Site, Kodiak Island, Alaska. *Anthropological Records* 17:1. Berkeley: University of California Press.

Kroeber, A. L.
1952   *The Nature of Culture*. Chicago: University of Chicago Press.

Platzman, S.
1992   Objects of Controversy: The Native American Right to Repatriation. *The American University Law Review* 41 (Winter):517–58.

Pullar, G., and P. Knecht
1990   Continuous Occupation of Larsen Bay/Uyak Bay by Qikertarmiut. Unpublished manuscript on file at the Native American Rights Fund, Washington, D.C. Office.

Scott, R.
1990   Continuity or Replacement at the Uyak Site, Kodiak Island, Alaska: A Physical Anthropological Analysis of Population Relationships. Report prepared for the Department of Anthropology, U.S. National Museum of Natural History, Smithsonian Institution, Washington, D.C.

Tylor, E. B.
1871   *Primitive Culture*. London: Bradbury, Evans, and Company.

Wagner, R.
1981   *The Invention of Culture*. Chicago: University of Chicago Press.

13

THE LARSEN BAY REPATRIATION CASE AND COMMON ERRORS OF ANTHROPOLOGISTS

I am a member of the Penobscot Indian Nation in Maine. As an attorney, I represented the Larsen Bay Tribal Council in its efforts to repatriate the grave offerings and human remains that had been removed from a burial site near the Alaska Native village at Larsen Bay on Kodiak Island. In this chapter, I want to draw on that experience to identify and examine basic mistakes that anthropologists tend to make when they deal with Native Americans. The days when men like Aleš Hrdlička could run roughshod over Native Americans are long since past. Members of the anthropological community must recognize that a new era has dawned. Tribes now control the disposition of the remains of their ancestors, and anthropologists must learn to work cooperatively with tribes or risk losing all access to the object of their interest.

New federal laws empower tribes and, for the first time, permit tribes rather than academics to determine the ultimate disposition of Native American human remains. A policy decision has been made by Congress to place tribal social values over the interests of science. This chapter briefly discusses the legal restrictions placed on anthropological treatment of Native American human remains. It also cites specific instances in which, during the course of the Larsen Bay repatriation case, the conduct of Smithsonian officials offended the Alaska Native people of Larsen Bay and made a mutually acceptable solution to repatriation impossible.

Legal Restrictions on Treatment of Human Remains

Common law has long held that there is no commercial interest in dead human bodies [*Dead Bodies,* 22 Am. Jur. 2d 4; 25A C.J.S. 2]. One cannot own a human body but one can have the legal responsibility to provide for the final disposition of human remains [*Matter of Moorehead,* 10 Kan. App. 2d 480 (1985)]. Most of the cases of which I am aware involve bodies that were relatively "fresh," but there is no legal nor ethical distinction, in my view, between a dead body that is less than one year old and one that is 500 years old.

The same rule of law applies to grave offerings. American common law holds that burial goods, if removed from the grave, are the property of the person who buried the deceased or of the descendants of that person [*Busler v. State,* 184 S.W.2d 24 (Tenn. 1944); *Ware v. State,* 121 S.E. 251 (Ga.App. 1924)]. Again, the law does not recognize a distinction between items that are recently buried and those that are ancient.

In a recent Louisiana case, it was held that an amateur archaeologist did not acquire title to human remains or funerary objects that he discovered and excavated [*Charrier v. Bell,* 496 S.2d 601 (La.App. 1st Cir. 1986), *cert. denied,* 498 S.2d 753 (La. 1986)]. The Louisiana Court of Appeals held that the human remains and burial goods were the property of the tribe of origin. The tribe had no intent to abandon the human remains and artifacts, and the modern-day political successor of the tribe of origin was held to be the owner.

Historically, anthropologists have not shared this view. At the risk of overstatement, it seems that dead Native American bodies have greater scientific value to anthropologists than they have human value. Bieder (1990) cites repeated instances, particularly during the post-Civil War era, in which the graves of dead Native Americans were violated for scientific purposes. Not only were ancient Indian burial sites violated, but fresh burials were targeted as well. Bieder (1990:19) cites several instances where fresh burials were unearthed to acquire the head of the dead Indian.

It is well documented that Robert Peary brought six Greenland Eskimos to New York City after one of his Arctic explorations and housed them at the American Museum (Harper 1986).[1] Of the six Eskimos, four died almost immediately. Franz Boas, along with Aleš Hrdlička and others, boiled the flesh from these bodies to permit study of their remains. One of the deceased Eskimos had a son named Minik. This eight-year-old boy survived and, in order to convince him that his father's remains were being respectfully interred, Boas and Hrdlička staged a fake funeral and burial. Many years later Minik discovered the ruse when he saw his father's remains in one of the museum's displays (Harper 1986:97). Despite Minik's protests, the remains were never returned to him (Pullar 1989).

While these activities may not occur today, Native Americans are aware of these and other indignities that have been suffered as a result of scientific inquiry. On a personal level, when I was a college student I visited a state museum in Maine and observed the skeletal remains of one of my tribal ancestors. I do not recall how old these remains were, but they were quite ancient. Despite their antiquity, I was genuinely shocked at this display. I thought it was morally wrong, but I had no idea what to do about it.

Not all tribes have the same cultural views about human remains that I express here. Based on their broad support for the Native American Graves Protection and Repatriation Act (NAGPRA), however, it appears that many tribes do share my outrage and object to the manner in which these remains and burial offerings were obtained and also to the way they are presently treated. If anthropologists believe that it is only the uneducated or misinformed that do not understand their profession's attitude toward dead Native American bodies, they are mistaken. Many tribes share my feelings about at the indignities heaped upon Indian dead. The advice that I provide in this chapter may well prevent anthropologists from offending the Native Americans with whom they must work if they want to continue to practice their chosen profession.

Before examining the kinds of basic mistakes that anthropologists make when dealing with tribes, I want to review two repatriation laws that have been enacted recently. The first is Public Law 101-185, 103 Stat. 1336, Section 11, of the National Museum of the American Indian Act. This act requires the Smithsonian Institution to inventory the Indian remains under its control and to notify the tribe that is culturally affiliated with the remains. The tribe then has the option of having the remains returned to them for reburial or other disposition.

The second is Public Law 101-601; 104 Stat. 3048, the Native American Graves Protection and Repatriation Act. This statute is a continuation and extrapolation of the approach developed in P. L. 101-185. It affects all federal agencies and all private museums that receive federal funding. In addition to the inventory and notice requirements that are found in P.L. 101-601, the law also provides for the protection of Native American burial sites discovered on federal and tribal lands. It further prohibits trafficking in Indian human remains and provides for jail sentences of up to one year for the illegal transport for sale or profit of Indian human remains.

While I do not intend to review these acts in detail, I cite them to establish the fact that Congress has made a policy decision that represents a sea change in the traditional balance struck between scientific interests and the fundamental human values of tribes. Tribes have federal legal rights now with respect to the disposition of Native American remains, and they are aware of those rights. Anthropologists must recognize that tribes now control decisions about who can excavate and study the remains of their ancestors. Congress has mandated that anthropologists work cooperatively with tribes both in excavating new sites and in studying the remains already in their possession.

Lessons from the Larsen Bay Repatriation Case

As an example of what *not* to do in repatriation cases, the Smithsonian's handling of the Larsen Bay request is instructive. I believe the Smithsonian made many errors, and I have seen these same errors made by other museum personnel as well. A general, but I believe important, example concerns the way anthropologists frequently dehumanize the object of their study. They often refer to skeletal remains as "material" or "specimens." Anthropologists must not lose sight of the fact that, to many Native Americans, these remains are respected ancestors with whom they have a direct connection, even if the remains are ancient. While anthropologists may consider the remains to be the objects of scientific curiosity, tribes tend to regard the remains as people who were once living, from whom they are directly descended, and who are entitled to respectful treatment.

Most tribes are fairly small, even today. Most people within a tribe are related to one another. When a person dies in a small tribal community, it is a loss for the entire community and not just for the immediate family. In large cities, if a person dies, 99.9 percent of the city population neither knows nor cares. In a tribe, death is more personal.

Because of these factors, tribes tend to see all of their members as ultimately related to all others. If an individual was once a tribal member and his remains are treated with disrespect, all tribal members are insulted. It is, therefore, most appropriate for anthropologists to refer to these ancient remains using terminology that shows respect. This attitude must permeate all anthropologists' dealings with tribes.

Between 1931 and 1938, Aleš Hrdlička, director of physical anthropology for the Smithsonian Institution, removed approximately 756 human remains from a site adjacent to the native village of Larsen Bay. He did this without permission and over the objections of the native peoples of Larsen Bay. All of the remains were shipped to the Smithsonian Institution for study.

In July of 1987, the tribe formally contacted the Smithsonian to request the return of the remains. The Smithsonian refused to comply. This set in motion a series of events that ultimately resulted in the reburial of those remains.

When the tribe first contacted the Smithsonian, Adrienne L. Kaeppler, then chairperson of the Department of Anthropology, asserted in a letter to the Larsen Bay Tribal Council, dated September 25, 1987, that "field records indicate that the local people not only were aware and informed of the work but also assisted by directing or taking Hrdlička to old sites and [working] as paid field excavators" (Appendix). This statement directly contradicts the recollections of several of the local people. Dora Aga, the matriarch of Larsen Bay, remembers Hrdlička well, though not fondly. When she was informed of the claims made by the Smithsonian, she vigorously disputed them (Pullar 1989:10). In a small community like Larsen Bay, where many of the families have been in residence for generations, it was possible to ascertain the truth of the Smithsonian's assertions about Hrdlička. Tribal leaders could simply ask the people who had lived in the village in the 1930s.[2]

The first important lesson of the Larsen Bay case is that claims from a tribe must be taken seriously. To suggest that Hrdlička's removal of human remains was based upon permission was a mistake, first, because it was probably not true, but also, and perhaps more importantly, because it is irrelevant. Under existing federal law the tribe would be entitled to possession.

The Smithsonian made another significant error in its initial response to the tribe. In the same letter, Kaeppler states the following: "As you are no doubt aware, the issue of deaccession is a complex one, which the Smithsonian must consider in light of the Institution's responsibility to hold its collections in trust for the benefit of all people, *not just discrete interest groups*" [my emphasis added].

The second lesson, illustrated in the above excerpt, is not to insult the tribe by minimizing tribal status or its interest in the remains. Tribes resent being referred to as "discrete interest groups." Tribes are separate semi-sovereign governmental entities with special status under the law. They have a jurisdictional status that is separate from states, and they retain all attributes of their aboriginal sovereignty unless it is specifically reduced by the federal government. Tribes are not simply "a discrete interest group."

The third lesson is that it is not necessary to balance scientific and public interests in the human remains with those of the tribes. Federal law has decided how these interests will be balanced and tribal concerns now outweigh those of the general public and the scientific community.

In a 1988 letter from Kaeppler to the tribe,[3] the Smithsonian raised the possibility that the remains were (1) possibly not burials at all, (2) not culturally connected to the present-day tribe, and (3) not recent. (See the Appendix.) This was another error.

The fourth lesson here is that when anthropologists communicate with tribes, they should not assume that they have better information about a site than the tribe. The reverse many actually more often apply. The Smithsonian asserted that the Larsen Bay site was not occupied at the time the excavations occurred, but the local people knew this was not true. There had been a cannery at the Larsen Bay site since at least 1888 (Roppel 1986). The native people of the village fished for that cannery just as they do today. Rather than accept or even investigate the possibility that the local people were correct, Kaeppler chose to rely on the statements of Hrdlička. Citing Hrdlička, Kaeppler wrote in the same letter that the site was not occupied and the local native people "did not know its name and had no traditions about it . . ." The Smithsonian ignored the fact that these statements were self-serving and failed to consider the possibility that the local native people may have had very specific reasons for withholding information from a known grave robber about a local burial site. If anthropolo-

Henry J. Sockbeson

gists ignore the fact that local knowledge is superior to theirs in many cases, they run a substantial risk of alienating the tribe.

The fifth lesson of the Larsen Bay case is do not try to convince tribes that they are no longer culturally affiliated with ancient remains because of contact with non-Indians. Contemporary Native Americans are proud of their identity and proud of the fact that their ancestors occupied this land from time immemorial. The Smithsonian's director, Robert McC. Adams, wrote the following to me in a letter dated April 27, 1990: "As Dr. Ortner discussed with you, the Institution is certainly prepared to transfer all materials reliably associated with the historic period, i.e., since 1750 A.D." (See the Appendix.) This offer was apparently an attempt to reach an accommodation with the tribe, but it only resulted in the further hardening of the tribe's position. What this, in effect, said was that with the arrival of the white man, the cultural connection between the tribe and their ancestors had been severed. This was a major error that, in combination with "the battle of the experts," made it impossible for the tribe to reach any subsequent agreement with the Smithsonian.

This brings me to my last point which is that tribes are not interested in establishing, to a scientific certainty, that the remains are culturally affiliated with their tribe. While tribes do not often want to be responsible for the reburial of captives or visitors who are clearly not members of the tribe, they will see attempts to definitively establish the cultural affiliation of ancient remains as an act of bad faith. As will be shown, the law supports the tribe on this point.

The Smithsonian tried very hard to divide the Larsen Bay human remains on the grounds that, at some ancient date, a new wave of people had come to occupy the Larsen Bay site and broken the chain of cultural connection. This was a mistake and was not required under the law.

P.L. 101-185 requires that the Smithsonian identify the tribe of origin for all Indian human remains and cultural items in their possession "using the best *available* scientific and historical documentation" [my emphasis added]. The law does not require that the origins be established to a scientific certainty but only that the decision be based on the best available data. The Smithsonian did not accept this approach. The tribe made a showing that the best available scientific and historical documentation supported the return of the remains. The Smithsonian hired two experts and attempted to argue that there was a division within the collection. The problem with this approach was that one could never resolve this question to a scientific certainty.

Whether there was mass migration from Asia thou-sands of years ago, or whether or not there existed a land bridge that permitted such a mass invasion will never be resolved to the complete satisfaction of all anthropologists. Different theories will find more or less general support until they are displaced by other theories. Even established theories are subject to challenge based on the discovery of new evidence or a new technique of evaluating new evidence. This situation was acknowledged by Congress when the standard for identification was adopted. This standard relies on the existence of available data. It does not call for new studies nor does it call for definitive studies. If the available data support repatriation, then that is what must occur. A museum has no liability if a repatriation request is granted based on the best available evidence and later it is discovered that the return was in error.

To its credit, the Smithsonian eventually came up with the right decision, but it was too late to suggest alternatives to reburial. Because the tribe had been alienated by the communications it received from the Smithsonian and because of the resistance the Smithsonian exhibited, the tribe eventually hardened its position to the point that it was impossible to agree upon a method of reburial that would have left open the possibility of subsequent study. Money was, of course, a significant factor as it always is. But it is my belief that a method of reburial that was economical and yet allowed future study could have been agreed upon.

In conclusion, the Larsen Bay repatriation case is significant because it is the largest repatriation request acceded to by the Smithsonian Institution to date. It foreshadows repatriation decisions and events that will be occurring throughout the country as a result of new federal laws. Mistakes were made with the Larsen Bay request that can and must be avoided in future dealings with Native American tribes. I urge anthropologists to examine some of the lessons I have highlighted and to try to apply them in future dealings with tribes.

In my experience, tribes are interested in their history, and they can and will cooperate with anthropological efforts. Philomena and Rick Knecht, as well as many others, have worked cooperatively and successfully with tribes. It can and must be done.

Notes

1. Skeletons in Our Museums' Closets, by Douglas J. Preston, *Harper's Magazine*, February 1989.
2. Dr. Kaeppler's statement was not even supported by Hrdlička's own account of his work. In *The Anthropology of Kodiak Island*, Hrdlička (1944:105) complained that the lack of local help in digging the site forced him to procure help from student volun-

teers. Hrdlička also states that the Jones Point site was shown to him by Mrs. Gordon Jones, wife of the local cannery manager and not by Alaska Natives from the village. Hrdlička further complained that local people gave him intentionally false information in an effort to prevent him from locating grave sites. These statements were apparently ignored or overlooked. Hrdlička's report is also informative for what it does not contain. Despite six years on the site, remarkably little is said in his book about the local native people (1944:120).

3. Letter from Adrienne Kaeppler, Chair, NMNH, Smithsonian Institution, to Frank M. Carlson, Larsen Bay Tribal Council, February 16, 1988) (Appendix).

References Cited

Bieder, Robert E.
1990   *A Brief Historical Survey of the Expropriation of American Indian Remains.* Bloomington, Indiana.

Harper, Kenn
1986   *Give Me My Father's Body: The Life of Minik, The New York Eskimo.* Frobisher Bay, Northwest Territories and Newmarket, Ontario: Blacklead Books.

Hrdlička, Aleš
1944   *The Anthropology of Kodiak Island.* Philadelphia: The Wistar Institute of Anatomy and Biology.

Pullar, Gordon L.
1989   The Hrdlička Legacy and Koniag Spirits. Paper presented at the Circum-Pacific Prehistory Conference, Seattle.

Roppel, Patricia
1986   *Salmon from Kodiak: An History of the Salmon Fishery on Kodiak Island, Alaska.* Anchorage: Alaska Historical Commission Studies in History.

Rosen, Lawrence
1980   The Excavation of American Indian Burial Sites: A Problem in Law and Professional Responsibility. *American Anthropologist* 82:5–27.

14

SENSITIVITIES AND PRACTICAL CONSIDERATIONS IN THE RETURN OF HUMAN REMAINS

We hear a great deal about the issue of repatriation and how museums and other institutions are making decisions regarding the return of human skeletal remains. Much effort is being devoted to establishing the cultural affiliation of the remains and the biological distance between the populations in question. Field notes, collections records, and publications are being carefully examined for relevant information. Heads of departments or agencies are communicating with tribal, government, and legal representatives to negotiate which remains should be returned to whom and on what time schedule. The repatriation laws provide more guidance now than was available when the Larsen Bay request was first made, and standards and criteria for the decision-making process and subsequent negotiations are beginning to take shape.

The decision-making effort, however, is only half of the repatriation transaction. Planning for and discussion of *how* to return the remains must follow. Although the practical considerations of preparing remains for transfer and maintaining information about their return is of considerable importance to all affected parties, these aspects can be easily overlooked. In failing to explicitly address these matters, erroneous assumptions can easily be made. How well an institution completes a repatriation transaction is an indication of its compliance with the spirit of the law. It is also an indication of its professionalism. The respect with which the remains and their recipients are treated sets the tone for future interactions.

Once the basic decision to return human remains has been made, some key issues need to be discussed by all parties involved in the transaction. These issues will determine how all subsequent work is done. Rapid and clear resolution of these points will simplify the task for the museum staff, smooth the way for the transaction, and ensure more satisfactory results. These key issues include the following:

What will the final disposition of the remains be?
Are the remains destined for a repository or for reburial?
What is the time schedule?
How will the remains be transported?
Should catalog numbers on skeletal remains be removed?
Who will prepare and pack the remains?
How should the remains be packed?
Is their condition after transport highly significant?
Should individuals be packed in separate containers?
Are there groups distinguished by age and sex that should be indicated?
Are there ceremonial procedures that the museum will need to accommodate?

What are the wishes of the recipients concerning publicity versus privacy during the transfer of remains?

In the rest of this chapter, I will discuss the various effects that these issues have on museum planning and preparation of human remains for repatriation.

The final disposition of remains will determine, in part, how they can be packed. Human remains destined for continuing examination and use should be transported in a "cavity pack" system. Such a system is suggested by conservators to minimize potential damage during transport. Cavity packs are prepared by cutting a hole or cavity in the shape of the bone in a sheet of foam. The foam sheet is fitted into a container and the bone is placed into the cavity. Pieces of foam padding are placed around the bone if necessary. Very sturdy transport containers, such as crates, should be used. Some conservators advocate the use of a chemical consolidant to harden the bone while it is being transported. Any numbering system on the bones should be maintained so that existing information may be matched to the remains. Organizational control must be maintained in order to keep the remains in meaningful groupings. Preparing bones in this manner is expensive, both in terms of resources and time, and such treatments need to be taken into account when scheduling completion and transportation dates.

Remains destined for reburial present different considerations. If the bones are to be buried in their packing containers, biodegradable materials should be used. It is undesirable to put non-biodegradable materials into the ground. This argues against the use of the more protective cavity packing approach, as well as packing bones in plastic bubble wrap or thin sheets of microfoam, even though these materials generally provide good protection. At the National Museum of Natural History (NMNH) we have tried to find a middle ground between compliance with our conservators' packing standards and the unnecessary creation of solid waste—by packing bones destined for reburial in plain, unprinted newsprint paper. Plain paper will eventually decompose while plastic and foam material will not. The recipients of the remains, however, need to be informed that bones packed only in paper are more likely to be damaged in transit. This is an additional point to consider when discussing resources, timing, potential damage to the remains, and the needs of the recipients.

At NMNH, a variety of different approaches have been used in preparing human remains for transport. For example, the skeletal remains returned to Hawaii were prepared by the Hawaiian delegation during a closed ceremony. The museum staff was not involved in packing the remains, although they did remove the remains from collection storage areas, ensured that they were the correct individuals, and prepared a private room for the ceremonies and packing. If the recipients prepare the remains themselves, they may bring their own supplies or they may request that packing materials be made available.

The recipients may also wish to group the remains according to any number of different criteria. If the museum staff prepares the remains, they should ask the recipients if any special groupings should be employed, e.g., age or sex. One recent transaction at NMNH required that the age and sex of each individual be marked on the outside of each packed box so that they could be buried by tribal custom according to their initiation status. If such distinctions are required, the staff preparing the remains must be capable of making reliable assessments of age and sex.

We have established an internal museum standard of packing one individual per container. The only exceptions are individuals who are represented by only a portion of their skeletons; in these cases, we group the various skeletal elements together in a container only after we have consulted with the recipient group. Skeletal remains can always be grouped together at a later time, but separating out distinct individuals from a mixed set takes a great deal of time and knowledge. It is better to maintain the remains as discrete individuals, if possible, than to have to recreate the proper organization at the last minute.

The museum staff will need to ask the recipients if the identification numbers should be removed from the remains. The removal is a time-consuming process, and the results are not always fully successful. Many institutions use India ink for numbering because of its permanency. Some cover the number with a varnish. The removal of these substances can damage the surface of bone. If the numbers must be removed, the removal should be done as a last step before packing to prevent confusion.

The types of ceremonies to be conducted and the amount of publicity desired will vary from tribe to tribe. When the Smithsonian repatriated 136 sets of human remains to the Hawaiians in 1991, the Native Hawaiian delegation that came to receive them prepared the bones for transfer during a closed, nighttime ceremony. Although press coverage of the event was not specifically requested, several local papers picked up the story because of a flamboyant counter claim made by a separate interest group at the last minute.

The Sisseton-Wahpeton Sioux officials who came to Washington in 1991 to receive the remains of 24 individuals were accompanied by a delegation of about 50 people. Separate public and private ceremonies were conducted. NMNH staff were invited to attend the public portion of the ceremony, but preparations

Carol Roetzel Butler

done immediately before the removal of the remains were closed to all but a select group of individuals.

No ceremonies were performed at the museum before the transfer of the Larsen Bay skeletal remains. A Russian Orthodox ceremony was, however, conducted at the reburial site on Kodiak Island and the event received considerable coverage in the state and local press. At the request of the descendants, there was no publicity of any kind in the Smithsonian's earliest repatriation, which occurred in 1984 and involved the remains of five Modoc individuals. The Blackfeet, at the other end of the spectrum, held a news conference when 16 sets of remains were repatriated to their tribe in 1988.

As these examples of completed repatriations suggest, museum staff must remain open to the possibility of being asked to arrange meetings between representatives and officials, to reserve rooms for ceremonial events, and to perform a variety of host-like tasks. As the details of returning skeletal remains are negotiated, museum staff would be well-advised to ask if the return is to be kept private or if public notice of the event may be given. Prior knowledge of what to expect overall will reduce the potential for embarrassment and misunderstandings, although the staff must be prepared for last minute changes.

Before you consider a repatriation transaction to be closed, you must do some maintenance work on your information files. This work has a cost just as preparation work has a cost. I have found that records' reconciliation takes nearly the same amount of time as the preparation of remains. You will need to update all your collections records, paper files, catalog cards, and databases to show that the material has left your custody. Include the date, the recipients, and the circumstances. There should be no ambiguity about the status of remains that have been returned. Future users of any of your filing systems should find consistency and clarity. If remains were on exhibit, you must immediately update your labels and any signage, pamphlets, or promotional materials related to the material. Most importantly, you cannot rely on oral tradition. You must create a reading file for all people who provide the public and/or target groups with current, accurate information on the status of your collections. Any reports on remains that have *not* been in your collections should also be in this file. All new staff members need to know about this information.

Although such attention to documentation may seem excessive, the museum staff is likely to continue to be asked about skeletal remains that were once in its custody. NMNH staff members, for example, regularly receive requests for information on the remains of Mangas Coloradas and Captain Jack. The museum has never had custody of Mangas Coloradas's remains, and Captain Jack's skull was returned to a descendant in the 1980s. But because these individuals are well-known historic figures who are linked to the Smithsonian in various books and other publications, the perception that the Smithsonian retains custody of their remains will persist as long as those publications are available. Finally, the museum staff may receive inquiries from family or tribal members who are unaware that remains have been returned. In these cases, the staff must be able to provide them with accurate and complete information.

During the course of these activities, all museum personnel involved must maintain professional standards and attitudes. Regardless of the final disposition, all skeletal remains must be handled carefully and respectfully. If any scientific study or verification is done during this period, it must be responsible research. Discussions and negotiations with the recipients of the remains must remain professional, and the same attitudes and standards must be maintained after the transaction has been completed. The different groups who have or who had custody of the remains will be forever linked by this transaction.

At the NMNH we have returned the remains of approximately 1,300 individuals in nine separate repatriation transactions. Each case has been different in its details. With each case, the museum staff has learned how to better accomplish the task. It has learned that the use of basic principles of professional responsibility, courtesy, and informed planning are vitally important. As we all learn to give equal energy and attention to both halves of the repatriation equation, we will have increasingly satisfactory results.

15

REPATRIATION AT THE NATIONAL MUSEUM OF NATURAL HISTORY

Present and Future

The Smithsonian Institution received the request for the return of Larsen Bay skeletal remains and grave goods in July 1987, almost two and a half years before Public Law 101-185, the National Museum of the American Indian Act, was signed into law. At the time of the request, the Smithsonian's repatriation policy called for the return of the remains of known ancestors to their lineal descendants and for the return of communally owned sacred objects. P.L. 101-185 substantially broadened that mandate to include human remains and funerary objects that could be demonstrated to be culturally affiliated with a contemporary Native American group. It also called for the establishment of a major Institution-wide program of repatriation. In order to implement the mandate, the Smithsonian established the Repatriation Office within the National Museum of Natural History.

When the Smithsonian made the decision to return the entire skeletal collection, together with associated grave goods, from the Uyak site in April 1991, the outline of the repatriation program was still in the developmental stage. When the museum had nearly completed the deaccession in September 1991, the newly created Repatriation Office had just hired the first two staff anthropologists of the present 15-person staff. The space intended to house the office was still being cleared of the more than 30,000 ethnographic objects from Africa and Asia that had been stored there for many years.

The fact that the Larsen Bay repatriation was un-

folding during the time the NMNH program was being designed and staffed had an important effect on the form and scope of the office's responsibilities. Drawing on its experiences with the ongoing Larsen Bay case as well as earlier repatriation requests, the NMNH set about building a program that would (1) be able to marshal the documentation necessary to respond to such requests more promptly, (2) meet both the needs of the requestors and the museum more fully, (3) provide a thorough and fair review procedure for assessing the results of documentation efforts, and (4) avoid the miscommunication, misunderstandings, and ill will that unfortunately surrounded many aspects of the Larsen Bay case.

P.L. 101-185 mandated that the Smithsonian establish a repatriation program that would conduct an inventory of Indian skeletal remains, as well as associated and unassociated grave goods, in its possession. The program was charged with assessing the degree to which these remains and funerary objects could be shown to be culturally affiliated with a contemporary Native American group, notifying the affiliated group of the existence of these collections, and expeditiously returning the remains to the appropriate group, if so requested.

In addition, the new law specified that a Review Committee be appointed. The major responsibilities of the Review Committee as given in the law were: (1) to ensure that the inventory of collections is conducted in a fair, objective, and comprehensive way,

(2) to review findings relating to the origin of the human remains and objects, and (3) to facilitate the resolution of disputes with respect to the return of remains or objects.

Beyond this simple outline, the law provided little guidance on how the repatriation effort was to be accomplished. This landmark legislation was the culmination of years of discussion on the issue of Native American rights in the repatriation of museum collections. It was left to the Smithsonian to find a way to carry out the mandate.

Basic Requirements for the NMNH Repatriation Program

A basic requirement of the NMNH for the Repatriation Office was that it be established as an independent division, reporting directly to the Director of NMNH through the Deputy Director. As the organizational chart in fig. 15.1 shows, the Repatriation Office was purposefully separate from the research and collections divisions of the museum. In this way, it is structurally removed from the seven scientific departments, including the Department of Anthropology, which are under the purview of the Associate Director for Science. The museum felt that such an independent status was needed to avoid any appearance of conflict of interest between the Repatriation Office and the departments affected by repatriation. In addition, it was done to ensure that the repatriation effort was treated as a finite task to be performed within certain time limits and not be intermingled with the day-to-day affairs of any given department.

An effective repatriation effort, however, also carried the seemingly contradictory requirement that the staff conducting the repatriation effort have a detailed knowledge of the scientific and technical aspects of museum and departmental operations. Repatriation could not succeed if it was not functionally integrated into the machinery of departmental operations or did not have the full cooperation of all museum staff, particularly the Department of Anthropology, whose collections would be most directly affected by the repatriation efforts. Moreover, the staff needed to have an anthropological knowledge of documentary research to be able to build upon the department's previous repatriation experiences, anticipate the various demands that the repatriation effort would make on museum resources, assess how best to meet increased interest in and use of the museum's collections and records by outside investigators, and develop procedures for what could potentially become a major program of deaccession.

The Department of Anthropology had some requirements as well. The primary one was that the inventory and documentation effort be conducted in a professional and thorough way that addressed both the interests and legal rights of the claimants, as well as the legal fiduciary and scientific research responsibilities of the museum. Another important requirement was that the considerable effort required to carry out the repatriation mandate not overwhelm all other departmental research, collection, and outreach initiatives. The need for added support was especially important for the two major departmental units that were most likely to be affected by repatriation activities: the Collections Management Unit and the National Anthropological Archives. Because both units were experiencing staff vacancies of between 30 to 40 percent at the time, they were having difficulty meeting even routine demands for their services, let alone the vastly increased demand that a major repatriation effort promised.

A final requirement placed on the repatriation program was that it establish open and easily accessible lines of communication with the Native American community. Not only must it respond to queries about the collections and requests for return fully and promptly, but it also must develop ways to disseminate information about NMNH collections, repatriation procedures, and the wide range of resources available within the museum for Native Americans. The program would have to make a concerted effort to learn more about the concerns and interests of the Native American community, and such information would have to be incorporated into the museum's overall efforts in repatriation and its general programs involving research, collections, and outreach.

Organizational Structure of the Repatriation Office

The organizational structure that resulted from these decisions is shown schematically in fig. 15.2. The solid lines indicate the lines of supervision and dotted lines symbolize lines of communication.

Although the Repatriation Office reported to the NMNH Director's Office as an independent division of the museum, a conscious effort was made to ensure that the Department of Anthropology was involved in all steps of the repatriation process.

The Repatriation Office is headed by a program manager, who not only reports to the NMNH director but who also works closely with the anthropology department's chair and curatorial staff. The office has an administrative staff comprised of a program assistant who is responsible for fund management, personnel, and general office organization; and a secretary.

Case officers and other related documentation staff form the core of the office. Case officers are re-

National Museum of Natural History
Organization Chart

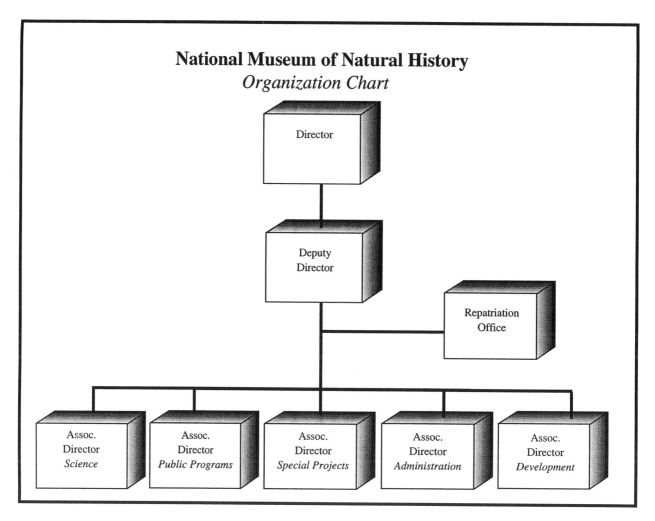

Figure 15.1. Organization chart of National Museum of Natural History. (Courtesy of the Department of Anthropology, National Museum of Natural History, Smithsonian Institution)

sponsible for compiling and presenting documentary information about collections potentially subject to repatriation. They are assisted by the anthropology department's curatorial staff in setting inventory priorities and providing background information on collections and their contexts. There are currently three case officers—two with backgrounds in archaeology and ethnohistory, and one with training in physical anthropology. In some instances, the office issues independent contracts to specialist consultants. Currently, an ethnologist and an additional physical anthropologist are working for the office on contract.

The case officers are assisted by seven technicians who are responsible for the collections management aspects of the repatriation efforts. The technicians are trained and advised by the anthropology department's collections manager and staff. Three technicians are charged with compiling catalog and accession information, locating collections, and packing

and shipping collections that are being repatriated. Two others assist in the documentation of physical remains. One of the individuals conducts computer queries, downloads information from the central database, and uploads updated information. Another performs registrarial activities related to the repatriation process, in particular those involved in deaccessions.

Most of the original field notes and pictorial documentation for the collections are stored in the National Anthropological Archives. Because only very cursory finding aids are available for several key, and as yet unprocessed, archival collections, the Repatriation Office has added two archivists and an archives technician to its staff. The archivists provide case officers with both archival reference and processing support critical to the repatriation process. Although these staff members are part of the Repatriation Office and are supervised by Repatriation Office person-

168   *Melinda A. Zeder*

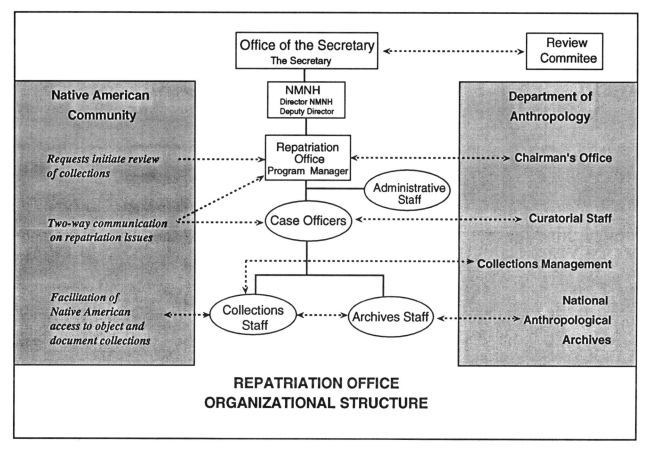

Office of the Secretary
The Secretary

Review Commitee

Native American Community

NMNH
Director NMNH
Deputy Director

Department of Anthropology

Requests initiate review of collections

Repatriation Office
Program Manager

Chairman's Office

Administrative Staff

Two-way communication on repatriation issues

Case Officers

Curatorial Staff

Collections Management

Facilitation of Native American access to object and document collections

Collections Staff

Archives Staff

National Anthropological Archives

REPATRIATION OFFICE
ORGANIZATIONAL STRUCTURE

Figure 15.2. Organizational structure of Repatriation Office. (Courtesy of the Department of Anthropology, National Museum of Natural History, Smithsonian Institution)

nel, the Archives Director and staff have been actively involved in training and coordinating the conduct of repatriation activities in this unit.

In addition to the internal processes of inventory and documentation, the repatriation effort also brings about increased interaction between the museum and the Native American community (see fig. 15.2). The new linkages go beyond repatriation requests and ensuing consultations to more general and more frequent information exchanges and onsite investigations of collections and associated documentation. Recognizing the importance of these interactions, the Repatriation Office's collections and archives staff has as primary responsibilities responding to inquiries and helping visitors gain access to object and documentary collections.

As noted earlier, a founding premise for the Repatriation Office was the need for direct, two-way communication with tribal communities. Many of the tensions between museums and Native Americans have been exacerbated by a lack of communication and by the absence of a shared understanding of the other's interests and concerns. Though generated in

part as a result of those tensions, the repatriation effort also offers an opportunity for forging a new understanding between museums and Native Americans. In the past year, case officers have made several trips to tribal communities in the Pacific Northwest, Northern Plains, Alaska, and Oklahoma, visiting with groups actively engaged in repatriation discussions with the NMNH, as well as with other communities that might potentially have an interest in its collections. The goal of these efforts is to shift the venue of interaction from Washington to the tribal communities, to work more directly with tribal people to understand their concerns, and, in turn, to convey the concerns of the museum to Native Americans. In addition to the off-site visits, there have been a number of Indian delegations that have traveled to Washington to meet with the Repatriation Office and the Department of Anthropology staff to discuss the collections and issues of concern.

Other efforts designed to encourage Native American participation in the repatriation process include sponsorship of short-term, repatriation-related research projects conducted at the NMNH and intern-

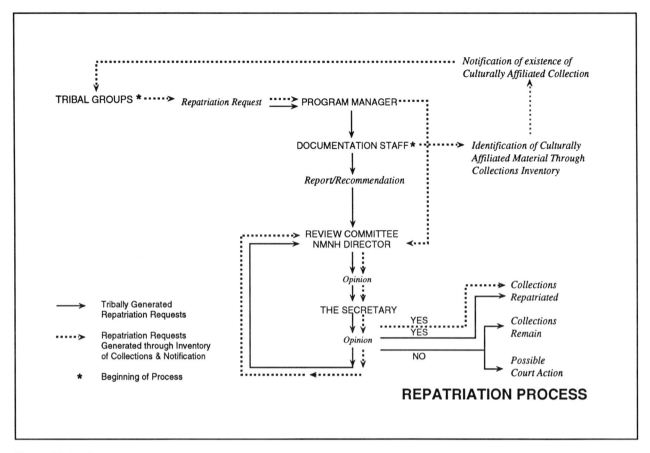

Figure 15.3. The repatriation process. (Courtesy of the Department of Anthropology, National Museum of Natural History, Smithsonian Institution)

ships for Native Americans in the Repatriation Office. The Repatriation Office has sponsored seven Native American interns and contractors to date. In a collaborative venture between the Doyon Foundation of Alaska, the Tanana Chiefs Conference, and the Repatriation Office, financial support was provided to two Native Americans to research skeletal remains from native villages along the Yukon River that involved an extensive review of the papers of Aleš Hrdlička. In separate studies, Native American students have researched Army Medical Museum documentation and worked on summary inventories of ethnographic collections in the museum. An individual from the Umatilla Tribe is currently engaged in a major effort to organize and extract information on mortuary contexts from River Basin Survey records.

Repatriation Process

The actual process of repatriation is schematically represented in fig. 15.3. Solid lines represent repatriation cases generated by Native American requests; dotted lines are repatriation cases generated inter-

nally as a result of the inventory process; an asterisk indicates the beginning of the process, and the potential outcomes are found on the right-hand side of the chart.

When a formal request for repatriation is received from a tribal group, the request is channeled through the Repatriation Office's program manager and assigned to a case officer who, with the aid of repatriation collections and archives staff, is responsible for compiling the available documentary information about the collection. The result of this investigation is a report containing all relevant information about the case and an assessment of the degree of cultural affiliation between the collection requested and the contemporary claimant group.

The Repatriation Office's report is forwarded to the Department of Anthropology for review and comment, and then to the Deputy Director and Director of the NMNH. The Director forwards the report and comments, along with his own recommendation for action, to the Secretary of the Smithsonian Institution, who renders the final decision about the disposition of the collection in question.

If there is agreement that the collection in ques-

Melinda A. Zeder

tion should be repatriated under the conditions of the law, it is promptly readied for deaccession and shipping. If an agreement cannot be reached, or if the Institution decides against repatriation and the requesting group wishes to press its claim, the case is forwarded to the NMNH Repatriation Review Committee. As specified by law, the Review Committee is appointed by the Secretary of the Smithsonian Institution. Formally constituted in May 1990, the committee is comprised of four members whose nominations were put forward by tribal groups and one member whose nomination was submitted by the scientific community.

The Review Committee, which can draw on the expertise of outside consultants if necessary, reviews all the evidence provided by both the Institution and the claimants. It then issues its recommendation for the disposition of the collection. The committee can also be called upon to help facilitate the resolution of a dispute between multiple claimants or to review specific findings of the Institution at the request of any affected or interested party. In any event, the committee is kept informed, through regular biannual meetings, of repatriation cases in progress and reports being prepared.

The Review Committee's recommendation on disputed cases is submitted to the Secretary, who is responsible for the final decision to repatriate or to retain the collection. Should the Secretary decide against repatriation and the Native American group still wishes to pursue its claim, it has the option of seeking legal recourse.

While the repatriations that occur are often generated by external requests, they may also come about as a result of the internal inventory process mandated by the law. This process begins in the Repatriation Office with the identification of a collection that, under the provisions of the law, is deemed to be affiliated with a contemporary Native American group. The office notifies the affected group of its findings, informs it of the collection's potential for repatriation, and provides instructions on how to proceed should the group wish to file a request. If the group formally requests the return of the specified materials, its wishes are conveyed to the NMNH director and the anthropology department. Pending NMNH and institutional approval, the collection is then recommended for return.

First-Year Accomplishments

In its first year of operation, a large part of the Repatriation Office's efforts were necessarily directed toward hiring staff, creating office space, developing databases and organizational structures, and estab-

lishing protocols for the documentation of skeletal remains, funerary objects, and ethnographic collections. Despite the substantial start-up effort required, the office made major in-roads in the inventory of collections and in the processing of requests for return.

The office currently has 37 active requests for the repatriation of NMNH collections. At the end of its first year and a half of operation, it had completed seven case reports, six of which had completed institutional review. In all six cases, the NMNH has agreed with the recommendations of the Repatriation Office and suggested that the remains in question be offered for return. Three repatriations have been completed and the office is awaiting responses from several other affected tribal groups.

The Repatriation Office has also established a schedule for completing the inventory of the Native American skeletal remains and funerary objects housed at the NMNH. Highest priority is given to the more recent historic and proto-historic collections, especially those collected by the Army Medical Museum in the late 1800s and subsequently transferred to the Smithsonian around the turn of the century.

In addition, the NMNH has adopted as policy the repatriation provisions contained in Public Law 101-601, the Native American Graves Protection and Repatriation Act, signed into effect in November 1990. This law extends the mandate of repatriation to sacred objects and objects of cultural patrimony and sets deadlines for the completion of collections inventory summaries. Claims for items of cultural patrimony and sacred objects are processed in the same way as claims handled under P.L. 101-185.

Conclusions

Repatriation has presented the NMNH with a challenge. Can the NMNH find a way to meet, on the one hand, fundamental ethical and social responsibilities and, on the other, its responsibilities to science as custodian of the Nation's cultural heritage? While perhaps not fully satisfactory to all, can repatriation be carried out with a maximum degree of fairness, thoroughness, and integrity? For all the controversy over the Larsen Bay repatriation, the NMNH learned some valuable lessons that will help it meet the demands of doing repatriation, now and in the future. For all the controversy that surrounds repatriation in general, there still remains a need for increased communication between and sensitivity towards the different parties affected. There exists a unique opportunity to create a common ground of understanding, one that hopefully will be the ultimate legacy of repatriation at the Smithsonian and in the Nation as a whole.

Part 4

Reflections on Larsen Bay

16

RELATIONSHIPS, AFFILIATIONS, RECRIMINATIONS, AND LESSONS LEARNED

Comments on the Larsen Bay Repatriation Case

From listening to and reading these papers, I have learned a great deal about Kodiak Island's past and about repatriation procedures and problems. I am grateful to the organizers for coordinating and organizing this symposium, which addresses legal, political, administrative, anthropological, and biological concerns. I think that Native Americans, scholars of Alaskan history and prehistory, museum administrators, and anthropologists in general will all be able to apply some of the lessons of the Larsen Bay case to our mutual advantage.

I am reminded of a traditional tribal leader who wrote a letter to a museum asking for the return of several items of cultural patrimony. After some delay, he received a reply denying his request. The leader was angered, more by the letter than by the denial. He told me that the person who had written the letter had questioned whether he was really a tribal leader, as well as his right to speak for the tribe. This apparent offhand dismissal of the leader's credentials was a blow that he could not tolerate. He perceived it as a specifically targeted personal attack—after all, the museum curator was an anthropologist and should know something about the tribe. Since I was familiar with the museum, as well as the author of the letter (someone I considered a thoughtful person), I was shocked and asked if he had somehow misunderstood the letter. He assured me this wasn't the case. He showed me the letter so that I could see for myself. As soon as I read it, I saw the problem. He had been sent a form letter indicating that, before discussions could proceed, he would have to provide some proof of his tribal position. The letter was the kind that institutions routinely send out when they aren't sure with whom they are communicating. In effect, the author *was* questioning the leader's standing, but it was not the intentional or personal slap that he inferred. It was a poor choice of letter to send, and I wonder if the museum official even knew that it had been sent. In all likelihood, it had been sent by an assistant or secretary who had replied to the letter "out of the blue" with a "boilerplate" response. The institution assumed that there was no point worrying about a request until everyone properly established their bona fides. Unfortunately, museums often don't understand the impact of such letters.

The story doesn't end here. After showing me the letter, the leader indicated that he was so incensed that he wrote a letter to the President (President Bush at the time). President Bush, he told me, responded immediately, properly, and with great concern. Given that I had never thought of President Bush as particularly attuned to such matters, I asked if I might see the letter from the President. It was clear that it, too, was a form letter. Although it actually said and promised nothing, it did so in a very conciliatory, respectful, and concerned way.

Some might suggest that the moral to be learned from this story is that anthropologists and museum officials should *never* write letters; indeed, letters have consistently provided the initial stimulus for many problems in repatriation cases. Others might recommend that museum and other administrators should hire some of former President Bush's protocol people and letter writers. More constructively, institutions should understand that they must take every repatriation request seriously, must answer each request with a personal letter in a timely fashion, and should try to meet personally with the individual or individuals making the request. It is easy to insult someone when both parties are a bit frightened, concerned, and wary.[1] Finally, I would recommend that one try to avoid dealing with mediators or go-betweens in these situations; instead, a personal relationship should be established between the people making the request and a person in a position of authority at the museum. It is for this reason that I particularly enjoyed and welcomed Butler's paper. I hope people will follow her advice carefully and apply it more broadly than as a simple pragmatic guide for packing bones for return.

I have grouped the papers presented in the session into the following topics, which will be discussed below: (1) the context of the Larsen Bay repatriation request (Killion and Bray, Ortner, Pullar, Talbot); (2) the problems of cultural affiliation and the problems of the case (Bray and Grant, Speaker); (3) the history of Kodiak Island, and especially of Larsen Bay (Donta, Dumond, Pullar, Scott, Simon and Steffian, Urcid); and (4) lessons learned or to be learned (Butler, Sockbeson, Zeder).

Context of the Larsen Bay Repatriation Request

The Smithsonian has accepted the responsibility for many of the problems that arose during the resolution of the Larsen Bay case. Nonetheless, Ortner makes several important and relevant points: (1) the request was made before the National Museum of the American Indian Act (Public Law 101-185) was passed, and the request was outside the scope of the policy and procedures of the Smithsonian at the time; (2) institutional policy and national law were rapidly changing during the period that the request was being reviewed; and (3) changes in the administration of the Department of Anthropology exacerbated the situation by causing long delays. These points are not offered as excuses. They merely provide the background context of the case. I doubt that the Larsen Bay people cared about these points one way or another, but they may have been somewhat more tolerant of the Smithsonian's response, or lack thereof, if they had been informed of the context.

Like many institutions, the Smithsonian has fence-mending to do and changes to make. To its credit, the

Smithsonian has moved into the present and is in the process of trying to modify many of its policies and what some see as past errors, i.e., practices that don't coincide with the views of the end of the twentieth and beginning of the twenty-first centuries. Pullar is correct when he says that the Larsen Bay repatriation case is a perfect example of conflicting world views. Although the Smithsonian's representatives, as anthropologists, should have been aware of some of these conflicts, it has to be remembered that the Smithsonian is also part of the federal bureaucracy, which is not known for its quick responses and changes.

No one disagrees on the basic facts of the case. The Larsen Bay people made their request in July 1987. They were rebuffed on several occasions and, eventually, they had the Native American Rights Fund represent them in their negotiations with the Smithsonian. In 1991, after the passage of P.L. 101-185 (and, subsequently, P.L. 101-601, the Native American Graves Protection and Repatriation Act), the Smithsonian agreed to return the Larsen Bay human remains for reburial. Unfortunately, this decision did not help clarify the Smithsonian's policy on repatriation. The decision, as indicated by Secretary Adams in his April 8, 1991, letter to Henry Sockbeson (Appendix), was not based on the application of the new laws, changes in policy, or scientific evidence; instead, it was the result of a series of negotiations and the acknowledgment that bad feelings had resulted from the length of time the Institution had taken to properly respond to the request. In this sense, the Larsen Bay case has technically set no precedents. Nonetheless, the return had a major impact on subsequent actions of the Smithsonian; it also stimulated the reexamination of the Larsen Bay data from a variety of perspectives.

Before discussing the problems of the case, I would like to raise an additional issue. Although Ortner and others allude to it, no one has directly asked why the Smithsonian and other institutions cannot answer seemingly simple questions about the artifacts and human remains in their custody. Several authors question why the Smithsonian had to study or examine anything. They point out that the Larsen Bay people presented a case and that should have been sufficient. After all, the Smithsonian had had the remains for 50 years, certainly enough time to examine the bones. As Ortner notes, however, it is unusual for a single research project to resolve all the important scientific issues and questions related to a collection.

More significantly for this and other cases, it is critical to recognize that data are not inherently present in any object or bone. What one records or measures or examines depends on the questions being asked. Although the Larsen Bay skeletons had been studied by a number of researchers since Hrdlička, the questions and issues they addressed were not specifically oriented to the nature of the relationship between modern Larsen Bay people and the burials excavated by Hrdlička. Hrdlička thought the groups were not related, but his methodology was known to be faulty. Indeed, in several studies, researchers have stressed that the remains were not included in certain analyses because of problems with Hrdlička's methodology. This does not mean that the skeletons were ignored during those many years. As Ortner points out, the collection has great biomedical significance and was the focus of a number of different studies. The point is simply that it is impossible for any institution to guarantee that it will have a specific class of information ready for anyone making a repatriation request; the availability of such information will depend on the type of research that has been conducted in the past. In the case of Larsen Bay, the studies that had been done were contradictory in terms of the relationship of the Larsen Bay people to all of the human remains excavated by Hrdlička. The Smithsonian had a responsibility to have scholars independently address the question by reexamining the data. The fact that Hrdlička's field methods and his treatment of local people were poor is an important, but separate, issue and does not enter into questions of affiliation.

Problems of the Larsen Bay Case

Sockbeson questions the Smithsonian's motives behind hiring experts to examine the Larsen Bay data, pointing out that the law requires only that determinations be made on the basis of available data and that new studies or definitive assessments are unnecessary. However, the available data had to be organized and evaluated. Attorneys for the Larsen Bay people also hired scientists as contractors (in fact, if Pullar's figures are correct, a roughly equal amount of money was spent by both sides). To put it simply, it is not unreasonable that the Smithsonian would invite scholars who are familiar with the collections and have conducted long-term research in the region to provide an objective reexamination of the data. Coordination of information on a collection of this size and scope is not unreasonable or suspect. While Indian interests may be primary, all opinions deserve a fair hearing.

Speaker, as well as a number of the other authors, make it clear that there are serious problems with Hrdlička's data and with his approach to excavation and analysis.[2] Their studies outline the problems and biases and demonstrate that we must be careful when interpreting Hrdlička's data. In particular, if we want to use the data to examine questions of site structure, it will be necessary to reconstruct the data and adjust it for biases. Nonetheless, Speaker's analysis suggests that Hrdlička's data can be used or salvaged to some degree with careful sorting and matching. I think it would be especially worthwhile to try to coordinate Speaker's work with that of Simon and Steffian. Since Simon and Steffian now have good control over provenience at Uyak, it should be possible to integrate Speaker's revised Hrdlička data into their framework. Although data resolution might suffer somewhat, the overall benefits should be great.

Bray and Grant, as well as Ortner, tackle the problem of cultural affiliation on a general level, while Scott, Dumond, and Donta address it for Larsen Bay specifically. Sockbeson argues that the determination of cultural affiliation under the law is a straightforward procedure, but I think the reality is more likely to be a set of conflicting and differing views of cultural affiliation, often based on the same sets of evidence. Conflicting views are particularly likely in situations where substantial research has been undertaken over a number of years. I share Bray's and Grant's view of the irony that cultural affiliation is being used as the basis of repatriation, especially when it is used less and less as a significant anthropological concept. I also agree that the solution to the problem of cultural affiliation is dialogue and a mutual construction of the concept. Unfortunately, once a request for repatriation is made, it may already be too late for any such mutual construction.

Scott makes the important point that one must look at many different kinds of information. He presents his data in a clear, objective manner, indicating where other kinds of data may contradict his views or be interpreted differently. Scott is to be commended not only for his objective analysis but also for placing the results of his work within the context of various extant views of Larsen Bay cultural affiliation and history.

History of Kodiak Island and Larsen Bay

The studies that fall under this category represent a variety of data, all of which are valid for use in the determination of cultural affiliation. Donta focuses on the continuity of items of ceremonial material culture. Dumond reviews the archaeological and linguistic evidence. Pullar reviews some of the oral history of the Larsen Bay people, as well as the natives' perspectives on Hrdlička's work on the island. Scott reexamines teeth in an attempt to determine biological relationships over time. Based partly on recent excavations at the Uyak site, Simon and Steffian try to develop a model of mortuary behavior for the Kachemak tradition. Finally, Urcid reevaluates the question of Kodiak Island cannibalism on the basis of an examination of the now-repatriated Larsen Bay human remains.

These studies represent the impressive array of analyses that can be conducted in a search for cultural affiliation. Not surprisingly, their findings do not match specifically or completely, although there is a surprising degree of complementarity among and between them. Instead of reviewing each study, I summarize what I think are the six most significant conclusions.

1. Biological continuity. Scott's dental data suggest ties between the living inhabitants and the earlier populations. The upper levels at Uyak are related to the modern Koniag populations. The biological data for the Pre-Koniag or Kachemak population are less clear. Scott concludes that both Pre-Koniag and Koniag samples fall largely within the Eskimo-Aleut biological sphere and that biological continuity over time is a reasonable conclusion. Scott also indicates that this biological continuity must be seen on a broad, rather than narrow, scale; movements of people within the region may have occurred. Also on the issue of biological continuity, Pullar argues that no distinctions exist for the Larsen Bay people themselves; the dead taken from the Uyak site are their dead.

2. Cannibalism and mortuary practices. Simon and Steffian, as well as Urcid, make strong cases against the presence of cannibalism, which Hrdlička originally hypothesized for the Uyak site. If cannibalism was practiced at all, it was likely in a ritualized form. More importantly, both papers provide abundant evidence for the presence of a range of mortuary treatments and extensive processing of the dead. Secondary treatment, whether or not it resulted in reburial, was a common occurrence, at least for some portion of the population.[3] Strengthening this conclusion is Donta's ethnohistoric analysis of Koniag ceremonialism and treatment of the dead. Simon and Steffian further argue that secondary treatment may be the result of the use of mortuary crypts and likely was a ritualization of territorial claims through a demonstration of ties with ancestors.[4]

3. Continuity in ceremonialism. Donta presents extensive data documenting continuity in ceremonialism from A.D. 1300 until A.D. 1870. He cannot, however, reliably extend this continuity back to the Kachemak tradition, although some Kachemak ceremonial artifacts suggest that a longer continuity is likely.

4. Prehistoric discontinuities. Something happened in the Kodiak Island area around A.D. 1000. Dumond reaches this conclusion from the archaeological data, arguing for an influx of people from the Alaskan peninsula. It is significant that this view is *not* contradicted by Scott's dental data.

5. Discontinuity in settlement. Based on available data, Dumond demonstrates archaeologically that there is no continuity of residence between the abandonment of the Uyak site and the arrival of Europeans. He suggests that this abandonment may be due to differential resource availability and needs. Dumond's conclusion does not necessarily mean that the modern Larsen Bay people came from elsewhere or are unrelated, but merely that Larsen Bay itself was seemingly uninhabited for a period of several hundred years before Europeans arrived.

6. Variability in types of data. Scott makes the important point that archaeologists, linguists, and physical anthropologists have disagreed on Kodiak Island's population history because researchers have focused on different sets of variables that change at significantly different rates.

Having reviewed the papers in this volume, I admit to some surprise. Based on my previous knowledge of the literature, I assumed that the case against continuity was a strong one. These studies, however, convince me that there is continuity and a relationship between the modern residents of Larsen Bay and the human remains excavated at the Uyak site, even though the people at Uyak may also be related to others in the region. Additionally, these studies point to a variety of significant and important questions that remain unanswered. These questions are relevant not only to anthropologists but also to the people of Larsen Bay. In my opinion, some of the more interesting and significant questions are: What is the precise nature and meaning of Kachemak and early Koniag mortuary ritual? What caused the abandonment of the Uyak site up to the arrival of the Europeans? Why was the site inhabited successfully for so many years and then abandoned?

Lessons Learned or to Be Learned

Sockbeson has attempted to outline a series of lessons for museums and other institutions. His lessons are valuable ones, some of which I believe have already been learned by members of the museum and academic community. Arrogance and the appearance of condescension is something that angers most people, and I think it is especially important for museums to remember that they might not have better information about a site than a tribe. This is especially true for sites excavated many years ago.

My only caveat to Sockbeson's paper is that, although institutions would do well to listen to his lessons carefully, institutions must also be concerned

Lynne Goldstein

with the museum profession and with proceeding in a professional manner. While it is true that the law requires only a preponderance of evidence and weighs the balance in favor of tribal interests, the law also indicates that there are many different kinds of evidence that might be used in a case for affiliation. Institutions have always had an obligation of responsibility for the items and human remains in their care. Their responsibility is to their institution and to their profession, as well as to Native American tribes and nations. This is an important point that Zeder makes in her discussion of how the Smithsonian structured the Repatriation Office. An early, face-to-face meeting between the institution and the tribe, in which problems, concerns, and issues are addressed, might make a big difference in understanding. Similarly, the institution and the tribe may well disagree on the issue of cultural affiliation, and both groups may present data from a variety of sources to document their claim. The law does not specify that simply because a tribe makes a claim a return is automatically mandated. There will be disputes, and there are mechanisms specifically provided by the law to handle such disputes. Unfortunately, in the Larsen Bay case, none of these mechanisms were operational at the time.[5]

The last point raised by Sockbeson—that there is no need to establish cultural affiliation with certainty and that there is no need to conduct investigative studies—is one that will continue to be a source of problems in the future. It is important and proper to get a number of different views and, because this is the nature of science, people will continue to do so. Furthermore, I think that tribes will be interested in studies that link them more definitively to remains. One of the most impressive aspects of the Larsen Bay case is that, in general, new studies were *not* done. Indeed, one might argue that the only really new study was the excavation at Uyak sponsored by the Larsen Bay people. People reexamined the extant data and came to conflicting conclusions. That is reasonable and predictable. The problem in my mind was not that the Smithsonian undertook those reviews but that the Smithsonian did not talk with the Larsen Bay people to explain why they were doing what they were doing.

Unfortunately, the Smithsonian and the Larsen Bay people never really did talk to one another. What could have been a positive experience for both sides was a disappointment for everyone. The Smithsonian was certainly to blame for errors of communication, but I don't think it is productive to place all blame squarely at its door. Pullar's paper has effectively demonstrated that blame is not necessarily a useful concept in this case. Pullar is correct—different world views were in operation and the Smithsonian missed what might have been a wonderful opportunity.

The papers by Butler and Zeder demonstrate that the Smithsonian has learned its lessons from this case. Many of the criticisms leveled by Pullar and Sockbeson have been directly and specifically addressed in the organization and operation of the Smithsonian's new Repatriation Office. In many ways, the Larsen Bay case can be viewed as having had a positive effect on the Smithsonian.

Finally, I want to reiterate my positive impression of Butler's paper. If we return to the story at the beginning of this commentary, it is relatively easy to see that concern for the kind of details outlined by Butler will likely do more to reinstate the good name of the Smithsonian with Native American tribes and nations than any grand scheme or program. Simple communication, manners, and concern can avoid major confrontations and litigation in the future.

Notes

1. One of the more interesting things I have learned from my own experience is that it seldom occurs to either side that the other is terrified. Museums and other institutions are routinely afraid of Indians, and tribes are often intimidated by museums. Realization of common fears might improve the situation and its resolution.

2. Several authors comment on the fact that women were omitted from Hrdlička's studies. While I am not comfortable judging someone in the past by modern standards, I would note that, given the descriptions of how Hrdlička undertook his study, it is not surprising that women did not allow him to examine and measure them; it is instead surprising that any men agreed to be examined.

3. I appreciate Urcid's attempts to provide specific examples to argue against a cannibalism conclusion, but I fear his examples are equally extreme and perhaps as fanciful. Extensive processing of the dead occurs in many cultures and in a variety of forms. It is not unusual or extreme behavior. Although Simon and Steffian indicate that the articulated nature of some skeletal segments argue for primary inhumation rather than for secondary burial of disarticulated bones, I would suggest that secondary burial does not have to be represented by, or associated with, disarticulated elements. Part or all of an individual may still be articulated when reburied.

4. In making their case for a link between a corporate group structure, ancestor worship, and territories, Simon and Steffian cite work done by Arthur Saxe and by myself. Although their citation is accurate, one of the critical aspects of my reformulation of Saxe's original hypothesis was in the directionality of the hypothesis and the importance of the nature of the mortuary facility—the disposal area must be permanent, specialized, bounded, and used exclusively for the dead. To the degree that this is true, it is likely that there is a corporate group structure, etc. The less formal, specialized, etc., the disposal facility is, the more alternative interpretations may apply. In the case of Kachemak sites, the range of mortuary behavior and the presence of the facilities intermingled and within the habitation area suggests that it is not a permanent and exclusive facility. Although Simon and Steffian make a case for a territorial, corporate group structure and ancestor worship, the case cannot be so strongly based upon the so-called Saxe-Goldstein hypothesis.

5. The Smithsonian Repatriation Review Committee had been appointed before the Larsen Bay return was made, but the Committee had not formally met nor established its rules of operation. Nonetheless, Secretary Adams could have referred the case to the Committee if he had wished to do so.

17

DO THE RIGHT THING

On a warm June evening in 1902 a force of several hundred free Yaquis struck at four haciendas near Hermosillo, Sonora, and liberated over 600 of their relatives held in forced labor. The Yaqui retreated northward, defeated a column of soldiers sent to pursue them, and took refuge in the rugged country south of Ures, Sonora. Here the fighters took up a defensive position while the women, children, and a small guard of armed men set up camp to their rear. The Yaqui fighters were far from home and they had chosen their ground poorly. In the dawning light of June 16th, a superior force of Mexican soldiers attacked the camp of non-combatants, driving the handful of armed men, the women, and the children into a canyon. In a running fight they killed many of the Yaqui and captured most of the surviving women and children. The soldiers gathered the captured Yaqui fighters, stood them up against the canyon wall, and shot them to death.

Three weeks later an American physical anthropologist, escorted by a group of Mexican *rurales*, visited the battlefield. Aleš Hrdlička (1904:66) came to the killing field in search of skeletons and he found them. He counted 64 Yaqui bodies, including 12 women, a little girl, and a baby still in its cradle board. He gathered up the weapons and other possessions that the Yaqui had abandoned in their flight and he packed up the bodies of the dead. All of this he shipped to the American Museum of Natural History in New York City.

Nearly 30 years later, the same Aleš Hrdlička, now

with the National Museum of Natural History, came to Larsen Bay, Alaska. Here he conducted his excavations at the Uyak site, mining the graveyards, ancient and modern, for bones. His finds included 3,000-year-old skeletons and the bodies of the Waselie family (Pullar this volume), who died during the flu epidemic of 1918. He either did not hear or chose to ignore the objections of the Qikertarmiut people who lived on the bay.

As Killion and Bray point out in their introduction to this volume, archaeologists and physical anthropologists are often dismayed by the dark images reflected back in the mirrors that Native Americans turn on us. We want to see ourselves as liberal and altruistic social scientists, while Native Americans often see us as running dogs, following close on the heels of the colonial master. The histories that the Yaqui and the Qikertarmiut people recount the invasion of their lands, the destruction of their way of life, and the killing of their relatives. The histories end with the anthropologist picking over the bones of the dead on the killing fields. Our histories begin with anthropologists in pursuit of knowledge, building the sciences of archaeology and physical anthropology, and then using this knowledge to combat racism and prejudice. We divorce our anthropological ancestors from the colonial context that created them, and ourselves from living Native Americans. This process of divorce was well underway by the time that Hrdlička rode onto a Mexican battlefield.

Hrdlička's methods of data collection were neither

new, unusual, nor extreme for his time (Gould 1981). He was simply one of the best at what he did and one of the most prolific. He rose to a high position in the National Museum of Natural History and thus had considerable institutional power in the field. He is often regarded as one of the founders of modern American physical anthropology. As Ortner (this volume) points out, Hrdlička "laid a solid foundation for future research in many areas of human biology."

Hrdlička and his contemporaries worked with a categorical idea of human physical variation. They were equally interested in the bones of Native Americans and of others, whether 3,000 years old, 30 years old, or three weeks old, because they saw these remains as representative of a human type or race. Hrdlička asked questions about the origin of the race of "American Aborigines" and about the physical variation within it. He did not ask questions about its future because like most Americans of his day he was convinced that Native Americans were vanishing, both biologically and culturally (Dippie 1982).

Native Americans, however, did not vanish. In episodes like the Larsen Bay repatriation they have forced archaeologists and physical anthropologists see that our research is a study of people—people whose interests are different than, and often contrary to, our own. As anthropologists, our paramount responsibility is to these people but we do not yet know how to "do the right thing" in a dialogue with them. We are entering into a process of dialogue, negotiation, advocacy, and scholarship that will be difficult, fraught with failure, constantly renegotiated, and ultimately beneficial to the discipline.

The ideology of the vanishing American separated living Native American peoples from their pasts (McGuire 1992). Native Americans, as primitive people living in a state of nature, could not survive the onslaught of civilization (Dippie 1982). Civilization corrupted them with drink, and poverty reduced them to a debased condition. Native peoples could only escape this misery as individuals if they assimilated into the American melting pot. In either case, they were rent from their past, and that past became the object of anthropological research. As Deloria (1973:49) noted, "America's Indians . . . no longer exist, except in the pages of books." But, of course, native peoples did not vanish. They continued to teach their children their native histories—histories that ended with the anthropologist picking through the bones.

Over the last decades two sorts of histories have existed for Native Americans. One has been a public history, researched in universities, written in books, and taught in schools. The other has been a covert history taught by elders in the home. Physical anthropologists and archaeologists did not know the covert histo-

ry because they saw their research as the study of things, bones and artifacts, not of living peoples. They tended to assume that real Native Americans had vanished, or were vanishing, and they saw themselves as the preservers of dead cultures. Most anthropologists were honestly shocked and confused when Native Americans began to obstruct digs and demand the return of the bones of their ancestors. The anthropologists recoiled from their reflection and fell back on the myth of the vanishing American. They questioned the authenticity of Native American leaders, the ancestral connection of modern populations to archaeological remains, and the factual basis of covert histories.

In the early 1970s Native Americans made public the histories that had been covert (Deloria 1973). They informed anthropologists that the pasts we study are the pasts of living peoples. We did not listen well. It took us over 20 years to come to the realization that our discipline is the study of people, not just things, and that these are people who have a present and a future as well as a past. We can no longer practice archaeology without consulting and involving the people that we study.

The story of the Larsen Bay repatriation is important because it documents, through example, the process that opened our ears to the covert histories of Native America. I wish I could say that this was primarily a process of dawning self-awareness. But in reality it took federal legislation to open the door to repatriations like Larsen Bay, and many anthropologists still voraciously oppose such repatriations.

In the end, the Smithsonian Institution did the right thing. The bodies of the Waselie family have been returned to their home. The Smithsonian not only amply documented the collection before it was returned but also answered questions of scientific interest. They turned the loss of the collection into an opportunity to reexamine questions that might never have been explored again. The Larsen Bay repatriation led to the establishment of procedures in the Smithsonian that will guide future repatriations and serve as a model for other institutions.

Many people might wonder why it did take so long for the Smithsonian Institution to do the right thing? As the papers in this volume amply document, this was clearly a complex process. It was rife with misunderstandings, differences of perception, and contradictory good intentions. Several of the authors lament that the process involved so much pain and struggle on both sides. It is not hard to do the right thing. The real difficulty lies in knowing what the right thing is. Perhaps we should be suspicious when individuals come too quickly, without pain and struggle, to that knowledge.

The individuals who sought to retain the Larsen

Bay collection at the Smithsonian did so for good reasons. Twentieth-century American anthropology has been one of the major intellectual forces combating racism and prejudice in the western world. At the core of modern western liberal philosophy is the anthropological notion of cultural relativism, and the anthropological finding that race, language, and culture are separate entities. Anthropologists have been able to advance these concepts in western culture in part through their study of collections like the one from Larsen Bay. They have championed these concepts in opposition to racist and fascist world views that permeate western culture. In 1935 Aleš Hrdlička was one of three anthropologists (along with E. A. Hooton and Franz Boas) who drafted and circulated a statement among American scientists denouncing Nazi racial theories and policies (Barkan 1988:189). Hrdlička based his support of the 1935 statement on his analyses of bones and anthropomorphic measurements.

As long as these scholars saw osteology and archaeology as the study of things, the remnants of a vanished or vanishing race, they did not have to confront the terrible contradiction hidden in this research, namely, that the practice (methods, categories, and theories) used to reach this liberal philosophy has been too often insensitive and racist. Their experience was the handling of objects and for them these objects were data, not mothers, fathers, aunts, and uncles. This contradiction has always been readily apparent to native peoples because their experience of this practice was different. They live in a context of regulations, bureaucracies, poverty, and discrimination that denies them the ability to determine their own lives and futures. In this larger set of relations the archaeologist's authority over Indian pasts is simply another aspect of their selves that has been taken from their control.

It is painful to face the contradictions between our intentions and our actions. Having done so, though, we should admit and make amends for our errors. What Hrdlička did at Ures, Sonora, and Larsen Bay was wrong. It was wrong both because he did not consult the people he was studying, and because he would never have been allowed to dig up white victims of the 1918 flu epidemic.

We should not only recognize Hrdlička's achievements as a scientist but also realize that this recognition should not prevent us from examining the contradictions in his work. Hrdlička could have conducted his research and made most of the same contributions by using different methods than he used at Ures or Larsen Bay. For example, Hrdlička (1925) conducted a major anthropomorphic study of "Old Americans," that is, white Americans whose ancestors had come to North America before 1830. For his study he took measurements on elite individuals who had been recruited, at least in part, through the offices of the Daughters of the American Revolution (DAR). The study was only possible because of the support of elite organizations, such as the DAR, and individuals, such as Theodore Roosevelt, who wished to be measured. He did this study without excavating graves at Williamsburg or picking through corpses at the Argonne. If we argue that Hrdlička's achievements depended upon insensitive and racist methods, then we affirm the claim that our research is inherently racist and destructive. If we ignore the contradictions in his research, we also blind ourselves to similar contradictions in our own inquiry.

The Larsen Bay repatriation teaches us that our research is the study of people and not things. Based on this lesson, we can learn to address and transform the contradiction between our intent and our methods. But we still have a long way to go to do this. I am not sure that the Smithsonian, or most of our profession, yet realizes the full meaning of the step taken in the Larsen Bay repatriation. Repatriation entails more than just the return of bones and objects to native peoples. More importantly, it means that we can no longer carry out our research as if native peoples did not exist or had no interest in it. Their demands for repatriation show us that they do have interests in the past, that these interests are different from our own, and that these interests are now supported by the force of law.

I was very struck by the differences in the papers presented by archaeologists and physical anthropologists and by Pullar, especially in the use of illustrations. The anthropologists' papers contain pictures of skulls and artifacts, but Pullar's paper is filled with pictures of people. I have to wonder what the people in Pullar's photographs will think of the anthropologists' pictures of skulls, discussions of cannibalism, and reconstructions of their ancestors' rituals. Were they asked for their thoughts? If not, why not, and if so, where are their answers?

The Smithsonian took a big step with the Larsen Bay repatriation, and it marks a fundamental change in the discipline. If we recognize that the pasts we study are the pasts of living communities, then we must also recognize an obligation to serve the interests of those communities.

The American Anthropological Association's (1983:1) statement of professional ethics asserts that "in research, anthropologists' paramount responsibility is to those they study." If, as anthropologists, we accept that as our responsibility then, I must ask, who are these people and who speaks for them? By detaching the pasts of Native Americans from living Indian people, archaeologists have struck mute our subjects. Archaeologists who define our obligation as being to

Randall H. McGuire

the people of the past or the people of the future (Meighan 1985; Goldstein and Kintigh 1990) conveniently identify persons who cannot speak to their interests as objects of study. This leaves scholars free to express scientific interests as theirs. Archaeologists have ethical obligations to a variety of communities—to the profession, to the general public that pays for research, to students, and to the people who are studied. The people we study are Indian people and as anthropologists we have a significant responsibility to their living descendants.

Recent legislation profoundly alters our access to and control over mortuary remains and sacred artifacts. Both Public Law 101-185, which established a National Museum of the American Indian, and the Native American Graves Protection and Repatriation Act of 1990 recognize the interests of Indian people in burials and sacred objects and requires that scholars consult and abide by these interests. The laws in essence mandate that archaeologists will have to work closely with Indian people in the future. It will no longer be possible to engage in archaeology without involving Indian people.

We should engage in a dialogue with native communities that will lead us to ask questions about the past that address the interests of these communities. Such a dialogue requires long-term and intensive relationships with these communities. We need to rethink how archaeology students are trained and train them more as anthropologists who can engage in archaeology as a human endeavor and not simply as the study of material culture. Our publication and dissemination of results need to consider the sensitivities and concerns of the communities that we serve. In this process we cannot abdicate our expertise, we cannot lie, intentionally ignore information, or simply make up stories that fit a given political agenda. Indeed, if we did, why would anyone believe us? Such an abdication risks self-deception and compromises the integrity of our own scholarly community.

There will be more repatriations. The Yaqui have not yet recovered their relatives who died in the early morning light of June 16, 1902. These future repatriations will hopefully benefit from the lessons learned at Larsen Bay. The Larsen Bay repatriation embodies the struggle and pain that was essential to knowing what the right thing to do is in these situations. The challenge before us now is to do the right thing in a dialogue with native peoples. The road towards realization of what "the right thing" is finds its direction through dialogue. The "right thing" is not, in the end, a platonic, essential principle but instead a dynamic understanding that must continually be critically examined and renegotiated.

References Cited

American Anthropological Association
1983   Professional Ethics. American Anthropological Association, Washington, D.C.

Barkan, Elazar
1988   Mobilizing Scientists against Nazi Racism, 1933–1939. In *Bones, Bodies, Behavior.* G. W. Stocking, Jr., ed. pp. 180–205. Madison: University of Wisconsin Press.

Deloria, Vine Jr.
1973   *God is Red.* New York: Delta Books.

Dippie, Brian W.
1982   *The Vanishing American: White Attitudes and U.S. Indian Policy.* Middletown: Wesleyan University Press.

Goldstein, Lynne, and Keith Kintigh
1990   Ethics and the Reburial Controversy. *American Antiquity* 55(3):585–91.

Gould, Stephen J.
1981   *The Mismeasure of Man.* New York: Norton.

Hrdlička, Aleš
1904   Notes on the Indians of Sonora Mexico. *American Anthropologist* 6:51–89.
1925   *The Old Americans.* Baltimore: Williams and Wilkins Company.

McGuire, Randall H.
1992   Archaeology and the First Americans. *American Anthropologist* 94:816–36.

Meighan, Clement W.
1985   Archaeology and Anthropological Ethics. *Anthropology Newsletter* 26(9):20.

18

REPATRIATION MUST HEAL
OLD WOUNDS

In the past, Indian peoples have been looked upon by museums as suppliers of material culture or as performers to celebrate the opening of exhibitions. Few museums have actually developed their policies and programs with native peoples in mind. Although American Indian topics are a major part of the educational mission in over 400 United States museums, the communities discussed have not been perceived as part of the public trust of those museums. Despite their centrality to the museum world, American Indians are often viewed as being outside the fiduciary and moral mandate of those institutions. This must change, and repatriation has begun to open the doors to a new relationship with the native people of this land.

The majority of museums have failed to identify native communities as their primary or target audience. Few have attempted to develop educational programs for people living on reservations or sought to circulate their collections among native communities. Fewer still have American Indians in decision-making positions. The lack of emphasis on establishing relationships or providing educational opportunities for Native Americans has led to a communications gap between museums and Indian people.

Discussions surrounding the issue of repatriation within the museum profession have generally been very anti-Indian. This is true to the extent that American Indians seeking the repatriation of remains and objects have not infrequently been labelled as accul-

turated militants, and their requests categorized as political rather than religious in nature. The story of the Larsen Bay request is a case in point. This type of defensive reaction on the part of museums is a way of discrediting the moral basis of the repatriation request. It raises questions about the moral obligations of museums to respect the religious concerns of those they study. It also foregrounds the question of the museum's educational obligations to assist in the cultural rejuvenation of the communities that produced the objects of interest in the first place.

Many of the museums' arguments against repatriation suggest that these institutions consider Native Americans to be outside of their institutional mandates. Should Native Americans be excluded from a museum's fiduciary or legal responsibilities? Are American Indians part of the public trust envisioned by museums? Is there not a moral obligation for museums to assist in the cultural development of American Indians as well as the general public? The failure on the part of many museums to address such questions, and their general response to the repatriation issue, has had the effect of casting Native Americans as anti-social, anti-science, and anti-progress.

Museums must stop thinking of Native Americans as adversaries and begin to view them more responsibly as constituents. American Indians must become part of the program mandate for museums with Native American collections. Museums must develop new partnerships with American Indians for the sake of cultural management within American Indian communities. This partnership needs to be based on the recognition of the fact that museums possess objects that are critical to the spiritual, cultural, and social well-being of American Indians. Native American identity is often manifested in these objects. The loss of these objects from native communities, ritual sites, the classrooms, and homes has caused great deprivations within American Indian society. The museums' possession of our dead and our religious objects has become the main wound that exists between our peoples. The time for healing has come—as mandated by Congress.

In the Larsen Bay case, the Smithsonian questioned whether there was a "reasonable relationship" between the contemporary native community that had made the repatriation request and the human remains in question. Prior to legislation, the Smithsonian would only consider the return of human remains in cases where direct descent could be proven or the name of the individual was known. Embedded in this policy was the assumption that modern native people lacked sufficient ties to their ancient ancestors. The irony is that scholars have defined American Indian cultures on the basis of archaeological evidence and created such entities as "paleo-Indians" as if they were genetic and cultural mutants that had no relationship to modern Native Americans. The denial that there is any spiritual affinity with native ancestors who died before the arrival of the Europeans is in itself unreasonable.

With regard to cultural patrimony, the validity of Indian beliefs is often questioned, bringing the resistance to repatriation to a new level of paternalism. Indian concepts of sacredness, spirit, and religion differ from those of other cultures. Some scholars have questioned those beliefs and want to act as judge, jury, and executioner in order to dismiss American Indian notions of sacredness. Yet their own scholarship identifies native concepts of community property as different from those of Western cultures. Museums know that there is a spiritual relationship between Native Americans and the objects they created or they would not be interested in collecting the objects in the first place. Their own research describes the emotional, spiritual, and cultural importance of ritual objects to Native American identity.

The possession of native dead is seen as a violation of a sacred trust of an entirely different kind. Coming to grips with that reality can lead to new perspectives on the value of information and an increase in knowledge among native people, as demonstrated in the Larsen Bay case. The repatriation of the human remains from the Uyak site stimulated research on the native people of the region and forced anthropologists to think about the significance of the remains.

The difference in this case was that new voices were heard and questions about morality were seriously addressed. In the end, both science and religion were advanced.

The museums claim that the repatriation process will take several years and more than $60 million to identify and investigate Native American remains, funerary offerings, sacred objects, and the cultural patrimony of American Indian nations in their possession. They claim that they do not know what they have, yet they argue that these sacred materials are essential to maintaining the integrity of their collections and that the remains of our dead are part of the national heritage. How do you create respect and understanding for American Indian burial customs by desecrating their beliefs? How do you present American Indian grave materials intelligently given the professed lack of information?

The integrity of American Indian religious practices must be taken into account. Museums must examine their legal and moral responsibilities to ensure the preservation of American Indian culture where it still exists. It is hard to imagine that museums are willing to stand by and watch American Indian languages disappear, witness the dismantling of Native American religious freedom, or think of living elders as potential specimens for the future generations of archaeologists and museum collections. There must be museum professionals who want to assist American Indians in these matters. It is time for those people to step forward.

This is not to say that some museums have not taken a proactive approach to assisting American Indians in their cultural development or that human remains and sacred objects have not been repatriated successfully. Where such events have occurred without the force of law, one is apt to find more secure relationships between the native community and the museums in question. The Smithsonian Institution and the New York State Museum are two examples of institutions that have successfully negotiated the return of sacred objects. Native Americans have actively participated in and benefited from such initiatives. The public is also better served insofar as their awareness of modern American Indian traditions and concerns is increased, and a more realistic education about contemporary American Indian culture achieved. In responding to the real needs of Native Americans, museums come to be seen as a social force for cultural development rather than simply as temples of the past.

In most cases, however, it has only been the force of law that has brought museums to the negotiating table. The history of the relationship between American Indians and museums proves this to be true. Only when Native Americans arm themselves with lawyers can they obtain audiences with museum boards of trustees to discuss their concerns. The majority of museums will return items requested by American Indians only if legally required to do so. The Larsen Bay case and the other acts of repatriation by the Smithsonian send a positive signal to both the Native American and the museum community. The Smithsonian, in reversing its previous stance on the repatriation issue, is setting a national model. This precedent must be seen in the broader context of other issues of religious freedom with which native peoples are still struggling. The use and protection of sacred sites, the right to participate in religious ceremonies without fear of persecution, and the right to define one's own culture and beliefs all play a part in the relationship of Native Americans to other Americans. Museums must do more to reflect current social, political, and religious trends in order to better educate museum visitors about the dynamics of contemporary native cultures.

Despite some unethical practices in the past, museums will have served the long-term educational needs of American Indians if they now proceed to assist American Indian communities in the creative use of archival material, objects of cultural identity, and other educational resources to help foster a new era of cultural development for American Indians. By creating new opportunities for American Indians to learn about their artistic, religious, literary, and musical traditions and beliefs, museums will share the responsibility of preserving American Indian culture for many generations to come.

Museums have preserved many objects of American Indian pride and belief. The time has come to recognize that this act of holding objects has really been for the sake of the American Indians themselves. This generation of Native Americans needs to be asso-

ciated with those objects. It is critical. Time is taking its toll on tribal elders who still remember when many of the contested objects were in native hands. If we wait much longer, much of the remaining oral traditions surrounding these objects could be lost.

Museums can have a positive impact on the future cultural diversity of this nation. They hold the balance of power. They retain the objects that American Indians believe are essential for their survival. If museums fail to respond, they will have to bear responsibility for the demise of the American Indian cultures that they profess they want to preserve. American Indians have made their interests in these matters very clear over the last 100 years. The time has come for museums to act.

American Indians also have a responsibility in resolving these matters. As we have seen in repatriation cases around the country, native peoples have taken different approaches to the problem based on the initial responses they have received from museums. The museums that want to lock dead Indians in and keep live ones out will find themselves faced with Native American lawyers and mired in court battles. Those that show genuine concern and negotiate in good faith will find that Native Americans will share in the responsibility of the resolution. We have made great strides with human remains and the dead are now returning home to their original resting places. Ironically, the recognition of American Indian religious rights has led to greater self-awareness within the native community. The act of reburial is a highly charged emotional and spiritual event. The fulfillment of this simple moral act opens the doors to museums to participate in the cultural management of Indian communities while at the same time acknowledging the rights of native peoples to manifest their own spiritual destiny.

APPENDIX

Larsen Bay Repatriation Letters

Larsen Bay Tribal Council Resolution No. 87-09, May 29, 1987

LARSEN BAY TRIBAL COUNCIL RESOLUTION NO. 87-90

WHEREAS, the Larsen Bay Tribal Council represents the Native indigenous people of Larsen Bay and Uyak Bay, Kodiak Island, Alaska, who have inhabited these places continuously for thousands of years; and

WHEREAS, we honor and respect our ancestors and their traditional ways, which enrich our personal and spiritual lives today as they will strengthen the lives of our children and our children's children in years to come; and

WHEREAS, several decades ago archaeologists excavated and removed the bodily remains of hundreds of our Native ancestors who had been buried here, the burial artifacts that were found with their remains, and many thousands of other cultural and spiritual items as well, and

WHEREAS, the work of Ales Hrdlicka and others is documented in several books and publications which all attest to the massive removal of our ancestors' remains and artifacts; and

WHEREAS, years after the archaeological research was finished, the remains of our ancestors and associated burial items excavated with them are on record as stored in the Smithsonian Institution; and

WHEREAS, the skeletal remains, burial objects, and artifacts held by the Smithsonian Institution belong to us, the Native people of Larsen Bay and Uyak Bay, who have the traditional right and spiritual responsibility to reinter our ancestors' remains; and

WHEREAS, recent court decisions elsewhere in the United States have upheld the rights of Native people to their ancestors' remains, burial objects, and other artifacts;

NOW THEREFORE BE IT RESOLVED that the Tribal Council of Larsen Bay seeks redress to a wrong that was committed years ago when ancient village sites were plundered in the name of archaeology, and we now demand the immediate return of the items held by the Smithsonian Institution; and

LET IT BE FURTHER RESOLVED that a copy of this Resolution be transmitted to Senators Murkowski and Stevens, the members of the Senate Select Committee on Indian Affairs, Congressman Young, the members of the House Committee on Indian and Insular Affairs, Governor Cowper, State Senator Zharoff, and Representative Davidson.

Enacted on the 29 day of May, 1987.

Signed: Frank M. Carlson, Tribal Council President

Letter from Anthropology Department Chair to Larsen Bay Tribal Council, September 25, 1987

September 25, 1987
Larsen Bay Tribal Council
Post Office Box 35
Larsen Bay, Alaska 99624
Dear Sirs:

In response to your letter of July 12, 1987, one of our staff archeologists has researched our records pertaining to the work of Ales Hrdlicka in the region of Larsen Bay, Alaska. We know that Hrdlicka visited that area during the 1930's and conducted archeological testing of four sites that are located within the general vicinity of Larsen and Uyak Bays. Those sites are identified in our records as Chief's Point, KAR-025, Jones Point (also called KOV-145), and KOD-157. The approximate number of human skeletal remains recovered from each site are respectively 16, 4, 793, and 1. Our records indicate that most, if not all, of the material recovered is prehistoric, dating as far back into prehistory as 1300 B.C.

The primary documentation for the Hrdlicka collection is his narrative field journal. Subsequent investigators in the region have relocated some of the sites he visited. However, relating specimens in the collection to locations in the narrative is not always possible. Furthermore, many locations are difficult to identify or relate to modern localities because of inconsistent designations, variations in place name spellings and vague descriptions. Also, there have been settlement shifts or discontinuities and modern residents of a location may not be direct descendants of former occupants. Some of the places from which he collected were actively being destroyed by river bank erosion and likely no longer exist.

Field records indicate that the local people not only were aware and informed of the work but also assisted by directing or taking Hrdlicka to old sites and as paid field excavators. In his field journal, Hrdlicka mentions passing over cases that he thought were recent and where disturbance of the burial might cause offense. He was looking for the oldest material he could find. In general, he collected from places that were considered "old," meaning long abandoned. He avoided graves of known individuals, and even those thought to be of known individuals. His excavations

were over 50 years ago. Thus, it is not likely that a close relative of anyone living today is in the Institution's collection.

Our records indicate the Kodiak collections include approximately 2780 archeological artifacts from sites throughout Kodiak Island. These specimens were recovered from Hrdlicka's excavations into site refuse middens which also contained buried human skeletons. To our knowledge none of these artifacts were grave inclusions, although this question has not been researched in detail.

As you are no doubt aware, the issue of deaccession is a complex one, which the Smithsonian must consider in light of the Institution's responsibility to hold its collections in trust for the benefit of all people, not just discrete interest groups. Before we can seriously consider such a request, we must be presented with compelling legal reasons justifying the transfer of human remains from our collections. Such reasons may include, for example, proof that particular remains in our collections can be linked directly to the tribe requesting their burial. Without that fundamental information, it would be difficult for us to transfer materials from our collection without also compromising our trust obligations.

We hope this information is useful to you. Please contact us if you have further concerns.

Sincerely,
Chair
Department of Anthropology

Letter from Anthropology Department Chair to Frank M. Carlson, February 16, 1988

February 16, 1988
Mr. Frank M. Carlson
President
Larsen Bay Tribal Council
Post Office Box 35
Larsen Bay, Alaska 99624
Dear Mr. Carlson:

With apologies for the extended delay in doing so, I am responding to your correspondence dated October 27, 1987 in which you request the return from the Smithsonian [of] all human skeletons and artifacts taken from the region governed by the Larsen Bay Tribal Council. We have carefully reviewed your request, checked the archaeological records pertaining to the collection, and also consulted with archaeologists familiar with the prehistory of the Larsen Bay region. We are aware of the concerns expressed by some Native groups and also have an appreciation for the scientific importance of this particular collection. As a department we follow specific guidelines governing the deaccession and transfer of human remains and artifacts. These cases involve circumstances where the original recovery has been deemed unethical or where the identification of the remains can be directly linked to living descendants. At this time, we are carefully reviewing the documentation for the human skeletal collection as a part of this initiative, and would welcome any information that you may have in this regard.

The stewardship of the Smithsonian collection is a serious concern and an obligation of the Institution because collections represent irreplaceable resources. Scientists learn a great deal by studying living and past populations, the latter being completely dependent on the preservation of well documented human remains in museum collections. Through research based on the Smithsonian collections, scientists have contributed an enormous and diverse array of information about human behavior, the epidemiological history of many diseases, and biological similarity and diversity. It is of mutual interest that collections in our nation's research institutions be preserved for ongoing and future investigations that will be of benefit to everyone. Of importance also to Native people, skeletal remains have provided legal evidence needed for the successful resolution of land claims.

Our letter of September 25, 1987 to the Larsen Bay Tribal Council described the sites listed in our inventory and gave the approximate number of human skeletal remains recovered from each site, as well as the number of archaeological artifacts recovered from throughout Kodiak Island. We also noted that Dr. Hrdlicka's field reports indicate that at the time of his excavations local people were aware of his work and directed, or in some cases, led him to sites considered ancient.

Dr. Hrdlicka's initial visit to the Uyak Bay area was in 1931, he mentioned then that only a few people lived on the bay. In his Kodiak Island book, Hrdlicka describes Jones Point (also called the Uyak Bay site or "Our Point"), the major focus of his excavations, as a site that "became extinct before or during the very beginnings of the Russian times, for the remaining nearby natives did not know its name and had no traditions about it, nor had anyone ever recovered any Russian objects from it."

This statement indicates that Dr. Hrdlicka interviewed local people about previously occupied sites. Other comments made by him show that he endeavored to explain his activities to local people with whom he interacted during his expeditions.

Dr. Hrdlicka worked openly at Jones Point for several years, and in the records offers no evidence that anyone there objected to his work. It appears that visitors to the site were frequent because his records mention setting up a display for visitors. Photographs of the site and of the vicinity do not show any houses

nearby, and there is no other evidence of recent or historic occupation of the location. The evidence suggests that the site is not one of ongoing occupation, continuing from the past to the present in the immediate area.

Dr. Hrdlicka excavated many kinds of sites, not just burial grounds. The Jones Point site was one that contained burials amid habitation remains. The dead were often buried outside the house walls or in abandoned house pits. It is also quite possible that the skeletons found in the Uyak midden are not the remains of the occupants of the site. The lack of formal burial procedures, mass burials, and pre-burial dismemberment are all indicated by the disposition of the skeletons. This contrasts with the careful and elaborate burial rites practiced by the Natives of Kodiak Island for their own people, and suggests that many of the Uyak skeletons are of outsiders captured in warfare. Historic records indicate such captives could have come from as far away as the Aleutian Islands, Prince William Sound, or the Northwest Coast.

The ethnic and cultural history of peoples of Kodiak Island is a very complex one that is currently being investigated actively by anthropologists, archaeologists, and physical anthropologists. Because Kodiak lies within the sphere of influence of Eskimo, Aleut, and Northwest Coast peoples, who are known to have traded, fought, taken slaves, and engaged in a variety of ceremonial and social activities, it is not easy to say for certain who, physically, might be represented by skeletal remains at a given site, particularly one (like Jones Point) that is not a designated burial group. Recent studies by Christy Turner on teeth from Jones Point suggest that the early people found at Jones Point are more closely related to Northwest Coast Indians than they are to, for instance, Eskimos or Aleuts. During the last thousand years, it appears that Kodiak Island people had a culture that was most similar to that of Southwest Alaskan Yupik people, which is where linguistic affiliations also lie. As you can see, sorting out the population and culture history of Kodiak Island is not a simple task, but is one that is actively being researched. Collections like those from Jones Point figure prominently in these studies.

Judged by both the documentation and the artifactual materials, our conclusion that the sites excavated by Dr. Hrdlicka are not recent is well supported. It is important to reemphasize that Dr. Hrdlicka's accounts clearly indicate that he avoided graves of known individuals and was specifically interested in prehistoric sites. We are always open, however, to review any other information or materials that would shed additional light on those accounts.

Please be reassured that the Hrdlicka excavations were not undertaken out of idle curiosity, but with specific research problems in mind, and that human remains and artifacts continue to be integral components of ongoing scientific investigations. Furthermore, these investigations are not limited to the academic concerns of a few scientists, nor are they trivial to the interests of the general public, including Native people of the United States. The skeletal collections housed at the Smithsonian Institution have provided critical data in the investigation of biological relationships of Alaskan Native peoples and basic biological problems including research in medical science directed toward understanding diseases that affect Native populations. The collections represent populations from throughout the world, and include all races and ethnic groups. They are respectfully maintained and regularly examined by scientists and physicians throughout the United States and from other countries for the historical and biomedical information they provide. The collections are not accessible to the general public, nor are they subject to mishandling. At present, a study of ancient dietary practices is being conducted at Harvard University with skeletal remains recovered by Hrdlicka.

We acknowledge your concern for your heritage and would point out that it is one which we share. In late March two of our anthropologists, Dr. William W. Fitzhugh, and Aron Crowell (who has worked with the KANA—Bryn Mawr archeological project on Kodiak) will be at the forthcoming conference. Both would like to meet with you during their visit to further explore these issues.
Sincerely,
Chair
Department of Anthropology

Letter from Anthropology Department Chair to Gordon L. Pullar, May 30, 1989

May 30, 1989
Mr. Gordon L. Pullar
President
Kodiak Area Native Association
402 Center Avenue
Kodiak, Alaska 99615
Dear Mr. Pullar:

Secretary Adams has asked me to thank you for and respond to your correspondence of April 10, 1989. We recognize that there are indeed concerns about the curation of skeletal remains from Kodiak Island, and would like to work with you to address them.

The human skeletal collection curated in the Smithsonian's National Museum of Natural History is an important resource for medical and orthopedic research. Through access to these materials, health professionals, forensic scientists, and physical anthropologists have conducted medical, forensic and historical research on a variety of topics including temporal and regional variation in human anatomy and physiology, growth and development, paleopathology, time interval studies of bone healing and response to infection, epidemiology, population genetics, and nutrition. Biomedical research publications based on this collection has contributed to our understanding of the historical dimensions of disease, the role of disease in human adaptation, and how diseases affect the human skeleton. Because of recent advances in medical technology, this collection offers ever-increasing opportunities for research in human anatomy, pathology, and medicine.

The Smithsonian's human skeletal collection contains human skeletal remains representing black, white, Native American, and other groups from throughout the world. Much of the collection consists of material recovered through archaeological investigations and represents prehistoric populations hundreds or thousands of years old. The collection includes North American white and black human skeletal remains acquired through forensic anthropology investigations for law enforcement agencies, medical school anatomical collections, and archaeological excavation of historic period Euro-American cemeteries.

Bone is not an inert structural framework that is impervious to the external environment. A hard matrix comprised of organic and inorganic components, it is sensitive to a variety of influences such as infection, nutrition, biomechanics, metabolism, neoplasms, and trauma. For this reason, health care professionals, including orthopedists, radiologists, pathologists, and physicians benefit through studies of human skeletal remains; the effects of disease appear clearly in tissue-free specimens. Examination of anatomical collections not only enhances our understanding of skeletal structure, but offers a broader understanding of how disease processes affect bone. Access to entire skeletons is particularly helpful because the pattern and distribution of the morbid condition in all areas of the skeleton can be studied in detail.

Large components of the Smithsonian collection predate the accomplishments of modern medicine, such as antibiotics, antisepsis, recent innovations in surgery, orthotics, and physical therapy. They contain examples of deformities and morbidity that reflect the degree of knowledge and level of sophistication at the time, as well as diseases that no longer exist, were more virulent, or were in more-advanced stages than normally are encountered in contemporary clinical practice.

The study of bone pathology in archaeological materials adds a chronological dimension that is essential to our understanding of disease and its role in human adaptation. The opportunity to study pathological conditions in prehistoric groups, in conjunction with paleodemographic and archaeological information, allows reconstruction of life ways and health problems in the past. The correlation of paleopathological data with knowledge from archaeology and clinical medicine help to elucidate the diseases of mankind in antiquity and in the modern world.

Because the human skeletal collection at the Smithsonian represents diverse populations living in different environments and with different genetic backgrounds, it is an invaluable and irreplaceable resource for medical and biological research. Well-documented skeletal samples are important for quantitative statistical studies that constitute the basis of modern scientific investigation. Questions can be addressed in terms of the frequency of occurrence and variability of traits within and between populations having different genetic and environmental non-western groups because understanding the historical dimensions of disease and how disease affects the human skeleton contributes to modern clinical medicine and our perspective on the maladies of twentieth-century mankind.

The Kodiak Island series is an important research collection representing prehistoric Kachemak Tradition people. The collection has been examined to obtain many different kinds of information, and we hope that this exceptional resource can continue to be available for future study. Please reassure the Koniag people represented by the Kodiak Area Native Association that the collection is carefully maintained and is only examined for medical and scientific research. It is not subject to any mishandling.
Sincerely yours,
Chair
Department of Anthropology

Letter from Robert McC. Adams to Henry J. Sockbeson, April 27, 1990

April 27, 1990
Mr. Henry J. Sockbeson
Native American Rights Fund
1712 N Street, N.W.
Washington, D.C. 20036-2976
Dear Mr. Sockbeson:

I recently met with Dr. Donald J. Ortner, Chairman of the Department of Anthropology at the Smithsonian's National Museum of Natural History, regarding the request from the Larsen Bay Tribal Council for the transfer of archeological human remains and associated funerary objects excavated primarily from the Uyak site in the Larsen Bay, Alaska, area. The ar-

cheological issues in this request are complex. The burials in question range in archeological age from 800 B.C. to the historic period. While your consultants have made a strong case for archeological continuity, there is other evidence that is at least equivocal on this issue. Furthermore, the archeological evidence does indicate significant cultural change during the time in question. In addition, the introduction of Western culture after 1750 A.D. has resulted in substantial cultural change in the historic period that may raise the question of the extent to which continuity is, indeed, the dominant factor. The obvious problem is to determine if there is an appropriate point in time after which cultural links are clear and generally accepted; research conducted thus far was not designed to resolve this question with the precision needed for such a decision.

There are, however, several options for resolving this issue that, on the one hand, deal fairly with the limitations of current evidence but also respond to the urgency felt by the Larsen Bay Tribal Council. As Dr. Ortner discussed with you, the Institution is certainly prepared to transfer all materials reliably associated with the historic period, i.e., since 1750 A.D., which is not to suggest that we would not go further as various questions are answered. One burial in this period is associated with a coffin that may be culturally associated with the people of Kodiak Island.

The Uyak site remains represent one of the most intensively studied samples in our collection. The biomedical research already conducted provides an important base of data for even more significant research in the future as new problems arise and new methods are developed. Might it be possible for the Larsen Bay people to explore with us ways of preserving the material for research while conveying control to them?

Possibilities for doing so might include sequestering the material in our collections storage area and providing access to scientists only with approval by the Larsen Bay Tribal Council or its representative. Another possibility might be to transfer the skeletal material and associated funerary objects to the new museum planned for Kodiak Island for permanent storage and care with similar arrangements for ongoing access by biomedical scientists for research only when approved by the Tribal Council.

The Institution has a deep concern for the long-term scientific value of the Uyak site material. Recently, at Smithsonian laboratories, DNA and human immunoglobulins have been recovered from archeological human remains. Data of this type is of great potential relevance in solving some of the medical and public health problems that affect Native American people today.

I hope to encourage a process for resolving these

complex issues in a way that is, first and foremost, responsive to the concerns of Native Americans. However, we hope to preserve a remarkable source of biological and historical information of great importance to Native American people and to the biomedical scientific community. In the context of this goal, I hope that we can reach an agreement that satisfies the Larsen Bay people but also responds to the very real need for future research on the material. If we can preserve this potential in a way that responds to the concerns of the Larsen Bay people it will be an important achievement.

Sincerely,

Secretary

Letter from Secretary of the Smithsonian to Henry J. Sockbeson, April 8, 1991

April 8, 1991
Mr. Henry J. Sockbeson
Native American Rights Fund
1712 N Street, N.W.
Washington, DC 20036-2976
Dear Mr. Sockbeson:

As we have already discussed by telephone, I am pleased to tell you that the Smithsonian Institution has finally completed its consideration of the request of the Larsen Bay Tribal Council for the repatriation of certain materials. The materials in question are, as you know, human remains and associated funerary objects from a site at Uyak Bay, Alaska, that was excavated by Ales Hrdlicka between the years 1931 and 1938. Our decision has not been an easy or uncontested one, and as you also know it follows from an exhaustive review involving a number of outside specialists. Now with the full concurrence of the Director of the National Museum of Natural History, however, I have concluded that the balance of some fairly complex considerations supports a return of these materials to the Council.

You have expressed the belief, with which I can sympathize, that this case has taken an excessive length of time to resolve. Frankly, an awareness of the negative effect this delay is having on our desire to maintain cordial relations with many Native American communities has played a part in the decision to conclude our deliberations on the Larsen Bay claim without convening the Review Panel that has been established for this purpose. A major problem for us has been the difficulty in recruiting the supplementary staff needed to expedite our own internal research on claims. That problem is slowly being over-

come, but we must recognize that substantial recruitment delays will always be inherent in Federal hiring processes.

But there have been other, more substantive reasons as well for the length of time that has been devoted to this case. The scientific evidence, while voluminous, does not lend what any fair-minded person would regard as absolutely conclusive support to any position on the repatriation issue. Without going into details, the record of the original excavations at the site presents many ambiguities, making it very difficult to decide on the likelihood of possible breaks in the occupation there, or on the possibility that older population elements may have been substantially or wholly replaced by new ones during the course of that occupation. Particularly for this reason, I have also felt it was necessary to weigh the evidence for general continuity of Native American occupation in the immediately surrounding region, from the aboriginal period until the present. Once again, no conclusion on this matter can be as clear-cut as one would like. But I think the sum of the evidence (if not all of its details) supports the judgment I am reporting to you herewith.

Issues like those mentioned above had not been anticipated in detail, I should point out, in the legislation mandating our review. Partly because they are so new, we have felt the need to think about them very deliberately. At the same time, now looking to the future, this experience leaves me with a growing sense of the particularity of each of the repatriation claims that are likely to be addressed to the Smithsonian. One would hope that each case would help us to develop broad principles, presently enabling us to handle subsequent cases with less uncertainty and delay. But I am no longer so confident that this hope will be easily realized.

Please be in touch with Dr. Frank Talbot, Director of the National Museum of Natural History, in order to discuss arrangements for the return of these remains. I do hope you understand that all of us at the Smithsonian, while obviously conscious of the scientific loss that we believe this repatriation represents, view the act of repatriation itself with the deepest sympathy and respect. It is our earnest hope that you, your colleagues and constituents will recognize in our action an expression of good will and good intentions that will lead to an improvement of our relations in the future.

Sincerely yours,

Secretary

Appendix

INDEX